THE CLIF

CORRESPC

1792—1846

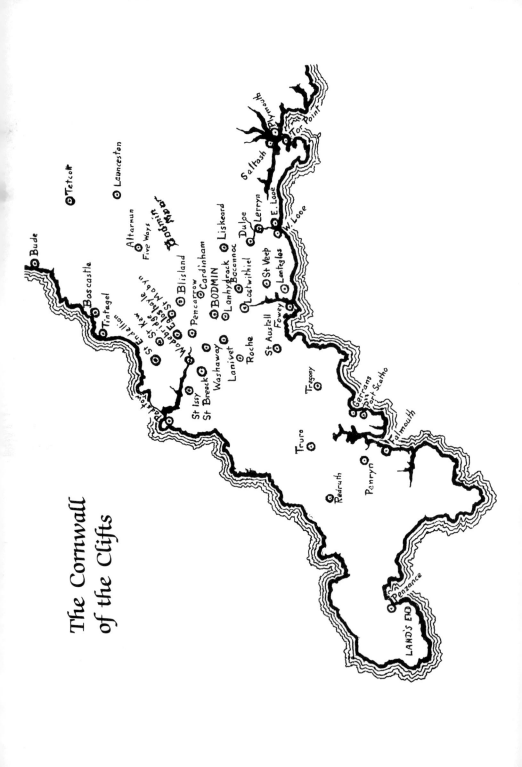

The Cornwall of the Cliffs

Bude
Tetcott
Launceston
Boscastle
Tintagel
Altarnun
Five Ways
St Endellion
St Kew
Wadebridge
St Mabyn
BODMIN MOOR
Blisland
Pencarrow
Cardinham
Liskeard
BODMIN
Lanhydrock
Boconnoc
Duloe
Lerryn
E. Looe
Saltash
Plymouth
Tor Point
W. Looe
St Veep
Lostwithiel
Lanteglos
Fowey
St Issey
St Breock
Washaway
Lanivet
Roche
St Austell
Padstow
Tregony
Veryan
Port Scatho
Falmouth
Truro
Penryn
Redruth
Penzance
LAND'S END

THE CLIFT FAMILY
CORRESPONDENCE
1792—1846

edited by
FRANCES AUSTIN

Centre For English Cultural Tradition & Language
The University of Sheffield
1991

British Library Cataloguing in Publication Data
Austin, Frances
    The Clift Family Correspondence 1792—1846.
    1. England. (Family). Clift.
    I. Title.
    929. 20942
    ISBN 0-907426-04-2.
    ISBN 0-907426-03-4 Pbk.

CECTAL OCCASIONAL PUBLICATIONS NO. 5

ISSN 0263 4805

Centre for English Cultural Tradition and Language
University of Sheffield
Sheffield S10 2TN

Typeset in Garamond by Wilson Hunt, East Stour, Gillingham, Dorset.

Printed by Remous Ltd., Sherborne, Dorset.

For
Bernard

CONTENTS

Acknowledgements xi
Sources of Text xiii
Notes on the Text xiii
General Introduction xvii
The Clift Family 1

Foreword 19
Letters
   Section I. February to June 1792 23
   Section II. June to December 1792 40
   Section III. January to August 1793 52
   Section IV. August to December 1793 69
   Section V. January to December 1794 85
   Section VI. January to December 1795 103
   Section VII. January to December 1796 123
   Section VIII. January to December 1797 148
   Section IX. 1798 to 1799 166
   Section X. 1800 to 1802 186
   Section XI. 1805 to 1817 198
   Section XII. 1818 to 1836 208
   Section XIII. 1837 to 1846 230

Brief Biographies 255
Bibliography 258
Index 260

Illustrations

1. The Cornwall of the Clifts — *frontispiece*

2. William Clift — *21*
    Drawing by his son, William Home Clift.
    By permission of the Trustees of the British Museum.

3. Burcombe Mill, Bodmin — *25*
    Watercolour by Isabella Mary Alms 1900.
    By permission of the Committee of the Bodmin
    Museum.

4. John Hunter's establishment in Leicester Square — *45*
    1792.
    By permission of the President and Council of the Royal
    College of Surgeons of England.

5. Priory, Bodmin — *62*
    Watercolour by William Clift.
    By permission of Lady Thompson of Winsford,
    Minehead.

6. John Hunter — *78*
    Attributed to John Zoffany.
    By permission of the President and Council of the Royal
    College of Surgeons of England.

7. Specimen of John Clift's handwriting — *87*
    By permission of the British Library.

8. Church Stile, Bodmin — *94*
    Watercolour by Isabella Mary Alms 1900.
    By permission of the Committee of the Bodmin
    Museum.

9. Specimen of Robert Clift's handwriting. — *120*
    By permission of the British Library.

10. Nancy Gilbert — *130*
    By permission of Lady Thompson of Winsford,
    Minehead.

11. Specimen of William Clift's handwriting — *156*
    By permission of the British Library.

12. Specimen of Elizabeth Clift's handwriting — *174*
    By permission of the British Library.

13. Specimen of Joanna Clift's handwriting 195
   By permission of the British Library.

14. Pencarrow 203
   Early nineteenth-century print.
   By permission of Lady Molesworth-St Aubyn.

15. Royal College of Surgeons of England 218
   By permission of the President and Council of the Royal
   College of Surgeons of England.

16. Street map of Bodmin 248

ACKNOWLEDGEMENTS

I am indebted to many institutions and individuals for help in the course of editing these letters. The Cornwall County Records Office, Truro, has afforded facilities for looking up parish registers and verifying dates, as also has the Royal Institution of Cornwall. It is with pleasure and respect that I record an inestimable debt to the late Leslie Long, for many years Honorary Curator of the Bodmin Museum. It is sad that he did not live to see this volume of one of Bodmin's most famous sons in print. Mr E.L. Smith, Honorary Secretary to the Committee of the Museum, has continued to give help, especially in the matter of suggesting and locating illustrations. I am also indebted in this search to Miss K. Pethybridge and Mrs Margaret Topping. I am grateful to Lady Thompson of Winsford, Minehead, for providing the portrait of Nancy Gilbert and William Clift's painting of the Priory, Bodmin, and to Lady Molesworth-St Aubyn of Pencarrow for the print of Pencarrow House.

I should like to record my thanks to the Librarians, past and present, of the Royal College of Surgeons of England, Mr W.R. le Fanu, Mr E.H. Cornelius and Mr Ian F. Lyle. They have given me ready help over more than twenty years and Mr Lyle has been particularly helpful in making available illustrations. Similarly, I am indebted to the late Miss Jessie Dobson, formerly Recorder of the Hunterian Museum at the College and the biographer of William Clift and John Hunter. The help she gave me has been continued by her successor in the Museum, Miss Elizabeth Allen.

For his encouragement and enthusiasm at a time when it was most needed I am very grateful to Professor A.J. Harding Rains, for many years Editor of the *Annals of the Royal College of Surgeons of England*. His willingness to publish articles on the Clift family in the *Annals* was an incentive to pursuing the task of editing these letters.

To the late Dr F.D. Omanney and his sister Mrs Mollie Medcalfe I owe thanks for the help and interest they have shown in these papers of their great great grandfather's family.

For help in the early days with methods of editing I must thank Dr Jean Bromley, formerly of the University of Southampton, and also Professor N.E. Osselton of the University of Newcastle-upon-Tyne, who supervised my first research on the letters and has continued to be an enthusiastic advocate of the Clifts ever since. The late Norman Davis, sometime Merton Professor of English at the University of Oxford, also has my thanks for his encouragement of the work and its publication from the beginning. For support over what at times seemed no more than an academic exercise I record my thanks to Professor J.E. Cross, Emeritus Professor of the University of Liverpool.

Again, for continued interest and encouragement I am indebted to Professor Norman Blake of the University of Sheffield, and for the most practical help of all I have to thank Professor J.D.A. Widdowson, Director of The Centre for English Cultural Tradition and Language, also of the University of Sheffield. Professor Dr Gertrud Walter of the University of Erlangen started me on the original quest and without her these letters might never have come to light. Of the individuals who have helped me, many unnamed here, I conclude with my thanks to Dr Bernard Jones, Honorary Visiting Fellow of the University of Southampton, who has given generously of his time and knowledge and has kept me on the path that has led to the completion of this lengthy project.

Finally, I gratefully acknowledge the assistance I have received from the University of Liverpool and the British Academy for grants which have made possible the considerable journeyings and visits in search of materials and verification of data. In addition, the British Academy has awarded a subvention which has made the publication of the letters finally possible.

SOURCES OF TEXT

The letters are contained in two main collections: the British Library Add. Mss 39955, and The Richard Owen Correspondence Vols 7 and 8, which are housed at the British Museum (Natural History). The fragment of William Clift's Autobiography comes from the collection of William Clift's papers preserved in the Library of the Royal College of Surgeons of England in Lincoln's Inn Fields. Grateful acknowledgement is made to these institutions for permission to print the manuscripts here. In addition, permission to reproduce illustrations has kindly been given by Lady Molesworth-St Aubyn, Lady Thompson, the Committee of the Bodmin Museum, the Trustees of the British Museum, the British Library and the Royal College of Surgeons of England.

NOTE ON THE TEXT

The transfer of handwritten materials to print raises many problems and absolute consistency is virtually impossible. The primary intention in presenting the Clift letters has been to furnish an accurate text that represents the letters as nearly as possible as they left the writers' hands in so far as this is compatible with readability and understanding. For this purpose the following guide lines have been adopted.

Lay out. The original lineation has not been kept except in addresses, greetings and subscriptions, which have been represented as closely as possible in appearance to the originals. In certain instances, where, for reasons such as an unexpected abbreviation, the end of a line may be of interest, it has been indicated by a diagonal stroke, thus: /. Robert Clift's letter No.78 has been treated in this way because he raises the final letter at the end of each line regardless of whether the word is abbreviated or not. Paragraphs have been regularly indented. Postscripts are frequently written round the edges of the sheets and in any available space. All these have been placed below the signature without comment. Alterations and deletions have not generally been shown. Where deletions affect the meaning they have been included in sloping brackets: /dear/. Insertions, too, have usually been silently incorporated into the text, but where they are of significance they have been included thus √also/. Many deletions and insertions occur in William Clift's final letters, which are in draft form, but these have been omitted. Deletions and insertions in an early draft, Letter No.86, have been included to show the care with which he composed his letters. Duplications of words, even when clearly unintentional, have been included as written, except where a word is repeated at the beginning of a fresh page as a catch word — a frequent practice of some of the writers. In these cases the repetition has been omitted. Conjectural readings, where the ms. is torn, the writing is obscured by the seal or is simply indecipherable, have been placed between stars: *the*. Where even a conjectural reading is impossible a gap, roughly equivalent to the number of missing letters has been left: *the d   *. Conjectural readings and omissions have been kept to a minimum as far as is possible without danger of misrepresenting the original text.

Spelling. The original spellings have been retained as far as possible. Where there is doubt I have adopted normal usage in most cases, e.g. *a* and *o* are often difficult to distinguish; likewise *e* and *i*. However, where a writer's spelling of any particular word habitually varies from the norm, the idiosyncracy has been maintained in cases of doubt. Long *s*, when used, has everywhere been rendered by short *s*.

Capital letters. These cause difficulty, especially in certain cases, e.g. *S, C* and *M*. The practice of normalizing for proper nouns and beginnings of sentences has generally been followed unless a clear indication to the contrary appears in the holograph. Certain words, such as Sister (but not *brother*) are invariably written with a capital by most writers. I have tried to follow the usual practice of each writer where uncertainty arises. For instance, the two sisters frequently use capital *C* in words like *Ceep* (*Keep*) and *Cind* (*Kind*). Honorifics, such as *Mr* and *Mrs* have been capitalized everywhere, although in the case of these two examples it is often difficult to tell if a capital is intended.

Raised letters and abbreviations. It is frequently impossible to tell if letters are raised or not. Here, therefore, I have attempted to adhere to a consistent policy. With most honorifics, e.g. *Mr Mrs St* (Saint) and *Dr* the raised letters have been lowered without any punctuation to indicate an abbreviation. The same policy has been adopted with the ordinal numbers in dates however they appear in the mss., thus *2nd* and *4th*. Abbreviations of names of months have been printed thus: *Feb^ry; Jan^y*. Elsewhere, raised letters have been retained, e.g. *W^m* for *William* or *y^r* for *your. M^r, M^rs* and *S^r*, where they represent *Master, Mistress* or *Street* are always raised to differentiate them from the honorifics *Mr, Mrs* and *St*. Abbreviations connected with pounds, shillings and pence sometimes have the signs written above the figures. These have been normalised to the practice generally used before the introduction of decimal currency, e.g. *£8. 11s. 2d.* or *£8.11.2*. Otherwise, the presentation of amounts of money has been kept as nearly as possible to the original.

Dashes, stops, commas, etc. In the letters of the two women writers there is generally little punctuation and what appears has often been added by another hand, almost certainly that of William Clift. In these cases the fact has been noted and the punctuation included in the text. Hyphenated words which occur when words are split across lines are usually punctuated with double hyphens: =. These have been silently omitted. WC frequently uses dashes of varying lengths, especially in his later letters. Here again a regularising policy has been adopted. Dashes following full stops have been omitted; those after a colon or semi-colon have been restricted to a short dash immediately following the punctuation mark, e.g. ;– or :–. Similarly, between words a single dash has been printed, e.g. *goes – Joanna*. Only at the end of sentences where there is no stop has a lengthened dash been used. These frequently indicate paragraph breaks.

Underlining. WC increasingly underlined words in his later letters, frequently to indicate some form of word play. At the risk of tedium these words and phrases have all been placed in italics.

Dating. Many of WC's letters have two dates. The first, at the head of the letter, is usually not in WC's hand if he has dated the letter at the end. As these dates have almost certainly been added later they have been omitted.

Coded letters. A slightly different practice has been adopted for the early letters that WC transcribed into a Letter Book in code. The code itself is a simple numerical one that works as follows: 1=a; 2=e; 3=l; 4=o; 5=u; 6=h; 7=r; 8=t; and 9=y. All other alphabet characters are retained as normal. In transcribing the letters, WC has substituted his own spelling and inserted punctuation. He has retained the syntactical and morphological forms of the originals even where his own usage is different, e.g. *hath* for *has*. The letters have been rendered as he wrote them, with the substitution of the relevant characters for numbers. Any obvious slips in his transcription, such as three *es* in *seeing* have been silently corrected. The use of capitals when a word starts with a number has been normalised. With dashes the same policy has been followed as in WC's other letters.

Editorial notes. These are included in square brackets thus: [*sic*].

GENERAL INTRODUCTION

The publication of the Clift family letters is no insignificant event. In 1936 H.C. Wyld wrote:

> We want minute studies of such documents as the Verney Letters and the Wentworth papers and also of other similar letters and diaries of the same period, and if possible, of more recent collections covering the period from about 1740 to the first quarter of the nineteenth century.[1]

This was over fifty years ago but the number of writings by members of the lower and working classes published since then has been relatively few. Wyld was speaking of their importance for the study of language but the same point can be made for many other areas of scholarship.

William Clift himself is known as the last apprentice of the founder of modern British surgery, John Hunter (1728-1793), and the first Conservator of the Hunterian Museum in Lincoln's Inn Fields, where the Royal College of Surgeons of England was built specifically to house it. The first letters contained in this volume are those that he wrote when he came up to London from Cornwall as a raw country lad of just seventeen. The letters of his three brothers and two sisters represent the writings of that substratum of ordinary people whose observations and opinions are rarely available for scrutiny. Together they constitute a first-hand record of life in the late eighteenth and the first half of the nineteenth century in both country and metropolis. Apart from providing a wealth of diverse material for specialists, they give a readable account of life at that time for the general reader. The early letters, in particular, have a liveliness and vigour that is reminiscent of the novels of such writers as Fielding.

For the student of English language the letters are a mine of information. They contain late survivals of morphological and syntactical forms that have previously been considered obsolete by that date. Older forms of verbs in the past participle, proscribed by the eighteenth-century grammarians, and third person singular endings in -*th* abound. The use of *be* with a motion verb in phrases such as *I was down to Priory* or *I was to Liscard* occur. This was probably obsolescent in the late eighteenth century in standard English but remained in dialect. This is well attested but other uses are less so. There is an unusual occurrence of the continuous tense with the verb *seem*. The continuous tenses had by then only just reached their full potential with the addition of the passive forms, so it seems strange that the use with a verb still noted as not possible in the 1970s[2] should appear in the letters at all. This construction is found in the sentences: *the trade is seeming to be going on a great deal better* and *Mr Eyres family are seeming to be in a decline*. Again, idioms, such as *was a week* for 'a week ago' are to be found. This was current in late eighteenth century dialects but was fast disappearing from all forms of polite and educated English, if it had not already disappeared.[3]

The letters also show the language in a process of change, not only as the writers themselves grow older but by reason of the difference in age between the eldest sister, Elizabeth, and the youngest brother, William, a gap of eighteen years. More complex issues are raised, however, since these two have also more forms in common than those of the other writers, presumably because Elizabeth was in a sense a mother to her young brother, whose real mother died when he was eleven. The closeness of family bonding is seen overriding the normal linguistic process.

Survivals of epistolary formulas, which go back to the eleventh century, are found here, although they had not appeared in the letters of educated writers for virtually a couple of centuries. Some of these formulaic greetings and phrases are parodied in the letters of lower class characters in *Joseph Andrews* and *Humphry Clinker* and, as they do not even exist in the letter-writing manuals of the time, it may be wondered where they come from, but here is clear evidence that they existed in the letters of the illiterate and semi-literate. The word 'illiterate' is here purely descriptive and has no overtones of belittling. The very last vestiges of the formula for ending letters were still to be found until after the Second World War and the present editor was taught at school, much to her disgust even then, to subscribe herself 'Your affectionate niece', although not, happily, 'till Death', as in the letters of the Clifts. Indeed, the formulas are already in an advanced state of decay in the Clift letters and were finally abandoned by most of them.[4]

Dialect is another aspect of these letters. Dialect words are surprisingly few. Perhaps already it was felt, even among the unlettered, that they were out of place in the written language. Much may, however, be learned of the grammar as already noted and even more perhaps about pronunciation from the phonetic-type spellings, used in particular by the sisters. Spellings such as *beet* for *bit* and *feeting* for *fitting*, for instance, seem to endorse Wright's conclusion that monosyllables with a medial /i/ became lengthened in the South West to /i:/[5], but *coop* for *cup* does not appear to fit in with his statement that /u/ in this position became shortened to /ɒ/. This would lead us to expect the spelling *cop*. The whole matter of spelling, like so much else in the language, is more complex than at first appears and the immediate impression may not indicate the actual pronunciation for various reasons. *Tay* for *tea* is clearly a survival of the earlier eighteenth century pronunciation of this word, made famous by Pope in *The Rape of the Lock* (1712):

Here thou, great ANNA! whom three realms obey,
Dost sometimes counsel take — and sometimes Tea. III, 7.

It is, of course, known that the pronunciation survived a long time in dialects and can, indeed, be found today. Here is evidence of its continuing history in days for which tape recordings of pronunciation are not available. One interesting feature that occurs just occasionally in the letters of the two sisters is an initial *sh* for *s*, indicating a pronunciation [ʃ], in words like *such*. These are usually crossed out and the normal spelling substituted. The phenomenon is noted as occurring in South West dialects, although not as far west as Cornwall, by Norman Rogers.[6] It is not noted by Wright. Other curious spellings occur, such as *imeadently* more than once for *immediately*.

Folklorists, as well as dialectologists, will find the letters of interest, both for local Cornish customs, such as the mention of Bodmin Riding, and also for accounts of the London amusements, such as St Bartholomew's Fair and Greenwich Fair, the latter graphically described by William Clift. A number of sayings and catch phrases are used by the writers, some of which have defied identification and which may be hitherto unrecorded. One of these is the phrase *Bother and Turf*, which William identifies with Ireland. There are allusions to traditional tales, some well known, such as Dick Whittington and, again, some unidentified and tantalisingly incomplete, such as that of the Original London Apprentice, whose daring exploits with a lion Clift relates to his own activities. William Clift's later letters contain references to the games they played as children round the old Bodmin Butter Market, as well as to local customs and superstitions. These provide a picture at first-hand of children's amusements in the 1780s.

At some remove from the specialist areas so far mentioned is the valuable information the letters afford for the medical historian. The account of the fate and fortunes of John Hunter's Collection of biological specimens, now known as the Hunterian Museum, is of particular importance. Its early history before it was bought for the nation under the terms of Hunter's Will is faithfully recorded by William Clift, alongside his personal anxiety for his own future. Even earlier in the correspondence a few brief glimpses of Hunter himself as seen through the inexperienced and naive eyes of a country boy add to the picture of one of Britain's most eminent surgeons. Clift's acquaintance with Hunter may have been brief but it inspired a lifetime's devotion to the surgeon's work and indicates something of the magnetic personality of the man. The account of Hunter's death and funeral and the subsequent confusion into which that event threw his family and immediate dependent circle gives us an intimate picture of the household of this great but unassuming man that is almost certainly unrecorded elsewhere. Of the nature of the Collection itself relatively little emerges except in a letter from Joanna, who was clearly surprised by what she had heard of for so many years without forming any idea of the nature of its composition. Obviously to the uninitiated layman (or woman in this case) it seemed as if a great deal of fuss was made about a curious assortment of 'Thousands of Large Bottles with both Fleash fish and fowls . . . with a quantity of Scelletons great and small'. Her younger brother by this time (1800) well understood its importance for the history of natural science as well as for medicine. In addition, John Clift's letters in particular give details of remedies used in the early nineteenth century for various ailments, some of which differ very little in their ingredients today, although probably sold under brand names that conceal the ancient pedigree of their constituents.

There can be no doubt, however, that it is for the social historian that the letters are of the greatest importance. There is so much material of historical interest and a large part of it is so casually embedded in the correspondence that it is not easy to indicate relevant areas. The writers naturally write of what concerns them most and, apart from specifically family matters, these are such things as the price of food, the grain riots of the 1790s, the fortunes of the Royal Navy, especially the activities in the Mediterranean, the war with France, and many similar everyday matters which impinge on public life. Most of these are already amply recorded but it is the freshness and immediacy of the expression that is of peculiar interest here. The naked facts take on life because they are recorded by people whom they directly affected.

There are also particulars of other matters. One is the way in which local justice was administered. Bodmin was an Assize town and the writers are clearly very interested in the court proceedings, often delaying their letters until they can give news of any trials of interest. Naturally, they are most concerned when any of their own acquaintance are involved. Many other aspects of rural life mingle side by side with glimpses of life in London. The differences of life between town and country are remarked on. In London meat could be bought quite cheaply 'ready dressed' and clothes 'off the peg' were already a feature of everyday life. In the metropolis there was the obvious danger of sudden and fatal fevers, one of which is recorded in detail. Danger lurked in the streets for the unwary in other equally sinister forms. Young Clift records an incident which involved the luring of men into a bawdy house after which they were seen no more by their families but secretly shipped off to serve in the army of the East India Company, according to the account given here. But these seamier sides of life did not apparently affect the essential *joie de vivre* of the ordinary London citizens. Everyone, high and low, engaged in a round of amusements at Sadlers Wells, Vauxhall Gardens and the annual fairs. They enjoyed the spectacle of royal pageantry, which attracted almost as much notice then, in relative terms, as it does today. Processions of any sort, including funerals, were events to be witnessed and written about.

Running through the letters is information about the journeys to and from Cornwall and the capital, the various methods of transport and the means by which letters were conveyed. The constant exchange of news at such a time may come as a revelation to the ordinary reader today. There is, too, ample evidence of the general exodus from the country to the town as the effects of the Industrial Revolution came to be felt. In the later letters there are frequent references to railways and journeys by rail and steamship. Clift's letters contain snatches of information about the growth of London, which had not reached as far as Kensington Palace when he arrived there in 1792. The spread into the suburbs is clear, as well as improvements in sanitation, water supply and urban roads. Information about many other matters, such as education, trade disputes, religion and the ordinary everyday organisation of rural life, in particular, may be gleaned from these artlessly written pages.

Above all, however, the letters afford information about life at that time with a freshness and liveliness that at its best would be difficult to match anywhere else. Facts are presented not in the objective and statistical manner of a textbook but with first-hand knowledge and rapt concern. They incorporate the writers' attitudes, and these are of the utmost importance in any attempt to reconstruct the past with understanding of the way in which people actually lived. Attitudes to religion, the class system, employers, government policies and so on are all set down, although, naturally, not under those headings or even with a direct indication of what is being written about at any one time. The information has to be dug out of the morass of gossip and sometimes repetitious manner of the writing, but it is there for anyone who wishes to find it.

Less important matters from a public point of view, such as reactions to the behaviour of other members of the family, neighbours and townspeople are all expressed. The writers are free with their opinions and often give them at length. They quarrel and support each other, take sides with one person against another but, in the final analysis, the family bond holds them close in ties of affection over fifty years of separations. These are real people with feelings and responses akin to our own. Their writings evoke the spirit of the past in a way which no objective account of historical facts can ever do. It is hoped that readers of many types, the specialist and the general reader alike, will find something here of value.

NOTES   INTRODUCTION

1. H.C. Wyld, *A History of Modern Colloquial English* (Oxford, 1936), 186.
2. See, for instance, Randolph Quirk et al., *A Grammar of Contemporary English* (London, 1972), 96.
3. See F.Th. Visser, *A Historical Syntax of the English Language* (Leiden, 1963), I, 15, n. 1 and Frances Austin, *Studies in the Language of the Clift Family Correspondence,* unpub. diss. (Southampton, 1969), 394–95.
4. See Frances Austin, 'Some Epistolary Features of the Clift Correspondence' in *English Studies* (Amsterdam, 1973), 9–22; 129–40.
5. Joseph Wright, *The English Dialect Grammar* (Oxford, 1968), 70.
6. Norman Rogers, *Wessex Dialect* (Bradford-on-Avon, 1979), 27.

THE CLIFT FAMILY

The Clift family of Bodmin in Cornwall is remembered because in 1799 William Clift (1775-1849) became the first Conservator of the Hunterian Museum of anatomical specimens, now housed in the Royal College of Surgeons, Lincoln's Inn Fields, London. Clift was the youngest son of a Cornish miller, and it is chiefly from his letters and diaries that one learns about the family's background and social standing in the eighteenth and nineteenth centuries. A fragment of autobiography, begun in later years, introduces the present volume. William Clift's son in law, Richard Owen, who was responsible for separating the natural history collections from exhibition in the British Museum to their present home in his 'Cathedral of Science' at South Kensington in 1881, wrote an obituary on Clift's death in 1849.[1] *The Gentleman's Magazine*, the *Annual Register*, the *Illustrated London News*, the *Proceedings of the Geological Society* and the *Lancet* all carried obituaries. That in the *Gentleman's Magazine* betrays unawareness of Clift's Cornish upbringing and of his true relationship to John Hunter (1728-1793), the great surgeon. The obituary was written over half a century after Hunter's death, and Clift had been absorbed so completely into the London scientific establishment that thoughts about his Cornish origin had become of no account to the writer. On the other hand, this obituary is useful because it points out the esteem in which Clift was held by such leading scientists as Joseph Banks, William Wollaston and Humphry Davy. There were, of course, many other admirers, as the following pages will show.

The contributor of the Clift entry to the *Dictionary of National Biography*, William Prideaux Courtney, used the obituary from *The Gentleman's Magazine*, but he also took the trouble to find out a little more about Clift's early life, and recorded something of his Cornish background.

It is probably true to say that because Clift's daughter — he also had a son who predeceased him unmarried — became the wife of Richard Owen, William Clift was for a long time overshadowed, and all but dropped out of sight.

There was no biography of him until the middle of the twentieth century, although a two volume biography of Owen came out as early as 1894. Victorian adulation of Owen has indeed in several ways worked against a full estimate of Clift and his work. Not only was Owen the personification of all that the natural sciences stood for in the second half of the nineteenth century — he was even named by Charles Kingsley in *The Water Babies* — but by marrying Caroline Amelia Clift he inherited all Clift's papers. Inasmuch as this kept the papers in the family in 1849, when Clift died, nothing better could have been hoped for. Caroline, however, died in 1873, some twenty years before her husband. Clift's papers, therefore, became part of the mass of Owen's papers, and over the years it seems that the Owen family was not above selling portions of them.

It is some measure of the eclipse of Clift — and of the superabundance of Owen's papers — that the Clift sections were not particularly sought after. This is not surprising. As a populariser of science, Owen has had few equals. He brought to it a religious fervour that can seem humourless, and even at odds with the spirit of the lighter episodes of his early years. But it was Clift who had at heart Hunter's ideals and who fostered them unswervingly from first to last, just as he gave unqualified personal loyalty to all members of Hunter's family. Yet there is some reason to be thankful for the temporary eclipse of Clift if only because it meant that the family papers were not thought worth removing by speculative collectors from the mass of Owen's. They are not, indeed, to be found under one roof, and a few items have made their way to America and the Antipodes. But at least they are mostly in London still.

From what has been said, it is clear that twentieth-century writers on Clift have had to start work more or less from scratch. The first essay length sketch was Sir Arthur Keith's Vicary Lecture, 'The Life and Times of William Clift' in 1923, which was the basis of an account in the 'Annual Report of the Royal Cornwall Polytechnic Society' of the same year. Then, in 1954, Miss Jessie Dobson, at the time Recorder of the Hunterian Museum, and long its devoted servant, at last brought out a detailed biography of William Clift in volume form. Clift had finally emerged from the shades of the past and, taking hints from Miss Dobson's book, enthusiasts all over the world began to be drawn to his quirky yet straightforward and shrewd character.

Even so, twentieth-century writers hitherto have relied perforce upon the writings of William Clift alone. Sometimes indeed they have been led astray by his hazy sense of time. In a late letter to his sister Joanna, for instance, he told her that she could not be more than four years older than he, but she was in fact ten years older. This same vagueness with regard to time can be seen in Clift's 'Autobiography'. He says that his mother died when he was eight and his father four or five years earlier. His father was buried on the 24th May 1784 when he was nine, and his mother nearly three years later on the 10th February 1787, just before his twelfth birthday. Examination of parish registers and discovery of the letters of William Clift's brothers and sisters make possible a fuller and more accurate chronicle of a poor and relatively uneducated family till now unknown. Want of formal schooling, however, should not lead one to think that the Clifts were generally unintelligent or unable to write spirited letters that, even when technically 'illiterate', convey a vigorous zest for life.

Family background

William Clift was the youngest of seven or eight children, six of whom outlived childhood and wrote letters that survive in one form or another. The

2

most prolific writers were William, Elizabeth, John and Joanna. Thomas, it seems, wrote rarely and briefly. Only three of his autograph letters are known, although several others were included in a letter-book containing some 27 letters transformed into code by William during his early years in London. Robert's letters, too, it seems, were spasmodic and few, although he claimed that he wrote more often and that letters were lost at sea. This may or may not be true. Four of his five letters are in the same hand. The other is shorter, and could have been written out for him by a midshipman or junior officer. Of the first letter in the sequence of five, John wrote to William:

> his letter was not wrote by himself. It was wrote by a masterly hand but very illiterate spelling. I should think he might improve very much if he was inclined to learn in the place he is now, but I suppose he never will now.

Robert had been away some years when he wrote this first letter, and his handwriting may have altered enough for John not to recognize it. Certainly, four of his letters are in this same hand whether or not it was Robert's own. It is clear that writing was not his strong point. The family correspondence, therefore, consists of numerous contributions from the two sisters and two of the brothers, and occasional and slight interjections from the two remaining brothers. It should be a help to have these respective writers of letters set down in some kind of order.

The Clift brothers and sisters in order of birth are:

1. Elizabeth   1757-1818
2. John   1759-1819
3. Thomas   1762-1835 (or 1836)
4. Joanna   1765-1846
5. Robert   late 1768 or early 1769-1799
6. William   1775-1849

The four older children were born at Glynn, near the tiny parish of Cardinham, the others at Burcombe Mill, to which the parents moved between the births of Joanna and Robert, and which is even nearer to Bodmin than Glynn. Another sister was born, and possibly another brother, although they take no part in the family correspondence. The death of Richard Clift was entered in the Bodmin parish register for 1782, but so far no baptismal entry has been found. He may have been born away from home and baptised in a parish other than Bodmin or Cardinham. On the other hand, he may have been a relative — an uncle, perhaps — who died on a visit. The third sister, Bridget, was born in 1772 but lived about eighteen months only. She died in 1773 before William was born. This meant that William was some six years younger than Robert, his immediate senior in the family. In a large family this is a considerable gap that left William very much the 'baby'. Between William and Elizabeth, on the other hand, the gap of eighteen years was enough to make Elizabeth, in the course of a few years, virtually a second 'mother' to the boy. And here the span of eighteen years shows through in the language of the letters. There are many instances of Elizabeth, John and Thomas retaining older grammatical forms and phrasing, whereas Joanna, Robert and William use a rather more modern idiom.

Of the mother of these children we know little apart from the fact that before she married their father she was Joanna Courts, and that she met her husband at Cardinham, to which he came from the village of his birth, Alternun. The children followed the marriage, and the mother died in 1787 just before the twelfth birthday of the youngest. This youngest child found a little more to write down about the father. His name, wrote William, was Robert, and he

> could read well, and write very tolerably, which was much more than many of his compeers could boast of at that period.

This little passage is worth quoting again, for, if — as is likely — it is true, it suggests that the seeds of cultivation were sown in the family home, as well, of course, as William Clift's own passion for reading and writing. As a miller, however, Robert the elder was not successful. Perhaps the reading and writing atrophied the competitive spirit that was to characterize all the doings of his youngest child. Even after moving from Glynn to Burcombe to be nearer the Bodmin trade, the business failed and he resorted to becoming a journeyman. For a few extra pence he would peel sticks for fishing rods, make walking sticks or set hedges. He died in 1784. The older boys must have been at work by this time, whilst the mother and her daughters earned about fourpence a day spinning and carding wool in their own cottage.

As William Clift tells us, his mother continued to stint herself that he might stay on at school, even though he had to take his turn with the wool in the evenings. But, as noted, William's mother died in 1787, and there was no longer money for schooling. Had not Clift in later life written the fragment that introduces this collection, it would have been hard to understand anything of the attitudes to learning in his home, apart from certain exchanges in the correspondence itself. As things are, it is unlikely that parents who sent their youngest child to school were indifferent to learning, and one wonders what kind of education his brothers and sisters came by. However, in understanding a collection of letters, some knowledge of the schooling and education of the writers is a matter of general importance. Rather than hold up the narrative of the family fortunes here, therefore, schooling and education will be looked at separately further on.

When schooling ended William Clift, as he recalled in his fragment of autobiography was put to work in a nursery garden. The abrupt end to this first venture must have been a bitter blow to Elizabeth, who somehow seems to have kept going the family home in Bodmin, and who must have been relieved that William was safely launched in the world. Indeed one imagines her scolding her brother soundly for being dismissed through the folly of caricaturing unflatteringly his first employer. Yet, paradoxically, the cause of his dismissal was the very same gift that would later take him away to a successful professional career in London.

After this episode, William took any work he could find, fetching and carrying in the neighbourhood of Bodmin. These various employments he embellishes colourfully fifty years later. He would seem to have served as general *factotum* for one of the Bodmin tradesmen, almost certainly for Joseph Eyre, the man who had earlier employed his mother and sisters as carders and spinners. Joseph Eyre is, indeed, an interesting link with the strong dissenting interest of the time. His eldest brother, John Eyre, although ordained an Anglican, was turned out of Bodmin by his own family for preaching a fiery sermon. Thereafter, he founded a well-known non-conformist theological college at Hackney and became a founder member of the London Missionary Society. The letters show that William's opinion of some of his own cousins from Fowey who, by strange coincidence, sailed with the first mission of the Society to the South Seas, was neither flattering nor familial. All one can say is that his opinions mellowed with time, and that contact with the Fowey family was resumed on a more charitable basis.

Whatever William Clift's formal schooling may have been, it was enough for him to become John Hunter's last apprentice in 1792. Mrs Gilbert of Priory, Bodmin, was a schoolfriend of Hunter's wife, some of whose poems Haydn set to music. As Nancy Hosken, Mrs Gilbert was the daughter of a former Vicar of Bodmin. She left the town on her marriage to the Rev. John Vivian, of the Manor at Glynn, only a few miles from Bodmin. Unhappily, she lost her husband early. Later, in 1783, she married Walter Raleigh Gilbert (1752-1837). As Mr or Colonel Gilbert was a descendant of those illustrious Elizabethan explorers, Walter Raleigh and Humphrey Gilbert — and Gentleman of the Bedchamber to King George III — it has often seemed natural to think that Nancy Vivian married the squire of Priory. The truth, however, is that Priory was bequeathed to Nancy by her uncle, William Pennington, so that she became lady of the manor by inheritance. Gilbert was a worthy man in every way, but the manorial property was his wife's.

Although she married twice, Nancy Hosken left no children. A child by Gilbert died in infancy, and she must have reconciled herself to childlessness early. Perhaps this personal circumstance led her to notice a little boy who seems to have had the run of the downstairs servants' quarters at Priory. He clearly had some artistic flair and, in general, a lively intelligence. The little boy, of course, was young William Clift, and when Hunter's anatomical draughtsman decided to emigrate, Nancy Gilbert recalled William's drawings and mentioned him to Anne Hunter. William was soon ceremonially and legally bound apprentice, and embarked on his London life. Both Mr and Mrs Gilbert, therefore, are often named in the early Clift family correspondence that began when William joined the Hunter household in London. When in later life the erstwhile apprentice visited Cornwall, he and his wife stayed with the Gilberts at Priory. There was indeed real affection in this relationship, which, surprisingly, began in the Priory kitchens, for Nancy Gilbert left William a small sum as a token of it in her Will. Moreover, her husband kept up the friendship until his own death in 1837.

At the time William Clift went up to London, his brothers and sisters were scattered about Cornwall and the West Country, and Robert was at sea in the Royal Navy. Thomas made shoes in Bristol. The letters will show that he later made his way on foot to London. He took in Portsmouth and Southampton on the journey, and paid for his keep by cobbling in the several places he passed through. In London, he married — possibly twice — and at one time at least lived quite near to William. He stayed on in London until his death in 1835 or 1836. John had been apprenticed to carpentry and building, and was to become general foreman or steward for the Molesworths on their family estate at Pencarrow. The house is still one of the homes of the Molesworth-St Aubyn family — which also owns St Michael's Mount — today. The sisters are not as easy to follow. Almost inevitably they eventually went into domestic service. Joanna had been in such service for some years already in 1792, but Elizabeth seems to have managed to keep going the Clift family home in Castle or Cas Street, Bodmin, until William left for London. Soon afterwards, however, she was abruptly evicted from her home. She found a place in the household of Joseph Eyre and his wife, who had already employed her and her mother in the cottage woollen trade. It is much to the credit of the Gilberts — given the way of the world at the time — that not only did they give William the chance of a lifetime, but were also not above 'knowing' Elizabeth, or, for that matter, their own servants. Some of William's early drawings that had been praised by the Hunters were sent to Priory. Nancy Gilbert called in Elizabeth to show them to her. Elizabeth was allowed to choose the pictures she wanted to keep, and shared others out among servants who had known the artist and his work before he set out for London. Much later, after she too had spent some years in London, Joanna returned to Cornwall and married. Her husband was for a time part owner of a Cornish fishing boat. Elizabeth left London to join her sister in 1818 and died there later the same year. John died almost exactly twelve months later. After the death of her first husband, Joanna married an old acquaintance of her youth, much to the annoyance of William and returned to her native Bodmin. The marriage seems to have been unsatisfactory, and they separated after a short while. William apart, therefore, the brothers and sisters did not rise above the social level into which they had been born.

Within twenty months of William's arrival in London, however, Hunter died unexpectedly. His death in October 1793 was followed by the break-up of his household — some fifty people, counting family, servants and pupils — in Leicester Square and Castle Street. Anne Hunter moved out to a smaller and more economical house at Blackheath. In the meantime, Robert Haynes, Clift's immediate superior in Hunter's private museum, was kept on by the trustees in the Castle Street establishment, with William to help him, to ensure that the biological specimens did not decay. Hunter left his Collection to the nation, but for the sum of £20,000. The government was at war with France and unwilling to pay the price. Then, early in 1795, Haynes was dismissed for some petty theft — old clothing or something of the kind — and William was left, as he wrote to Elizabeth, 'cock of the walk'. The trustees, however — Everard Home (Anne Hunter's brother), and Dr Matthew Baillie, Hunter's nephew — seem to have overlooked the plight in which William had been left by Hunter's death. On a basic level, they seem not to have noticed financial hardship, whilst on a higher they probably gave no thought to the fact that Clift had lost the training that he would have received had Hunter lived. Both Anne Hunter and Nancy Gilbert assured William that he would not be forgotten, but government haggling went on for six years and he several times wondered if he would not be too old to embark on another career were he to be eventually turned away. However, despite his fears, he had caught some spark from Hunter's genius, and when the nation finally paid £15,000 for the Collection in 1799, it was said to be in even better state than at the time of Hunter's death. William, therefore, was made first Conservator of the Collection in 1800 at a salary of eighty pounds a year. His future was settled.

Shortly afterwards, he married Caroline Harriet Pope. She was then living in London, but she came from the village of Mells in Somerset, and impressed Elizabeth and Joanna as rather a 'fine lady'. There were, as noted, two children of the marriage, Caroline Amelia (1801-1873) who married Richard Owen, and William Home (1803-1832), who was named after Anne Hunter's family, and particularly after her brother, Everard Home, the boy's godfather.

William did not lose touch with his family, although the difference of condition must often have been painfully obvious to the other brothers and sisters. For many years between 1801 and 1818, indeed, Elizabeth, Thomas and Joanna all lived within easy reach of each other and of William in London, Elizabeth even taking service for a time in William's household. But whereas William started with eighty pounds a year and ended with £400, the sisters could never earn more than four or five pounds a year and their keep.

In 1810, William moved his household into quarters at the Museum designed by George Dance for Hunter's Collection in Lincoln's Inn Fields. Between 1801 and 1818 family letters almost cease. Robert had died in 1799, and John at Pencarrow was not a regular letter writer. Indeed from this time the distinctly family letters largely move forward into the generation of William's children, although William's correspondence with Joanna continued until her death in 1846.

Joanna and Thomas alone lived on to know of the important events in the later lives of William and his wife — his election as a Fellow of the Royal Society at the Instigation of Davy in 1823; the appointment of their son as Assistant Conservator — 'by acclamation' — of the Museum, also in 1823; the death of that son in a coach accident in 1832; and the marriage of their daughter to Richard Owen in 1835. William Clift and his wife finally gave up their quarters in the Museum for a house of their own, Stanhope Cottage, Hampstead Road, when William partly retired in 1842.

7

From the amount of space given to — and the amount of knowledge of William Clift — it is clear that he was the 'bright' one of the family. The letters show, indeed, that his position was acknowledged and accepted by his brothers and sisters. Yet they all, of course, came from the same background and, although one need not speculate that the others would have become as cultivated as William had they been given his chances, it is not unlikely that all of the children started their education in the same way. The word 'education' here is used in the widest sense to cover learning at home, at school, and that most important kind of education that one gives oneself.

There is William's word that their father was a relatively literate and reading man, and that their mother starved herself rather than take him away from school. Here an important division must be noted in the light of the attitudes of the time. Boys would have been treated differently from girls. However, this difference would not greatly affect the home education of the young Clifts. They would have been taught to honour their parents, to make themselves useful to the household, and to pay attention at Church. This background, based on the precepts of a religious upbringing, is both confirmed and commented on by William in a letter to his daughter Caroline Amelia, written in 1841. She was on a tour of the West Country with her husband, Richard Owen, which took in a visit to the Fox family, Quakers, of Plymouth, about whom William also writes, and details of which are to be found in *The Journals of Caroline Fox*, or *Memories of Old Friends*, to give it its proper title.[2] Of the idle moments he spent during divine service looking round Bodmin Church, William writes:

> There were many wise Saws concerning Consanguinity written on the same Wall, in a Diagram stile, and in which all People that on earth do dwell, were forbidden *ever so many* things that would never have entered any shallow head unless the church had in its kindness and foresight so properly reminded us of the glaring impropriety. It began thus:-
>
> A Table of Consanguinity.

A Man may not marry his Grandmother.	A Woman may not &c
&c. &c. &c.	her Grandfather.

Apart from obeying the Commandments and other tenets of the Church, the young Clifts would have been taught to respect learning for its own sake. According to individual aptitude, they would probably have started to scribble, to learn their letters and numbers, and even to read a little. At this stage it might even have been possible to foretell that William would in the end go far beyond his brothers and sisters in both literary and general cultivation.

The next stage, that of formal schooling, is the one in which most people show the keenest interest, and in the reading of such a collection as the Clift family letters, it is obviously of the utmost importance for its influence on the writers' differing degrees of literacy. Historically, the eighteenth century falls into a period for which documents about school education are hard to come by. The founding of the free grammar schools of Tudor times, such as those Shakespeare attended at Stratford and Wordsworth at Hawkshead, made school histories possible for such establishments, but foundations stopped in the time of the Stuarts and some of the schools were in a questionable state by the late eighteenth century. On the other hand, the Clifts were born rather too early for the charity schools that began to spread at the end of the century. In short, documentation of the institutions that did exist is so often defective that it is impossible to be sure just what kind of school the Clifts attended with anything like confidence.

The lack of documentation, however, does not excuse patient enquiry and the business of setting out the possibilities. Before doing that, however, it is worth remembering that when documents are wanting, their place can often be filled imaginatively from hints in the letters and writings of others from the same period. Frequently, this imaginative reconstruction can give a truer impression than rote-like examination of such documents that do exist without reference to what can be gleaned from other sources. The period of the early lives of the Clifts, especially William, is indeed full of impressions of this kind. Shenstone's 'The School-Mistress' is no longer widely read. The poem first came out in 1737 and it was revised several times up till 1748. It clearly shows that the village schoolmistress had already become established in the pattern of society, which could no more be thought of without her than it could without the parson. Even more telling, perhaps because it is still read, is Goldsmith's 'The Deserted Village'. People still argue about what village Goldsmith had in mind but no one doubts the existence of the schoolmaster and the parson, and that they were keystones in the arch of eighteenth century society. Indeed, it is rather alarming to recall that the poem came out in 1770, the year in which Wordsworth was born and five years before the birth of William Clift. For Goldsmith those glories had already departed and his diagnosis was in general well founded. But the passing of the pastoral way of life that he lamented did not in fact immediately annihilate the village school teachers and parsons who turned their hand to basic teaching or the squires and their ladies who were active in seeing to the needs of the children of their poorer neighbours. With such impressions in mind, one can turn to the documentary evidence for any light it casts on the general picture.

Bodmin had had a free grammar school since before 1548.[4] However, records of it in the eighteenth century, apart from the names of its masters, which are given in Maclean's *Parochial and Family History of the Parish and Borough of Bodmin*, have been lost.[5] Again, no trace of a charity school, as such, can be found in the Bodmin records. However, that Bodmin was without some sort of elementary school throughout the eighteenth century is unlikely. On the 25th of November 1799 the following advertisement was printed in the *Sherborne Mercury*:

9

Schoolmaster wanted for writing school. Corporation gives £10 per annum for education of 5 poor boys.

It cannot be proved that this school opened before 1799 because the Corporation accounts from 1701 to 1798 are missing. The placing of the advertisement in the *Sherborne Mercury*, which at first sight may seem surprising, shows that some member of Bodmin Corporation knew where they were best likely to find a teacher for a writing school, for by accident or infection, a number of related trusts had set up 'schools' in Sherborne and the neighbouring villages that set great store by handwriting. This seems to have been a local freak but there is no doubt that Sherborne and its locality had a high reputation for the quality of instruction in handwriting. It will be learnt that William Clift boasted that he could beat not only his schoolfellows but his teacher at 'print hand'. This modest school, then, could have been in existence in William's boyhood, but without the Borough records no proof is possible.

Clift's aptitude for learning and success in later life have led people to surmise that he attended the grammar school, which was housed in the Chantry of St Thomas in Bodmin churchyard. This seems unlikely. In later letters, William named his schoolmaster as John Salter. During the years in which he would have attended the grammar school, however, the headmaster, according to Maclean's list, was Moses Morgan (1781-89). Moreover, William outlined what would now be called the 'core curriculum' and it was, not surprisingly, perhaps, the three Rs — reading, writing and 'casting accounts'. On the whole, then, what William learned from John Salter would better match a writing school than a grammar school, which, by definition, would pay some attention to the classics and principally Latin.

At the same time, one must not overlook the changes taking place in the grammar schools at the end of the eighteenth century.[6] Wordsworth owed his early dedication to *English* poetry to one of his Hawkshead masters, and the reading and writing of English, as well as arithmetic, were beginning to find their way into the lower forms of the grammar schools. Strangely, the schools often charged for these elementary subjects as 'extras' comparable with, for instance, dancing, because they had for centuries concentrated solely on the classics. Frequently the Parish Clerk would be appointed to serve as 'usher' for these younger boys and John Salter was, in fact, the Parish Clerk of Bodmin. Could he then have been in charge of the lower forms of the grammar school after all? It is possible although he was also, apparently, a hairdresser and wig maker.

It is clear enough that William had some schooling and that he could come by it either at the Corporation writing school — if it existed before his mother died in 1787 — or in the lower forms of the grammar school. To attempt to teaze out the possibilities further without documentary evidence is probably a fruitless exercise. One important point seems worth making and that is, given William's character and the store he set on learning generally, it seems unlikely that, if he had attended the grammar school — even the lower forms rather than the school proper — he would not have mentioned it in the letters in which he recalls his early education. There is additional evidence that John Salter ran his own school that was separate from the grammar school. In a letter to Joanna of 1845 William writes about the Fifteen Balls public house which, he says, is 'in Prison Lane opposite my *good* Mr Salter's School'. Yet even if different readers make different deductions about William's education, the really important facts are that the basic type of education he received is known and that the death of his mother brought it to an end when he was only eleven years old.

If the precise details of the schooling of William, the youngest of the Clift family, are in doubt, those of his brothers and sisters are simply lost in the mists of time, for there is no record that they had any formal education at all. However, if the parents sent William to school, it would be reasonable to suppose that they also sent his brothers. The letters of both John and Thomas show a distinctly higher level of literacy than do those of the sisters, and they both had a pathetic yearning for a 'correctness' that they could not always attain.

Robert is the enigma. His five letters give one little to go by. But if the four of his letters written in the same hand were indeed written by him, they show that he was the least literate member of the family. If they were not written by him, then it would seem that he possibly could not write at all, or at least that he could not write well enough for him to dare to write letters to his brothers and sisters. Robert's uncertain predicament is particularly sad, as the rest of the family made a fetish of the physical act of writing with their own hands. Even at the end of her life, Joanna struggled to write to William:

> my Dear Brother I hope you will please forgive my Bad writing as I Can scarsly Hold my pen haveing almost lost the use of my right hand by the reumatic and my sight is Just as Bad But rather than suffer another to write for me I have bin several days writing this miserable scrole.

One senses the proud spirit triumphing over the flesh. Spelling mistakes and scattered capitals have no power to undermine Joanna's determination to write 'this miserable scrole' herself. Robert may simply have been inattentive at school (if he went) or could have suffered from being born just when his father's fortunes were beginning to decline. Because of this he may have missed such formal schooling as his brothers had. From the remarks of John already quoted, however, it seems that his brothers and sisters had decided that little could be expected of him. Yet it is touching to note that the first thing he did on returning to England after years in the Mediterranean was to send a letter to Elizabeth. But in 1797 he deserted from his ship, the *Echo*, at Yarmouth and lost any remaining goodwill from the family. After a fortnight he was back on duty. Whether he returned voluntarily or was caught is unknown, but when he got back the *Echo* had sailed to Cuxhaven. Whilst waiting to rejoin his ship, it is almost certain that William visited him. What took place at the meeting is unknown. William was remarkably silent on the matter and Robert apparently never communicated with his family again.[7]

If the brothers received only a sketchy formal education, it would seem likely that the sisters had less or none at all. Their home education must have been much the same as that of the boys, and when they grew up they could read and write with vigorous if incoherent fluency. Of the period between, in which no formal education has been surmised, one ought to raise a point that may have affected not only Elizabeth and Joanna, but also William among the boys as well. Much later, in 1814, John wrote that Nancy Gilbert paid the school fees of some of the local children:

> she was with the Children which she pays Schooling for — Examining their work.

Nancy Gilbert did not inherit Priory until 1789 but her father, the Rev. Anthony Hosken, was Vicar of Bodmin, so that her mother, the Vicar's wife, may well have shown interest in the education of the poorer children of the parish and her daughter may have helped her. Nancy Gilbert was indeed some seven years or so older than her second husband, Walter Raleigh Gilbert. She was born about 1745. Consequently, as she was about twelve years old when Elizabeth Clift was born, she was quite old enough to take a hand in helping both Elizabeth and Joanna with reading and writing. She signed the register at a marriage conducted by her father when she was about fifteen years old. She was never long away from Bodmin and later she certainly had a quick eye for William when he made himself at home among the servants in Priory kitchen.

Nancy Gilbert was neither the first nor the last vicar's daughter or squire's lady to take an active part in educating and schooling the poorer children of the parish. She was simply carrying on a long established tradition of parsonage and manorial philanthropy. Pedantry may smile at Elizabeth's manner of writing and at some of the wilder flights of both sisters. On the other hand, much may be said for any kind of education that enables the young to absorb — to read, mark, learn and inwardly digest, as both Elizabeth and Joanna did — the language of the Bible and the Book of Common Prayer. If they owed this to the parson's lady or the squire's lady, then that lady did not live in vain. This pattern of patronage has a long history. A squire's wife claimed later that she had taught Thomas Hardy his letters and was hurt when his parents sent him to a school away from his native village. The urge to do good must always be praiseworthy however it comes about. Both Nancy Gilbert and Julia Augusta Martin, Hardy's 'first teacher', were childless, and it would not be too far-fetched to imagine that their open-hearted affections went out to the children of others. Nor has the visit of the lady of the manor to look over the needlework of a village school yet fallen altogether out of living memory.

As for Elizabeth and Joanna, Elizabeth seems slightly the more illiterate of the two as far as spelling goes. Yet she wrote astonishingly prolifically and frequently when one takes into account her disadvantages and the postal charges of the time. It is true that many letters were carried by fellow servants in other households, who often travelled between Bodmin and London.

Joanna, going into service earlier, may perhaps have picked up the more spirited style of her early letters from other and younger servants. At least, one senses a slightly later form of English informing her writing.

Because William Clift did not go to university, it has been hinted that he may be an early instance of the climbing technocrat class, somehow, possibly just emancipated from the ranks of the artisans, but not quite of professional standing. Such hints are unhistorical. What Clift did was utterly conventional: he found a patron, or patroness, in Nancy Gilbert. His distinction is that he made the most of his good fortune. Had John Hunter lived longer, William would most likely have become a surgeon and nothing would have been heard of his being not quite professional. The Royal College of Surgeons was very much the equivalent of the university anatomical departments at the time, just as the Inns of Court were the equivalent of law departments. Those in the best position to know treated Clift as an equal. Not only Nancy Gilbert left Clift a token bequest but Ann Abernethy, the widow of one of the foremost surgeons of the time and one of Clift's most intimate friends, also remembered him in her Will. William Clift was a professional among professionals.

This discussion has swept straight past one of the most important stages in any education, that is, the education one gives oneself. The letters will show certain discussions of books among the writers but clearly William, as in all intellectual matters, outstripped his brothers and sisters. In the 1790s he laid the foundation of a passion for the theatre and the round of the London season. In the early London years he listed some of his reading: *Tom Jones, Joseph Andrews, The Vicar of Wakefield, Roderick Random, Tristram Shandy, Robinson Crusoe*[8] . . . here, surely, were the makings of a respectable course in fiction, and later Clift undoubtedly kept his reading up to date well into the Dickens and Thackeray era. In his retirement he writes of re-reading his forty odd volumes of Walter Scott. He learned French at some time and was several times in France. William, it has been noted, made the most of his chances. His brothers and sisters did not have such opportunities and their level of culture remained consequently on a lower plane. Apart from the mechanics of spelling, punctuation and handwriting, about which John, in particular, was deeply concerned — he once admonished his youngest brother that without correct spelling the most impeccable handwriting was of little worth — it cannot be said that any formal schooling greatly influenced the style or even layout of the family's letters. The many grammar books intended for school use that were published during this period simply show, like so many similar school text books today, that they were too remote from everyday usage to affect family correspondence and informal writing. William, as always a compulsive learner, deliberately set out to better himself when he went up to London, and he may have adjusted his usage by studying such grammars as that of Lindley Murray, which came out in 1795 and stayed in print throughout Clift's lifetime. Consequently, only his early letters can be considered comparable with those of his brothers and sisters.

Style of writing

Schooling apart, there are possibly three formative influences at work upon the Clift family letters. The first was undoubtedly the religious atmosphere of their background. In early years, the Bible and the Book of Common Prayer would have been regular reading. Soon after William arrived in London, Elizabeth asked in one letter,

> when you write let me know if you have bought the prayer book.

Then, there were the week after week, season by season, readings from the Bible in Church services, and sermons — good, bad and indifferent — drawing heavily on the wording, phraseology and cadence of the English of Cranmer and the early seventeenth-century translators of the King James Bible, an English that made its way through half-closed eyelids and brains dulled by tiredness to become the listener's own means of expression. A passive receptivity is one of the surest methods of absorbing the spirit and essential sound of what one hears. Elizabeth and Joanna in particular seem in their letters to be echoing the Scriptures and the Liturgy.

A second influence was that of 'letter-writers', that is handbooks of sample letters compiled to show how one should write in any number of particular circumstances. This kind of book is still found even today. Such books could have been used at school but it is not likely that they were. One of the Clift letters luckily names one such handbook owned and used by the family. In an early letter from Elizabeth, coded by William, she tells him that Thomas is going to write to him:

> I have heard from Brother Thomas and he is very well. He sent home for me to send *The Young Man's Best Companion* and desired to know where to direct to you.[9]

The book so titled was written by George Fisher and it ran through many editions in both Britain and America between about 1735 and 1853. This might mean that the book had originally belonged to the Clift parents. Such books, indeed, led long lives, for interestingly, as late as 1874, Hardy named Fisher's book as part of Gabriel Oak's library in *Far from the Madding Crowd*. In it are arithmetical instructions, rules for spelling and punctuation and specimen alphabets, all of which must have been seen by the Clifts. Even ciphers and 'secret writing' were dealt with. This could have put into William's head the notion of coding the earlier of the letters he received in London, although the simple numerical code he uses, which was understood by other members of the family, has not been found in copies so far examined. The number of specimen letters in any edition seems to have been few. The 1763 edition, for example, gives seventeen. Fisher's layout and approach may have influenced the Clifts, but none of the surviving letters conforms with any of these 1763 specimens or any others in different editions. Even Thomas's writing does not reflect any evidence of using them as models in spite of his request. Of the family, John seems to have been the one most influenced by Fisher's sample letters, as his two first letters, typical of those 'from an Elder

Brother to a Younger on his Leaving Home', with their good advice, show. *The Young Man's Best Companion* was a source of much miscellaneous information and was clearly very popular. The earlier editions were based very closely on Mather's *Young Man's Companion*, which was published early in the eighteenth century. It would be interesting and useful to identify the edition owned and used by the Clifts but this has not so far been possible.

The third influence on the letter writing of the Clifts may be called traditional family usage. Layout, along with opening and closing formulas are frequently passed on from parents to children even when schools seek to teach other ways. The Clift children, then, probably adopted much of their epistolary modes from their parents. This would account for the formulas many of them have in common. It may also account for the fact that the styles they adopt can be found in upper class letters of an earlier period, although they differ markedly from those of contemporary literary and more educated writers.[10] In all linguistic fields, the usage of the less educated is far more conservative and changes more slowly than that of the educated.

It will have been noted that all three of these fundamental influences on the letter writing of the Clifts were firmly based not on book learning, or what may have been taken in at school, but upon usages of the parents and the family in general. Whatever other influences may have played a part, the home background always showed whenever pen was put to paper.

However, following family usage does not mean that the Clifts were unselfconscious letter writers — if such people exist — and John and William, in particular, had notions of what letters required, especially in spelling and handwriting. John's comment on Robert's letter has been quoted and his advice to William mentioned. William, all his life, made much of a good hand. Of John Salter and his family he wrote in a late letter:

> They were all excellent kind-hearted people but I beat them all at print hand by their own unaminous confession,

and of his grandson, Willy Owen, he wrote to the boy's father:

> Willy will write, if I don't mistake, a very legible hand — pray encourage him in it.

Writing from Hunter's dictation was one of William's chief tasks when he first went to London. Indeed, his handwriting as well as his drawing ability led Nancy Gilbert to recommend him for the situation. The many volumes in his hand in the Library of the Royal College of Surgeons, copies of Hunter's manuscripts made mainly between 1793 and 1799 when he was looking after the Collection, show his facility and compulsiveness. When he wrote letters, he often drafted and corrected them, tightening wording and phrasing for the posted copy. 'I am almost tired', he writes of one letter,

> with writing this twice over as it did not please me the first time.

And again:

> I have sent my second letter with this because I had not time to write it over again.

Such was his mania that he sometimes corrected the spelling and punctuation of letters he received. Elizabeth's letters were particularly subjected to this treatment and, without considering her educational drawbacks, he once wrote her a bad-tempered rebuke:

> but I shall never be convinced to the contrary of what I now think, by you, unless you learn to mend your Orthography or spell better; because no person on earth I am very certain can understand the true meaning of what they read unless they read it right and unless they understand its true meaning it is impossible their Ideas of things can be rightly formed.

This graceless condescension must have wounded the person who had mothered him through later boyhood. The coded letters are particularly revealing, for when transliterated into ordinary prose, they show that William changed spelling and punctuation to match his own, but left untouched idioms and grammatical forms, such as *hath*, that he never used in his own writing. John often apologises for mistakes and of one letter writes:

> I hope you'll excuse this abrupt old fashioned letter, or I rather should have said new fashioned, for I am sure you never saw one like it from me or any person else.

As it happens, this apology is neatly turned and gives the impression of a mind in the act of thinking. It shows, indeed that John had in him the makings of as natural a letter writer as his young brother.

In spite of likenesses drawn from their common background, the Clifts developed distinct styles of their own that, if hard to define, are usually easily recognisable. John is careful, concise and deliberate; Joanna is flamboyant, helter-skelter and convoluted; Elizabeth plods, often repeating herself, although she arrives at her intended goal after numerous meanderings and digressions on the way. William is lively, graphic, racy and humorous — qualities that he later developed in letters to his wife and children into a fine art and one, incidentally, that he bequeathed to his son, William Home Clift, in whose letters it reached its apotheosis. Only Robert and Thomas remain shadowy. As a mere five letters from Robert remain, there is little room for self-portraiture. All that one is given are details of shipping movements and naval battles — the latter Robert mostly contrived to miss. One learns of a constant longing for letters from home, a longing shared by hundreds of thousands of seamen in the vast fleets of the Royal Navy at that period. In general, Robert's letters are typical of any seaman's letters of his time. Likewise, few of Thomas's letters have survived and these are even shorter than Robert's. There is not space enough for the language to bear any markedly individual stamp of the man's personality.

Between the letters of the four most prolific letter writers among the Clift brothers and sisters, certain grammatical and syntactical differences can be seen. There are three main trends and they divide the writers into three different groups. The most obvious division has already been mentioned, the difference in ages that separates Elizabeth, John and Thomas from Joanna,

Robert and William. The second division has also in fact been referred to, and that is the difference in education that separates the sisters from the brothers. The third division at first seems surprising. This, too, has been hinted at, but that it should have any linguistic bearing would seem to run counter to the age division. This is the separation of Elizabeth, the eldest, and William, the youngest, from the other members of the family. On several occasions Elizabeth and William use forms and phrases — especially opening and closing formulas — that are not found in the letters of the others. The only possible explanation seems to be that when their mother died, Robert at roughly eighteen was a man; William, on the other hand, at eleven was still a boy. Elizabeth, however, was twenty-eight or twenty-nine — in other words, she was old enough to be William's mother. Elizabeth clearly took her responsibilities in bringing up this youngest child seriously, as Joanna later was to recall:

> I well know I never had it in my power to merit your kind attention as you know well my sister Did and its Equally known to me that she has bin a friend to the friendless and as a Tender mother to the Motherless Child.

This tribute — perhaps one senses a touch of envy in it, for it seems that Joanna herself was childless — is probably decisive. The bond of affection between Elizabeth and William shows through all their letters, even when they were having what William called a heated 'paper war' about religion. Elizabeth was hurt and William proud, and the letters stopped for over a year. But William, proud 'cock of the walk' as he was in London, grasped at once the first chance that Elizabeth gave him of making up the quarrel. Elizabeth clearly held the Bodmin home together until William went to London, and it was she who saw to it that his indentures of apprenticeship to Hunter were properly and legally drawn up, and she who noted, in a roundabout way, the time at which they expired. The others left Bodmin earlier than William, and so Elizabeth's influence on him was greater than on them. Many of their shared expressions were dropped by William, one by one, as he established himself independently in London. But in the early years the likeness of expression of William's letters to those of Elizabeth is often surprising and can only be accounted for along some such lines as have been surmised here.

This separation of Elizabeth and William on grounds of usage is unexpected and, by the same token, almost certainly the most interesting linguistically, even though its grounding is biographical. But the people are ultimately inseparable from the way they use their language. As has been remarked, the Clifts who have left behind a substantial body of letters can be differentiated by a grammatical usage here and an idiomatic usage there, but other differences defy definition. No matter how laboriously their letters are combed for distinguishing features and no matter how illiterate some of them are, they elude complete description as inevitably as do the no less distinctive personalities of the writers themselves.

NOTES
THE CLIFT FAMILY

1. Richard Owen, Obituary of William Clift in the *Proceedings of the Royal Society* (1849), V, 876.
2. *The Gentleman's Magazine* (August 1849), 209-10.
3. *The Journals of Caroline Fox 1835-71,* a selection ed. Wendy Monk (London, 1972).
4. See A.F. Leach, *Educational Charters and Documents 589-1909* (Cambridge, 1911), 476-77.
5. John Maclean, *Parochial Family History of the Parish of and Borough of Bodmin in the County of Cornwall* (London 1870), 102.
6. See further D. Robson, *Some Aspects of Education in Cheshire in the Eighteenth Century* (Manchester, 1966) 43-65, esp. 54-56.
7. See Frances Austin, *Able Seaman Robert Clift of Bodmin 1790-1799* (Dorset, 1983), for a full account of Robert's life and letters.
8. These were probably instalments of the *Novelist's Magazine,* 1780-88 and later. *Phillip Quarll* was also included in the series – see Foreword, p.19. Peter Longueville, *The Hermit or the...adventures of Phillip Quarll.* 1st pub. 1727 under the pseud. Edward Dorington.
9. George Fisher, *The Instructor; or, Young Man's Best Companion* (Edinburgh, 1763). 1st pub. c.1735.
10. See Frances Austin, 'Some Epistolary Features of the Clift Correspondence' in *English Studies* (Amsterdam, 1973), Vol. 54, 9-22; 129-140, for the origin of these formulas, particularly the opening and closing formulas.

'FOREWORD'
BY
WILLIAM CLIFT F.R.S.

I cannot but think, that a short account of my Life would interest
many people:– not equalling in adventure that of Robinson Crusoe, or Phillip
Quarll;– but perhaps no less useful; being more within the every-day
occurrences of every-day life; (and yet not an every day occurrence in many
particulars:) and consequently may be as useful though not so entertaining as
the before-mentioned celebrated individuals; in setting an example to many,
who like myself may be cast adrift on the Wide world, and at last be taken in
tow by an almighty & beneficent Providence which generally affords assistance
to those who show an inclination to provide for themselves, and struggle
against adverse fortune.

My father I have every reason to believe, never having heard a whisper to
the contrary, was a very honest man;– one tolerable reason why he did not
succeed better in the world;– He was born at Alternon in Cornwall in the year
1720 and having been educated in the best manner that his poor parents could
afford, for he could read well, and write very tolerably, which was much more
than many of his compeers could boast of at that period, he was probably
apprenticed to a miller; at all events that was his calling. When he became a
young man he went to seek his fortune, and engaged a Mill on his own account
at Glynn, about four or five miles from Bodmin in Cornwall and Cardinham
being the nearest Parish Church, (or at all events the prettiest girls in the
parish were to be met with there; I recollect that when a child the young men
came from far and near to Cardinham Church.) There he became acquainted
with my mother Joanna Courts, whose father was a Carpenter and she was,
even within my recollection, after much distress and privation, a good looking
woman; and two of my Aunts that I have seen that were better off, were
remarkably good looking women and had very passable families. At all events
my father having taken possession of the Mill at Glynn must needs have a wife,
and most of my Sisters and Brothers were born at Glynn:– but the mill being at
the distance of four or five miles from the nearest market towns, Lostwithiel
or Bodmin though it possessed a beautiful & never failing stream of Water, did
not yield sufficient profit to support an increasing family, and an opportunity
offering of a mill at Bury-combe, or Burcombe, within a mile of Bodmin
Market, my father removed to that situation: and there I had the good or bad
fortune to be born (after one or two others.) This unfortunate Mill had the
misfortune to be situated about three quarters of a mile further from the

Town than John Jeffery's Mill which, as a matter of course, took almost all the poor people's corn to grind on account of the distance; and consequently my poor father got but little to do, though in addition he was under the necessity of keeping a horse to fetch and carry that little, to and from the Town. After struggling on for some years he was obliged to resign the Mill, and became a journeyman miller wherever he could find employment, and occupied his leisure hours in making fishing rods and walking sticks, or building hedges, at which he was considered a very dexterous architect. My poor mother, and sisters occupied themselves in carding and spinning wool, which was the staple employment of most of the poor people, during the Winter months, and haymaking and harvest during the Summer which afforded but miserable and scanty sustenance, as the greater number of employers gave only four pence a day, very few indeed gave six pence, and no food or drink! And farmer's men, with a family, got only a shilling a day in summer, and ten pence a day in Winter:– and no perquisites except perhaps a few turnips:– potatoes being too precious to give away.

Notwithstanding this miserable state of things, my poor mother contrived to starve herself to afford me three–pence a week for schooling – though I was obliged to work over hours in winding the yarn she had spun during the day, into skains, to be rendered up to the owner on Saturday. And at length, when my poor mother died, (my father having died of Pleurisy four or five years previously) I was obliged to seek for employment in a nursery when about eight years old, where I worked steadily for about two years at four pence a day; and became a tolerable botanist and horticulturist. Unluckily for me, Mr King the Nurseryman was a great lover of Brandy and water, or rather brandy without the water, and when he had had a sufficient quantity he became exceedingly boisterous and domineering, and as he had for many years been a martyr to the gout he was obliged to ride over his domains to look after his foreman and workpeople and usually in a violent ill humour, he never scrupled to strike whoever offended him, or came in his way, every one lived in fear of him except the foreman (Mr Williams) who on being threatened with a beating like the rest of the workmen, threatened in return to pull him off his horse, and consequently he (George King) never offered to strike him (Mr Williams) afterwards: but laid it on double, on those who were afraid to resist: as there were no understood laws for assault and battery in that part of Cornwall in those days.

Under Mr Williams's auspices I had learned many things that the other boys could not so readily acquire, such as budding and grafting, putting down layers, transplanting seedling plants, and various other light work in which I was favoured by the foreman who had taken a fancy to me, who even occasionally entrusted me with his gun and powder horn (no small favour to a boy of twelve or thirteen years old,) but these *halcyon* days were not to last, though there were no *King's fishers* to shoot at) King George, though he durst

William Clift F.R.S. by his son, William Home Clift

21

not resent Mr Williams's using the Gun, could visit his sins upon every one else; and one day in a fit of ill humour he endeavoured to knock me on the head with his everlasting long cane – but having excellent use of my legs, and knowing that he durst not gallop over the cucumber frames and glass shades which protected the young cuttings of Geraniums and Myrtles I took to my heels, leaving him to vent his rage on his white horse, or the next comer. This he did not forget; and to make the bad worse, I drew a caricature of my good master and myself with a label coming out of my mouth "Running for my Life." This tickled the fancy of my good friend Mr Williams so much that he gave me the largest sum I had ever possessed (a shilling) by way of encouragement; and though he showed it to every body in the town, and raised my character as an artist, it boded me no good, and did not make my fortune; for on the next Monday morning on going to work as usual, Mr Williams told me with a very long and grave face that Mr King had heard of my Drawing (in fact he had shown it to him, as a good joke, not thinking of the consequences) and he had desired him to say that he was not in want of a Botanical draughtsman and that I had leave of absence. Well, thought I, I'll go for a soldier! Many a better and taller fellow than I have done so:– but on second thoughts, that scheme would not exactly do, as I found on stretching myself to the utmost I did not measure five feet by an inch or two: and they did not enlist fifers. Mr George Wills the Drum major always contrived to fill the ranks with his own begetting and I was not strong enough to carry a Drum. So as neither George King, nor King George, would accept of my services or give me a retaining fee, I got a new master within half a day, and became a most useful jack of all trades, sometimes as courier, carter, plowboy; and became expert at harrowing, plowing, sowing, reaping, haymaking, and all other country pastimes; and as my new Master had a most ample choice of employments, and occupied half the workpeople in the Town I had great variety of occupations in a way much more to my liking, being chiefly among the horses, which was my delight, and many a hundred mile, and many a hundred pounds was I entrusted with, little urchin as I was, all round the country and frequently to the astonishment of the Country people and Turnpike keepers who frequently wondered at their sending such a child on such errands so many miles from home: and many times I had hair breadth escapes in consequence of these thoughtless sendings, and returnings at night among the Tin mines and stream works, from Luxillion, St Austle, Fowey, Wadebridge St Minver (Christening Cake) Launceston (in 2 hours) Liskeard, Lostwithiel, St, Blazey with Quick Lime – with drunken Carters, &c. & &c. but always escaped accident and robbery, or loss.

30th March 1840.

I. FEBRUARY TO JUNE 1792

It seems probable that it was Joseph Eyre, the prosperous Bodmin business man, for whom William became a general jack of all trades and errand boy after being dismissed by Mr King for his comic and offending sketch of the nurseryman. Apart from what he tells us of his childhood in his short autobiography, other youthful pranks and activities are recounted later in letters to his sister, Joanna, and his daughter, Caroline. From these we have a glimpse of the boy in church on Sundays, awaiting the entrance of the tardy parson and studying the table of consanguinity which was set on the wall for all to see, for the congregation was 'forbidden ever so many things that would never have entered any shallow head unless the church had in its kindness and foresight so properly reminded us of the glaring impropriety'. William Clift did not waste his time while the parson fussed because 'Mr Salter had not sufficiently curled frizzled & powdered his Wig or his hair'. Like generations of boys before and after him, he busied himself with cutting his initials into the church pews. On another occasion, finding the door to the belfry open, he climbed the steps and set the bells ringing, then ran for his life to watch at a safe distance as the indignant ringers rushed back from their ale mugs to know the cause of the disturbance. Once he fell off his horse and was knocked unconscious, only narrowly escaping the fearsome operation of trepanning. He says that he 'was obliged to walk as gravely as an old man for a year or two afterwards'.

His talents as an artist were suddenly in demand when, in 1789 as a result of Pitt's shop tax, every shopkeeper was obliged to display a sign in his window. But his skill in that direction was not unnoticed elsewhere. Mrs Gilbert of Priory observed how young William often drew pictures for the amusement of her maid servants, whom he frequently visited. His ability at handwriting was freely acknowledged by his former schoolmaster, Mr Salter, the Parish Clerk. When, therefore, Anne Hunter told her old school friend of her husband's difficulties in finding a suitable apprentice who could assist in drawing specimens and copying from dictation, Mrs Gilbert had no hesitation in recommending the sixteen-year old William, whom John Hunter agreed to take without the usual fee. So, the young 'botanical draughtsman' whose services were not required in the nurseries at Bodmin was set on the path to London, to join the household of the most eminent surgeon in England.

After the indentures had been signed, his sister Elizabeth and Mr Gilbert acting as witnesses, and all arrangements made, William set out early in February 1792 for Fowey, whence he was to make the journey to the capital by sea. Elizabeth and John accompanied him, and Elizabeth, at least, stayed with him at Fowey for a few days at the home of their Uncle, James Puckey, and his family. John probably travelled back immediately to Bodmin, where he stayed the night before going on to the house of his employer, Sir William Molesworth, at Pencarrow. From Bodmin he wrote his first letter to his young brother before he set sail.

The first two of John's letters contain advice and sentiments which were considered appropriate for an older brother to express to a younger one on his leaving home. We know this from the various letter–writing manuals, popular at the time, which frequently include among their model letters one headed 'A Letter from an Elder Brother to a Younger on his Leaving Home'. That the Clifts possessed one of these manuals is apparent from a letter in which Elizabeth tells William that Thomas has written from Bristol asking for their copy of *The Young Man's Best Companion* so that he can write to his brother in London. This was probably *The Young Man's Best Companion* by George Fisher, although this does not contain a letter of the kind written by Thomas.

After the voyage, William reached John Hunter's house in Leicester Square on February the 14th, his seventeenth birthday and the sixty-fourth birthday of Hunter, who was apparently indisposed at the time. William took up his duties in the museum under the assistant, Robert Haynes, who had been sent to fetch him from the boat, and after a few days he was initiated into his work as amanuensis to John Hunter himself. William was impressed by the size of the establishment in which he found himself and gives a list of the servants, but apparently he greatly underestimated the size of the household, which, counting family, apprentices, house pupils, servants and attached employees, numbered about fifty at this time. The premises extended from 'the front house' in Leicester Square to the house in Castle Street (now part of Charing Cross Road) behind, where William had his quarters with Haynes and a separate housekeeper, Mrs Adams.

William's first letters tell of his work and his impressions of John Hunter, to whom he was immediately attracted. He also relates his early experiences of London life and describes the sights with lively enthusiasm. Particularly notable is the description of the funeral procession of Sir Joshua Reynolds, who live in Leicester Square and died very shortly after William arrived in London. During these first months the brothers and sisters in Cornwall all made the effort to write to their young brother and we have the beginnings of the Bodmin gossip which is to continue throughout the correspondence. The names of the many people mentioned make little impact at first but gradually some emerge and take their places as characters in a saga of Cornish life. Catty Pinch, the 'prentice girl', who worked for Mrs Eyre, the turbulent Climo family, and William Tabb, the Gilbert's servant who frequently acted as the carrier of letters between Bodmin and London, all become a familiar part of the background. Other people whose names often appear among the lists of

24

Burcombe Mill, Bodmin, by Isabella Mary Alms 1900
Birthplace of William Clift

25

'enquiring friends', Thomas Arthur, John Ford and the curiously baffling 'Onion', remain names and nothing more.

This section ends with a single letter from Cousin James Puckey of Fowey to Elizabeth in Bodmin. No other letters written by him seem to be extant but he and his brother appear later in the letters and occasion a quarrel between William and Elizabeth so heated that the correspondence between these two virtually lapses for over a year between the end of 1797 and July 1799.

1. John to William. 9 February 1972. (Coded)

Bodmin 9 Feb^{ry} 92

My dear dear Billy,)

I hope you will excuse my not writing a long letter at present as I am very much fatigued with the journey, the roads being so very bad.

I went to Priory and gave your duty to Mr and Mrs Gilbert and left them know that we had a very agreeable journey, and I expected you'd sail the beginning of next week; I have been to see Joanna, and found her in much better spirits, than I expected. Kitty is just come home drunk, – I find Sir John is in town, and the repeated oaths that he makes use of renders me incapable of saying what I other wise might.

Please to give my kind love to Uncle & Aunt & Cousins and I return them my humblest thanks for the many favours we have received from them

May God grant all your undertakings may be crowned with success, which will ever give me the greatest happiness this world will produce or possibly ever can while I have existence—

I hope you will have a pleasant passage to London & I shall expect a few lines immediately after your arrival. I intended to have gone to Pencarrow to night, but as it is verry likely to be a wet night I shall defer it untill morning tho' I had rather sleep on a rock if I had you in my arms so may the Almighty bless, preserve, & keep you, which will ever be the constant prayer of your most affectionate Brother

John Clift.

P.S. I hope you wil be so good to send me a few lines when you sail. Mrs E Northy died since we left home.

2. William to Elizabeth. 19 February 1792.

Sunday London Feb^{ry} the 19th 1792

Dear Brother and Sisters/

I have taken this opportunity of sending you these

26

few lines hoping twill find you in good health as it leaves me at Present I have a
thousand things to write and I Can't tell where/ where to begin first – But I
think Ill begin from the time I left Fowey – Just as we was getting out of the
Harbour I saw you and Cousin Polly out at St Cathrines and I look'd at you till I
saw you get out at the Castle and sit down upon the Bank the other side and I
look'd and look'd and look'd again till you look'd so small that I Cou'd not
discern you scarcely only your red Cloak, when we got out at the Harbours
mouth the Vessel began to tumble and Pitch finely But I did not get sick till we
were Past Eddy stone – and after I was past that I soon knew what the Ship was
made of and began to Cry Oak Oak for my life and so kept to it for that day and
night and Part of the next day till Dinner time I went down in the Cabbin
when the men was at dinner and after I had Cast up all my accounts[1] I eat a bit
of a Bit of lean salt Beef and a Cold Potatoe and that so settled my Stomach
that I never Vomited afterwards, but I was Verry Qualmish that day and so I
went to bed and against the Morning I was Come Pretty well settled and so I
had some tea and at dinner time we had Pork Boild and then I made a Verry
Hearty meal and from that time I Recover'd and became quite well and Coud
Eat like a Horse, for the first night I slept (or lay) for sleep I Cou'd not, upon
the floor of the Cabbin *   * Evening when I went down *again* to Vomit
Bravely for I was a great Deal better when I was up in the air and so I lay down
upon the floor and there I lay till the morning which seemd a Month to me and
when the daylight came I Got up upon deck again And there I staid till dinner
time – I saw a little of Plymouth but we were a great way from it and so I Coud
not see much of it, I saw Stuart,[2] Portland, and the Isle of Wight we Sailed
almost Close by it but it is no great Prospect for tis nothing but great Hills – So
the third night I saw Dungeness there they make Great fires for a guide to the
Shiping and a little farther on I saw the south falling light[3] and In the morning
when I rose I found the Vessel at anchor Close by Deal town for in the night we
had Pass'd the straights of Dover, and so I did not see any thing of that but the
Castle and a little of the Town Back over the Hills – Deal is a verry Pretty Place
by what I Coud See of it for We were not on shore, there are six wind mills
about the town that I Coud see and how many that I Cou'd not see I Cant tell –
Just as we had lost sight of Deal another pretty View began to shew itself
Named Ramsgate which was a Brave little Round town enough – and Just as
we had past that we met with another pretty Town Called Broad stairs Then
we past that and Came in View of a Pretty Farm house Surrounded with
Thousands of Trees and Close by the Sea Side was a Plenty of the most
Beautifull Pleasure Houses ever I saw in my life and Just by that stood the
North falling light[4] – or North headland – then we turnd the Corner and
Came to Margate which was a Verry Pleasant Place But I Coud not see much
of it because where they Dont stop we Cant see much because we said out of
sight presently[5] and then we Came to the two Sisters which is a small Place
with a Church and Two towers at the End Close *by each* other and then in a

few Hours we got into the Thames and then to Gravesend where we Cast anchor and the *Capt* Mr Spicer and myself went on Shore – and then I had a good Prospect of it and all the Houses are Built with brick and Coverd with Tiles as are the Houses in Deal and Margate &c – from thence we with the morning Tide Reach'd Woolwich which is a verry Pretty Place and large as well – There is a Warren[6] for soldiers and Barracks/There the Capt Mr Spicer and I went on shore and View'd it all Round for they always Put me with them where ever they went from thence Jack and I went to greenwich by land (which servd to Raim[7] my legs a bit) to get a boat to tow us into London Where I Had a View of the Hospital Park &c &c &c – and from Woolwich they towed us into London with the Evening tide, and there I sent the Letter to Mr Hunter the next day – on tuesday evening we reach'd London on wednesday I sent the letter and on the thursday after Dinner they Came to fetch me One Mr Hains the Clerk whence we had a Coach and which Carried us to the kings Mew's which is almost Close by my masters House – I have not seen much of London yet – We have a great family indeed there is ladys Maid, Butler, two footmen, Clerk, Cook and three Servant Maids and Myself[8] Mr Hunter Has been poorly lately and I Have not seen him yet – I have seen Mrs Hunter & Mrs Gilbert and Will[m] Tabb and they are all Verry Well – Please to Remember me to Priory Maids and all Enquiring Friends I like my Place Verry well so far – I saw John Galty Chandler – I Cant write more for want of Room But next Time You shall Have more Particulars I Have been making Paper Boxes for Holding Preparations thes 2 Days and I supose When I see my Master I shall be put to Draw—
So nomore at Present from your affectionate
Brother William Clift

Please to Excuse this *   * Scrowl this time and *Next time* Ill write it
Better

*   * Direct for W Clift at John Hunters *at* Nº 13 Castle Street Leices[r]
Square

3. John to William. 26 February 1792. (Coded)

Bodmin Feb[ry] 26th 92

Dear Brother,
         I now take my pen in hand with the greatest pleasure to inform you that we (to our great satisfaction) have received your kind letter, and to return you a thousand thanks for writing so soon. I thank God for so favourable weather as you had on your passage. I am happy to hear you had so

28

good a prospect of the country, after you found what the vessel was made of. I am happy I did not see you out in the troll boat[9] at Fowey, as Sister informs me you were, I bless God who preserved you from sudden death, and hope he will bless & prosper you thro' life in all good undertakings; be sober & discreet in all you do, be kind & courteous to every one you have to do with, & let the remembrance of your God still have the first place in whatever you do, for that is the way to attain the truest wisdom, never absent yourself from your masters house by any means without his leave and always be attentive to his commands.

Charles Blake is just come home from Bristol, he says he saw Brother Thomas when he left Bristol in very good health. We have not seen Charles, since he came home, but I expect he hath no letter for us as he came to town Friday last; while we were at Fowey. Charles sent his mother a letter in which he informed her that he had seen Brother and he proposed to send something by him, but we do not hear any thing of it at present. I expected to have had a letter from him long ago as I wrote to him concerning your going to London.

Sister is now reading your letter to Tammy Bonny and she is laughing heartily to hear that you found it to be Oak. Sister is tollerable well at present, she has been poorly since she came from Fowey. I have got a bad cold at present and have for these several days past.

My dear Billy it will seem seven years before I see you again tho' I hope it will not be two, if every thing answers my expectation, which will be the happiest day I shall ever see if I find you so happy as I shall always pray for, Mr Rob[t] Hoblyn was buried this day week. Poor Sister Joanna had like to have been killed by her masters cow last week, she run her horn in under her arm a full blow, but happily did no material harm.

I hope by this time you have had the pleasure to see your Master and I hope he will like you verry well & you him – which will give me the greatest happiness. E. Yeo desires to be remembered to you, J[n] Ham is gone to Bristol to work & Rich[d] Hurden is going this week, I suppose to better his trade. I have found your magnet since you have been gone, we have sent the things to Cousin W[m] by Tammy Bonny to Fowey Fair.[10] I am glad to find Mr & Mrs Gilbert was in London when you came as it must be great satisfaction to you, to find any person there you knew, much more so them that should be always esteemd your best friends.

Sisters give their love to you, likewise all friends. I hope you will let me hear from you as soon as convenient so no more at present from your affectionate

Brother,
John Clift.

P.S. Please to give my love to W. Tabb.

29

Sister hath desired me to let you know that she went to Polkerries the day you sailed & staid but a few hours.
E Collins gave her love to you.

4. *William to Elizabeth. 5 March 1792.*[11]

Regency 1811-2
george III 1760-182

London February 5th 1792

Dear Brother and Sisters
I have this opportunity of sending you these few lines, hoping they will find you in good health as it leaves me at Present, I Bless god for it, I have been verry well since I have been here and likely to continue so, But William Tabb has been verry Ill almost ever since he has been here, at least for a fortnight and more, he was not out of door till yesterday was week, he had a Gathering in his neck and broke and then he had a Blister and Plenty of Doctors stuff to take but he is come very well again now I was up at Mrs Gilbert's house yesterday was week and Dined there, and that was the First time I saw Mr Gilbert, he was verry Glad to see me and Mrs Gilbert gave me a Shilling and I was in the Parlour with them for an Hour I Believe, and I have the pleasure to tell you, that Mrs Gilbert told me that when I had a letter to send to you that I shou'd carry it to Mrs Hunter and She would Frank it, because Mrs Hunter has Got a Frank and then twou'd cost you nothing, and that wou'd be a great deal of odds to you poor Soul so she said, and that I knew as well as she that sixpence was money to you and me too – I am verry much obliged to you for Post-Paying the letter but I hope I shall be able to make it up to you again one day or other – John, Mrs Hunters Footman told me on saturday last that Mrs Gilbert told him to tell me that If I had either letter to send home that she was Going to send home a small Parcel I think, and so she wou'd send it home without Costing you any thing, and so I was Glad of the opportunity because I shan't like to give Mrs Hunter so much trouble too often, – I had the pleasure to see Mr Hunter the day after I sent you the letter and I Go to Write almost every night from eight till eleven and by day Making little paper boxes to hold little shells and such things in because he is a verry curious man, and plain as well for he has hair as white as snow and has never got it drest, I believe there is not a bit of Pride in him and all his clothes so plain (But very rich) that I am sure you wou'd not think he was such a Grand Gentleman) For here the Barbers and Taylors and their wifes are All dukes and Dutchesses on Sundays, I suppose you have heard tell of Sir Joshua Reynolds that fine Painter,[12] well he will never draw any more, for he is dead and Buried at St Pauls church on saturday last and I was put by Mr Haynes to see the Procession and first there went My lord Mayors Coach then the Sherifs then the City Marshal all in red and Gold lace, then went the Hearse and then 42 mourning Coaches with lords knights and Dukes of all sorts, and then followd

all the gentlemens Coaches, that rode in the Mourning Coaches which was upwards of 120 more – well it was the finest sight ever I saw in my life at that time, But yesterday which was sunday Mr Haynes put Me to St James's and there I saw the king Queen and three daughters – well from there we went to See Westminst' abby which was the finest place I ever saw and the Monuments, well tis no use to tell, I wish you was here to see it, from there we went to Mr Haynes fathers, where we dined and drank tea and then we came home again –I wish you cou'd but see St James's Park and Hyde Park you woud delight your self, There is verry Great wages here I saw a girl that came to see one of our maids she was not 18 and she was complaining that she wou'd not stay only till she cou'd get another place because she had but 7 Guineas a Year, only to keep 2 Children neither – Pleas to remember Me to Priory maids & every other enquiring Friend,

｛ So no more at Present from ｝ W Clift
｛ Your affectionate Brother ｝

I Cant Write any *more* for want of Room But I have a Thousand things to write if I had

5. William to Elizabeth. 10 March 1792.

London March 10th 1792.

My Dear Brother and Sisters
                                    I am not willing to loose any opportunity of sending you a few lines at any time when I can catch it, I mean of Sending, not of writing because I can always make time to write and pen Ink and paper Cost me nothing I saw William Tabb one day this week and he told me that his Master and Mistress and himself was going to leave London on Monday next, and that If I had any thing to send home that I should bring it up at their house to Day or tomorrow and he would carry it for me, I have not any thing Particular to write only I have to tell you that I have a new Suit of Clothes making and I am in hopes I shall have it to wear to Morrow it is of a Dark brown and the Coat waistcoat and Breeches are of one sort, I have three new Shirts that cost Seven shillings Each they buy them here at the Shops ready made, I have 3 Neckcloths of the same sort of them I had of Brother John and I have 4 new Pocket handkerchiefs at 1.6 a Piece I have four Pair of Worsted Stockings The House of Commons in Ireland or the House of Lords I dont know which but twas one of them, was burnt Down last week, but I believe twas the House of Commons, – Please to remember Me to Onion and the Old Jee Onion and Thomas and to Kitty and Ann and Deborah and to John Ford and his Mother, and Jonathan Olver, and his Mother, Please to remember Me to John Chapman and his family and to Uncle Daniel and Amos, and Wm Wills

and William Roberts & his wife and to Mr Jo Elliot and to Mr Salter and his family – Please to remember Me to William Clemo, and to Rodney and his Mother and to Mrs Blake and to all and every other Enquiring Friend, Be Please to let me know in your next letter, where you have had any Letter from Brother Thomas, and if you have let me know where he lives at what N° and Street, Because I woud send a few lines to him and I Should be glad to know whether you have heard from Brother Robert or not, – Please to remember me to Robert, and Tammy, and to Katey Pinch, and Cath^r Row, and, please to let me know how Joanna likes her place, as for me I like mine very well so far, Please to let me know where Deborah's Club has shared their money because I want to know when I am to have that odd Sixpence, that she promised me; I wish you would be kind enough to send a line or two to Fowey and remember me to them and tell Aunt that I left the Jacket waistcoat and Breeches with bob Robins, and he told me he woud carry it to Fowey and so she may look for it when the Vessel comes to Fowey – I have Sent you a Ribbon enclosd in this letter, I have nothing at Present to send to brother John but If I met with any thing that I think worth Sending I Shall—

This being all at Present I Conclude with my Prayers to God for your health and Prosperity and shall ever remain your ever loving

and Affectionate Brother

W. Clift.

Saturday morning
11 OClock
Please to send me an answer
as soon as Convenient

6. *William to Elizabeth. 6 April 1792.*

London April the 6th 1792.

My Dear Brother and Sisters

I have taken this opportunity of sending these few lines hoping it will find you in good health as it leaves me at Present, Young Mr Hunter has been at the Colledge at Cambridge and is come home this week for the Holidays at Easter, he came in to our room Just now and told me that Mrs Hunter had sent him to tell me that she was going to send to Cornwall to day and that if I had a mind to send a letter I might, so I thought I would not let any opportunity slip, I have no great deal to write at present, but I was taken to the Park at St James's yesterday to see his majesty return from the Parliament house It was a most noble sight, he had a dozen footmen to walk before the State coach and a Company of Dragoons before them; and so behind and about a Couple o' Dozen of beef eaters or Yeomen to walk by the

Side, He was drawn by Eight Cream coloured Horses (from Hanover) and the harness all Red Moroco Leather and Gilt and ribbons all over and the Coach's top Red Morroco and on the top the tropic of war and a Crown and before and behind in full shape stood the God's, and on the Sides were All the Gods Painted and the wheels and all over it was beautifully Carved and Gilted and about 10 or 12 Thousand Spectators running after – William Tabb desired me to write to him and I was Just begun as Mr Hunter came into the room and Pleas, to tell him that John Adams the Footman left us last monday was Sennight, and that he is gone to the Westward about 60 miles but where Or with whom I Cannot tell for I have enquired several times of the Servants but they all tell me they cannot tell and tell him that there is nothing new nor pretty that I have to send, but Please to remember me to all Priory Maids and Richard Hocking – and to all enquiring friends

I expected to have had a letter from you this long time and I hope you will send one as soon as you receive this. And Please to let me know where you have heard from Brother Thomas or Robert or no, and let me know how Joanna likes her Place. Please to remember me to John Ford and his mother and all my old acquaintance/ I like London (or rather Westminster) for it is in the City of westminster that Leicester Square is) very well, I have no more at Present to write But must Conclude

Your most affectionate Brother till Death

W Clift

PS; Please to let me know where it is that Ge° Solomon lives when you write

Please to give my best Respects to Mr & Mrs Gilbert

7. John to William. 9 March 1792. (Coded)

Pencarrow March, 9th 92

My Dear Brother,

I hope your goodness will excuse me for not writing sooner, as I thought you would be glad to hear how the Assizes went on, I find Mr Pearce has escaped the halter this time, but I hear he hath committed a similar fault again already, by a near relation of his, but as to the truth I cannot assert at present, We are all tollerable well at present I thank God & I trust in God I shall hear by next post that you enjoy a good state of health which will always give me the greatest satisfaction to hear. We received your kind letter by W: Tabb, for which I return you many thanks, likewise sisters for your kind present enclosed as I suppose it is more than twenty times the value from another person. Richard Hurden is returned again from Bristol; we have received a letter a few days since from Brother Thomas and he says he hopes some person will be so good to shew him round the town that he may see the difference in work here and at Bristol as he expects there must be great Alteration since he left his native country. Brother Thomas presents his love to you & us, but, he forgot to shew his love to Sister in the manner as you did which I expect she will not forget to mention for some time to come, as he hath had many favourable opportunities of late to do it; but she shall not want a friend I hope, if please God to send me my health. We have not heard from Robert since you left us. Ann Climo is deliverd of a fine girl, is quite well & gives her love to you likewise Ann & Rich[d] Philp give their love to you as do all Priory servants & all friends at Bodmin of your acquaintance. I saw T: Arthur last night, he is verry well.

J: Clift.

This and the following were wrote both in one.[13]

8. *Elizabeth to William. 11 April 1792. (Coded)*

Bodmin April 11th 92

Dear Brother,

 I am very glad to hear that you are well & that you like your place so well. My Dear, you desired to know how Sister Joanna liked her place. She does not like it at all, she is coming away this week if they can get any body in her place, they desired her to stay till they can get some person or else she would have been off before.

 W. Tabb desires you will write to him. Dear Brother I was very glad that there was nothing particular in your letter you sent last, for I went down to Priory to fetch it, they had sent Richard up to tell me that there was a letter for me. Mr Gilbert asked very kindly after you & Mrs Gilbert desired I would let her see the letter if there was nothing particular in it, & asked me to stay to tea. So she read it and liked it very well, & desired I would write to you on Monday, but John said he was going to write to you and that he should be home on Monday but he was not so I went to Pencarrow yesterday to see if he had sent to you, he had begun to write as you see, so I brought it home with me & wrote these few lines. Brother Thomas is at the same place at Mrs Stockings Red Cliff Pit.

 When you write let me know if you have bought the Prayer Book. W: Roberts gives his love to you & desires to know if you have seen Mary. John Ford, W: Wills, Mr Joe, C: Rowe, Onion Kitty, Ann Deborah & many more that I cannot mention desireth their love to you.

 The Club has shared 41/ each. My dear I have a thousand things to write but time will not permit.

Yours &ccc E: Clift.

34

9. Elizabeth to William. 15 May 1792. (Coded)

Bodmin May 15th 1792

Dear Brother,)
      I take this opportunity of sending you these few lines hoping it will find you in good health as it leaves me at present I bless God for it.

I have not seen Brother John but once since I wrote to you last and that was on Sunday last. Joanna & I went down to see what was become of him, & he said the reason that he had not been home was that they had been very busy putting the house in order against the family came home. They returned from London on Wednesday last & that day he strained his foot, so that he was not able work for that week, but he is much better now he is able to work again. I have not heard from brother Robert since you left us. I have heard from Brother Thomas & he is very well, He sent home for me to send the Young Mans Best Companion[14] to him & desired to know where to direct to you, & I sent a few lines to him by Betty Ham who is gone to Bristol to Jonathan. Richard Hurden & his family are gone to London with Capt Banks & the next time he comes up again I believe Sally Bonady, (that was), is going to London to her husband he went there just after you did.

      Dear Brother, I hope you will not neglect writing to me every oppertunity you have, as there is nothing gives me so much pleasure as to hear from you & to here that you like London so well & that you have had so fine a prospect.

      William Tabb gives his love to you & desires you will write to him. Mr & Mrs Gilbert is very well & they were very glad to hear from you & Mrs Gilbert said she was very well pleased with you that you had not forgot me, she thought it was very kind of you to send home the ribbands Dear Brother, excuse haste, I have a thousand things to write but time will not permit, when I write again I'll send you all the news. Mr Mudge is married to Mrs Grace Belling. (I have inclosed six pence under the seal.) So no more at present from your ever affectionate Sister

E. Clift

This & the following were enclosed & sent by Thomas Hambly.[13]

10. Joanna to William. 15 May 1792. (Coded)

Bodmin May 15th 92

My ever dear Brother,
             With inexpressible happiness I have embraced this

35

opportunity of writing to you, which is indeed the greatest happiness I desire on earth & to hear of your safe arrival at London & the happiness & pleasure you enjoy in that dear port of which I shall ever glory in its name while youve a being in it. My dear you give us the unspeakable happiness to receive & read your affectionate letters, & tho' we are now at a great distance; my dear Billy I hope the distance will never lessen your affection to us but that you will always write to us, otherwise it will render us but miserable. My dear dear Billy if I had now the wings of a dove for then would I fly to you where I should be at rest, but the distance at present makes me quite hopeless of that rest.

My Dear, when this you see, youll think on me, tho' many miles apart, where ee'r I go where ee'r I be methinks your dear & tender face I see.

My dear Billy I left Mr Eyres's about a fortnight since, of which time partly I have been at Fowey & am happy to let you know they all enjoy a good state of health, which my trust in God is, that you enjoy the same blessing. Uncle aunt & Cousins all desired their kind love to you.

My dear Billy,
this being all at present
I conclude, your ever loving &
affectionate Sister till Death
Joanna Clift

P.S.   Dear Brother
    I return you many thanks for the favour you sent and am sorry I have nothing of which I can make you any return.

11. Thomas to William. 16 April 1792. (Coded)

Bristol April 16th 1792

Dear Brother,
            I have just received a few lines from Sister Betty by Jonathan Hams wife & she informs me where to direct to you & I am now happy to inform you that brother & Sisters are in good health, as I bless God this leaves me at present. I shall be happy to have a few lines from you as soon as you have a convenient opportunity & happy to hear of your welfare.

I have sent you this by one Edward Triscott a carpenter one of St Issey which came in the same ship with Hams wife from Padstow & telling me he was bound for London I was glad of the opportunity to send you this letter but time being short I conclude your affectionate Brother

T Clift

12. Thomas to William. May 1792. (Coded)

Bristol May 1792.

Dear Brother
　　　　　I have received yours, which gave me a deal of happiness to hear of your health likewise the prospect you had on your passage & happy to hear you like your master so well, & that delightfull situation you are in, as I believe there is no one dislikes it that ever have seen it. As for my part I like this place extremely well I never lived so happy in my life as since I have been in Bristol. Our boot men & glaze heel men are standing out for the wages and as soon as they get it we expect to stand out & think we shall get it too soon after. I should like to see London very well but as I have not been home for some time & as I can go from here to Padstow for so small expence I think to go home this summer. I have not heard from home since J Hams wife came up. R. Hurden intends coming here at midsummer. Tho⁵ Williams otherwise Face – George Wills & many others are here too tedious to mention
Yr⁵ &ccc
Tho⁵ Clift

13. William to Elizabeth. 23 May 1792.

London May 23rd 1792.

My dear brother & Sisters
　　　　　　　　　　I received your kind letters by T. Hambly on sunday Evening last, it being my sunday in, you must know there is two houses, the front house faces in the Square and the other in Castle Street, and so the Stables and yard between, and I belong to the back house, where Preparations are made so there is one Mrs Adams Mr Haynes and Myself that live in the back house, but I eat my Victuals in the front house, so we take it by turns to go out Sundays, Mrs Adams one sunday, and Mr Haynes and I another, well, as I said before, it was my Sunday in and as I was standing at the door, Thomas Hambly came up the Street and gave me your kind letters and Present, – Dear Sisters you need not send any money, for I shall but throw it away, but as for the rule or such thing as that I cannot spend it, and as I have always money coming to throw away you need not send any more, Our great room of Preparations has been shown these three saturday's past Last saturday to the Ladies and the other two to the gentlemen, and next saturday to the Gentlemen, it is Shown once in a year, that is the four saturdays in May.; I sent a Letter to brother Thomas, a day or two after I received your Last, and before he could have received mine there was a man, one of St Isey that came to bristole in the same ship with Jonathan Hams wife and so he sent a Letter by him to me and when the Man Came to London he could not find the way but brought a Man three

37

Miles *off* to show him the way, and he told me that my brother told him that I would pay him for his trouble so I had to pay the Man for bringing the Letter and the man for showing him the way, and if he had sent the Letter by the post it would not Cost above four pence, and he has not sent any answer to My Letter yet. There was a fire in Tavistock Street Last sunday was a week I went in the afternoon to see it where I met with Edmund Rickett he was in company with Nell Philp I was standing one side of the street and they was the other so he left Nell to come to speak to me, but Nell did not, and I believe he did not want me to see him for he was Looking very shabby. Edmund told me he had been here a month and desired to be remember'd to brother John I had no time to ask him any thing for he went to see for Nell and could not see him again.

Please to save my Piney apples on the Dresser and all the Letters I send till I come home again, and I'll save all yours – I Live a Great deal happier than ever I did in my Life – Please to Let me know all the News and how you go on in your next – Please to give my Duty to Mr & Mrs Gilbert and I hope they are well, and remember me to all the servants and to all other Enquiring friends & acquaintance – Please to tell Nancy Hocking in prison Lane that there is no such place as Cranver passage Leicester Fields but Cranborn passage and if that is it, Let me know in your next

The Coldstream guards do not Lodge in the Tower but are out at Quarters, I have not seen Corp' Silvey yet – Mrs Hunter has not Said any thing about my bringing my Letters to her since the Last and I shan't Like to Carry them without she asks me

Thomas Hambly works at N° 11 Little Drury Lane near Covent Garden it is not far from our house, John Henwood that Livd at Mr Ough's and William Trefry works in the same shop – I shall write to William Tabb soon

This being all at Present I remain
your ever Loving and Affectionate
Brother
W Clift

I think I was born to live in
Castle street all my Life time
For when I was home I Liv'd in
Castle street when at Fowey I
Livd in Castle street and Now
I Live in Castle Street.

14. *James Puckey to Elizabeth. 31 May 1792.*[15]

Fowey May ye 31st,, 1792

Dear Cousin,

I Wroute the these lines to you, Instead of Sally williams, as she

Desire^d me, because of not forgeting, her name,) Concerning going To london in Cap^tn Hayes,) and I have Seen him, and he tells me he expects to Seal for Plymouth, the beginning Of next week, and then Seall from their In About Aweek After,) Notwithstanding He Expects to Come to bodmin before he Seals from here, To see Mr Ham, and then She,^ld see him her self, as I have Told him her name, so you Can shew her the letter, He Arived home,) wensday Evening, Father & mother give their love to you and gla,^d to here You Are well, Fowey Town was shaken last saturday Night, Just About the same Time that bodmin was, Al,,tho wee did not Heer it,
I have nothing more Particular at Present
    But Rememb,^r me to Cous,^n John,
        So Conclud from your Sincear and Harty
           Well Wisher
                    Ja,^s Puckey Jun,^r
Willm Deeser,^d to be Rememb^d to you.
He will Sen,^d your Clouak by Galtey, or the Post, lickwise Mary bate Gives her love to you

NOTES SECTION I

1. *To cast up one's accounts* means 'to vomit'. The use is now obsolete but the *OED* gives examples up to 1808.
2. Probably Start Point.
3. The South Foreland light near Dover.
4. The North Foreland light between Ramsgate and Margate.
5. *Presently* retained the meaning of 'immediately' until as late as 1869 according to the *OED*.
6. *Warren* was formerly used as the name of the Woolwich Arsenal. It has been obsolete since the end of the 19th century.
7. *To raim* is a Cornish dialect term meaning 'to stretch' in the sense of walking or running.
8. According to Jessie Dobson, *William Clift* (London, 1954), p.5, Clift under-estimated the household, which numbered about fifty people at the time.
9. *troll boat* – probably a fishing boat. The word was confused with *trawl*. One meaning of the verb *troll* given in the *OED* is to 'trail a baited line behind a boat'.
10. *Fowey Fair*. There were several fairs each year at Fowey at this time. The one referred to here was probably the one held on Shrove Tuesday.
11. The letter is dated *February* by Clift, but this is clearly in error. He did not arrive at John Hunter's house until February 14th, 1792. *March 5th* has been written above the date in another hand.
12. Sir Joshua Reynolds also lived in Leicester Square.
13. Note added by Clift in his letter book. The letters have been kept in the order he transcribed them regardless of date.

14. The *Young Mans Companion:* see THE CLIFT FAMILY p. 14 and n. 9 p. 18.
15. The punctuation of this letter has been retained as closely as possible. Much of it is highly unusual and idiosyncratic. Capitalization is also extremely difficult to assess.

II. JUNE TO DECEMBER 1792

In the letters for the second half of 1792 the interest shifts a little from London to Bodmin. Most of the letters in this section are written by Elizabeth and John and, less concerned now with how their brother is settling down in his new position, they are almost wholly absorbed with local news. Although fragmentary, the events related give us a clearer picture of life in the Cornish town. Details of petty crimes, brawls and thefts take up much of the space. In an early letter John mentions the Assizes, an occasion of importance for all the local population. The interest of the writers in the fortunes of the various offenders is evident from the attention they devote to the trials and examination before the magistrates, which sometimes, as in Elizabeth's letter of September the 9th, have unexpected and alarming results. There is other local gossip. The first of the escapades of Catty Pinch, Mrs Eyre's maidservant, is hinted at by Elizabeth, and other similar scrapes of the local girls are recounted.

The letters also contain news of the family. Elizabeth and Joanna have monetary difficulties with their respective employers. John is still working for a Mr Chapple as well as for Sir William Molesworth of Pencarrow at this time, but no more is heard of this employer and presumably John leaves his service as he threatens to do. Joanna also changes her employment, leaving the Eyre family and going to a place with a family just outside Bodmin, the first of a long succession of moves. Thomas is expected home from Bristol and various rumours of the whereabouts of Robert, from whom nothing has been heard since before William set out for London, reach the family at Bodmin.

Meanwhile, William is evidently happily settled in the household of John Hunter and his letters to Cornwall are less frequent. An unusually long gap between July and October is explained by an illness which Elizabeth mentions after he has recovered. William reports on his progress in drawing and of the masters whom Hunter engages for him. He continues to tell of his outings in London, mostly taken in the company of Robert Haynes, but his attention too is centred on the affairs of the community he has left in Bodmin and he repeatedly asks for news of his home town. His last letter of the year, written on Christmas Eve, ends with a postscript: 'I have been in London 10 months &

8 days'. The careful calculation, the second in this group of letters, probably indicates the extent to which he was still missing his family and friends.

15. Elizabeth to William. 23 June 1792. (Coded)

Bodmin June 23d 1792

My dear Brother
        I am very happy to hear that you enjoy a good state of health as it is one of the greatest happinesses we can enjoy whilst here below. My dear I am very glad to hear that you are so happy & comfortable and that you like, & that your master likes you so well.

Mrs Gilbert has heard from Mrs Hunter twice since I received y^r last letter & she mentioned you both times Mrs G: said you was very well and that Mrs H: did speak very well of you which my dear I hope you will give them no other cause for if you behave well that is the way to gain the favour of both God & man. My dear always put your fear in the Lord & then you will never want a friend for he will never forsake them that put their trust in him. One day as I was down at Mrs G:s I was sitting down in the window, the Bible lay open by me I took it up & looked in it & it was in the Proverbs. I thought it was very remarkable you may find it in the 27 Chap: & 10 Ver:[1] – I was sorry to hear that brother Thos: was so unkind for I should think the postage of a letter could not be so much to him if he had put it in the Office.

I have had but 2 letters from him since you left me. One of them was dated New Years day & I did not receive it till Feb: 27th & then he sent it by Charles Blake & the other he sent by R: Hurden. Charles Blake is living home still with his mother, he makes a great show but I believe there is little foundation – he keeps very poor company. Billy Hockin in Prison Lane is coming to London in a fortnights time he is coming up in the waggon & so is Sally Bonady; they are afraid to come by water she told me she was coming the next week after I received your letter which was the reason I did not write till now.

Mr & Mrs Gilbert are very well & are very glad that you do so well. All Priory servants give their love to you. Peggy Jenkin that lived with Fanny Harvey has got a young daughter by Mr Williams the gardner & Molly Musgrove is *ll*ooking for child every day & they say it is his too. R Sowden is dead & was buried 11th inst. John & Joanna gives their kind love to you. He was come last Sunday & was very well but goes on just as usual. As for me I work at Mr Eyres's still but how much longer I dont know for we have not been to any account since you left me nor I dont know what I am to have a piece for warp^g[2] but I am resolved to know when he comes from Bristol & when I write again I will let you know how we go on. I have not heard from

Brother R^t since
So no more at present from y^r ever affec^t &c.
Sister Eth Clift

16. *William to Elizabeth. 24 July 1792.*

Dear Brother and Sisters)
I have this opportunity of Sending you these few
Lines hoping they will find you in good health as it leaves me at Present, I Bless
God for it, – I have nothing particular to write at Present, I have not had much
time to draw lately, but I shall have more time soon, for we have had a great
deal of work to do, for some time past; Mrs Hunter's footman told me last
evening that Mrs Hunter told him that if I had any mind to send, that she was
going to send a Frank to day and that I might send my Letter in it so I thought
twas as well to send as not, There was a great Rowing=match yesterday on the
river, (for a Wherry boat,) between 7 Boats, each boat 1 Pair of Oars, The men
all in Uniform dresses, Caps and Red Sashes, – and a Plenty of musick all over
the River, of all sorts, I was as far as westminster Bridge to see it, but that is not
far from our House; —^{3}
Please to give my duty to Mr & Mrs Gilbert and my love to all the Servants,
and I hope they are very well, and please to give my Love to Brother and Sister
and I hope they are as I am, that is, in a good State of Health and very happy.
Please to let me know all the good news when you write to me and which I
hope will be soon; Please to give my love to all my old acquaintance and all
Enquiring friends.
This being all at Present I must conclude with my prayers to god for your
health and Prosperity, and shall ever remain, your ever loving and
affectionate
Brother,
William Clift.

Leicester Square,

Tuesday July 24, 1792

17. *John to William. 5 August 1792. (Coded)*

Bodmin Aug^r 5th 92.

Dear Brother
I have once more taken this opportunity to enquire after your
health & welfare. I must confess I expected to have had a letter from you long
before now as you might well suppose it must be great satisfaction to me to

42

hear from one that was ever dear to me as life (but out of sight out of mind) as you desired in your last (as sisters inform me) to know where T: Boyne was he is gone to Swansey & is now engaged with an Uncle to him onboard a Trader that belongs to that place. C Solomon is eloped[4] from his Master, I find, & is home with his mother. He says he has a very good master but one of the servant maids & him had some difference, which is the only reason he gives for leaving his master but I hear he hath taken the liberty to get a letter writ to his Master to demand his indenture. As you desired to know all the good news, I shall let you know all I know of both sorts. Mr Jn[s] Arthur is dead since your last Nanny Giant, hath sworn the peace of R[d] Kefael & he is again down to the little Pallace[5] but it is thought he will be set at liberty again at the Assizes which begins tomorrow. Sister Joanna is gone to service at Mrs Mountstevens's at Towerhill which I am very glad for as I hope the place will do verry well. Mrs King tells me she intends to go to London as soon as the Assize is over & intends to call to see you, If she doth I shall send something by her. I hope you'll excuse this abrupt old fashioned letter or I should rather have said new fashioned for I am sure you never saw one like it from me or any person else but as Mr Tabb has been waiting for me almost an hour to go to Pencarrow & most part of the time spent before I could begin. Sisters & myself I bless God are all well at present as I trust in him you are the same we have not heard from B[r] Robert since we saw him. Mr & Mrs Gilbert & servants are very well & give their love to you as do all friends. So I must conclude y[r] ever loving affectionate Brother

John Clift

PS: M: Musgrove is in the fashion again.[6] T: Arthur gives his love to you.

18. Elizabeth to William. 9 September 1792. (Coded)

Bodmin Sept[r] 9 92

My dear Brother
      I am very happy to hear that you enjoy a good state of health & that the Lord hath blest you with all earthly blessings & I trust he will still continue his goodness to you & preserve you through this wilderness of time. My dear I am sorry to tell you that Billy Ough is in jail. tho he & I you know was not very friendly yet I am sory for him with my heart. You must know that in the assizes Billy Scantlebury was helping the ostler at Mr Joles's & the Sunday night or Monday morning after, the stable was robbd, the men always kept their clothes in the stable & Scantlebury saw the man put the clothes there the Sunday evening & the Monday morning as soon as they found the things gone

Scantlebury sat off & they went after him & took him at St Mabyn but found nothing upon him. They put him before Sr Wm Molesworth but as they found nothing upon him, they could do nothing to him. but it is most likely he had conveyd off the things before. But be as it will, the Wednesday morn^g it was found on Billy Ough & he said as he was going to St Mabyn to work the Monday morning Scantlebury met him down by Jeffery's mill pool[7] & desired him to carry this bundle to St Mabyn for him & told him that he was coming to St Mabyn to work as soon as Mr Jole was up but Billy Ough was put before Sr W^m & bound over to the Sessions, & Scantlebury was taken up again & put before Sr W^m again & he would have been committed if they could have had the least hitch upon him for they was very much against him & told him that he was certainly the rogue but he strongly denied it & his father swore that he was in bed the Sunday night by 11 oclock & did not get up till seven in the morning. Mr Cock & Cromwell saw him in the Fore Street by five & they told Mr Jole so, but just as they came home from Sir Williams, an accident happened which gave the people liberty to say that they had been swearing false – they were but just in when the room they lived in fell in, the beams broke off & the floor fell all down the beds cradle people & all together, the young infant was almost stifled when they found it. The cradle was turned upside down with it & Turpin was left sitting in the window & they were forced to get a ladder to get him down.

The things that were found on Billy Ough was a great coat to a London gentleman, jacket a p^r stockings & a silk handkerchief to the ostler, however he came by it I think he will suffer for it, It is most peoples opinion that he will be transported. Mr & Mrs Gilbert has been at Boconnoc these three weeks they are all very well. Mr G^t has bought all the Priory that belonged to Mr Eyre for £400, the mill is taking down & Mr Eyre is building one at Margate.[8] Priory maids give their love to you as also John Ford & his mother but John is in great trouble for the loss of his father, he died last week Parson Pomerys wife died last Thursday at Bath. Dear Brother I will tell you all the news I can. Wm Sweet & E: Kestallick are going to be married; their banns were called to day. Billy Hocking is coming up soon with Mr Sam: Stone. Joanna gives her love to you she is very well & likes her place very well. She has made a bargain for £3 a year she has a great deal of work to do. G: Wills is home & says Brother Thos is coming home soon but he did not send as much as a line by him. I have not heard from Robert. John goes on just as usual. Last Sunday Wm Roberts & I went to Polkerries to fetch home C: Pinch & the child & it came to such bad weather that we could not come home for the night so when we were there & I thought I could not be wetter than I was we took the horses & went on to Fowey & staid about half an hour there. Uncle, Aunt & Cousinds all desired to be remembered to you & Edward & Betty the same & they are all very well. Thomas Bate was here to day all their people are very well. I heard from Uncle John Leavers this week, he is very poorly. Cousin Jenny is married. All friends

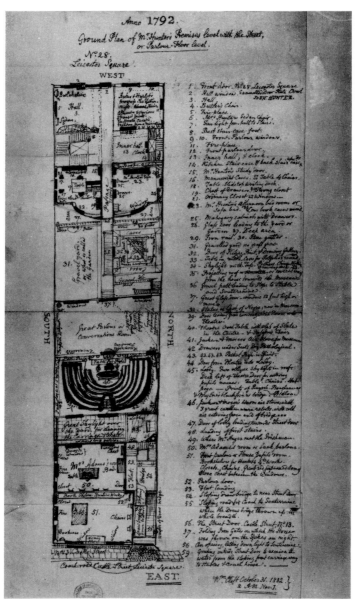

*Ground plan of Hunter's establishment in Leicester Square as it was in 1792.
Drawn from memory by William Clift 1832.*

& acquaintances give their love to you.
So no more at present from your ever affec^t Sister
Elizabeth Clift

19. John to William. 7 October 1792. (Coded)

Bodmin Octr 7: 92

Dear Brother
                    I hope you will be so good to excuse my long silence as I have
been full of business of late as I have had more to do since your absence than
ever I had in my life tho but for little profit as yet I am obliged to keep so much
acc^{ts} as one that had nothing else to do almost, for Mr Chapple & Sr W^m but
have not had the pleasure to settle my own acc^t with neither of them yet but I
have now just finished Mr Chapples work so of course we must come to a
reconing soon, for I have been just a year & three quarters in his service &
never been to no acc^t yet. Tho I hope there will be no mistake as no one can be
more correct in account than myself & I hope he is the same but for the future
I am resolved to ballance or acc^t once a month, be where ever I may, or Im no
longer Their H^{ble} Servant. I thank God I have more work ordered by S. W^m for
me at present than ever I had at once in my life tho' my goodlooking friend, Mr
T—b⁹ would rather I was some where else, but the worst is he cant do the
work I have to do, himself, I never was so much deceived in my man as I have
been in him for I have nurs'd a snake in my bosom that would even sting me to
death if it were in his power tho' I bless God his stings cannot have the desired
effect, but I shall not dwell any longer upon this subject as I hope I shall be so
happy to see you next spring rather than make any person uneasy on my acc^t &
wish he may take care to keep the place as long as he has already.
        I bless God I have injoyed a tollerable good state of health of late but have a
great cold at present Sisters are very well & give their love to you as do all
friends of our acquaintance Wm Tabb & his master have had some difference &
he is to leave his service. Betty Lestarick & W Sweet is married this morning.
The Millitia meets tomorrow. Wm Ough has taken his trial. Sentenced twelve
months imprisonment an old man for stealing corn was flogg'd yesterday tho' a
man of property therefore not much pitied. A young man for stealing a watch
was also whipt. Running the cat seemd rather tedious I suppose for he often to
poor Jack and walked backwards to favor the blows which made the old man
pray heartily.[10]
        We hear Brother is in Ireland onboard a ship called Cyron[11] – Joanna likes
her place exceeding well. I expect Brother Thos home about this time. My dear
Brother I must desire you to write me a letter as soon as you receive this &
please to let me know every particular for I can just know how you are by

Sisters letters & that is all for she is very carefull how she lets me see them. She is gone to Cardinham to day. I dont know of any thing more at present to write but conclude with my prayers to God for y^r health & prosperity & remain your

> ever loving & affectionate Brother
> John Clift

20. *William to John. 11 October 1792.*

London October 11th 1792

Dear Brother,

I have at your request taken this opportunity of sending you these few lines, hoping they will find you in good health as it leaves me at present, I bless god for it.

I have nothing very particular to write at Present, but I am very glad poor Billy Ough fared no worse, than he did for one Year is better than seven, as Sister told me that it was most peoples Opinion that He would be transported, I received your letter yesterday it was brought at the Front House in the Square, and our Butler Mr Duell told me that when I did write again, to tell you not to Post-pay the letters you send but to direct them at N° 28 Leicester Sq^r instead of 13 Castle street and then he would pay for them, for in so many letters as he takes in for Mr Hunter, they could not find out so few as mine, for I suppose the Letters that are brought to Mr Hunter in a Year dont amount to less than 3 or 4 Thousand, for sometimes when I am in his room writing at nights I see him burn twenty or thirty. I suppose you did not receive any letter from Brother Robert, as you told me you had heard from him, I believe that Was the Name of the ship we heard he was on board soon after the Cambridge was paid off; I suppose you have heard of St Bartholomew-fair[12] and Robin Goodfellow – I was at it with Mr Haynes, I believe it was about three weeks ago, and there I saw a great variety of all sorts and sizes. Wild beasts Wild-birds Rope dancing, and almost every thing that was worth seeing – So the next day Mr Hunter asked Haynes if I had been at the fair and he told him no, So he gave him half a Crown and told to take me, to see the Birds and Beasts, So as I had been the day before and the Butler wanted to go out for the evening an hour or two, (and as he is always very kind to me) I staid in and kept the door for him as Mr Hunter at that time slept at His country House,[13] and Mr Haynes told me that some night when I had not any writing to do he would take me to Sadlers wells or the Play or some publick place or other. Please to give my kind love to Brother Thomas If he is at Bodmin, and tell him to write to me for I have had but one letter from him besides that which the man brought, since I have been here which is now Eight months in 5 days time.

Please to give my kind love to sisters and I hope they are verry well – and remember me kindly to Nancy the coachmans wife when you see her, and to all enquiring friends and acquaintance, I do not suppose you will ever reach London for I suppose you are almost married by this time, but if you do I warrant you Ill put you far enough about London to tire your legs

Mr Hunter has provided me a Drawing master At last he is a little old Hump of a fellow, he is pro*   * My Lord, but he may not be the worse artist for all that but I have one good thing on my side I am sure he will not be able lick me for I am sure I am the best man of the two; he has given me some lessons 2 or three days ago and I have not seen him since. The people tell me I am Grown a great deal since I have been here – but I do not know where it is so or not, when you see me you will be able tell.)
Yours till Death W Clift.[14]

21. *Elizabeth to William. 13 November 1792. (Coded)*

Bodmin Nov[r] 13th 92

Dear Brother

This comes with my kind love to you, hoping this will find you in good health as it leaves me at present I bless God for it. My dear I saw Mr & Mrs Gilbert a few days ago & they are very well & she asked me how you was, & I told her that you writ you was very well & she said she was very glad of it for you had been very poorly indeed but she said she would not tell me of it till you was well because she knew I should trouble myself. When Mrs Hunter wrote to her that you was very ill she wrote to her & desired to let her know again soon & when Mrs Hunter wrote to her she said you was much better. & Mrs Gilbert desired I would give their love to you, & let you know that she was very glad to hear your master speak so well of you, & she said that she hoped would walk in the ways of the Lord, & that you would not be drawn aside by any wicked person, for that London was a very wicked place. My dear I can inform you where B: Rob[t] is, I heard from him by Kitty Musgrove who was here in the Millitia & he said he saw him at Plymouth-Dock a day or two before he came away; & very well & that he was onboard the Prince George[15] & that he belonged to the Admirals long boat. I think he might have sent just to let us know in so long a time for I suppose he has been no farther than Dock for the ship is a guard ship.[16] I sent him a letter by C: Musgrove & desired him to send as soon as possible but he hath not sent yet. I saw Brother John on Sunday last, & he is very well & gives his kind love to you – I saw Sister to day & she told me that she was coming away from her place when her month is out which is next Wednesday. She tells me they are so ill temper'd that she will not stay any longer with them. Mrs Gilbert has got a place for the young John Harries at

Fowey with the young Mr Graham he is to be bound for 7 years if he stays, but he was not very willing to go, he would rather stay at home & run about the streets. His father told Mrs Gilbert that he thought 2 or 3 years was enough & she said, John, how can you expect such a thing for he is to be put to school & learnt to read & write & so by the time he is brought to any thing to take him away. I believe she was not very well pleased. The boy went there last Sunday was a week & they were all a crying as if he was going a 1000 miles off. Milford was not here this meeting his time was out & so Kitty Climo looked after the Capt.ˢ house & did very well till the day before they broke up, he got drunk & got a fighting he went up to Strikes & challenged a man to fight & Strike came out & dragg'd him about & struck him & Kitty struck him again & then he sent him to the guard house & kept him there till next day & would have had him flogg'd had not the man broke up, so when he found he could not do any thing to him that way he went & swore the peace of poor Kit and he was committed to Bridewell & there he must have gone if Mr Mudge & Jnᵒ Bate had not been bail for him. Billy Hocking is not coming to London till after Christmas & then Ill send you all the news I can think of between this & that. There is going to be a great brewhouse made out of the old Bridewell it is new building it is as high as Bodmin Church. Mr MacCaule preached at Mr Barons meting twice this summer. All your friends & old acquaintance desire to be remembered to you. So no more at present from your ever affectionate Sister

Eliz.ᵗʰ Clift

22. William to Elizabeth. 24 December 1792.

Dear Brother and Sisters
                I have taken this opportunity of sending you these few lines hoping they will find you in good health as it leaves me at Present, I have had a great Cold for these two or three days but I am pretty well again now, I believe I told you in my last that I had a drawing master, but he did not come above once a week and then did not stay above two or three Minutes at a time, and Mr Hunter thought that would not answer the purpose and last Tuesday he gave me a letter to carry to one Mr Martin[17] Nᵒ 10 Great Marlborough Street at the Evening School, from 6 till nine where I am in hopes I shall get on a great deal faster, Mr Hunter says he shall see how I come on at the Evenings or else I shall go by day, but I might as well go by day too for I have scarce any thing to do but write and Draw all the day; I have (last week been drawing a bird from nature) for Mr Hunter has a great Collection of Stuffd birds and Mr Home, Mr Hunters Brother in Law, Mrs Hˢ Brother came into the room where I was drawing and said he thought it was done very well and Went through to the other house and told Mr Hunter, and in the Evening

when I went in to write he told me to bring it to him the next morning, which was Yesterday and he told me he was in hopes I should do very well in a little time, for as Mr Hunter has got some thousands of such fine drawings, that mine at present cannot seem as any thing to him as yet – To day morn^g Mrs Hunter sent for me to come to her in the drawing room and she said she thought I had done it exceeding well indeed and told me that she was going to send a frank to Mrs Gilbert tomorrow and If I would write a letter she would inclose it for you I have a new suit of Cloaths and a new hat and Shoes against tomorrow Christmas day—

Please to let me know in Your next whether you have heard from Brother Thomas or Robert since I received your last and where Joanna has got any place since she left Towerhill and let me know how somebody likes their winter quarters, I suppose You know Who I mean – Let me know how Brother John comes on and where he is working and let me know what Is become of Elizabeth Yeo and let me know how it goes on at the Head of St Nicholas Street on the right hand side and how your next door neighbour Mary Little, Sammys wife comes on – Please to give my kind love to brother and sister and desire them to write to me or I shall be very much affronted with them—

Please to let me know when you heard from Fowey and how all the people do there and let me know how all the People at Priory and Penbugle[18] do, please to give my kind love to them and let them know how Johny likes place Please to send me all the news in your next and if Billy Hocking comes to London after Christmas you can send a letter by him and then I expect John and Joanna will write—

This being all at present I must conclude your ever loving and affectionate Brother till Death

W Clift.

Leicester Square
Decr 24th 1792
Monday Evening

I have now been in London 10 Months and 8 Days—

NOTES SECTION II

1. *Proverbs 27 v.10:* 'Thine own friend, and thy father's friend, forsake not; neither go into thy brother's house in the day of thy calamity: for better is a neighbour that is near than a brother far off'.

2. *warp^g* i.e. warping. The *OED* gives two meanings of *to warp*, both marked as obsolete: 1) to weave; 2) to arrange yarn so as to form a warp; to wind a warp

beam. Either meaning seems possible here.

3. *a great Rowingmatch*: according to Clift, he saw this on 23 July. In spite of the discrepancy of dates it seems likely that it was the rowing match described in Chambers's *The Book of Days*, which was held annually on 1 August. This match, which was rowed upstream from London Bridge to Chelsea, was founded in the early 18th century by an actor, Thomas Doggett, to commemorate the Hanoverian succession. Only six competitors took part, watermen in their final year of apprenticeship, the prize being a coat of orange with a badge representing the white horse of Hanover.

4. *eloped*: as well as the usual meaning of *elope*, the *OED* gives 'to run away, escape, abscond'.

5. *little Pallace*: a dialect phrase used in Devon and Cornwall, meaning either a cellar for the storing of pilchards or a cellar or storehouse underground.

6. Molly Musgrove was expecting a baby. See Elizabeth's previous letter.

7. *Jeffery's mill pool*: Jeffery owned the mill a mile nearer Bodmin than that of Robert Clift senior that effectively put him out of business.

8. *Margate*: a farm about a mile east of the centre of Bodmin.

9. Mr Tabb was John's senior on the Pencarrow estate. What, if any, relation he was to William Tabb, who was a house servant at Priory, the letters do not reveal.

10. A line or some words appear to have been left out here by Clift as he transcribed the letter into code, leaving the sense unclear.

11. *Cyron*: Probably the *Syren*, but Robert was never mustered on this ship. At this time he was on the *St George*, which was stationed at Plymouth Dock.

12. St Bartholomew's Fair was held at Smithfield on 24 August each year. Originally a trading fair, it became an excuse for rowdyism and was abolished after 1855, having been in existence since the time of Henry II. It is probable that Hunter bought some of the wild beasts exhibited there for his menagerie at Earls Court.

13. Hunter's country house was at Earls Court, where he kept his menagerie.

14. The signature has been made with some form of chemical salts.

15. Elizabeth means the *St George*. As both ships were in commission at the same time the mistake is understandable.

16. A guard ship was a ship which did not go to sea but was used as a posting station. If what Elizabeth says is true, it was a temporary measure as the *St George* joined the fleet when it sailed in 1793 for the Mediterranean. There is evidence from contemporary records and letters of the Captain, Sir Thomas Byard, that the *St George* was used as a recruiting ship before 1793.

17. *Mr Martin*: there were three Martins, painters, working in London at this time. David Martin (1737-1798) seems the most likely candidate.

18. *Penbugle*: Penbugle is a farm about a mile north of Bodmin centre.

III. JANUARY TO AUGUST 1793.

At last, in January 1793, reliable news of Robert reaches Bodmin in the form of a letter from him but not, according to John written in his own hand. He is now serving on the *St George*, 98, a second rate ship of the line. News of the letter's arrival is passed quickly to William in London, who in turn passes it on to Thomas. The letter itself contains little information compared with those of the rest of the family and follows the stereotyped pattern of most seamen's letters of the period. It does, however, give the first indication that England is on the brink of war with France.

War was declared on February the 1st, 1793, and an immediate effect was felt in Cornwall with the shipping off of corn to other parts of the country and a corresponding increase in its price. John describes vividly one of the risings of the Cornish tinners at Padstow, in an attempt to prevent the corn being taken away. Elizabeth also mentions the corn riots and, like her brother, gives meticulous details of the current prices of wheat and barley. These were of immediate importance to the members of a community for whom bread was the staple diet. The militia are called out to settle the disturbances and these die down temporarily with the tinners apparently in command of the situation.

Another item of news which concerns the family at this time is the arrest of an acquaintance, Thomas Williams, living, like Thomas, in Bristol. This unfortunate young man had apparently strayed by accident into a riotous scene at a brothel following the bonfire celebrations on November the 5th of the previous year and was committed to prison along with the troublemakers. Here he remained awaiting trial for five months. Thomas describes his activities on behalf of his friend and there is considerable anxiety expressed about the sentence he could receive. Details of the sentence and the subsequent efforts of his father to free him are all faithfully recorded.

During this time William, when not commenting on the news in the letters from Cornwall, is busy relating the affairs of Billy Hocking or Hawking. Since the middle of 1792 Elizabeth had been giving reports of the postponed journey to London of this Bodmin boy, presumably of a similar age to William. He was coming to London to join his father, the mother and younger children remaining in Bodmin. Billy Hocking eventually arrives in January and there is one letter of his written to his mother after many requests passed on through Elizabeth to William. How much this letter was prized may be judged from the fact that it was copied out at least once, and probably more than once, for circulation among his family and friends. It is a copy made by his uncle which is included here. However, it appears a little later that it was William and not Billy Hocking at all who penned the letter and William is called to account for the deed by his sister. Billy Hocking's stay in London was destined to be short. After six months he fell ill with one of the typhus fevers prevalent at the time, as a result of the inadequate sanitation in the capital, and within a few days he was dead. The section concludes with Elizabeth's account of how his mother receives the distressing news and this brief and rather pathetic episode, which tends to dominate the letters in the first half of this year, reminds us of how these people were constantly aware of the precariousness of existence. Small wonder that letters with news of the writer's continued health and well-being were frequently demanded and eagerly looked for.

23. Elizabeth to William. 1 January 1793. (Coded)

Bodmin January 1 93

I have taken this opportunity of sending you these few lines to let you know that I received your letter last Thursday to my great satisfaction to hear that you are in good health, as it leaves me at present I bless God for it. I have been very much concerned to think what could be the reason that I did not hear from you for so long a time, for I was afraid you was ill & then I thought that Mrs Gilbert would not let me know of it because when you was ill last time she did not let me know till you was well again.

I saw Mrs Gilbert last Sunday, she sent for me to come down & she told me that she was very well pleased to hear your master speak so well of you as he do. My dear I have not heard from Brother Robert since – If he is at Plymouth I think it is very ill natured of him not to write as I desired him of all love to write & Kitty Musgrove told me that I might depend that he should see him in a day or two for that he came very often at his house – I have heard severall times from Brother Thomas since my last tho I have had but one letter from him & that dated Oct; 24th & I did not receive it till December 5th but I saw two that he sent to Jack Williams in Bury Lane concerning his son Thomas's misfortune. He has been in Bristoll working some time & did very well till this misfortune happened to him which is a great one indeed. The fifth of Novr there was bondfires & great rejoicing in Bristol & Brother said that there was a great deal of sailors & youngsters of the town to it, & after the fire was gone to decay, a great many of them went to Tower Lane which is a place of resort for bad women, & they broke in to the house & they carried off all the chairs, tubs barrells & the very bed steads to the fire, & the whores cried murder & alarmed the watchmen & constables & they seized all they found in the house and Brother said that Thomas W^ms was unfortunately coming by, just as they were crying murder & went in & he with many more were took, & sent to Bridewell where they were kept till the 10th when they where took before the Mayor & then Thomas & one more were sent to jail to stay till Assizes & all the rest were acquitted – His father is almost broken hearted for they think it will go very hard with them, & since he has been confined his father hath buried two of the youngest children.

53

Mr Moer died suddenly the Sunday before Christmas Day – Molly Little
goes on very well, she has a young son & I believe it will not be her fault if she
has not got more.

Fanny Climo would have sworn T: Boyne father, but Mr Frank Hicks would
not take her oath so he got off & went home & after he was gone Billy said he
had stole his clothes & carried them with him, & they went after him to Fowey
but he was gone to Padstow, & so they missed their aim – I believe the poor
fellow carried off nothing to them, nor Fanny was not with child, for after he
was gone there was nothing said about it.

Tilly Moor is with child again she hath sworn Billy Scantlebury father, &
they took him up & kept him one night & then they let him go again. The Revd
Mr Gilbert is now living in the house where Mr F. Hicks did. John Coppin is
off from Priory. Wm Tabb is coming off soon & then he hath some hopes of
seeing you soon after for he intends to come to London as soon as he is off
from Priory. Joanna is at Tower Hill still. I have not heard any thing of her
coming away since. She gives her kind love to you & will write when W. Tabb
comes to London – Brother John is very well, he is at Pencarrow still & I
believe he goes on just as usuall. I have not seen W.O since his triall but I heard
he was very well & that Mr Chapple was very kind to him. This being all at
present &cccccccc

E Clift

This last letter I received by Wm Hawking but after it was wrote & sent I rec^d
one dated the fourteenth which I rec^d before that by W^H & which I shall Omit
as they was very much alike, only saying that Billy Hocking had left Bodmin for
London. & that W: Tabb was going to bring it.

24. Robert to Elizabeth. 19 *January* 1793.[1]

St George hammoze the 19th 1793

Dear Brothers and sisters I now take the Oppertunity of wrighting these few
lines to You hoping the will find you all in Good health as I am at present
thanks Be to God for it Dear sister I am very sorry i have not heard from you
this seventeen months as often as i have rote to you and never had answer from
you Ever since which I hope you will not neglect wrighting to me this time or
Never more you need Expect no letter from Me after this Dear sister we
Expect to seal from hammoze Every Day But wheare wee are Going we
Cannot tell I would Be very Glad to Know wheare my ungest Brother is or
whether he is sent an aprentice or not and as for My Brother John I heard he
was working with Mr Chappel and I would Be very Glad to know whear My
Brother thomas is or wheare he is working which i would Be very Glad to

54

heare from you all But i hope with Gods Blessing to see You all if I live to see the ship payed of or if this Disturbance does not Continue which I hope there will Be nothing of it But i am Greatly in Dread there will as the are fiting oute a fleet as fast as possibel Be pleased to rember me to Mr pinch and his family & to Nanthannell George and his family And Be pleas^d to remember Me to Oner williamson and her wife and fammily & Christopher Climo and his wife and fammily So No more at present from Your loving Brother untill Death
                    Robert Clift

Be pleased to Direct Your letter to Mr Bellameys at the Sign of the welcom home Saillers in Brags ally Plymouth Dock For Robert Clift Now on Board of his Magestiys Ship St George Hamoze

25. John to William. 1 February 1793. (Coded)

                                        Pencarrow Feb^{ry} 1st 93

Dear Brother
              I have now taken this opportunity to enquire after your health & welfare which I trust in God you enjoy as I thank God we do at present, we have just received a letter from Brother Robert from Hammoaze, on board the St George man of war which he says is fitting out for sea as fast as possible he desired to have a letter as soon as possible & he says he hath sent many letters, but never rec^d any answer which I cannot believe, as I think if he ever put a letter in the Post Office it must certainly come safe his letter was not wrote by himself it was wrote by a very masterly hand but very illiterate spelling. I should think he might improve very much if he was inclined to learn in the place he is now but I suppose he never will now. He/he says if please God he lived to see the ship p^d off again he hopes to see us all again. Brother Thomas, we hear is coming to Bodmin about Easter to set on business & intends to bring a stock with him on purpose, he quarters with R Hurden in Bristol. Hurden I find hath 13s p^r week which is I think 7 more than I should wish to give him.
    We have had great confusion in Cornwall of late, occasioned by the tinners raising in order to put a stop to the shipping off corn[2] which they have happily effected for the good of the country as wheat was at twenty shillings p^r bush: before they stirr'd about it & was in a fair way to be thirty before next harvest. The tinners came to Padstow about a fortnight since – I think about 1500 when immediately the corn factors fled & the gentlemen of the town were obliged to be bound to put an entire stop to the exportation of corn for seven years & were verry happy they fared no worse, They got about fourty soldiers there thinking they could bid defiance to the Cornish heroes, but it only served to raise their undaunted spirits. When they first met the commanding

officer with his drawn sword, who bid them stand, one of them with his little shellelly club gave the sword a blow & told him come on if he was for that fun, but if they attempted to fire they would kill every man of them & level the whole town; so the soldiers & tinners were as friendly as men could be in a short time.

The tinners have surveyd all the neighbouring towns & markets & have set a price on the corn. For wheat that was 20/ about a fortnight ago is 16/ and barley which was 12/ is now sold for 8/. Otherwise they would not let them sell any. One of them being confined (by the gentlemen) as the ringleader of the tinners to take his trial at the Assizes, but his loyal companions attended the Sessions at Lostwithiel & demanded the prisoner whose name was Dyer when Sr W^m was Chairman but was glad to make the best of his way for they said they would have him (Sr W^m) living or dead, they came to a house where the coachman was & enquired where Sr W^m was – while they were searching for him in that house Sr W^m & Mr Gregor made their escape leaving thear carriages behind & the tinners were going to proceed on their journey to Launceston to take out the prisoner, at which the gentlemen gave Dyer's brother a release to carry to Launceston & take him out – then they gave three huzza's & said they had now got what they came for – The liberty of Dyer – & so every one departed in peace – so I must conclude at present being y^r ever affectionate Brother

John Clift.

26. *Thomas to William. 12 February 1793. (Coded)*

Dated Bristol Feb^r 12th 1793

Rec^d Feby 11th

Dr Brother

I have once more sent you a few lines hoping that I shall have the pleasure of an answer as I have sent several times & never rec^d any answer & I cannot think the reason. I have sent home several times to know if they had heard from you, or whether you was removed from the place I directed to you. So if you receive this I shall be happy to have a few lines from you as soon as possible, to know how you like London and some of the best news. I am sorry to inform you that our old neighbour Tom Williams is in Newgate here at Bristol since the 5th of November concerning of breaking into a house amongst the common prostitutes & taking tables & other things to help make a fire & there he is to continue 'till Aprill & then take his trial, whatever the consequence may be; which has been a great disadvantage to me for since he has been there I have been obliged to go to him two or three times a week to fetch work for him & to carry it to shop for him or else he might have starved sooner than any other person would have done it for him.

I am now living with R. & E. Hurden & am now in perfect health I bless God for it as I hope this will find you the same. I have appointed to go home severall times but never have brought it to bear yet & when it will be I cannot pretend to tell. This being all at present I shall ever remain your affectionate Brother

Thos Clift

Direct for me at N^r 5
opposite the Pump, Cherry-
-lane S James's, Bristol

27. William to Elizabeth. 16 February 1793.

February 16 1793

Dear Brother and Sister
             I have now taken this opportunity of sending these few lines hoping they will find you in good health as it leaves me at present I thank God for it – I received your kind letter by Wm Hocking on Monday the 21st of January he arrived in town the Friday before, he said Mr Stone came to Exeter before he expected him and so he was forced to pack up all his shirts which had been just wash'd and were very wet, On the monday Mr Stone came down and I went with him to his lodgings as he call'd it, it is a public house in cranbourn alley where Mr Hocking and Billy were seated 'till Mr Stone's return, so I had my letter and I stop'd while they drank a pint of Beer and then I set off with Billy that he might know the way another time to our house – I believe it was the next Day that I received your second letter which I found was to have come by Wm Tabb but I don't think he will ever leave Mr Gilbert's without some very uncommon thing happens I received the letter by a young man who said that Wm Tabb had thought of coming to London but he believed he would stay in his place he said he was footman to some relation to Mr Mountsteven at Towerhill and that william had sent it by him. I Received a Letter from Brother Thomas on the 11th Ins^t he does not say much concerning himself or any person else only he says he has to go and fetch and carry work to Thos Williams 3 or 4 times a week which puts him back a good deal and he says if he did not no body Else would and then he must starve where he is – he says he has often thought of going to Bodmin but when it will be he does not know but he does not mention any thing of going home at Easter, he says he has Sent several Letters to me but never had any answer, and a good reason for I never received any letter 'till now since May, he says he also sent several letters to you

to know if I had left my place or not but never rec^d any Answer

I let him know In my answer I sent him that you had heard from Brother Robert I told him where he was and that he was very well but that I did suppose it was no use to write as they was preparing for sea and might have saild before now, But I am all before hands with myself for I received a letter (two or three days before I received his) from Brother John who acquainted me with all this news as also of the riot at Padstow amongst the tinners about the Corn – I wish you would be kind enough to write to him as soon as you receive this for I wrote a wrong Direction for his letter being lockd in my box and it was almost too late to put it in the Post Box and I thought I knew it very well by reading it 3 or 4 times I wrote it and sent it away and I am afraid he will not get it but then you will know

His proper direction is, For Tho's Clift Cordwainer N° 5 Opposite the Pump, Cherry Lane St James Bristol—

Please to remember me kindly to all enquiring friends and acquaintance, and this being all at Present for want of Room I must Conclude your Ever loving and affectionate

Brother

William Clift.

Please to excuse me
now and I will will write oftener
for the future

28. *Elizabeth to William. 7 March 1793. (Coded)*

Bodmin March 7: 93

Dr Brother

I have now taken the opportunity of letting you know that I was very happy to receive your kind letter & to hear that you was very well & that I have rec^d another letter from Brother Robert 12th of February by Billy Musgrove, he was at Torpoint & saw Brother there at the publick house he gave him something to drink & desired him to come to the water side to him in the morning for he said he should be there with the long boat, but before Rodney³ came he was gone on board again, so he did not see him when he came away but he gave him the letter in the evening before Rodney says he was very well drest and had plenty of money Brother said in his letter that he was then onboard the St George but was going to be turned over to another ship the next week & then he was going to join the Admirals fleet & as soon as he did get on board the other ship he would write again he gives his kind love to you and says he hopes to see us all again if the Lord is pleased to spare him in 18

58

months time, & desired when I wrote to him to send your direction where to write to you. I believe pens ink & paper are very scarce in Bristol for I have had but 3 letters from Brother Thomas these 18 months. I have sent to him & desired him to answer it, but you know how kind they all were in writing to us when you were at home. R^d Levers that lived with T: Hicks the gardner is in Bridewell for taking some wheat from his master & carrying it to J Jeffery's to grind, they say it was 2 gallons. He is to take his trial at Truro Sessions. Lord Camelford was brought home to be buried last Saturday, & Wm May died last Monday. Jonathan Oliver & Jack Brewer at Nedy Bonds is gone to sea this week. Yesterday there was a great meeting at the Great Hall concerning the tinners but I think they had better let them alone while they are quiet for it is most peoples opinion that it will be very hard times in Cornwall, for the tinners are determined to rise again if they ship off the corn, & the gentlemen have agreed that it shall be shipped off for they say that the farmers cannot pay thear rents except they do. Sister is very well and gives her kind love to you. She is at Tower Hill still & Brother John is very well. Billy Hockins mother desired you would be so kind as to beg him to send a few lines to her as he promised, unknowing to his father & let her know how to direct to him so as his father may not know it, she thinks the best way would be to direct to you, & that she would be very glad if you would be so kind as to let her know when you write to me how & in what manner & where & with whom they live I think he is very unkind not to send to his mother in all this time. Priory people are all very well & give their kind love to you. I suppose you wonderd at the letter that was brought to you by the young man. I had wrote it some days before he left Bodmin to send by W: Tabb. He sent up to me in the morning for me to come down to Priory for he was going to London that day by the coach, so I wrote a few lines & went down & when I came down the maidens told me he had no heart to go for he had been up in town & heard that Mr Molesworth wanted a servant & that he was gone to see & if that did not suit, he would set out for London the next day. Mr & Mrs G. were at Lostwithiel on a visit & he called on them as he returned from Mr Molesw^ths & then they agreed he should stay again. Tho there was another come in his place. Please to let me know in your next, where my last letter was post p^d or not.

    Your ever affect^e Sister till death
E. Clift

29. William Hawking to his Mother. 17 March 1793.[4]

London 17th March 1793

My dear Mother,
        I have taken this opportunity of sending these few lines hoping they will find you in good health as it leaves me at Present. I was down

last Sunday to see Billy Clift and he told me he had received a letter from his Sister, and that you desired me to write as I promised to do, but the second week after I came here I went to work with father in the morning when he went, and do not leave work till he leaves work in the evening, and by that means I have not had any opportunity ever since. Father and I work with Mr Strange N° 108 St Martin's Lane, and we quarter at N° 38 Great St Andrew's Street, Seven dials at the house of Mr Hoe, watch glass maker. I should be very glad if, whenever you send any letter to father not to mention any of our lodgers to me again, for when father asked me who Nancy Randall was, I not thinking of any harm, harmlesly told him she was one of our lodgers, but as soon as I recollected myself, I told him that she had not been there long, and that I did believe she was going away again soon. I should be very glad if you would be so kind as to write to Exeter, and give my kind love to Uncle and Aunt, and my little cousin, and to let them know that I am very well, and that I like London very well. Please to remember my kind love to Grandfather and Grandmother, to Uncle and Aunt, and my kind love to Sisters. Please to remember me to Nancy Rendall, to Mr and Mrs White, and please to remember me and Billy Clift to Mr and Mrs Salter and family, and to my Uncle, Aunt and Cousins in Lostwithiel, and to Betty and Joanna Clift, and to all enquiring friends and acquaintance, and to all my old playmates and schoolfellows.

This being all at present I must conclude your ever loving and affectionate son till death.

Wm Hawking.

Please to direct to me (for Wm Hawking to the care of Wm Clift at John Hunter's Esqre N° 13 Castle Street, Leicester Square, London), I believe you will be forced to write the direction small or you will not have room. I should be glad if when you write to me you would carry it to Mr Salter[5] to direct it for you and then you will be sure of its coming safe.

Billy Clift gives his kind love to his Brother and Sisters, and says he will write to them soon.

Copy of a letter brought by Pearce.
It is written by his mother's brother.
Decr 29th 1847.

30. Thomas to William. 14 April 1793. (Coded)

Bristol April 14th 1793

Dr Brother
        After a long time I have sent you these few lines hoping they will

find you in good health as it leaves me at present tho I have been poorly for a week past with a cold.

Excuse me for not writing sooner, but reason is that every hour I have had to spare I have been with T. Williams and writing letters for him. Last Sunday I began to write this but I received a Letter from his father & he desired an answer so I was forced to drop it till now. Tom was tried on the 10th ins' found guilty, & condemn'd for death but his father has made great friends & had a petition drawn & sent to Lord Grenville to present it to his majesty & we hope that he will have a free pardon. Trade is very dead in all branches here at present tho it is not so with me as yet. I sent a letter to Brother Rob' since I heard from you but whether he received it or not I don't know for I have heard nothing from him. I shall be glad to have a few lines from you as soon as convenient to know how London agrees with you & some of the newest news.

Y^{rs} &cccc Thos Clift.

Mr Sainsbury's next door to the
Pump, Cherry Lane Bristol

31. William to Elizabeth. 15 April 1793.

Monday April 15 93

Dear Brother and Sisters.

I have taken this opportunity of Sending you these few lines hoping they will find you in good health as it leaves me at present. Billy Hocking was down here last sunday was a fortnight and he told me that he was going to Knightsbridge with John Gatty the next Sunday and last week I saw him again and he told me they had been at the House of Henry Bond, and he said that Mr Bond was married to the Maid that used to live at Cap^{tn} Peers at Churchstile & he said that she wished she could see me, so I knew at once that it was Grace Collins as I never knew any other maid live there. So yesterday afternoon billy and I went down there it is not above a mile from our house –It is not far from the road going to Mr Hunters Country house and as I was coming home from there one day I Met Mr Bond, and pass'd him without speaking to him for I could not tell who it was but I was sure it was somebody I knew – We went down there and drank tea and they were very glad to see me and very hearty – Grace has got a fine little Boy, My name sake – about 6 or 8 months old – I had the whole history of George Solomon of Grace she says when she lived at the other end of Town she did not live as far as from butter Market to Churchstile from where George lived, and that he used often to come and see her she says he had a very good place a great deal too good for

61

Priory, Bodmin as it was in 1792. Drawn from memory by William Clift c.1814.

him, for he was a very impudent saucy boy and he had alway a plenty of money, and a watch in his pocket and always a great plenty of Clothes he did not carry away any thing with him but his watch and that he sold to pay his way homeward. I suppose he wishes himself back again, before now. Grace desires to be rememberd to my Sisters and Mr Bond desires to be rememberd to Brother John, they live at N° 3 Little Exeter Street Sloane Street Knightsbridge – Please to tell Willm Roberts that Mr Bond told me that Mary is gone to Holland with her husband – and that Serjeat Burrows is made Serjeant Major in the Norfolk Millitia

I hope Mr and Mrs Gilbert are very well and all the Servants, You did not tell me in your last that Mr Renorden had been and Carried away one of the Miss Phillips's nor of all the Great buildings going on in Bodmin – Please to remember me kindly to all Mr Eyres People, to Deborah, to E. Yeo, to Kitty & Ann to Thomas Onion and her Mother and to Betsy Williamson, and all enquiring friends – Please to remember me to T Arthur John Ford & his Mother, to Tammy *Bonady* and tell Joanna now I hear she is out of place she will write to me or else I shall write to her soon Billy Hocking desires you will Give his Duty to his mother and that he will write to her soon

Be sure and let Brother John know that I have writ or else he will think I have surely forgot him, Please to send me all the Good and bad news in your next and write as soon as convenient, tell Joanna to write to me and let me know whether you have heard from brother Robert since or not – The Letter you rec^d last was a mistake in putting into the Office I gave the house keeper the money to put it in for me and She forgot to pay for it—

Y^{rs} &C Wm Clift.

32. William to Elizabeth. 24 May 1793.

London Leicester Square   Friday May 24th 1793

Dear Sisters and Brother

I have taken this opportunity of sending you these few lines hoping they will find you in good health as it leaves me at present I bless god for it. I received a letter from Brother Thomas about the beginning of May he was very well then he says work is very dead in Bristol but that he had as much as he could do as yet – he Informed be [sic] of Thos Williams's being condemnd on the 10 of April but that his father had made great friends and that they were in hopes of a free pardon but all this I suppose is Ropers news[6] to you.

Mr & Mrs Gilbert arrived in town on last monday fortnight and I saw them that evening they came at our house and they were very glad to see me and Mrs Gilbert desired me to come to their lodgings at N° 13 Charles St Grosvenor Square not far from their lodgings last year – I went there last sunday week which was my sunday out but when I came Mrs G was gone to the Chapel so I went to the same Chapel and when I came back she was not come in and then it was one OClock and there was a lady waiting for her too; so I could not *   * much of that time but she told me I should know time enough to write and send any thing to you when they did leave town and on Monday Mrs Hunters maid told me they did leave town on thursday so on wednesday I went up and carried my letter and some drawings for she desired me to let her see some) and I could not get out till 3 OClock I was so very busy and then Mrs G was dressing to go out and I could not see her but sent me word that she was not going till saturday. I suppose she will take some of the drawings with her and then I suppose you will see them.

On Tuesday I asked Mr Hunter for a holiday and went to Greenwich fair,[7] billy hocking told me last sunday that he was going on tuesday but I did not think of Going then and when I came to their house he was gone with the woman that belongs to the house they live in, and I never saw him all day. It is about six miles to Green^{ch} from London and I walk'd down and home which almost tired me I had a very pleasant journey and fine weather. In greenwich park is where the people all met and go to the top of a very steep hill and run down for a quarter of a mile and somtimes the girls come down such nice tumbles twould make you split your sides to see them come down with such a fall and running their full force down hill that as they fall their petticoats fly right over their heads before some thousands of both sexes – there is/is some very creditable looking girls run and tumble as well as the girls of the town – It is a delightful park facing the river Thames and when I came up with Capt Banks I went on shore there and then there was some hundreds of deer, but now, fair time they were put in the House.

I wish you would tell John and Joanna to let me know what is the reason they do not write to me all this time and beg them to send as sooon as they can

In Greenwich park when all the people was very busy in looking at the Girls running a pickpocket stole a pocket handkerchief out of a Gentlemans pocket and some of the young men saw him do it and they took him and drag'd him to a large pond in the park and in they sous'd him as it were into the belly of a Tulip over head and years and battered him with mud & Tabs[8] till they half killd him and would not let him come out till he had swam across two or three times

Billy Hocking desires to be remembered to all his friends at bodmin – I cant write any more for want of room and I am almost tired writing this twice over as it did not please me first time[9]

So no more at present from your ever
    loving and affectionate brother
            W Clift

In my answer to Brother Thomas's letter I desired him to send you some thing whin convenient but whether he will or not I must leave that to the Reader.

33. Elizabeth to William. 4 June 1793 (Coded)

Bodmin June 4 93

Dear Brother—
            I have taken this opportunity of sending you these few lines hoping they will find you in good health as it leaves me at present I bless God for it. Mr & Mrs Gilbert came home last Wednesday evening & on Thursday they sent for me & when I came down Mrs Gilbert told me that she had a letter for me & that she had brought home some of your drawings so they were brought to me to see them & she said I should chuse some of them/ them first & the servants should have the rest amongst them so I had three, that with the fruit, the woman of Monte Casino & the tarrantula dance[10] & then she went into the parlour and brought out the letter, and told me that there was money

in it for me. She said she was very well pleased with you that you had not forgot me & that she hoped you would do very well & that you was greatly improved & that your master did speak very well of you she told me that when you bro' the letter to her she said W^m it is heavy I believe there is money in it & you said it was a trifle for me & she told me that you was very well now but that you had been very poorly in the winter with the head ach, & that you was very happy in your place & that you liked your Master very well. My Dear Brother I return you many thanks for what you sent me. My Dear it is more than I have had of any one of all of my Brothers since you left me & as for Brother John he seldom comes to see me, for when he comes to town there is too many public houses in the way for him to come to see me. As for Brother Thos he has not wrote to me since Octr last, tho he has had many opportunity's for there has been of this town 10 I suppose that hath come home from Bristol but he never so much as sent a line to neither of us. I hear he is going to Monmouthshire & I suppose I should not have known any thing about it, if it had not been for John W^ms. He sent a letter to him the day after he rec^d yours to let him know what he has laid out for Thomas which was 20/ since his trial. He has 2 years imprisonment. Brother Thos desired John Williams to remember him to his Brother & Sisters and let them know that he had heard from you the day before & that you was very well, but he never sent a ribband nor the worth of one to sister nor me since he left Bodmin—

I have not heard from Brother Robert since. Joanna is working at Blissland about the bark. Mr Eyre has bought the wood just by the Church Town – she was home a Sunday & was very well & desir'd to be remembered to you. Mrs Eyre & Francis are gone to London to Mr John Eyres's[11] they left Bodmin on Sunday & Mr Barron is gone with them I was a mind to send a letter by them but as she did not say any thing, I did not know how to ask. I wish you may have the opportunity of seeing them before they return. I believe they will stay three weeks or a month.

The Millitia marched from Bodmin last Saturday morning for Exeter. T Williamson desired to be rememberd to you he was in light company. The maidens at Priory give their kind love to you & return you many thanks for the drawings W: Tabb desires to be remember'd to you

D^r B^r I cannot write any more for want of room so I remain your ever loving & affect^e Sister

E. Clift

34. *William to Elizabeth. ? July 1793.*

Sunday Leicester Square July 93

Dear Sisters and Brother,
                    I received your kind Letter on I believe the 7th of

65

June and happy to hear you are all well, as also of Mr & Mrs Gilberts safe arrival at Bodmin, Mrs Hunter had told me the day before I received yours that She had heard from them and that they were safe home. The day before I received your letter I had been at Covent Garden and as I was coming home just before our door in Castle Street who should I meet but Mr Barron – he did not know me at first but when I told him who I was he stopt and talked with me a good while and seemed very glad to see me; he told me that you was very well when he left home but he did not tell me that Mrs Eyre & Francis were in town nor have I seen any thing of them as yet, I suppose they are home again before now; I should have been very glad to have seen them before their return but it is such a way from our house that I should hardly get there and back again of a Sunday. it is near twelve miles forth and back to Hackney. Mr Barron said he would call on me before he did go and take any thing I had to send, for me, but I have not seen any thing of him since. Mr John Hunter My young Master is coming to Cornwall and was so good as to take this with him for you, our people tell me that he is going with a cabinet Maker of our Town, I suppose it must be Mr Barron, I dont know who it can be else, but he told me then that he was going back the next week which is near five weeks ago. Mr Hunter will be at Priory for some weeks I believe and then I suppose you will have the chance of Seeing him I wrote a letter then if Mr Barron had called but as I had not any thing particular to write it is no great odds.

I saw Thomas Hambly two or three sundays ago, he was very well and desired to be remembered to you – he invited me to come to see him, and that John henwood works in the same shop with him and that Sam Pope and Wm Trefry was in the same Street at another Shop. Billy Hocking desires to be kindly remembered to his Mother and Sisters and all his acquaintance—

I hope you will be so kind as to write to me whenever you hear from Brother, I think Brother John might have found time all this While & Joanna too,; why Mr Hunter dont take so long to write a large Book as they do to write a Letter – You will be able to send when Mr Hunter returns if you do not before, as it will not take up much room in his Trunk with his Clothes and then if they do not write by that time, I shall not forgive them you may tell them, for you will not have a better opportunity and you will be able send one each made up in one if you like—

Please to remember me to all enquiring friends & acquaintance, and let me know in your next when you heard from Fowey last and how all the people there are.

There were some young Whales caught in the river Thames since I wrote last we had one of them at our country house where I had a nice walk out and ride home with Mr H:^{r}/every day for a week—

This being all at present I must remain your ever loving and Affectionate Brother

William Clift.

Leicester Square July 15th 1793   Monday Morning

Dear Sister I have now taken this opportunity of sending these few lines hoping they will find you in as good health as it leaves me at Present – I have been waiting ever since I received your letter to have the opportunity of sending by Mr Jn° Hunter who leaves home to day for Priory, this is the third letter I have wrote since I rec^d yours – when I wrote the first which Mr Barron was to have Called for (but did not) I desired you to Remember Billy Hawking to his mother and in my second I did the same and to tell them he was very well, tho when I wrote the second he was very ill but I was in hopes he would soon get the better of it, – on Sunday last was three weeks he came down to see me and complained of a head ach but he believed it was with drinking some ale in the morning and when he went to bed and was scarce out of it again till on wednesday last when he was put in his Coffin, poor fellow he was ill of a violent fever which carried him of and he so soon became putrid that he was forced to be buried the next day – he died on Tuesday, at one oClock in the Morning – I went to Burrying on wednesday evening last the Eleventh Ins^t at 6 oClock he was buried about a Mile out of town I have forgot the name of the Church that the ground belonged to but I think it was St Georges, Hanover Square, the churchyards are not Joining to the Churches here in London they have a burying Ground some where out of town as nigh as they can get them. I must beg you will not mention anything of it to any body for fear it should reach his mothers years and then she would be frighted to death I suppose, I beg you will let her tell you of it first for I suppose Mr Hawking will send to her first and tell her that he is ill and then send again to say he is dead – for he did not write to her all the while he was bad because he was in hopes billy would get well again and She know nothing of the matter – I do not think there was any thing wanting to be done that any body could do for him I am sure his father left nothing undone for him that he could do and the poor woman of the house had almost tired herself to death watching up almost every Night he was ill – I have nothing else to write at present but must conclude &c

Wm Clift

P.S Mr John is going to set out I cannot
    write any more I have only time to write
    this – John Gatty and Richd Broughton was at the
funeral – Be sure and not let his mother hear any thing of it whatever you do –I have sent my second letter with this because I had not time to write it over again—

NOTES SECTION III

1. Robert's first extant letter is written in a hand other than his own, as John's somewhat acid comments make clear.
2. *shipping off corn*: i.e. to London. Under the Corn Laws of 1791 foreign corn could not be imported until the price in England had reached 50 shillings a quarter. This was to protect the interests of British farmers.
3. Rodney appears to be the Billy Musgrove just mentioned. The people frequently have two surnames but this is the only instance of two first names.
4. This letter, apparently written by William Clift, survives in a transcript made by Billy Hawking's uncle.
5. Mr Salter was the parish school master (not the Grammar School master) who had taught William Clift. He was also the parish clerk, a wigmaker and hairdresser.
6. *Ropers news*: i.e. no news. This is a west country saying and probably confined to Cornwall. It was recorded in 1879 in the *Folk-Lore Record* (ii. 203) as being particularly associated with Bodmin. Various forms of it appear in the letters.
7. Greenwich Fair was held at Whitsuntide annually. Like St. Bartholomew's Fair it was eventually banned because of the rowdy behaviour it gave rise to.
8. *Tabs*: according to the *OED* *tab* is a largely dialectal word and the most likely meaning recorded seems to be a short, broad strap.
9. One of the instances showing that Clift frequently redrafted his letters. Three or four lines are heavily blocked out below.
10. *tarrantula dance*: *tarantula* is the name of a poisonous spider. The *OED* says it has been used erroneously for the tarantella dance, which would seem to be the meaning here. Tarantism, which is a disease characterised by the impulse to dance, was popularly ascribed to the bite of the tarantula spider in the 15th to 17th centuries, so the two words are apparently connected.
11. John Eyre was the brother of Joseph Eyre of Bodmin. Apprenticed to the textile and clothing trade, he was converted to religion in its most evangelical form and as a result was turned out of doors by his father, John Eyre senior. He came under the protection of the Countess of Huntingdon's Connection and was trained for the ministry at her college at Trevecca. Later, he became a founder member of the London Missionary Society, in whose first ship the Clifts' cousins, the Puckey brothers of Fowey, set sail for the South Seas as missionaries in 1796. He was also responsible for founding the Hackney Academy at his home in Hackney but died before it got under way. This eventually became Hackney College, which trained ministers for the Congregational Church and survived until the Second World War. (The editor's father was trained there). Eyre himself remained an Anglican and was ordained by Robert Lowth, Bishop of London.

IV. AUGUST TO DECEMBER 1793.

The incidents of the second half of 1793 are overshadowed by the death of John Hunter on October the 16th. William writes to his sister of the event and its implications for his own future just two days later. Elizabeth replies in a letter full of concern for her brother. She has seen Mrs Gilbert and talked of the calamity with her. The Gilberts have appeared frequently in the early letters and Mrs Gilbert clearly continued to take a kindly interest in the boy whom she had been instrumental in sending to London. Now William is once more in need of the support of his first benefactress and he is to turn to her for advice many times in the next few years.

Before this overwhelming blow to William's expectations occurs, the letters continue to deal with family matters. John gives his version of a quarrel with Elizabeth in Billy Bonady's public house, the George and Dragon, and William repeats his account to Elizabeth almost verbatim. In the differences between Elizabeth and John, William invariably takes his sister's part. Sir William Molesworth is having a house built at St Marylebone Fields and John expresses the hope that he may come to London with the furniture which he has been making for it, a proposal not very warmly received by William. Joanna has again gone into service, having had a short spell working for Mr Eyre at his bark-stripping business at Lerryn. According to Elizabeth, Joseph Eyre was in financial difficulties and she hints that he is likely to go bankrupt. A strange prophetic dream which she relates in high flown biblical language is interpreted by William as portraying the downfall of the Eyre family, for whom he shows little liking.

One of the isolated pieces of information which is of interest is a list of books which William says he has been collecting in sixpenny numbers and which includes many of the classic writers of the eighteenth century. How much John Hunter discussed affairs other than those to do with his work with his young apprentice we shall probably never discover but in reading, as in other matters, it is likely that he exercised a considerable influence on William's development. After eighteen months under his direction William was in a way to advancement he could little have dreamed of a few years earlier, and there can be no doubt about the sincerity of his confession after Hunter's death that he will never like another master so well.

36. Elizabeth to William. 8 August 1793. (Coded)

Bodmin Aug[r] 8 93

D[r] Brother
      I have taken this opportunity of writing these few lines, hoping it

will find you in good health as it leaves me at present I bless God for it. Mr Hunter came to Priory the Thursday after he left you, by nine oclock in the morning.

He gave that which you sent to me by him, to Mrs G^r as soon as he came & she sent up Rich^d to me but I was down to Margate. In the evening when I came home they told me I must go down to Priory, & when I came down they told me that W^m had got my letter and that he was gone up to Mr Eyres's with it to me/ me & then Mrs Gilbert came into the kitchen & desired me to sit down till William did come back & she sat down & talked with me a good while, & she said you was very well & that Mr Hunter did speak very well of you and very much in your praise & that nothing did give her greater satisfaction than to hear you did behave so well & that you had your health, she said Mr Hunter told her that you should go out more in the air, for she was afraid too much confinement would hurt you as you was used to the country.

Dear Brother I was very happy to receive your kind letter & drawing & more so to find you enjoy your health so well my dear you are the only brother that taketh any account of me, I have not seen brother John but once since I wrote to you last & that was the week before our Assizes & then he was painting Mr Tabb's house; he is idler than ever; the Sunday before the Assizes he went up to Boney's & staid all night & there was a company of the Somerset Militia went thro' the town that night they came in at ten & went out by three in the morning & carried away a new pair of shoes a pair of stockings & a handkerchief from him & when I heard of it I went up to him but could not get him away, & then Sally Tabb went up & got him away & put him out of town & I have not seen him since. Sister is at Lerren working for Mr Eyre, she hath been there these six weeks so that I have no person of my own to speak to, as for John it is no odds if he was a 100 miles off for he never comes to see me nor takes any account of us let there be what there will amiss with us. I bless God I have my health much better than I used to. I was at Lerren last Sunday was a month to see Joanna & after dinner several of us went into a publick house to have some cyder & we were but just into the house before Uncle James & Jimmy came into the room. They were surprised to see us there & we were surprised to see them there; they brought up a Mr Broad in a boat from Fowey he came from London & is a brother to the man wher Joanna lodges Uncle & Cousin desired of us to go home with them, but Joanna could not for she expected Mr Eyre there early in the morning to load a barge with bark, so I went to Fowey that evening to see aunt & came back to Lerren in the morning with the tide & when I came back to Lerren sister told me that Mr Eyre was not there for his father was dead & that W Roberts was come there to load the barge. He was ill three weeks, taken ill of a Saturday night after he went home from market & that day three weeks he died, His children were all home just time enough to see him & that was all, Mr John was not in the house above half an hour before his father died. Mathew came home the Wednesday before with M^rs & Francis, he was buried the day poor Billy Hocking died

Mrs Eyres brother Mr Mitchell that Tregarden belonged to died the next week Mr Jn° Eyre is gone back to London & Andrew is gone with him. M^rs & Francis would have been very glad to have seen you if they could, the wrote home three times to know your direction & M^r forgot to write where you was when he wrote. He told me that Mrs Eyres uncle lived just by Leicester Square & there they spent most of their time; Francis said he would have sooner have seen you than all the people in London I believe they did not spend but little of their time at Hackney, they enquired of every person they knew if they did not know you but they did not know your Masters name nor what part of London you was in so they could not find you out. I had it finely when they came home that I did not give them your direction where to find you before they went away. The day they came out of London Master came into the room where I was & told me that Mrs Eyre had wrote home twice & Francis once to know where you was, for that Francis had been making his mother mad to see you & he had forgot to ask of me till then and then it was too late. W. Wills's time is out & he left Bodmin for Bristol last Thursday was a month. I sent a letter to Brother Thomas by him & last Sunday I received an answer to it by J: Ham. It was dated July 30th. He says he is coming home in 8 or 10 weeks at the farthest. I have not heard from Brother Robert since Jany. Sister was home last Sunday she was very well & gives her kind love to you & she will write to you soon. My dear Brother I was greatly shocked when I opened your letter & found poor Billy Hocking was gone I never let any person know of it till Mrs Hocking knew it which was not till last Thursday Mr Hocking directed his letter to Mrs Hockings father, & they received it the Thursday but as she was poorly they did not let her know of it but they told some body of it & desired them not to tell of it, but it was known all over the town before they told her of it. Saturday morning Dick Bray went in & asked Mrs Hocking if it was true that Billy was dead & said Par Hambly told him so & the poor woman was frightened almost out of her senses, she ran out of doors like one out of their parts to go up to Par to know if it was true & as she was going up Prison Lane she met Mrs Hawk who was coming to tell her that he was poorly, but if they had a mind to have brought it about they should not have told it to any person. As for me I did not as much as tell Joanna of it till Mrs Hocking knew it. Mrs Hawke desired her to go in & be reconciled so by that time she knew it was so she went in & fainted away & was very ill all that day & has been very poorly ever since. She desires you will give her love to her husband & let him know that the children are very well, but she is almost overgone with trouble, as for my part I cannot hardly bear to go into the house to see her in such trouble; My dear brother you may easier guess what her trouble is than I can describe it. She desired you would let her know when you write to me if Billy ever received that letter she sent to him, because he never answer'd that letter & how it was that he did not write

71

that letter himself that he sent to her, for she told me it was your writing. Tell Mr Hocking that she will write as soon as she is able for she is not able write for trouble at present. I have not seen Mr Hunter yet. Mr & Mrs G: & him are gone west. Polly Coule told me that he was very poorly she says he is just in the same way poor Bill May was & that he was not going to return for some time All the servants give their kind love to you. Henry Oliver & Betty Hoskin & T. Gatty & Becky were married on Bodmin riding[1] Sunday 21st July. Poor Deborah Lord is blind she is put home to Blissland Parish she has been blind these 5 or 6 months. Polly Godfrey is home & has a fine little boy that is able to run about she came home last Thursday. Her husband is at Hertford Bridge a recruiting she her mother & sister – Catty Rowe John Ford T Arthur, H Williamson & family give their kind love to you. There was but 6 prisoners tried at our Sizes 5 of them acquitted – the other 6 months imprisonment. Jn° Colwill is in Exeter Jail & he took his trial at the last Assizes for having bought the Kings stores from the dock yard there was a great fine levelld on him & not being able pay it he has got off with three months imprisonment. This being all at present I conclude with my prayers to God for your health & prosperity & shall ever remain your ever loving sister

E Clift.

37. John to William. 8 August 1793. (Coded)

Pencarrow August y^c 8th 93

Dear Brother

According to your request I have once more taken pen in hand to enquire after your health which I bless God we all enjoy at present I thought by this time you must have forgot my name but I find by sisters letter that you enquired after me when Mr Hunter came down. God knows who the fault is in I cannot say, but I really expected to have had a letter long be fore this time, which if you have sent I suppose my good humoured Sister hath taken up, but if you would be so good as to trouble youself with writing me a letter & direct it to me at Pencarrow perhaps I may have the pleasure to receive one once more from you – I find sister Betty hath had several from you but she thinks it enough just to say that you are well or something to that effect – Just in the usual temper she was so good as to let me have a sight of your drawings brought by Mrs G: which gave me a great deal of pleasure

I cannot say at present how soon but I hope shortly to have the pleasure of seeing you again as Sr W^m hath a house built in Mary bone Fields Westminster & I have been making furniture for it for some time past and as the family is going to town very soon I intend to come if I can get leave by any means, as Mr Tabb is got quite an old man by the gout I think he will hardly go so far from home. If I cannot get leave to go when the family do I think I shall go up with the furniture if possible I can as I find the goods are to be sent to Fowey by conveyance (I suppose) of Captn Banks as I should wish to see you if I were not to stay two days in Town – I have not said any thing to Mr Tabb yet about it but I have told several in the place my intention – I told him some time ago that I would not stay any longer but he will not listen to it, – for this reason I suppose – I find he hath told some person he cannot get another to suit the place so well. But I dont think he hath used me half as well as he might – nor indeed as he ought & proposed when we engaged; so when a master runs from his word I think it is time to run from such an engagement.

Sister & me had a little difference about a month ago since which time I have not seen her. The occasion of which was as follows. I had been at Mr Tabbs, painting against the Assize & when I finished I was going with an old pair of shoes and & stockings tied up in a handk^f. I called at the George & Dragon to get a glass of gin, & I just set down the parcel to rest for a minute while I went to the bar door, mean while a baggage cart stopt at the door with some soldiers, presently I found the parcel gone and no body could get account of it. Presently sister was come and abused me like a pickpocket & insisted on my going to door. I have a 1000 things to relate when I have the happiness of seeing you but I suppose there is a difficulty of coming by water at present but there may be an alteration in the course of three weeks or a month, when the things are sent to Fowey I shall write to you again. W: Tabb desired me to give his love to you likewise my best of friends Mrs Jeffery. Mr Tabb seems to show great respect for you I have not seen poor Joanna for I believe almost three months; I were at Bodmin Assize but she was not home She I find hath been at St Veep for some time past for Mr Eyre. I have not heard from/ from brother Thomas by letter but once since I saw you & then he told me he would write oftener as for poor Robt we shall not see him again for some time I suppose. I have lost my penknife and have only a pen as you may see by this abrupt scroll. I cannot recollect any thing more at present, we have a great number of French prisoners in Bodmin & I am informed that one of our town girls is to be married to one of them. I hope you will write me a letter as soon as you receive this.

From y^r most affectionate brother
John Clift.

38. Elizabeth to William. 4 September 1793. (Coded)

Bodmin Sepr 4 93
Wednesday evening 7 o,clock.

Dear Brother
This comes with my kind love to you hoping it will find you in

good health as it leaves me at present I bless God for it, as it is one of the greatest blessings we can enjoy whilst here below. Dear Brother I have been very uneasy for fear you are not well as you have not wrote to me since Mr Hunter came down. I wrote to you and desired you to send to me as soon as you could. As Mrs Hocking has sent to her husband & received no answer which makes her fearfull he is taken to drinking again. She gives her love to you and begs you will desire of him to write to her as soon as possible & when you write to me let me know what I desired of you in my last. Dr Brother I have not seen brother John since I wrote to you last. Brother Thomas sent to Jno Williams last week & he said he had been very poorly for a fortnight but was better again.

Sister is home from Lerren. She came home last Friday was a fortnight & Sunday was a week she went to Mr J: Billings to live she is very well & gives her kind love to you & she said if she had known that Mr Hunter had been going home so soon she would have wrote to you but now she has not time for I did not know it till last evening. Polly Coule told me that Mrs G^r expected Mrs H^r down soon & so we thought Mr H: would not have returned so soon. Dr Brother we hear that Brother Robert is gone to Matrion but I have not had any letter from him. The way we heard from him was by a young man that lived at Towerhill with Mr Mountstevens & he is gone to sea – he is onboard the Intrepid, the same ship Mr Edgvean is minister of, so we was acquainted with him when he lived at Towerhill & he used to say he would go to sea & if he did he would enquire for R^t & so he sent home that Robert Clift was at M—.

Mr Eyre's people are very well & gives their love to you & Catty Rowe & W Roberts & R Bescumb. I believe he is coming back to our house again. There hath been no person there since W Wills went away, but W Roberts and me. There hath been a great talk about Mr Eyres being bankrouted but I hope it will not be as some persons would have it. Mr Colwill & Mr Willis was partners with him in Barlandue wood which cost £1300 & when the money came to be paid they would not pay any of it, tho' they looked after the workpeople all the summer & went to & fro to the wood with him & acknowledged themselves partners with him or he would not have bought more than he could have paid for if it had not been for them for he bought £800 worth first & then they heard it was very cheap & then they desired him to buy the rest of the/the wood & that they would advance the rest of the money & he never knew any thing to the contrary till the day the money came to be paid I believe Mr Eyre is gone to London about settling it now, he went away last Friday so when I write again I will send you more particulars but as I do not know how it will be I shall say no more about it but I believe he will be able settle it. Mr & Mrs G: are very well & so are the servants who give their kind love to you. Dear Brother if I was to put down all their names that desired to be remembered to you I might fill the whole sheet with nothing else. Dear brother I hope you will be so kind as to send a few lines to me as soon as you receive mine to let me know if you have heard from Brother John or Thomas since you wrote to me last. This being all at present I conclude with

my kind love to you & remain your ever
loving & affectionate Sister till
Death. E. Clift.

Bodmin
Septr 4th: 93
Wednesday evening 7 oclock

The following is a dream which I saw as I lay on my bed. I thought I was standing at my own door & my father & mother standing by me & all at once I saw the whole street full of men drawn up in rankes & immediately I found myself in the church yard in the path just between the place where father & mother was buried & the tower & I still saw such a multitude that could not be numberd for the whole earth was covered with men all musterd up ready for battle & the weight thereof made the earth shake, for it could not bear the weight, & I saw the armies all fire at once & then dissappeared & it seemed to me as if the earth was sinking under me & I thought the world was at an end & I should see you no more. I had all things in my mind as perfect as if it had been real & then I thought I knew that father & mother were dead, & I then turned my self round & kneeld down to pray for I could see nothing for it was dark with smoke which proceeded from the fireing & as I was at prayer, I looked up & I saw as it were, the heavens open & I saw in my drear, the Lord descending from heaven in terrible majesty & I heard a voice to say, "the worst is to come

And then I fell down with my face to the ground & I saw the earth open and the sight which I saw is too dreadfull to mention. & with the shock I awoke, & when I came to my senses I did not expect to see the morning light, for with the shock I was as one dead. I lay a great while before I could move hand or foot for I had no thought of any thing but death, & I remained very poorly or some time, after, for I could not put it out of my mind, but that something more than common would happen. & now I cannot think of it without putting me in such a terrible shudder.

39. William to Elizabeth. 10 September 1793.

Septr 10th 1793

Dear Sister
        I received your kind letter dated August 8, and was very glad to hear that you enjoyed a good state of health as this leaves me at present. I

75

receiv'd a Letter from Brother John since I received your first in which he told me (ropers news)[2] that you and him had had a difference about his going up to Billy Bonadys, he said he only went in to get a Glass of gin just as he was going out of town, & that he put down an old pocket handerkerchief with an old pair of Shoes and Stockings in it, upon the bench while he went to the bar, and in the mean time a Baggage Cart with a Company of Soldiers stopt at the door and when he turn'd round he missed his Bundle and could not find it any where, and to add to his misfortune, you came in and abused him like a pickpocket and forced him out of doors. He says he intends coming to London when Sir W[ms] Family comes to town which will be in a Month or two's time and if he cannot come then he shall try what he can do when the Furniture comes, to furnish Sir Williams new house in Mary-bone fields – The furniture is coming by water from Fowey and then he says he will come if it is only for a day or two – but he does not consider how he is to get back again I suppose, for I daresay he will not save money enough to pay his carriage back tho' he gets it up, for nothing. I wrote him an answer that I am sure he did not like, I never wrote him such a one before but as I am not much afraid of his coming up to tell me of it I do not care. I have not seen Mr Hawking since I received your first letter, for as I do not go to Great Marlborough Street to draw as I used to, for I have a master at our house, he is a French Gentleman who was forced to leave his own country because of the disturbances there, and there fore I do not have time to call as I used to do for I am generally pretty busy all the morning till twelve or one o Clock and then I go to draw till dinner time at five and then I Go to write for Mr Hunter at 8 till 11, and on sundays I have for these several past been at earls court our country house to do any thing for Mr Hunter (as he always dines there on sundays) such as Catch Insects as Bees &cccc and if I was to call any week day at Mr Hawkings I should be sure not to find him in, and Billy would never tell me any thing of the manner how his father lived, who and what the woman was that lived with his father nor even her name for he always said he never knew. The reason why I wrote the Letter for him was because he desired me and said he did not know how to do it himself and then he would not have said half as much if I had not forced him to it. Mr Hawking does not work at the same place now as he did nor I do not know where he do work, for upon receiving your letter by Mr Hunter I went to the shop to see him if I could but they told me he did not work there, so I went home and wrote a note to let him know what Mrs Hawking desired me to tell him and carried it to his house for I was sure before I went that he would not be in and so I left it with a neighbour of his that lives in the same house as the Housekeeper was not in neither.

If I see him before I send this I shall tell you what he says. If he had been Ill I am sure I should have known it. I do not think he drinks scarce any thing now, or where it is only before me for fear I should say any thing when I write home I cannot tell, but he says he gets a great deal of money and what he does with I do not know, but I dare say Mrs Hawking gets but a precious little of it. You may tell Mrs Hawking what parts of what I have said, as you think fit. In Brother Johns Letter I desired him more than once to tell you that I was very well and told him to be sure and remember me to You and Sister and as I expected Mrs Hunter to go to Cornwall every day I defer'd writing as I had not the Cash to pay the postage for I have been taking in some novels that are publishing in weekly numbers at sixpence each I quite forgot to save any money to pay the postage. I have been saving every farthing I have been able to scrape together since Christmas last & now I am afraid I shall be forced to stop till Christmas comes again when I shall get a small donation from our tradespeople. I have got already the History of Tom Jones; Vicar of Wakefield; Joseph Andrews; Roderic Random; Tristram Shandy; and Robinson Crusoe, and now I can go no farther for want of a fresh Supply of Cash. it is a very pretty Edition fit for the pocket and Exellent Type and Very fine Engravings, one plate with each number. Dear Sister I was in a sad hurry about your last letter which you sent by the post for they charged it double and when I found it was single I was forced to let it go back to the General post office in the City where they had to look in it to see it was not double and then they sent it back with the overcharged Sixpence with J Wilson[3] Upon it, and so I had my poor letter again. When you write, please to fold it as thin as you can and write Single Sheet at the bottom and use thin paper. You seem to say that Mr Eyres family are seeming to be in a decline, now I do not think that I shall want a Coat any more than he do, at least I hope so, and perhaps that long neck may live to want that penny which she thought, and said, I had kept when I fetch'd the Bran from Betty Bonadys one night, I do not know whether you remember it or not, but I have not forgot it. Perhaps she has rared her own childeren too tender for what they may be brought to as she said of me one day to you. Why I think I can interpret your dream out of your own letter. First, as things were, Father and Mother were alive, Mr Eyre was such a governor that the world would hardly hold him when he used to bustle about, and the Soldiers were the work people, but now As things Are, you say there are hardly any people employ'd that is, they are vanished, and only you and Wm Roberts at the House and, As things will be, you say the voice Said, the Worst is not yet come. That will be I suppose when he is properly done over, for I always thought he was going a fair way to it.

 Dear Sisters

    this being all at present I must remain,

(with my prayers to god for your health and prosperity and to keep you from all such dreams for the future) your ever loving and affectionate Brother 'till Death

     William Clift

John Hunter, attributed to John Zoffany

40. William to Elizabeth. 18 October 1793.

Dear Sister

     I have now taken pen in hand to write but am at a loss for words to express my Ideas – what am I going to tell you when I say that Mr Hunter went from our house at 12 OClock on wednesday Morning[4] as well as ever I saw him – and the Butler came and beg'd me to run after Mr Hunter with his round (which is a paper that Mr Hunter used to put down all the places upon that he had to call at till he came home in the evening) and I overtook him in Charles S^t St James's Square where I saw him get into his Carriage as well as ever I saw him in my life, where they then drove to St Georges Hospital where there was to be a general Board held and Mr Hunter had not been there long before he was taken very ill and died in an hour or two. I believe our people would not like to have it known that he died till he was brought home which was about five OClock in the evening, in a Sedan Chair.

     All our family was at Brighthelmstone[5] at the time where Dr Baillie went that night and got there in the Morning and they all came home last evening except some servants who are left take care of the things left behind.

     Mrs Hunter and Miss and Mr John are almost breaking their hearts. I did not see Mr John till to day morning when he burst into tears and could hardly speak when I spoke to him. Mr Home was forced to go to Deal Last evening before Mrs Hunter came home and will not be back till to night, he went to see some of our soldiers that are come home from France wounded. I am afraid our house will be turned quite upside down now the wall and support is gone. I shall know how it is to be with me in a fortnight or so I suppose when all things are settled a little but I do not care how it is to be, I hope God will provide for me. I should like to live in London very much but I dont think I should ever like any Master as well as Mr Hunter. Perhaps Mr Home might take me to serve out my time with him to look after the dissecting Rooms but then all my future hopes of learning to draw would be quite put a Stop to, and I suppose I should never learn Anatomy under him for he is quite a different man from Mr Hunter as Mrs Gilbert well knows I shall be able give you a little better account of things perhaps next time I write but at present all thing are at a stand in our house. I suppose Mrs Gilbert will see the Account in the papers before you receive this and I suppose I shall get a letter from you before you get this, for it was in one or two of the papers of yesterday. Please to give my kind love to all friends.

     I am able write no more at present but shall ever

remain your affectionate Brother
till Death.
William Clift.

London.
Friday Octr 18th 1793

41. *Elizabeth to William. (Coded)*

My dear Brother

        I have not took a moments rest, since last evening when I received the melancholy news of the loss of your worthy master. I am not able to express the the distress of my mind on thinking of you my dear brother. Last evening about eight o clock I was at Mr Eyres's shop when Wm Tabb called me out & told me that Mr Hunter was dead & that his Mistress/ mistress had received a letter of the melancholy news; I was seized with such a cold chill & trembling all over my body that I could scarce stand, so I came home & should have wrote to you directly but I thought I would see Mrs Gilbert first, so to day I went down & she was not in, but they told me that she would be in soon so I sat down a little while, & Mr & Mrs G: came in, & Mr G: came into the kitchen & saw me there & spoke to me, & went into the Parlour & I believe he told Mrs G I was there, for she came into the kitchen & talked with me a little while. She is very low & wisht. She asked me how I knew that Mr H. was dead, & so I told her. She said you had lost a good friend & so had she, for he was a worthy gentleman & if the Lord had spared him she knew he would have been a friend to you, she said she hoped you would stay in the family still. She desired me not to trouble myself for that she would be a friend to you, & do every thing that lay in her power for you. She said she should hear again from London soon, that then I should know more about it. She told me that as soon as she did get a letter I should know it, – & told me to come down again, so my dear brother if you will have me mention any thing to Mrs G. tell me of it when you write to me again so my dear I hope you will write to me again, as soon as possible & I desire you will not straiten yourself to post pay my letters for if I had but that in all, I would gladly pay it, to have a letter from you. My dear brother I am much better satisfied since I saw Mrs G than I was before. I hope the Lord will be a friend to you & will support you under every trial that he is pleased to lay upon you, & since he has thought fit to take to his your worthy Master, I hope and trust he will raise up another for you, for as long as you live in the fear of the Lord he will be a friend to you & rise up friends for you unthought of, as he has in times past, for God it is that hath been our support in times past, & he it is that is our only friend, for he hath promised to be a friend to the fatherless & to all them that put their trust in him. My dear I hope you will do every thing in your power to oblige the worthy family you are in, for the sake of the worthy Mr & Mrs G: for I am sure they have been friends to you & me, & are always glad to hear of your welfare, & she told me just now that though you had lost your Master, you had not lost all your friends for she said she had done for you & would be a friend to you still, & see you taken care of she said you had always behaved well since you had been there, & that she hoped you would do very well yet; – I saw Sister Joanna this morning & told her of your Masters death, & she burst into tears & is very much affected for your loss. & I saw her again this evening, just as I had received your letter, & she gives her kind love to you.

Wm Tabb desired to be remembered to you I have not seen Brother John since' I wrote to you last. This being all at present I remain your ever affectionate and loving sister till Death

Eliz^th Clift.

42. *William to Elizabeth. 20 November 1793.*

Dear Sister

I have taken this opportunity of writing these few lines, hoping they will find you in good health as it leaves me at present I bless god for it. There has been great alterations in our House since I wrote last. I deferd writing till now for I did not see Mrs Hunter since she came from Brighton till a few days ago, and she told me that I need not make my self uneasy about any thing for I should be taken care of, and that she had wrote to Mrs gilbert and received her Answer and that I should stay with her till she heard of something better, for me, and that I should not want a friend as long as she did live. Mr Hunter was buried on the 22nd of October at St Martins Church, It was a very private burying for there was only a Hearse and two Coaches, besides Mr Hunters Chariot, but nobody rode in that, my cloaths was not made soon enough, to go to the Burying and none of the servants went to the burying but I was acquainted with the Undertaker and so I went to the Church and he put me into the vault with him – None of our people saw me there I believe and I did not want them to. Mr Hunters Coachman and footman and the Butler are discharg'd, and Mrs Hunters Coachman, for the Both Carriages and Horses are sold, and the Horses at the Country house are sold and since Mr Hunters footman has been gone I have had to go out any where for Mrs Hunter – two days last week I had to go to all Mrs Hunters Acquaintances with Cards – & yesterday I was out at Earls Court with Miss Hunter and the Ladys Maid to pack up some books and things to bring to town – I think it must seem very strange to Miss Hunter to ride in a Hackney coach, being used to ride in one that was reckoned the handsomest Coach that was at court when Mr Hunter had it new to go to Court in. I had a new Suit of Clothes which was brought home only a week before Mr Hunter died, and now I have a new suit of Black and a new Hat and not above 2 Months ago I had Six new Shirts – and this week I am to have some new Pocket Handkerchiefs. I believe Mr Home is not going to carry on the Lectures and Dissecting after this Winter, and then I suppose when that is over I shall have a place got for me. I have not any thing particular to write at present only I thought you would be expecting to hear from me before now.

81

I saw Thomas pinch here yesterday & he tells me he has been in town these 6 or 8 Months tell H: Williamson that he desired to be remembered to her, & remember me to all their family and to Kitty and Ann.

Give my kind love to Joanna and tell her that I expect to hear from her soon I think she might have found time in all this while – Tell her if it had been somebody else – I know, she would have found time to have wrote before now.

I have had a mind to write several times to Brother Thomas and I had wrote a letter to send to him the other day but when I went to direct it I did not know where to send it for I did not know whether he had left Bristol or no. – so when you write again I wish you would be so good as to let me know. Please to remember me to Brother John when you see him – I have not seen any thing of John Hawking, Billys father since you wrote to me about him – Please to let me know when you write, if you have heard from Robert since your last or not.

Dear sister this being all at present,
    I must Conclude, your ever
       Loving & Affectionate Brother
        W. Clift

Leicester Square }
Novr 20th 1793 }

43. Elizabeth to William. 30 December 1793. (Coded)

Dear Brother
           This comes with my kind love to you, hoping it will find you in good health as this leaves me at present, I bless God for it. I received your kind letter November 23rd and was happy to hear that you was in good health, & likewise to hear that Mrs Hunter is so kind to you. My dear, I hope you will do every thing/ thing in your power to oblige her & her good family, & I hope & trust the Lord will be a friend to you & order all things for the best.

I saw Mrs G: last Tuesday & she told me she had heard from Mrs Hunter, & that she said she had treated you as one of her own family & that you should stay with her till she could do better for you; she said she was very glad to hear that Mrs H: was so kind to you, but notwithstanding that, she should not forget you. She told me that she had heard from you every week & that you was very well & which I was very glad to hear. I did not tell her any thing which you mentioned in your letters to me. Wm Tabb tells me that his master & mistress are coming to London soon & he thinks he shall come with them & if he doth, I shall be able to send by him – Mr & Mrs Gilbert are very well. W^m & the maidens give their kind love to y. Brother John has not been home but once since the Assizes & that was the evening I received your last letter, & then he said he was sorry he should do so & ran on a plenty of it, & telling how good he would be, & what he would do for me, but he has not been home since. Mr Tabb sat out for London last Friday but I did not know of it till he was gone for if I had I should have sent by him; when you write I should be glad to know if brother John sent by him or not, & what he says, for he is very unkind to me, for he hath not been inside my door but once these six months. I have been very poorly for this month past, & I should not have wondered if I had been worse for I have had a great deal of forecause of late, for Mr Eyre has stopt the spinning & I have been about the bark or at Margate most part of my time these 6 weeks. We have been drying a great deal of bark on Francis Colemans kiln, & so I was at the kiln one day & at the pound another, & by that means I got a very great cold, but I bless God I am well again & I hope we shall finish the bark this week, & then I suppose I shall be most part of my time at Margate about the tucking[6] if he does not shut up. I cannot tell what he is going to do; if he does not put on the spinning again soon there cannot be any thing to do much longer for me & I would rather be off than there, if I was not to work at our own business. We have not worked by night for the winter. I have not heard from brother Robert since. Brother Thomas is in Bristol still & at the same place he was, in Cherry Lane next door to the pump. I heard of him last week C: Climo sent home a letter to Ann & he said he saw Thomas Clift & that he was very well & to be rememberd to me. I have not had a letter from him these three months. Sister is very well & gives her kind love to you; she is at Mr Billings still & she does not keep company with W.O nor hath not this year & half – I desired her to write to you & told her what you said; & she said you was the first in the world that she would write to if she had time, but if W: Tabb comes she says, she will make the time some how or other. If it was not for the child she would have time enough, she has always got that night & day.

Billy Hockings mother gives her kind love to you, & she hath heard from her husband since I wrote to you last. She got account where he was & wrote to him or else I believe he would not have wrote to her I have forgot where it is but I think it is in Soho Square. George Pearce & Thomas Arthur, John Ford & Polly Godfrey, Ann Climo & H: Williamson & all her family give their kind love to you. There is great alterations in Bodmin since you left it. There hath been more/ more buildings since you have been wanting than ever I remember before. Dear Brother I shall be glad to have a few lines from you as soon as convenient, & let me know if I must direct to you as usual or not.

Dear Brother this being all at present, I must conclude
your ever loving & affectionate Sister
Elizabeth Clift.

Bodmin
Dec[r] 30th 93
Monday evening.

NOTES SECTION IV

1. *Bodmin riding*: this local festival can be traced back to the 15th century when it was associated with the trade guilds. Both the activities and the dates seem to have changed somewhat over the years. It was held during July and has generally been connected with the Monday after July 7, St Thomas a Becket's day. The 21 July of the letter seems rather late but there is evidence that at certain times the Riding extended over several weeks and some writers speak of the middle of July. It incorporated a church service, processions of the guilds and sports. According to Richard Carew's *Survey of Cornwall* (1602), the sports were held at Halvager, a little way from Bodmin, and may have been associated with Bodmin Riding in the 17th century. These included a mock-trial or court. Other writers keep the Halvager Sports and Bodmin Riding distinct. A letter written by Walter Raleigh Gilbert, the 'Mr Gilbert' of the letters, in 1812, describes the Riding as he remembers it twenty or thirty years previously, the time of Elizabeth's letter. Then, it seems, the festivities also included a visit to Priory with a decorated garland and pole. The manuscript of this letter is in the British Library. The various accounts are confused and for a full discussion the reader is referred to *Bodmin Riding and Other Similar Celtic Customs* by Pat Munn (Bodmin, 1975), which includes a transcript of Mr Gilbert's letter. Sometime during the last quarter of the 19th century the Riding was discontinued but it was revived in 1974.

2. *ropers news*: see Section III n. 6 p. 68.

3. *J Wilson*: the meaning of this allusion is unclear. It is likely that it would be the name of the Post Office official who opened the letter but no one of that name who was employed by the Post Office in London c.1793 has been traced. Opening of mail was much abused, especially in the early days of the Post Office. By an Act of 1711 official opening of mail was made legal for various specified reasons, one being the refusal of the addressee to pay the postage due, as was the case here.

4. *Wednesday morning*: the day of John Hunter's death was 16 October 1793.

5. *Brighthelmstone*: Brighton. The name *Brighthelmstone* survived in official documents until the early 19th century.

6. *tucking*: one meaning of *to tuck* is to dress or finish cloth after it comes from the weaver, especially to stretch on tenters, i.e. frames for stretching the cloth evenly without shrinking. In the light of Mr Eyres's business pursuits, this seems the most likely meaning here.

V. JANUARY TO DECEMBER 1794

1794 was to prove a year of uncertainty for both William and Elizabeth. Following Hunter's death in the previous October, the great household in Leicester Square was broken up and only Haynes and William were kept on to manage the museum with Mrs Adams, the housekeeper. Mrs Hunter had moved to a home at Blackheath and the house in Leicester Square was to be let. We learn from William that negotiations for selling the museum with its collection of biological specimens were going on with the Government, to whom it was to be offered for the sum of £20,000 according to the terms of Hunter's will. While wondering about his own future, William is kept busy cleaning the Collection ready for the sale. He expresses a desire to Elizabeth to go with it when it is sold but at first this seems unlikely, although Mrs Gilbert and Mrs Hunter together promise to do all they can to help. Haynes has the prior claim and William knows he is pressing this with the two executors, Everard Home, Mrs Hunter's brother, and Dr Matthew Baillie, Hunter's nephew.

Meanwhile, life in Bodmin continues much as usual. John had not come to London the previous summer as he had hoped but now he states his intention of coming this year. No letters arrive from Robert but rumours reach the family that he is in the Mediterranean and, erroneously, that he is now on board the *Windsor Castle*. Little is heard of Thomas, who has not yet come home to Bodmin in spite of frequent promises to do so. Elizabeth is still working for Mr Eyre and she believes his financial affairs are improving in spite of local gossip. Nevertheless, the Eyre family has its own share of trouble when an accident befalls little John Eyre. Elizabeth describes how the little boy's skull is fractured and he undergoes the operation of trepanning, which he miraculously survives.

It is in July that Elizabeth suffers a personal misfortune when the house she lives in in Castle Street, Bodmin, is sold and she receives an eviction order. She has stayed on in what had been the family house ever since the rest of the family departed. Now she is faced with the choice of giving up her independence and going into service or finding alternative accommodation, which is costly and, as she says, 'houses never was so scarce in Bodmin'. She writes to William for advice but now we see an unexpected side of his character. He shows a reluctance to accept responsibility for his sister's affairs, a reluctance which is later to play a decisive part in shaping his own life. He delays his reply until after Elizabeth has had to make a decision and in the end she finds a room in Back Street, nearer to the centre of Bodmin, although as things turn out she makes little use of it.

The ordinary local news continues, but against this familiar background, one or two racier incidents stand out. There is another, graphic account of a corn riot at Padstow from John, in which the women of the town play a spirited part. Most striking perhaps, although partially obliterated in the manuscript, is Elizabeth's description of the advantageous marriage made by the chambermaid of the Whitehorse Inn. She attracts the attention of a Mr Bentley from London, who is investigating the building of the projected canal from Wadebridge to Lostwithiel, thus effecting a passage from the north to the south Cornish coasts. The strange courtship and wedding evidently cause a stir in the local community. This extraordinary episode, in spite of the naiveté of Elizabeth's account, is told with such verve that it reminds one of certain scenes in Richardson's *Pamela*. This story has a happy outcome unlike the incident at a bawdy house near Charing Cross, which is described by William. Here, unfortunate men are lured in and then conveyed secretly to the ships of the East India Company to serve as soldiers. The illegal goings on come to light when one prisoner makes an unsuccessful attempt to escape.

With this account the letters for 1794 come to an end and there appears to have been no further communication between Bodmin and London from September until the following January when William again writes to Elizabeth to ask why he has not heard from her for six months. His apparent unconcern at the long silence seems to indicate his increasing independence (he was now approaching his twentieth birthday) in spite of the uncertainty which hangs over his own future career.

44. John to William. 9 February 1794. (Coded)

Pencarrow Feby 9, 1794.

Dear Brother

having not heard from you by letter, for near six months I am very uneasy for fear something or other is amiss more than common or I am sure I should have heard from you long before this time. Sister informed me the other day that she had received a letter from you, in which you informed her of your worthy Masters decease, which I am exceeding sorry for, but I hope since God has been pleased to take your Master from you, you will submit with patience to his divine will, in whom we should set our whole trust & confidence, who is the best of masters & our constant friend. I hope you will continue still with Mr H^r as I suppose he would wish to keep you in the same way as you have been hitherto, which I shall ever pray for. I thought I should have had the pleasure of seeing you long before now, but I have been disappointed in what I expected, as I mentioned in my last, but it was Sir William's pleasure to send my old master instead of me, much against my will, but as soon as I found he was to go, I said to him Mr Tabb I hear you are to go to London soon, he replied yes he should, then I said I should not be long after him, at which he said he would advise me as a friend, which he would always be

myself in great hopes of haveing a Letter from
you, M#s Tabb & Daughters to Enquire after
Sally & M#s Williams (formerly Arthur) to enquire
about her husband who I find is in London with
Miss Hannah Beard his House keeper —
I were happy to have so Satisfactory an
acct of you by W# Williams but I thought
I shoud have had a Letter by him though
I had not writ you so long, I recd a letter
from Rich# Branch (Lady Molesworths
foot man a few days ago who (I am h...
to say) speaks highly in your favor —
he says I met your Brother the other
day who is Quite a Gentleman behav'd young
man I like his Solid manner verry
much —— I am really sorry for Brother
Robets misfortunes, I shoud be verry happy
if I could hear the same Character of him
as the above — please to let me know when
you write whether you know where he is
my love to Brother Tho#s &c & let him
know I shall Trouble him with a Letter
soon, please to let me know whether he
is / married at nor & how he goes on

Specimen of John Clift's handwriting

to me as far as his power extended and desired me not to leave Pencarrow in his absence, & he was sure I could make myself as happy there as any young man could wish to be, but if I chused to go to London this summer I should, which I hope I shall have the pleasure to do if please God give me health.

Pencarrow family is just arriver in London, I hope you will have an opportunity to call on them in the course of a day or, two, for I have sent an order by the coachman to give you a half crown when you call on them as he has money in hand due to me. Give my due respects to all the servants when you see them. I warrant they will be very glad to see you. Please to enquire for the coachman, he is one of the worthiest men I ever met with & give my love to him & let him know that his wife & children are all well & give their love & duty to him, but his wife has been very poorly for severall days past with a pain in her side & fellon[1] in her face. Sisters are in good health & I bless God I am at present & join with me in love to you. I must desire you will write to me as soon as possible. Brother Thos[s] is coming home about the middle of this month, I am informed by George Hoskin (who is our post) I believe I have not had a letter from him this twelvemonth. Nor do I know where to direct to him. We have not heard from brother Rob[t] since he went off but I expect he is up the Medditerranean & I found the St George was on the coast of Italy a small time since. A few days since the tinners rose and met at Padstow to prevent the shipping off barley, at which the corn factors sent for a party of Welsh Millitia that was in the west, at their approach the tinners set off immediately the farmers were busily employ'd in carrying the corn to the vessels again, but a woman of Padstow got a drum & alarmed the town, at which, all the women in the place were soon assembled, knife in hand & cut every sack they got in reach of insomuch that the soldiers were drawn up & the Riot Act read to no purpose, at last the soldiers were orderd to fire on them (unknowing to them without ball) at such an alarm all the men were soon in action & every thing soon quiet, as the soldiers were but few.

Sir W[ms] house is at Gloucester Place Portman Square, so I must conclude your affectionate Brother

John Clift.

45. *William to Elizabeth. 16 March 1794.*

Sunday March 16th 1794.

Dear Sister,

I have now taken pen in hand once more to write a few lines to you hoping they will find you in good health as it leaves me at present I bless god for it. This is the fourth letter I have wrote since New Years day and have sent neither of them, but I am resolved this shall go, The first I wrote I put a half guinea under the seal but I could not make it stop shaking about and I was afraid that If the Post master had felt it and taken it out that you would not get it, and I was resolved not to send the letter without a new years gift. I received a letter from Brother John about a month ago and he told me that If I would go to Mr Tabb he had orderd him to give me a half Crown Sir Williams house is near two miles from our house and Just as I had received his letter, I had to carry a letter within a Stones throw almost of Sir W^{ms} House; and Mr Tabb told me that he should go to cornwall in about three weeks so I wrote a letter to send by him and last week I went to know when he did go and he told me that he believed he should not go till May. So yesterday I wrote a letter again to send by the post for I thought it was no use to wait any longer, and when I had wrote it, it was too late to put it in the post, and there is no post here sundays, and to day morning I had a letter sent from Mrs Hunter to carry to Mrs Gilbert who came to town on friday but I did not know it till to day morning that I had the letter to carry, So I was obliged to write this fourth letter, and I think it was very lucky I did not send that last night. Brother John seemed very much vexed that he could not come to London with Sir W^{ms} Family but I think as Mr Tabb told me that he had much better Stay where he is for there are too many publick houses in London for him ever to do well here, and I told him so when I answerd his letter a day or two after I got his. I desired him to give my/my kind love to you and let you know I was very well and when you write to me again I would be glad if you will let me know whether he did or no for I daresay I highly affronted him and I dont think he will write to me again hastily about coming to London

Mr & Mrs Gilbert was not up to day morning when I carried the letter but I waited till they were, for an answer to the letter and Mr Gilbert sent down the servant to enquire if it was William Clift that had brought the letter and they immediately sent for me to come up stairs, before they were drest, they both came out in their Night gowns and was very glad to see me; Mr Gilbert says he thinks I am grown a good deal. They told me that they were going to blackheath on Tuesday to see Mrs Hunter, (who has lived there ever since Christmas and the house in Leicester Sq^{re} is to be lett.) and that they would speak to her about getting me a place and that they would do every that lay in their power for me; I was almost ashamed they should see me for it was in the morning before I had Cleaned myself and last week we have been cleaning the Collection, for the last time before it is sold which made me so very dirty. I was down at Blackheath last sunday week to see Mrs Hunter, but she did not say any thing to me about a place, nor did not give me any thing to put in my pocket, she never gave me as much as sixpence as yet and now I am obliged to pay for my own letters now she is out of Town, I shall enquire soon who is to pay for them for as they never give me any money they can't expect that I can pay for them. There is only the housekeeper left in the front house to take care of it till it is let and her and I, am upon board wages, She gives me a shilling now and then, for pocket money, but she might afford to give me a shilling a week if she had a mind, for I believe I have 7 Shillings a week. Mrs Hunter don't keep any carriage now, and only keep a Lady's maid, a fotman, and a maid of all work, they have a pretty little house, and garden and it is about 6 miles out of town so that it is a pretty walk, of a sunday to see them; the servants there are upon board wages too, so that I shan't like to go so often as I should if they were not. There has been a bill brought before the houses of Parliament and it has been recommended by the King, about the Collection so that I suppose it will be settled soon one way or the other, as the king of Spain has sent a person here to see it and if our Government don't buy it, he has a mind to it, Mr John Hunter has got a Commission in the army, and Miss Hunter is to be married soon to one Capt Cambell, I suppose Mr and Mrs Gilbert is come up to wedding – I think for my part that they have made too much haste about it so soon after the poor old Mans death. Every thing has been getting ready there for this some time past and the Bed and all is ready for them to get into I believe – You did not send any letter by Mrs Gilbert I believe, for she did not say any thing about one. If you should want any Money to pay the Rent or any thing if you will borrow it I will send some to you by Mrs Gilbert when they leave town & then you can pay it again, for I have been saving all my Money I have had given me at christmas for you but I do not know any other way to send it than by Mrs Gilb^t/ I must beg you will write as soon as you receive this, that I may hear how all things are going on at bodmin; I am to stay here till the Collection is sold and settled which cannot be done in a minute and so you will direct to me as usual till you hear to the contrary. So no more for want of room from your ever loving and affectionate Brother

W. Clift

I am afraid Joanna will forget how to write if she does not write oftener than she writes to me, – tell her so from me.

46. Elizabeth to William. 21 March 1794. (Coded)

Bodmin March 21st 1794

Dear Brother,
            I have received your kind & affectionate letter & I am very happy to find it left you in good health as this leaves me at present I bless God for it. My dear Brother a thousand thoughts hath ran in my mind concerning you since I received your last letter as you never left writing so long before. Sometimes I should think you had not rec^d my last letter & then I should think you was ill & some times one thing & sometimes another so I could not tell what to think & I should have wrote to you again but I was always in expectation to hear from you, as I thought Mr Tabb was coming home & you

was going to send by him, & I was not willing to send to you till I had heard from you & as I heard Mrs Gilbert was going to London soon I thought I would send by them but I did not know when she went away, nor I did not know she was gone till last Thursday, My dear I did not think it was out of neglect, but that you had some reason for not sending; last Saturday was a week Brother John sent to Joanna by George Hoskin that he had had a letter from you & that you was very well & you beg'd to be remember'd to her & me. He said he had not forgot us, & he was going to send us something for a new years gift, but that money was so very scarce with him, as for my part I never knew it plenty with him, & I am afraid I never shall. I was very poorly for five weeks, just after Christmas, I had a very bad finger for three weeks, my fore finger on my right hand, so that I could scarce do any thing for it, & if I had not been at Mr Eyre's I am certain I should not have got sixpence all that while but they were very kind to me, so that I did not lose my time for as long as I was there I was paid the same as if I was able to work ever so well. Sister sent to him to desire him to come home, that I wanted to see him, but he sent word that he could not come home then upon any account, but he would come soon but I have not seen him since I hear he is in town this evening, but I have not seen him. Brother Thomas sent me word that he was coming home 18th Feb^ry with Bill Bennet, but when Bill came his mind was alterd, for he says the days are short & the roads dead to walk. He sent me a letter by Bill & desired I would excuse his not coming, he desired an answer by Bill & so I sent him a few lines & I told him that I never should expect to see him home, as he had sent so many times that he was coming & did not & that I should sooner expect to see you or Brother Robt tho you was at the greatest distance, he has been wanting for these 5 years & half & never sent as much as a ribband to Joanna nor me, nor the value of one, but I hope we shall do as well as them yet, tho' they get a good deal of money they can make use of it all & more if they had it I believe. Sister is living where she did, & does very well, & I bless God I have my health a great deal better than what I used to. Dear Brother I could not read your kind letter without tears, to think of the difference between you & them. My dear you said you would send some thing to me, but I desire you will not straighten yourself, for I would rather want ever so much than you should I think it a great favour of you in paying my letters, & I hope I shall be able to pay the rent next week, tho' if John was to pay it for me he could not find the want of it, but he never asks me where I pay any or not & I believe he doth not care for any thing as long as he can get some money to spend. Sister & I have got our ribbands still that you sent us, we have not wore them yet & she says she will not wear it till she sees you again that she may always have something to keep for your sake, she gives her kind love to you & desires you will not be angry with her for not writing & she will write soon. Wm Tabb is off from Mr G:s but I suppose you know it already, & so is Polly Coule she is now living at Truro. Mr Eyre went away the fast day & came home last Tuesday, I believe he was at

London, we thought he was gone to buy the house he lives in of his brother John, but he hath not. There was a survey for it the evening he came home but it was not sold. Bennet Mitchell was the best bidder. There is a great talk that he is broke but how it is I cannot tell, the trade is seeming to be going on a great deal better than it has of late, he hath bought in a great deal of wool, & Robt Popham is come to work for him, this is the first day with him. W Roberts & I thought we should been off before now but he was not willing for us to go, for he said he should have work enough for us again, & so he hath now, but how long it will last I cannot tell. I have not ran but one chain² this six weeks we have got no worsted now but he is going to put out some next week & we have put out spinning again & so I look after the spinners or any thing just to keep myself employed. Mrs Eyre hath got another young son, he is nine weeks old, it is to be called Humphry Robins. Mary Arthur is married again to W W^{ms} the blacksmith, & Jack Every is married to Joan Craddock – & Mr Frank Hicks's wife is dead. Mrs King is living in Mr Moor's house & John Coppin is living, in hers.

Dear Brother I hope you will send as soon as ever you hear of another place or there is any alteration, for I shall not be happy till I hear you are settled, for I am always thinking about you, but I hope the Lord will provide for you as he hath already done, far beyond our expectation. This being all at present

from your affectionate sister till Death

Elizth Clift.

47. *William to Elizabeth. 30 March 1794.*

Sunday March 30th 1794

Dear Sister I have now taken this opportunity of sending you these few lines hoping they will find you in good health as it leaves me at present I bless god for it. I went to see Mrs Gilbert this morning who Informed me that she intended to leave town about wednesday or thursday and that if I would get a letter ready and bring it on Tuesday Morning she would take it for me and as I am very busy at present a Cleaning the Collection I set about writing it now, for fear I should not have time tomorrow

Mrs Gilbert told me that she had been at blackheath to see Mrs Hunter who told her that I was to stay where I am till the Collection is disposed of and then Mrs Gilbert says that she shall do every thing in her power for me to go with it, if our Government buys it and Mrs Hunter says the same, which I should very much like, as it is what I have been employed at and what I have learnt more of than any thing else, since I have been here. Mr Haynes My fellow servant has been very Ill this fortnight and he was taken ill just as we had begun Cleaning the Collection and now I have to do the rest by myself.

It would be a nice easy place to look after the Collection, as there would be very little hard work to do; I have often wished to go with it but I never entertained any hopes of it till now, as Mr Haynes told me that Mr Home and Dr Baillie[3] had been speaking to him about it and he intended to go to look after it, but now since he has been bad he says he shall go into the Country as soon as he gets well enough. I have nothing very particular to write just now but as soon as I hear of any thing particular I shall write again – I hope you will find safe enclosed what I promised you, and if I had any better convenience of sending any thing I might be able to send you a handkerchief or ribbon or something or other besides but I hope better opportunities will offer when I shall have better opportunities of Getting any thing to send, Please to give my kind love to Sister Joanna and to every enquiring friend, This being all at present I must conclude with my prayers to God for your Good health and better prosperity, and hopes of better times from your ever loving and affectionate Brother

W. Clift

P:S: You need not say any thing to any body about the half guinea for if Mrs G. asks me what is in my letter I shall tell her it is only two or three Shillings to help pay the rent, for she desired me not to send any thing, to put me out of pocket Money, she gave me half a Crown, for she knows Mrs Hunter dont give me any.
when you have read this Scratch it out.

48. Elizabeth to William. 14 May 1794.

Bodmin May 14th 1794

Dear Brother this Comes with my Cind Love to you hoping these few Lines will find you in Good health as it Leves me at Preasent I bless God for it Dear Brother I Received your Cind Letter and Preasent wich you sent by Mrs Gilbert I am sorry I have not had the time to writ to you before as you must think me very ungrateful in not answering you Cind Letter before now but when you know the Reason you will readely Excuse me it is a Great missforting wich hapned a Good friday to Littel John Eyre my Dear Brother Mrs Gilbert Came home on a tusday an the thursday she sent for me to Come down but if I had known she had been home I should not have Given her the troubel to *have* sent for me if I had known she had been home I should have Gladly Gone down to Inquier for you for thire is nothing in this world Gives me so much Pleasuear as to hear from you as you are the only Brother I have that takes anny acount of me my dear I am shoure I Canot a nough Regard an Esteem you for your Goodness an thoughts towards me as for my other

Church Stile, Bodmin, by Isabella Mary Alms 1900

Brothers they scarce Enquer for me nor Care I Belive wether they have a sister or no I have not seen Brother John but once since I wrot to you an that was the Sunday after Easter he was in town an some Person told him that I had had a letter from you so he Came in to Masters to me to ask for you I was in the dining Room with the littel John so sister an he Came up to me an I told him he was very Cind in Coming to see me when Joanna sent to him that I was very Bad he said he never new any thing of it nor he had not in town but once since he saw me Last but I Could tell him of four or five times he had been in town an where he was he desird sister an me to come out to see him the next Sunday but we have not been out nor seen him since nor I have not hard from Brother Robert nor Brother Thomas since my dear Brother I was very happy to hear Mrs Gilbert to speek so well of you she told me that if I was to see you I should be surprisd to see that thir was no more alteration in you she said one would not think to see you that you had lived so Long in London she told me she Liked your dress she said you did not dress taudrey but neat an she Liked your Good behavour to wards the famely she said she had no dout but you would answer her Expectations in Every thing she told me she had a Great deal of talk with you an she did hope you would due very well she said she would due Every thing in her Power for you she told me she had talked to Mrs Hunter Consarning your Being setteld she said Mrs Hunter said you should be setteled as soon as the Collection was disposd of an she would due her indeauver for you to Goe with it if our Goverment did by it an Mrs Gilbert said if you did

94

not she had talked with two or three Gentelmen Consarning you an I was very happy when I had *read* your Letter that they had Menchoned a bout your Going with the Collection as I found in your Letter that it is your desire to Goe with it my dear I hope the Lord will Provide for you Mrs Gilbert told me she desird you not to send any thing to me for she was afraid you would want it wich I should be very sorry for if you was to I saw Mrs Gilbert yestarday down at the Church stile she asked me if I had hard from you since she Came home I said no she said you was very well an you was with Mrs Hunter still but she did hope you would be settled soon My dear Brother as I menshond be fore that there was a misforting hapned it was a Good friday witch I think is very unproper day to work but Master had ordred his work Peopel all down to margret to work that day ther was three Carpenters an two Masons an Eight Labrours and whin I Came home from milkin in the morning they told me that master was Gone to margret and he Left word that I was to Come down with his diner and bring down the Children with me they new it was athing I did not Like to work on that day so I was not working so I was to Goe down for a walk with the Children so I had to Carry down dinner and Every thing to Make tay in the afternoon so I had them to tend to dinner and tay to make for them I had Fransies an Joseph an John with me an when Master an the Cilldren had drank tea he said I should Give Mr Conic a bason of tea an Mr Eyre and the Children went out and I had not time to Power out a Coop of tea be fore the Cildren ware Goot up stares a bout the Mesheen so I went up to the hier End of the Room and thir was a trap hatch an ther was a tabel just under so I steept up to see what they ware about an I Cald to Frances to be quite for his father told me not to Let them Goe in to that Room so Frances an Joseph Run out an John went to run after them an fell down throw the trap hacth an fractuard his scull so master Cald bill Secomb and Robert Popham to bring him Home an I was afraid he would die before we Got home for he never spook all the way home an as soon as we Goot home I Cald Mr Hambly an when he Came he went to bleed him but Could not for his blood was Conjeld he went out an soon returnd with Docter Hall they Examined his Head an said it was fractuard so he Ley that night an never spook an by the next morning his right Eye was turnd in his head the Docters said his head must be opned or ther was no safe for him Master an Mistress was very unwilling to have it d*u*d they ware afraid he Could not under Goe the upration so he Contiened in that deplorabel Condition till the tusday morning when his head was opned an four Large Picesis of his scull tuck out his head was opned from one Ear to the other an from his fore head to his Crown thare was five Docters the upration was an our an three quarters in duing I bless God for it he is mutch better an in a very God way Jenny Dave an Catty Rowe an me have watched by him Ever since in our turns we ware not abel to leve a minet by his self for three wickes

Dear Brother I Conclud with my Prayers to God for your Health an Prosprity

This Being all At Preasent from your Ever Loving an affectionate
Sister
      Eliz Clift
PS
      I should be glad of a few Lines from you as soon as Conveanyeant Thomas
      arther is off from Mr Liddels he did not be have well

49. William to Elizabeth. 11 July 1794[4]

Dear Sister
                I hope these few lines will find you in good health as it leaves me at
present; I write now to keep you from thinking that there is any thing the
Matter with me for not writing before, but I have not any thing worth the
Postage, to tell you. I suppose I have to stay here where I am till next May or
June for it is not likely that we shall hear any thing about the Collection till
then. We are very busy just now in getting the Collection to rights, and Mr
Haynes has been verry Ill for some time past and Is very poorly now and so we
are getting every thing in order in the Collection for him to go into the
Country. I have no time to do any thing to Drawing now but I hope I shall get
more time for it, in the Course of a few weeks but then I have not any person
to show me any thing, since Mr Hunter died and I can't get on as I ought by
Myself and as I am not quite sure of Going with the Collection, tho' I suppose I
shall stand a Chance for it, I think I am loosing time, for If I am to go with the
Collection I ought to be taught or Set about drawing but Mr Home never asks
whether I do or do not draw, nor never asked me whether I should like to go
with the Collection or not, nor that I am to go, nor any thing else. I never knew
such a Man as he is, for he hardly ever comes to our house, now and when he
does he hardly ever speaks ten words. I have not any thing worth writing but I
must fill up the Paper. When you write let me know if you have heard any
thing of Brother Robert & whether he is on board the St George or not, I
know a Person here in London who has a Brother a Lieutenant on board the St
George, now if you can tell whether he is onboard that Ship or no, I can ask
this Lady to ask her brother when she writes to him to enquire for him and if
he is there to desire him to write to me I do not know where the St George is
now, I thought the last time you heard any thing of him that the ship was going
to join Lord Howe's or Lord Hoods fleet,[5] I find his ship was not in the Great
Engagement on the first of June[6] and I likewise find that it is very likely we
shall be forced to give up the war to the French in the End after so many
Thousands of poor fellows being kill'd & perhaps Brother Rob[t] amongst them,
but I think he was always too wicked to get hurt, & that we shall see him again
for all this. When you write again please to direct it to the Late Mr Hunters N°

13 Castle Street, Leicester Square for we have not any thing to do with the House in the Square now. You need not let these foolish complaints of Mine reach any bodys Ears but your Own. I trust I shall see better days yet tho' they are not amiss now I am very well off just now for I dont want for any thing and I should not think about what is to come. Please to remember me kindly to Sister Joanna and let me know how you all do, and go on, both in town & Country be sure and send me every thing worth writing. I Suppose you have read of Whittington and his Cat If you have not, I have – last sunday was a week I went with Mr Haynes to Highgate, about 6 Miles out of Town where we had a most delightful view of London from the top of a very high hill so that we could see all over it at once and in our way home, for we took a great round about to it for the sake of the Walk, there I saw the stone that was set up to the memory, on the Spot where Sir Richard Whittington sat down by the road side when he had ran away from his place when the Cook maid broke his head with the Slice the place where the Stone is put up is where he sat down when he heard the bells ring "Turn again Whittington Thrice Lord Mayor of Great London" – Please to remember me kindly to every one that Enquires for me

    Write soon and let me know all the newest
       news and I shall ever remain your ever
         affectionate brother.
                William Clift

Friday July. 11th
1794.

Please to let me know how poor little Johnny Eyre is and remember me to all their People—

50. Elizabeth to William. 31 July 1794

Dear Brother
this Comes with my Cind Love to you hoppin it will find you in Good health as this Leves me at Preasent I Bless God for it I recived your Cind Letter the 12 of this Instant and I was very happy to find it Left you in Good health for I thought you was Ill or that thir was somthing more then Coman the Matter that I had not hard from you so Long an as you are the only Brother that takes any acount of me for I am Shore I have no frend on Earth but you my dear I hope you never will refrain writing to me as Long as we booth due Live and are at Such a distance an Canot see one a nother it is the Gretes Pleasuear I have to heare from you an to hear that you are well my dear I am sorry to think that thir is no altration yet But I hope the Lord will be afriend to you and Provide

for you beyond our Expectations for he hath all readey Provided for us things
that we never thought of I have not hard from Brother Robert since but I hard
that he was onboard the Winsor castel when he saild from England an that he
had a very good berth it was somethin be longin to the gunner I know but what
I have forgoot he is in Lord Hoods fleet an so is the St Jorge I belive for they
saild just to Gather thos williamson was home a bout a month Past from
Macker Camp an he told me that he was at dock an he saw the Poosser⁷ Clark
belongin to the Cambridge an he told him that Brother Robert was very well
when he saild an that he was on Bord the ship I have menchend Brother John
hath not bin home since he Goes on just as yousal I saw him once since and that
was the Sunday after I sent to you Last I was at Pencarrow with the nurs that is
at mrs Eyres she is a sister to Mary the diary maid an then he told me he was
Coming home the next wick but I have not seen him since he told me then that
he had had a Letter from Brother Thomas an I asked him what he said on his
letter but he told me he Could hardly tell for he just lookt it over an burnt it
for he did not like it for he Supposd he said he had had a letter from you or som
boddy by his writting he would not tell me any thing that was on the letter for
my Part I have not hard from Brother Thomas since the 18 of febuary Sister
Joanna is very well an gives her Cind love to you she is at Mr Biling still But I
Belive she will not Stay no longer then her year she sais it is to littel wages she
has but 50 shilings a year Mr Hewett the organist hath Bought the house I live
in at Midsomer last an then he sent a notice Paper to ous to leve the house at
Christmas next we had not had the notis a bove a wick before he was Come up
to see if we had Got a house and told Ann that if we did not goe out he would
onroof the house an he hath not left ous quite one day since an last Satuarday
was a wick they Cald me in to there house an asked if I had got any Place or not
an he said it did not signifie for he must tare it down next wick or the wick
after to the farthest I told them I would goe out as soon as I Could geet any
Place to goe I told them they should not have given ous a half years notis an
then to look for ous to goe out derictly they said they Could not help it for
they were injacted out of ther house an that Mr Hickes had sent a notis Paper
to them an if they ware not Gone out of it by Michlmas that thir should not
one stone stand on a nother she said she was very sory to distress ous an she said
it was hard upon she to be distressed so by her own Brother she told me that I
should Come down there an Have a room to live in as longe as they did stay but
I told them that was no youse for me to Come down there for a wick or to an
them to be turnd out of dors for I Could not Expect no other as they must
Leve it them selves he said it was very hard that he had bought a hous an Paid
for it an Could not Come in to it he said he suposd he might Cary his Goods
down in the butter Market for he Could not geet any Place in town I told them
I would Goe out as soon as I Could geet a house to Goe in to an since she was in
to Master to desir of him to desir of me to Goe out of the hous an since that a
gain they have bin to Joanna for She to desir me to Goe out they told her they

98

hoped that I did not mean to Put them to troubel for the rest of the tenants
had a busd him an told him they would Cause him troubel be fore he should
geet them out She said I did not mean any such thing but that I would Goe as
soon as Posabel they told her that if I Could geet a room they would Pay a
quarters Rent for me or if I Could geet any Place to stay before the hous is
fitted I should Come and live with them for they should Ceep a maid an the
work would not be hard thir would be but to to tend and a Cow to milk an thir
ground is not far an what I shall due I Canot tell for I have tried All over the
town to geet a hous but I Canot I belive houses never was so scarce in Bodmin
before for thir is so many strangers in the town an houses is at such a rate now
that Cannot tell what it is best to due Mrs hewett was up hear yestarday an told
me the same as she told Joanna but if I was to sell what I have an to Goe to
servis then if I was sick or bad I should have no Place to Goe to an what to due I
Canot tell they Canot Put us out till Christmas if we have no mind but if we
due not they will *   * Dear Brother I should be Glad if you would writ
soon an tell me what you think is Best for me to due I should have wrot to you
before but mr Eyre an I have not bin to account never since you went away an I
was in hopes to have settled it last wick an I intended to let you know but we
have not but I belive we shall be to in short if he will not I am askin them but
they are alwis puting it of but I am Resolved not to be put of no longer

Mr Thomas Telomick is dead an the old Mr Lewis Marshal an the old Sally
Ley since I wrot to you last an Jemmy Merryfield is dead he Came up to see his
ants an he was took sick an died hear aUncel William Rundel is dead he died
sudenly he was at dula[8] working in the woods an his son an other men with
them an they make houses in the wood an sleep in it an one eving the wood
men had somthing to drink a mongest them selves an they went to bead they
had to Beads in this Room one at one End of the Room an one in the other
uncel will an his son slept to geather an they suposd to have bin in Bead a bout
an our when Cosen william a wacked an found his father dead by his side I
supose you have hard a bout the Cannells that going on hear[9] thir was to
gentelmen Come from London hear a bout it the Name of the one *   *[10]
an the other name was Bentley they set up at *   * an they had not bin long
hear befor Mr Benley *   * Ill an no Person Could tell what was the
matter he took to his Bead but he would not have the doct *or   * Person
to tend him he was viseted by the best of the t*   * Could not Pervail on
him to have a docter but *   * Eving Mr Winn that is he that Ceeps the
whith *   * he went up to se him an desird him to have somth *ing   * said
he should send up a tumbler of negers to him *   * Chamber maid but she
said it was not Prudent for *   * a woman to goe in to the gentelmans
lodgin *   * desird the waiter to Carie it to him an when he Came to him
he asked why betsey had not brought it to him an the waiter told him that she
thought it was not Proudent but he would not have any thing Except she
brought it to him so her Master desird she wold Care up somthin to him an

99

that Mr Winn stay at the Chamber door an when she Came to him she asked him how he was an he said he was very Ill she asked him to have the docter he said thir was none but she Could due him any Good an if she would not have him he must die for he could not live without her after some time she Consented to have him but mr Brown an Mr Walish *an* many more tried to Preswad him agenst her telling him sh was not a Girl worthy of him for she was a Poor girl she had not lived in servis but 5 wickes she is a sister to Harry Hoskin an Jenny that did live with master Eyre but all they Could say was no youse he said he had Enough to make them both happy an if she would have him that was all he disrd he asked if they thought he was mad or why they did Preswad him so mutch a genst her for he said she was the girl he would make his wife Mr Brown would not grant the Licence so he went to Mr gilbert the Justice an he Granted them an it was the grandes weding that hath bin in Bodmin a Great while for he had a Coch to Carir her to Church an now he hath maried her an drest her like a Lady John Eyre is head is all most hole.

    I must conclud your Ever Loving Sister
Eliz Clift

July 31th 94

  51. William to Elizabeth. 27 September 1794.

September 27 1794.

Dear Sister

      I have now taken this opportunity of writing a few lines to you hoping they will find you in good health as it leaves me at present I bless god for it I have nothing particular to write or I should have wrote long before now. I am Just in the Same Situation as when I wrote last, that is, I am Still in the House in Castle Street and It is not likely we shall hear of any alteration for several months yet. I saw Mrs Hunter, for I was at Blackheath, tomorrow was a Month ago, and she Said that she hoped it would be all settled soon and that she hoped I should go with the Collection, and she said she had heard from Mrs Gilbert that week and that Mr & Mrs Gilbert were very well then and who I hope are very well now, and to whom when you see them you will give my duty. Brother John says in your last that he Supposes that I had Sent to Bristol or that Brother Thomas would not have Sent him such a letter I have not heard from brother Thomas since the beginning of April and then I believe I answerd his letter but I have not wrote Since. I thought I would not write to you when I received yours because I would let you take your own advice about either going to live with Mr Hewet or take another Room, because I thought If I had advised you to have gone to live with them, then perhaps you would

  100

have said why now I cannot go where I wish either of an evening or on a Sunday and now I am forced to be up early and late and perhaps to go to milking in the rain against my will and a great many other little things that you would not have thought of If I had not persuaded you. Then if I had advised you to stay at a house of your own, then (if you had taken my Advice) you would Say why If I had gone to Service I should not have had all this rent to pay, I should have had a good fire (perhaps) to sit by without paying for it and as many other things to ballance the other Scale, and so I have left God and yourself to settle it and I hope you have settled it for the best, be it which way it will, and which I hope you will let me know as soon as convenient after you have Received this. I wish you and Sister Joanna were settled in good places here in London. I thought Joanna promised to write to me, and that when I left Bodmin she would not be two years behind me, Now our Housekeeper Mrs Adams has a daughter here and she got a very good agreable and a very easy place in Leicester Square and has got nine Guineas a year and I am sure she cannot do more work than Joanna if she had a Mind. Please to tell her from me that If she do not write in a Short time I shall give her up and strike her off my lists for I am sure if she does not write oftener than she writes to me she will soon forget to write at all. So much for her, and to her, from me. WC.

You said in your last you Supposed I had heard of the Canals that are a going on near Bodmin I wish you would let me know in your next where and what it is for. I cannot suppose that they are to bring the Tide up from Warbridge to Priory pool and so I wish you would let me know all the Newest and best news you can find for we get hardly any thing but very bad news here, – There has been a great deal of Rioting here of late but it is pretty Quiet here now again. at Charing Cross which is not far from our house there is a little Court which is no thoroughfare and so at night when all people are quiet there is scarcely any person goes into it, the Court is Call'd Angel Court but I think it was pretty well filld with Devils before there was a riddance made for there was a woman in it that kept a Bawdy house and where the Girls decoyd in people and then they would Strip and Rob them and *th   *m to the East India Company for Soldiers who as *   * talk had a passage under ground to this house from the river Thames where they would take them away by night and put them on board a Ship and keep them down in the Hold, where no body could see them till they were out at sea. The beginning of these riots was occasioned by a man who they had decoyed in, he had been Stripped almost naked and his hands tied behind, and his hair cut off to disfigure him and had been put into a Garret by himself and locked in and he, to get away Jumped out at the garret window and as his hands was tied he could not save himself and therefore knocked his brains out in the fall. Somebody came by at the entrance of the Court and heard him groaning and so they raised a Mob presently and tore down the House where they found severall men almost starved to death with their hands tied and Chained by the legs, one poor young man tied in a Chair almost dead with the Small pox. The Mob from that house went and tore down almost all the recruiting offices in London to search for more kidnappers for the men that did help this old bawd was drest in soldiers Clothes and pretended through the day to be recruiting Officers

There are several poor fellows under Sentence of Death for helping to discover those wretches by breaking down the Houses Tho' I think it is a great pity they should be hang'd for trying to rid the World of such Monsters as would steal their fellow Creatures to sell them and I think it would be a great service if they would rather them for doing. The poor Man that was kill'd by his fall, was an excise man and had a Wife and several small Children near London—

Yours W: Clift

NOTES SECTION V

1. *fellon*: or *felon* is a small abcess or boil or an inflamed sore.
2. *chain*: apart from the unit of measurement, in weaving *chain* means the longitudinal threads in a woven fabric, the warp.
3. Matthew Baillie was the co-executor of John Hunter's Will with Everard Home. He was the son of John Hunter's sister, Dorothea. See Brief Biographies, p. 255.
4. Someone has attributed the letter to 1796 but this is clearly a mistake.
5. The *St George* was with Vice-Admiral Lord Howe's fleet in the Mediterranean.
6. 'The Glorious First of June' was the name given to the naval battle in the Atlantic of 1 June 1794 against the French, when the successful British fleet was commanded by Richard Howe. It is surprising that Clift should even have imagined his brother could have been involved, unless he was showing off to impress Elizabeth.
7. *Poosser*: the Purser.
8. *dula*: presumably Duloe, a village between Liskeard and Looe.
9. These were the Padstow-Lostwithiel Scheme and the Polbrook Canal Scheme to connect the River Camel with the River Fowey from Dunmere on the Camel to Lanhydrock, north of Lostwithiel. After various suggestions and alterations to the schemes they were tacitly dropped. See Charles Hadfield, *The Canals of South West England* (London, 1967), pp. 176-78.
10. Thomas Bolton and George Bentley were the two surveyors initially called in (1793-94) to examine the possibility of the canal.

VI. JANUARY TO DECEMBER 1795.

By 1795 William was writing to his sister in Bodmin at about six-monthly intervals and in the section for this year there are only two letters written by him. That he wrote to his other sister and brothers in the West Country as well as to Mrs Gilbert is clear from his comments and those of the other writers but these letters have all apparently been lost.

William's first letter, dated January, conveys the news that Robert Haynes had been dismissed the previous October for petty theft and that William is now in sole charge of the Collection. This clearly increases his chances of staying with it when it is sold but the negotiations drag on and by October, when he writes again, he is in considerable financial difficulties. He complains that the seven shillings a week he gets for board wages is scarcely enough to keep him in food and that he frequently goes without a midday meal. The five pounds a year he is supposed to have in addition has evidently not been paid and he is working in the evenings for Dr Baillie in order to earn a small sum of money to augment his scanty income. Anything he does manage to save he spends on paper for writing and drawing and he is copying out whatever he can lay hands on, especially the writings of John Hunter, for his own improvement.

William is not the only one aware of the rising cost of living. Thomas and Elizabeth both comment on the increase in prices, especially corn, an increase undoubtedly occasioned by the war. Joanna is the only one to report that she is living comfortably in her new place in Liskeard, where we learn that Catty Pinch is also working. The young maidservant had run away from Mr Eyre's house after she had been found parading in her mistress's clothes. The story is told by Elizabeth, who after her departure finds her own work increased. Elizabeth is now living with the Eyres and intends to give up her room in Back Street at the end of the year. The fortunes of Mr Eyre have not improved. In July Elizabeth tells William that he is selling off his 'shop goods' at a cheap rate and later in the year trouble arises between him and his brother Thomas, each accusing the other of owing money. In consequence, Elizabeth's master, Joseph Eyre, is arrested and later freed on bail.

Little is heard of John, whose relations with his sister in Bodmin do not seem any more cordial. She finds it hard to forgive him for not visiting her when she had a bad hand while her cousin, Thomas Puckey, took the trouble to send her money. However, in November John is taken ill and Elizabeth hastens to his bedside, not leaving him until he is showing signs of recovery.

The final excitement of the year is caused by a letter from Robert, from whom nothing has been heard for over two years. Earlier in 1795 Elizabeth had been under the impression that he was on board the *Windsor Castle* but his letter confirms that he is still serving on the *St George*, which is now in the

Mediterranean. There is evidence that he remained on board the *St George* all through its campaigns in the Mediterranean in spite of repeated rumours to the contrary. The letter, written in July 1795, has taken five months to reach its destination. William first receives news of its arrival from Joanna and her letter is closely followed by one from Elizabeth in which she carefully copies the letter out for him. Robert mentions successful encounters with the French fleet and is particularly anxious for details of a galleon which they captured and for which he should receive prize money. Elizabeth asks William to seek information in London since she can find out little in Bodmin. She follows the request with a copious list of things which William is to tell Robert when he writes to him with the news he has succeeded in obtaining about the galleon. At this point the letters for 1795 come to an end and we have to wait until the following year to discover how William sets about his errand.

52. *William to Elizabeth. 3 January 1795.*

Dear Sister

I have been expecting to hear from you for a long time past, as it was your turn to write, for I sent an answer to your last letter which was dated July 31st 94, and you desired that I would write to send my opinion of what it was best for you to do, as you said Mr Hewet was wanting you out of the House. I expected you would have wrote long before now, that I might know how you was going on

I have nothing very particular to write, though there has been a small alteration in the House since I wrote last.

In the first place – There was a fellow whose name was Duell that liv'd as Butler at our house when I first came here, – when he left our house he went down near Southampton to live and keep a Shop and sell all kinds of old Clothes, and new &ccc So Mr Haynes went down there Just by, to see his father and Mother last summer, and took down several things which belong'd to Mr Hunter and gave them to Mr Duell, so before he came back Haynes and Duell fell out and then Duell wrote up a letter to Mr Home and told him of all the things that Haynes had brought down to him. So just before Haynes came home – Mr Home sent for me to come to his house and asked me if I knew any thing of what Haynes had taken away and I told him I did not and he said he did not suppose I did for he did not think that Haynes would let me know of it without it was by chance that I saw any thing. So says he Haynes does not come back to our house any more and as I believe you are honest and well inclined towards our Family, whenever the Collection is settled I shall do whatever lies in my power for you. So when Haynes came home about the Middle of October it was on a lecture night and Mr Home calld him into the parlour and then he read part of the letter to him and did not tell who it come from but said that as he was one of Mr Hunters executors he could not in justice to the

104

family do less than tell him that he had no longer any need for him, and that he might sleep here that night but no longer. and so Haynes has been gone from here ever since and I am left Cock of the Walk, and do my work at my own time, but when he was here he did nothing himself but only kept me at work so that there was the name of two to work and not much done—

A few nights ago Mr Home when he came here at Lecture asked me if I ever had any money now, or if I used to get any of Mr Hunter and I told him that I had not got any nor that I never had any of Mr Hunter and that since Mr Huger (who used to be in the House and give me some sometimes for doing any thing for him) had been gone I never got any – So he said it was not right that I should be without money now, and so he gave me a half a Guinea for a Christmas Gift, for the trouble I got in the time of his Lectures which is three times a week but I had rather have twice the Trouble than lose the Hearing of them.

I spoke to him about some new Clothes the other day as I was coming rather Bare, and so he said I should wear my best clothes every day as they would be growing too little and that I shall have others against they are done.

I have a long Job to do this winter by Myself. there are Seventeen Thousand preparations and upwards in the Collection which are all to have numbers marked upon them with paint and when that is done Catalogues are to be made of them.

I must beg you will not show this letter to any Body as they would say I was growing proud of Myself and that I had no business to meddle in family affairs. The great end I had in letting you know was to show you that I have still some friends which I hope I shall endeavour to keep. and that I have more promised me now, and consequently I have more to expect than ever I had before. Please to write to me as soon as you get this and let me know how you go on and how you are settled.

Tell Joanna that I expected to have had a letter from her *by* this time if she had only wrote a word in a week.

Dear Sister Please to accept of my kind love to yourself and give it to all enquiring friends and I wish you a happy new Year. I would send you a new years Gift if I had an opportunity, but when I get an opportunity I hope it will be as welcome and as much in my power.

Mr John Hunter saild for Gibraltar about the Time I wrote last and there has been no accounts of him since

I remain your ever affectionate Brother

Wm Clift

Late John Hunter's
13 Castle Street
Leicester Square London
  Jan^{ry} 3d 1795

53. Elizabeth to William. 18 January 1795.

Bodmin Jan^r 18 1795

Dear Brother this Comes with my Cind Love to you hoping it will find you in Good health as this Leves me at Preasent I Bless God for it I was happy to receve your Cind Letter but I am sorry that I had not the Opurtunity to answer your First Letter till now tho thir hath not aday Past since I wrot Last to you but I have thought upon you an would have wrot If I Could but the first of September I went to Lerren to Look after the Bark an did not return till the 2 of october an when I retund Mrs Eyre said she was very Glad I was Come home for the Nurs had used her very Ill an an if I would Come an wean the Child I should sleep thir a fortnight an then I should take the Child home withe me by night an she an she would Pay me for it the Child was 9 Months old when it was weaned an three wickes an four days after she was brought to Bead of a nother young son But it did not live But one day it was named Jacob an they have no Maid sinse the nurs went away so I have bin In the house since oct the 18 night an day an you may think thir is Enough to due I scarce see the fore dore from one End of the wick to the other Sister Joanna is Living in Lescard Pareish it is a half mile from the town with one Mr Moon she hath a very Good Place I have had to Letters from her and she went to her Place the 3 of Sepr But I have not wrot to her till Last wick when she wrot to Rose Butler to desier Her to know what was be Come of me she said she had sent three Letters to me an received no answer I have not seen Brother John but twice since I wrot to you Last the first time I saw him was the wick I Came home an the Last time I saw him ws a Bout the Midil of Novr when he Promist me to write a Letter for me an send it to you the next day if he was Living but I find he did not wich I shall Return him thanks for when I see him as he knew I Could not I have not hard from Brother thomas since Febuary 94 Nor I have not hard Nothing of Poor Brother Robert since I have troubled my self a Great deal Conserning him when I hear of the dreadful Clamityes that are a Broad tho I am Surting that the Loard Can Presearve him in the midst of the Enemy as safe as if he was home for I am seurting that he is afrend to all that trust in him I am shore he hath Bin afriend to us an hath Providid far be yond our Expectations an I am very hapy to find that the Lord is still rising up frinds for you I hop I never shall be so Long with out writing to you I Left Castreet the 25 of August an went down in the back street in a room to Nany Jient I have the Chamber an *aney* hath the Kitchin I Give 26 shilings a year I have not sleept But three wickes in the room since I took it the Gardner williams is Maried to Tame Bonady John ford remembers to you an desirs to know if you have seen thos Pearce since he hath been in London Mr an Mrs Gilbert an all ther famly is very well I have not been to Priory this long time for I Canot Goe no Place without the Child if it had not Been for that I should have Gone down Long a Gone to have inquird for you an to have known what she said a Bout you But I hav not the time to

Goe out side the door I hav not been to Meeting but once this three Months an then I had the two young Children as for Mr an Mrs Eyre atend no Place of worshop at all as for my Part I have all wise Got the Child night an day so I Canot writ no time for she will not Let me stay up after she is Gone to Bead Dear Brother I hope you will Excuse this Scroll for I have wrot this with the Child in my arms the talk is that the Canells are Going on foorth with they say it will Come from Wadbridg to Priory Pool an from Loswithel it will be brought to hall Gower an from ther to town

I moust Conclud for the Bell has rung for me to Come to Bead

So I Remain Your Ever Loving

an affectnot Sister till Death

Eliz Clift

54. Thomas Puckey to Elizabeth. 24 January 1795.

Fowey Jany 24th 1795.

My Dear Cousin,:

Having hard that you have been Indispos,d lattley,) I have sent you 2 shillings by the Post Boy to be left at Mr *   * for you / I Trust the lord will Never let you Want But Above All;. I Beseech you to Labour To Enter In to the straight Gate; that leads To Everlasting Life, Of which so few Do find;) And since their are but few sav^d, Let Us labour to be of that happy Number.) We see what Destruction sin has made In the world:) Surely saith Isaiah c1 v9 If the lord of hosts had not left us a Very small Remnant, We should have Been like Sodom & Gomorrah long before No;) But Glory be to his holy Name Marcy is his Darling Attribute

I Must conclud from your sincear frind

Thos Puckey Junr

You May send Word or a line by the Post to know how you are

Father & Mother & Brother is fit

55. Elizabeth to William. 6 April 1795.[1]

Dear Brother I am Happy to have this oppurtunity of sending thes few lines to you Hopping these few Lines will find you in Good health as this Leves me at Preasent I bless God for it I have not Enjoyd so much health since I saw you as I have this winter tho it hath bin a very sevear one I Bless God I have not wanted for any thing I have bin now 24 wickes in the house the first 8 wickes I had 3 shilings awick and 16 wicks I had 4 shilings an now she would have me Bargin for a year in the house as they have shutt up Bisnes they are selling of the shop Goods at Prime Cost an she told me that they Intended to Goe to London in a bout a year she told me so to monthes a gone mrs Eyre an frances are Coming to London In June John williams receved a Letter from Brother Thomas an he said he had bin very Bad for ten wickes he said he had sent to you an John an me an had receved no answer from nether as for my Part I never receved any Letter from him this fiften monthes he said he is better But Desred If he had a brother or a sister in Bodmin they would writ to him I have wrot to him Sister is very well an in the same Place Brother John is much a yousal I Beleve he will never Be a Changerlain[2] I never here from Brother Robert

           Dear Brother this Being all at Preasent
        I Conclud Your Ever Loving
             and affectionate Sister
             Eliz Clift
             April 6th 1795

Nance Hocking Gives her Cind Love to you an would be Glad to know if you have seen her husband Latley or Can tell where he is quartered

56. William to Elizabeth. 3 May 1795.

Sunday May 3rd 95

Dear Sister,
        I take this opportunity of sending this, hoping it will find you in as good health as it leaves me at Present, I received your Kind letter by Betsey at Mrs Gilberts, tho not 'till they had been nearly three weeks in Town, and it was then, that I first knew of their Arrival, by Mrs Hunters maid who had come to Town from Blackheath and had been at Mrs Gilbert's with a Letter. Mr Gilbert was taken very ill a day or two after they came to Town, and which was the reason that I did not know sooner, of their being in Town, for Mrs Gilbert was not able go out, and Betsey did not know the Town, and their Servant was sent to Our house in Leicester Square and they told him they did not know me. I have seen Mrs Gilbert since Mr Gilbert got better, and she told me that Mr Home had called upon them, and that he had spoken very much in my favour to them; that I was to have five Guineas a Year & My Clothes – till the Collection was settled, and then whatever lay in his power, he said he would do for me; – When my Salary commenced I don't know, but I should think it ought to have begun from the time of Mr Hunters death. but about this Mrs Gilbert will be able give you a Better account than I can.
        I do not see Mr Home above once in a Week now as there is nothing particular going on at our house in Castle Street now. I have done very little to

my drawing for these twelve months past but I am in hopes I shall get some spare time very soon to do a little to it again I do not hear of any thing being done towards the disposing of the Collection I have had a great deal to do to it this winter to get it into repair.

Last Sunday Betsey (Rowe, I believe) and I took a long walk together, we went into Hyde Park, Kensington Gardens, St James Park and then to our House, where I show'd her the Collection, but it was so dark that She could see very little of it as it was so late before she could get out.

In the Letter you sent by her You say that Mr & Mrs Eyre intend coming to London to live. If it is so I think you had better come with them.

If Mrs Eyre & Francis should come here in June you must not forget to give them my Directions – As to a Letter from Brother Thomas I have rec^d / none since 13th April 94 but as He said then that he intended to Leave Bristol I did not know where to write to him. When You write to me which I hope will be soon, you will be so good as to send me his address if you know it, and also that of Joanna and I will write to them both.

I should have thought Joanna might have found time in two years to Write me a letter. As to Mr Jack Hawking I have not seen him but once or twice since Billy died, for as I think he is not quite so good, either to his family or himself as he should be I do not trouble my self to find him out, or look after him, for I do not consider his acquaintance any great Honour. The Last time Mr & Mrs Gilbert was in town (before this) she desired me not to have any thing to do with him. but however if I knew where he was I would willingly let you know for the Sake of his Wife & family.

Dear Sister My finances being very low at Present I know you will readily Excuse my not sending what I could wish but I hope e're long I shall be able send you something to keep in remembrance your ever loving and affectionate Brother

W Clift

I have not seen Mrs Hunter this great while, she is Still at Blackheath and Mrs Cambell her daughter is living next door to her, but is going to leave it soon as Mr Cambell her husband is going into Chesire to Join his Regiment – He is lately made a Colonel. Mr John Hunter is now at Corsica, he is made a Lieutenant, and is in good health and likes his situation very much.

Please to Wish Mrs Williams (late T Bonady) joy for me, and I hope she will be as fruitfull a Plant as her Husband has in his Nursery. I thought upon John Williams at Priory, till Betsey informed me of the Contrary as you wrote Mr W^{ms} the Gardener, if you had said Nurseryman I should known at once who you meant.[3] Give my kind remembrance to every one who enquires for me and tell John Ford that I have not seen T Pearce. I believe Betsey has seen him and all the rest of our Townsmen near Drury Lane.

I seldom take to the trouble of going to find out acquaintances, for as it is generally very inconvenient to have any visitors coming to see one and as I can always find something in London to amuse my self without any ones assistance, and as I like retirement and solitude best, I always like to keep myself to Myself.

Every thing is very dear in London Though we have the advantage of the country in this, that here is *almost* every thing to be had for Money. Beef Steaks – are 7^d a Pound, Mutton Eight Pence and every thing else in Proportion so that I can scarce live on 7 Shillings a Week. Be so good as send Joannas direction when you write again as also that of Brother Thomas's —

And let me know every thing worth writing

W Clift

---

57. Elizabeth to William. 5 July 1795.

Bodmin July 5th 1795

*   *Sunday

*   *ing

Dear Brother this Comes with my Cind Love to you hopping it will find you in Good health as this Leves me at Preasent I bless God for it I received your Cind Letter by Eliz Nichols an I was happy to hear you Enjoy your health an happy to hear of your Conduct an Good behavour for that will stand by you an be afreind to yo when friends may seem to fail But my Dear I hope the Lord will allwaise be a freind to you for we have no other frend to trust to but him an he is a freind at all times to them wich Put thir trust in him I Can speek it by Expearyence for Blessed be his name he hath Given me my health much better then Ever I Expected I did not think once that I Could have Gone throw such a house of work as I now due for thir is M^r/ and Mistress an 5 Children an Cat Pinch is Elopd[4] from us Ever since the thursday be fore whisantid an Last monday her sister brought her home from Liscard to see if Master would tak her but he would not an then they aplyed to Mr Geteat[5] an he sent for Master an told him they had bin to him with a complent of Ill yousag an he told Master that thir was a metting on wensday at washaway an desird he would meet him ther Master not being home at the time she runaway he did not know what she was beat for nor what she had don so I was obliged to Goe to testifie what she was beat with an what she roonaway for she was beat with acane wich was not Larger then areed tho she deservd it wors for she had looked her Mistress is Clothes out of her drawers an waring it an mistress said after she was very Glad she had found it out for *that   * not the first time she had found her Clothes mising an she might have Condemd me or any other servant as son as she when we Came to washaway ther was two justis Mr Gilbert an justis molswoth an as Master reffused to take her back she had her discharge an they are not Going to Ceep no servent but me while they stay in Bodmin wich I belive will not be Longer then Christmas if they Can dispose of the Shop Goods they have Gave out the secent notis Papers to return thanks to thir frends an Castners[6] an to ashure them that they are selling at Prime Cost an many things under an that the house an shop wich they were in is to be Let for 14 or 21 Ears from Christmas or sooner if they Can dispose of the shoop Goods but where they are Going I canot tell Master an Mistress are very Cind to Me I shall yeld up the room I have Goot as soon as the year is out I took it by the wick but Nanny Jient will Make me Pay the years rent wich is one Pown five shillings an I never sleept in it but three wickes I bless God I have the monny to Pay her but in seven years she will not be that the better nor I shall not be that the wors Sister is Living in Liscard town with mr Hocke a Gentell Man he youst to Ceep shoop just by the Market but now they Live in dean street next door the Presbeteuryan meetting I was to Liscard the third of may an I was to see uncel John Leavears an he was very well an desird to be rememberd to you an Cusen Peggy an Philly Bate are Living in Liscard an they Give ther Cind Love to you uncel James an aunt an Cousen James an bill are very well an Give ther Cind Love to you I was very som time a Gone I had very bad finger an Cossen James[7] sent me 2s by the Post wich was more then Brother John did I very seldom see him he is at Pencarrow still the Last time I saw him it was five wickes since an he was very angery with me an all of us he said he sent you a Letter by the Coach man an asmall Preasent he said you had not answerd his Letter I belive he thinks I have Put you in head a Genst him he said I had had many Letters from you since he had anny I told him he had a Letter from Brother thomas an he did not answer that was nothing but an Excuse for we did not take any acount of him so when you writ be so Cind as to Let me know wether you recevd that he sent by the Coach man or not an whether you have wrot to him or not I hard from Brother thomas just after I wrot you Last an he was very Poorly then an he said he was Coming home I wrot to him the 8th of June an diserd an answer as soon as Posabel but I have receved none wich makes me think he is wors I shall writ this wick to him this is the drectons At Mr Wilkins upaset the three Cups Reed Clift pitt Bristoll Mr Gilbert an Mrs Gilbert an all the family are very well I have not seen Mrs Gilbert to speek to her since you saw her betty Nichols Gives her Cind Love to you an returns you thank*s for* the Cindness and favours you shood to her my Dear you Cald her Row but she is Cald Nichols John foord Gives his Cind Love to you Mr George Brown is dead he was Berried at Blissland a whitson monday I have not hard from Poor Brother Robert since nor Canot Geet any acount of him

Dear Brother I shall be Glad to have a few Lines from you as soon as Conveant this Being all At preasent I remain you Ever Loving an affectnot Sister

Eliz Clift

Dear Brother dont troubel your self about me for I hope I shall Due very well if the Lord is Pleasd to send me my health

Every thing is very dear at Bodmin Corn is very scarce an dear wheat is 27 shilings a Bushal an Barly is 15 an not to be had for that ther was but 7 bushels of Corn in our market yestarday Beef an mutten has bin six Pence a Pound ther Never was shuch in Bodmin since any one Can remember for Poor sools Canot Geet bread for monny the Corn that is Brought in is divided in to to or three Gaollons Each acording to thir famly the Milers an Backers are not a Lowed to by any thir was som flower brought in to famlmouth an the Genteel men have sent an bought som an it is deliverd out once a wick to the Poor in habitance so many as they be in famly so many 5 Pounds

58. *Joanna to William. 19 July 1795.*

Dear Brother
Since you have taken the trouble to write to me I,ve taken the Pleasure of writing you an answer and First you should Like to know Where I woud go to Buy an Excuse for not writing Before In which I with shame and Confusion i Confess tis not In my Power to get an Excuse that would by worthy your Exceptance after Shuch an ill treatment from a sister But since you,ve Condesended to humble yourself to write to Me I Must hope that when you write to Me again that you,l send me an Excuse and Pardon My Neglect and In so doing you,l obledge your Ever Affectionate Sister

But when you wrote your Letter I suppose you thought to teaze me as you did John yet I hope you Dont think me alltogather of my Brothers Disposition tho when first I Perusd it over I Could not help thinking it a Pretty Smart Punishment for my neglect Espeshely when I Could Reflect on no person but My Self for it but Indeed I hope you,l never have Cause to remind me any more of my Long silence

My Dear I,me realy sorry to hear that the times are as hard with you as tis with us tis verry Bad Indeed and when twill be better god only knows an we can have no Idea of it at Present

I think My self as hapily sitiuated as any one Living I Bless god I have a good M^r and Mistress and nothing to Provide for yet I Pity Every one who does not Enjoy the same hapiness

I wish But for one thing now to Compleat my hapiness at Present that Is nothing Less then the Picture you Mentioned in yours and if Posible you Could Enclose it *For* Me in a Letter if you think twou,d Come safe I woud receieve it with *unspeakable* hapiness and think My Self forever obledged to you for so great a favour

this being all time will Permit me at
Present
I Conclude your Ever
Affectionate Sister
Joanna Clift

Liscard July the 19th
Dean Street

59. Robert to Elizabeth. 26 July 1795.

St George Forensey[8] July the 26th 1795

Dear Brothers & sisters I know take the oppertunity of Wrighting these few lines to you hoping the will Find You in good health as i am at Present thanks Be to god for it i have sent several letters home and am Very much surprise[d] You could never have an oppertunity of sending me an answer Dear Sister I would Be very happy to know in what part of England My Brothers is in & Espesial my Brother william I would Be glad to know in what part of london he is in as i have a Better oppertunity of sending to him than i have to You we rea tooke a spanish galoone[9] from the french When first we saile[d] from England we hear she is condem[d] But Cannot Be sertain of it I would Be glad to hear from you a tru account from you whether she is or Not or how much she will Be a man to Us we had three Engagements with the french fleet since we have Been Up the medetrania But alwase proov[d] Victories over our Enemys we tooke two sail of the line & sunke one and as for frigates is Unaccountable—[10]

Dear sister I would wish that you would take Care of this letter an it might Be of service to You if in Case I Should Be kille[d] or should never return which i hope there is No fear of that my number on the ships Bookes is N° 77 Which would Be of great service to You in regard of geting my Wage[s] and prise money By aplying to the Commisoner of Plymouth Dock Yard and in Case such a thing should Happen I hope you will Eaqualley divide it among you all Dear sister i would Be Very glad to see you all in good Health which with the Blessing of god it will not Be Very long Before i do for i am in hopes the war will Not hold out much longer for i am in hopes it is almost at an End Be plase[d] to remember me to Mr pinch and His family & mother williamson and her family – and all Enquireing friends Dear sister when you wright to me you must direct on Board of His M.S. st George leghorn or Els where So Nomore at Present from your loving Brother
Robert Clift

Be plais[d] to send me all the News you can & the particulars of Every thing you can

Dear Sister

I suppose you think I have quite forgot you, but I assure you it is not so. I have been so very busyly employed of late that I have scarce had time to write to you if I had the mind, for I have had a great deal of writing to do for myself and other people and therefore every spare minute I had, I was employed in writing. A gentleman[11] who lived in this house at the time of Mr Hunter's death has been taking in a work which treats of all the arts and Sciences and he is just come back from his travels and he has been good enough to let me have those parts of it which are about painting, &cc. which I have been copying for myself, and as he is going away to America his native country in a few days I have been obliged to set up almost all night for two or three weeks to get it done before he went and I have not finished it now, as some of his books were sent away before to America and the rest are now packed up as he is gone into the country and when he comes back he sets off for his own Country, and this last week I have been writing for Dr Baillie a relation of Mr Hunters family who got leave of Mr Home for me to go to his house in the evenings and write from 5 to 11 oClock. It will take me 8 or 9 Nights in all, for which I am to have a Guinea when it is finished, besides he is very kind to me, I have a nice Room to myself. Ring for any thing I want, get tea brought me at 6; table laid and a good supper at 9 – Dr Baillie is the other Executor, as Mr Home is one, and as he is a very good kind of man I think of speaking to him as soon as I have finished the writing to give me more board-wages for I cannot live at all upon 7 Shillings a week; as I do not work hard I frequently go from breakfast to tea, and get no dinner and yet I find that at the end of the quarter I am several shillings out of pocket more than my board-wages, and as they do not give me any pocket money I cannot afford that. I have not received any wages yet, and as Mr Hunter has been dead almost 2 years there will be £10 due I should suppose; and I think of asking Mr Home for part of it to buy a watch – I dont like to keep money by me when I get it. I had saved a guinea & more a little while ago, but I laid it all out in Paper & one thing and another, and now as there are no gentlemen in the house it does not come in again, therefore at times I am very poor. They never say any thing to me about my Drawing nor did they ever buy me, or give me money to buy materials, but I hope I shall do well enough without their aid. As I have not an over deal of work, and Mr Home does not come to our house once in a week hardly, I make time to practice a good deal upon what I have already learnt.

I wrote to Joanna when I received her direction in your last and she has since wrote to me, when she wrote she was very well it is a month ago now, & I suppose you have heard from her since I have wrote to her again to day. I sent a letter to John when I wrote to Joanna last, I put them both in the office at the same time; but he has never answered it I dont know whether he received it or not. It was dated the 25th or 26th of July.

This London is a strange place. I have not seen any one that I knew before I came here, since Mr & Mrs Gilbert left town. I hope they and all their family are very well and I hope you will be so good as write me as soon after you receive this as possible or convenient and let me know every thing new, How you go on, & how all Mr Eyre's family do. Please to remember me kindly to all enquiring friends Let me know how Kitty & Ann are, and the children; and Hon[r] Williamson & the young Onion & Betty and all our old acquaintance are, and when you heard from our friends at Fowey. & How Aunt Polly Leavers' family are

> This being all the particulars I have to write
> at present I remain your
> ever loving & affectionate Brother
> William Clift

13 Castle Street
Leicester Square, London
4th of Oct[r] 1795
Sunday.

PS   I intended to have gone to Blackheath to see Mrs Hunter *today* but it being a rainy day here (I dont know what it is with you) has prevented me, and has given me an opportunity of writing to you.

Mrs Hunter's Mother died since I wrote you last, I believe. Their sorrow did not reach as far as our house or at least so far as to give us any thing the colour of what I am writing with. My fellow servant Mrs Adams sat up with her four or five nights running but they did not give her as much as a ribbon for her trouble. You may guess their good nature.

61. *Thomas to William. 22 November 1795.*

Bristol Nov[r] 22 95

Dear Brother
                I have took the opertunity of sending you those few lines Hoping that It will find you in good health as I Bless god this leaves Excepting a Cold which I have Had for this fortnight past which has Been the general Complaint of most people here of late I hard from home a few weeks past By John Scantlebury othirwise Madicks which *   * Brought a gentlemans horse to Bristol, Sister Betty was in good health but as for aney other person I Could have but little tidings of our ould Neigbours Tom Williams otherwise face has left me and is gone to sea about 6 or 8 weeks agone he is on board the Melpomene Friget I shall be glad if you will send me a few Lines as soon as

Convenient—

And let me hear some of the Best News you have in town and how times *governs* with you whether it is worse with you then it is heare if it is it is bad anough for Every thing is so Excessive Deare that I have a nough to Do to geet vituals at present and send me Down word whether you think thare is roome anought in town to hold me if I should Come up after Christmas

this being all at present
I Conclude with my prayers to you
for your health and prosperity
and remain your Ever Affectonate
Brother Thomas Clift

Direct as Before with Mr wilkins opsite the three Cups Red Cliff Pit Bristol

And please to Excuse Me for Not sending sooner

62. Elizabeth to William. 3 December 1795.

Bodmin December the 3 95

Friday morning one o Clock

My Dear Brother

this Comes with my Cind Love to you hoping it will find you in Good health as this Leves me at Preasent I Bless God for it Brother John Has been very Ill I was to mrs Jefferys three days with him he was so Ill that he did not know me for a day an a night after I Came it was the first of nov^r I was sent for whin I Left him he was abel Seet up an he Promisd me to writ to you the next day he recevd the Letter you sent him I receved aletter from sister Joanna the 5 of Novr she was then very well she said she had receved your Letter but had not time to answer it a bout the midel of oct^r Jack Scantelberry was at Bristol an saw Brother thomas he said he was much better then he had been for a Great while he desird him to Give his Cind Love to me an to tell me he intended to Come home in the Spring I hope I shall Hear from Brother Robert if he is on Boord the winsor Castel for Suckey willis Mrs Borros is Niss has abroher on Boord the same not abraham I think he is Cald George he has a wife at Dock she had a Letter from him in April an she wrot to her husband in August an be fore she wrot she sent to miss Suckey to let her know then Miss wills Left me know it then she wrot to her Sister Law to desir her when she wrot to her Husband to inquer if ther was any such one on Boord the winser Castel so she has Promised me as son as she hears from her Brother if Brother Robert is ther I shall know it I hard from our Peopel at fowey Last wick By Billy musgrove he is working ther the old Mr Pomery is Going ther to Live so Bill is thir making the Gardens an they ware All very well Cousin Peggy Bat is maried to a solder

and aunt is al most Broken harted a bout it Mrs Gilbert has bin very Poorly Mr
Gilbert an she has Bin at Bath 5 or 6 wicks Betty an william has bin with thm
they Came home Last friday I have not seen her to speek to her but once since
she Came home from London an that was as she Post by our door I have bin
down twice but Could not see her nether one of the times she had Company
with her I am very sorry to think you are not settled no Better I think it is very
hard you should not be Put som Place or other to Lern or to have som Person
to instrouct you But my Dear Brother I hop an trust the Lord will be afreind to
you and Provide som way or other for you for he hath Promised to be a friend
to All them that Put ther trust in him when all others fail I Believe if I due not
Leve Bodmin be fore our Peopel it will be a Good while first if they due not
Leve it soon I belive I shall for the work is so hard that I am a slave to them you
know they used to Ceep two Maidins an work Enough when Sister lived with
them Cat Pinch was then with them when I Came with them to Live she said I
should only Look after the Children when Catty went a way they told me that
they should not Ceep a servant in the house but that it should make no
difference to me for they would Ceep som Person an Give them so much a
wick an Provide them selves so Nancy *Caig* was with us a littel while an now
they have no one but me nor they are not Going to Ceep but one I have had a
God Place of Profit this yeare I had 9 shilings to the sizes I have had more than
five Pound this yeare but the ill tempers of one an the others it is scarce to be
beared with the day before I went to see brother John M^r an I had many words
so much that I will not take so much of him no more nor would not then if
John had not bin so ill he said while he had aservent he would be waited on an
be fore the wick Came round he was waited on to his hearts Content the day
after I Came home he was a rested for a hundred Gineas by his Broher thos
there was two bailes to wait on him from thursday till friday night I watched
thre nights that wick to nights *g*owling[12] with Brother an one with him I
should have thought he Could not for Geet in so littil atime for 5 wickes an
four days be fore this he Could not showe since august his Brother thos was
Put to Preasen the Lawe was against them for one hundred an Eighty Pounds
Each he Gave bail after he had Ceept of so long an I may Justly say I had not a
nights reast in all that time he hath Given Bail a Gain Mr Liddel an Mr Broad
was the first Bail an Mr tuck an Mr Climo for this Last he sais he Due not owe
his Brother any thing but that his Brother owes him fifty Pounds an More I Be
live there is no one knowes how it is be twen them but thir selves the house we
live in is advertized to be Let from Christmas next for 14 or 21 Ears the shop
Goods is Great Part of it sold of they have bin selling by oucton an Prime Cost
this six monthes

    I Can writ no more for want of room
     so I Con Clud your Ever Loving an
    affectnot Sisster
      Eliz Clift

John Foord desirs to be remembrd to you

E willmson is very ill in a dicline*a*ney an her mother Gives ther Love to you ann and Citty is very well

Dear Brother I hope you will be so Cind as to writ to me soon

63. *Joanna to William. 17 December 1795.*

Liscard Decr the 17th 1795

Dear Brother

I Suppose you think me still neglectfull in not writing to you before but at the time I receieved yours My Mrs Brothers were Just Come from Lisbon and her sisters and their uncle from Saltash, what with them and the Constant visits of their friends that Live in Liscrd I Can assure you I had anough to do they'd been gone but a few days before M^{rs} was seized with a violent fever yet I Bless god She is restor,d to her health again she,s realy a good Mistress as I Ever had yet while I,me writing you this I am impatient to Lett you Know I,ve Just now receieved a Letter from Sister with the Most happy news of her having receieved a Letter from our dear brother Robert on friday Last It being Dated July the 21st 95 – he was then in good health as I trust in god he still remains he said they^d had Many Engagements with the french Fleet since they have bin In the Midetrenian Sea but they have allways got the victory and that they had taken two sail of the Line and Frigitts out of number when he wrote he was then at fransey[8] but that Sister was to direct for him at Leghorn or Elswhere onboard the St george he desir,d to know where we all were and how we was but Espesialy his dear Brother william and that he Longed to write to you but he knew not where to direct and desired Sister to give him where to direct to you as he Could a great deal better send to you then he Could to us so My dear william be speedy In writing to him as soon as you receieve this

Which being all at Present
I Conclude being your
Affectionate Sister
Joanna Clift

PS   Sister is verry well, I suppose you will hear from her soon Poor soul I Beleieve she has anough to do; she is still at Mr Eyres and no other servant; she does not think of staying there much Longer, as the work's so hard, I hope she will Come to Liscard soon; I Could get her A Place allmost at any time, but My fellow servant Talks of Leaving us soon, and then I would soon get her In the house with me. Kate Pinch Lives here in Liscard, and she has a verry good Place Indeed. Cousin Philipia Bate Lives in Liscard, and her sister Peggy Lived here in Liscard for some time But she Is Lately Maried to A Soldier and gone off with him

Poor Betty williamson is dead and buried She died Last friday Morning and was buried the sunday

Poor old *oney* and the young and Both Living Still[13]

My Dear Brother you will Please to Excuse what Ever you see In this as tis now one o Clock in the Morning and I hope to have more time when I write to you again and hope you,l write to Me soon as Posible as I Longe to hear from you

So farwell J.C.

64. *Elizabeth to William. 20 December 1795.*

Dear Brother

I have sent you these few lines, Hoping it will find you in Good health. I have been very Poorly with the rumatick in my Legg, for this fortnight Past but I bless God for it I am much better. Dear Brother I have receved a letter from our Poor Brother Robert, whome I never thought to hear from any more but blessed be the All mighty who hath Preserved and Ceept him in the midst of so many an Great dangers as he hath been in a Coppy of his Letter I am Going to writ he is still on board the St George tho we ware informed he was on Board the windsor Castle[14]

St George Fransey July the 26 1795

Dear Brothers an sisters I know the oppurtunity of writing these few lines to you hoping the will find you in Good health as I am at Preasent thankes be to God for it I have sent several Letters home and am very much suprised you Could never have an oppurtunity of sending me an answer Dear sister I should Be very happy to know in what Part of England my Brothers is in an Especely my Brother william I should be Glad to know in what Part of London he is in as I have a better oppurtunity of sending to him than I have to you we retook a Spanish Galoone from the French when first we saild from England we hear she is Condemd but Canot be sertain of it I should be Glad to hear from you a true a Count From you wether she is or not or how much she will sheare a man to us we had three Engagements with the frich fleet since we have Been up the mediterranean But allways proved victoureas over our Enemys we took two sail of the line an sunk one and as for frigates is unaccountable dear sister I should wish that you would take Care of this Letter as it may be of servies to you in Case I should be kild or should never return wich I hope there is No feare of that my number on the ships books is N°. 77 wich would be of great servies to you in regard of geting my wadges and Prise money by applying to the Commishoner of Plymouth Dock yard and in Cause such a thing should happen I hope you will Equally divide it amogest you all Dear sister I should be very Glad to see you all in Good health wich with the Blessing of God I hope it

119

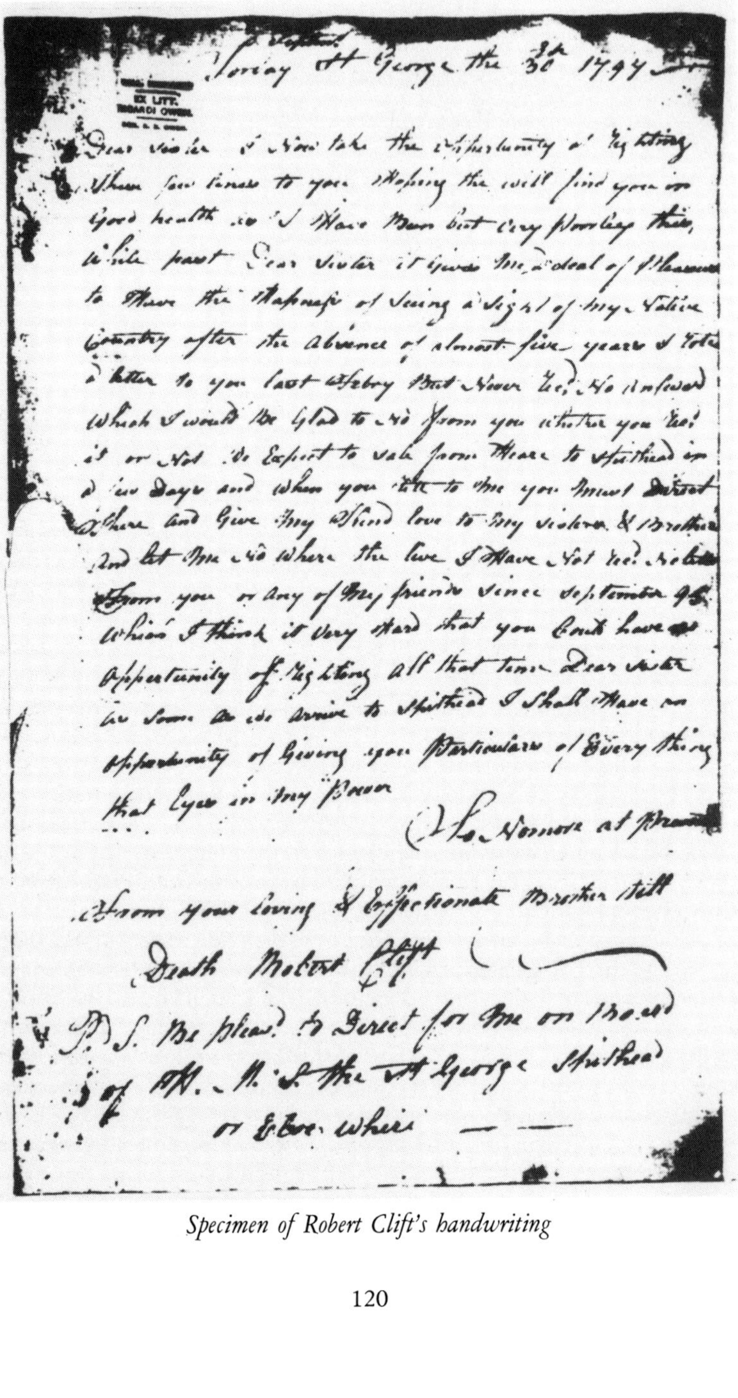

Specimen of Robert Clift's handwriting

will not be Long be fore I due for I am in hops the ware will not hold out much Longer for I am in hopes it is all Most at an End be Pleased to remember me to Mr Pinch an all his famly an to honear williamson an all her famly and all Enquiring friends dear sister when you writ to me you must direct on Board of his Magestys Ship St Gorge Leghorn or Elst where So nomore at Preasent from your Loving Brother

Robert Clift

PS

Be Pleasd to send me all the Newes you Can an all the Particulars of Every thing you Can

Dear Brother I have Put down Every Particular as I Must desire you to answer it for me as I Canot Geet any true acount a bout the Spanish Galoon wether she is Condin[15] or not an as I hope you Can I shall be very thankful to you to answer it for me an Give my Cind and affectnot Love to him an tell him I hope and trust the Lord our God wich hath been with him and Preserved him this far will be with him still and Bring him back to his native Land a Gain to enjoy what he hath Labourd hard for tell him it will be a happy day two us all to see him once more home we never thought to hear from/ no more tell him we never receved any Letter from him If I had I should Gladly have answerd it tell him I did not receve this Letter till the 11 of December tell him Broher John is at Pencarrow an Brother thomas is at Bristol an sister Joanna is at Liscard with mr hocke she has avery God Place and I am at Mr Eyres a servant Bodmin

dear Brother I should have wrot sooner but I was so Poorly in my Leags that I was not abel to Goe out in town to Enquir about the Spanish Galoon I sent afew Lines to Brother John an he sent me word he would se me in a day or two he said he was very well but I have not seen him since nor Canot tell the reason it was ten days a Gone I sent to him tell Brother Robert that Poor betty william is Gone to be no more in this troubelsom world she died the Morning I receved his Letter in the Eving the Poor old anny is very Porly anny is very well an Gives her Love to him an you an Citty an Ann an Mr Pinche an all his famly Gives ther Cind Love to him tell him Polly Pinch is maried to Mr George Fisher the tin man Roger Crapps hath not been home since that time Brother saw him at tor Point nor his mother Canot Get any acont of him she Gives her Love to Brother an if he should have the oppurtunity of seeing him he would when he writs hom a Gain Menshon it an Polly Levears Gives her Cind Love to him an to Let him know that her son Richard is on boord the Corageux now at Leaghorn and if he should have the Chance of Ever seeing him he would desire him to writ to her she has receved but one Letter from him since he hath Been to sea an that was in July 94 an then he wrot from Fransey the way she know he is at Leaghorn Mrs hussey at Blesland had a Letter from her soon who is on boord the same ship an he said richard was very well the young housey has sent

121

his mother many Letters wich she has receved and Carefully answerd Every one of them an he has never recevd one an now she has a direction from som Gentelman who told her it would Goe she mit depend the driction is at Leaghorn or Elst where by sea or by Land dear Brother you said some time a Gone that if Brother was on Board the St Gorge that you Could send to him so my dear Brother I hope you will writ to him as soon as you riceve this if you Can if you Can Geet the acount of the Galoon if not writ me as soon as posabel how Ever I should be Glad of a few Lines as soon as Posabel an Let me know if you received the Letter I sent to you the 4 of december yestarday *I* saw richard at Priory he told me that Mrs Gilbert received a Letter from you an she had sent answer to you an I should be Glad to know if thir is any thing the mater Dear Brother desire of Brother Robert if he should Chanc to fall in with the Intripid she is the ship Mr Robert Edgeman was Chaplin of that he would if any time should be on shore if he might Meet any of her men he would Enquire for one Thomas Teauge he is a worthy young man

Dear Brother I fear you Can not read this it is so badly wrot but I have no tim to writ but after I am in bead I am a blidged to Goe in to Bead to quite the Child

I Conclud your
affectnot Sister
E Clift

Dec^{br} 20 1795

NOTES SECTION VI

1. This letter has been written over, almost certainly by Clift and probably as he was reading it. Spelling has been altered, punctuation added, etc. At times it is virtually impossible to decipher the original.
2. *Changerlain:* chamberlain? This would seem to imply a house servant but John's skills were carpentry and estate maintenance. There is no indication in the *OED* that the word could be used of an estate foreman, which would seem the natural end of John's career.
3. Clift worked for Mr Williams, the nurseryman, when he left school at the age of eleven. See his Autobiographical Sketch, p.20.
4. *Elopd:* see Section II n.4. p.51.
5. The ms. is quite clear at this point but surely *Gilbert* is intended.
6. *castners:* customers.
7. *Cossen James:* it seems to have been Thomas Puckey, not James, who had sent Elizabeth the money. See Letter 54. Thomas was probably the brother of James and William Puckey, who visited Clift in London and sailed as missionaries for the South Seas in 1796. Thomas is not mentioned elsewhere in the letters except by John, who reports his death in 1806. See Letter 104.

8. *Forensey:* St Fiorenzo, Corsica. Also spelled *Fransey* and in various ways.
9. *a galoone:* a galleon, probably the *Imperieux,* 38 guns, taken off Genoa on 11 October 1793.
10. The ships taken off Genoa in March 1795 were the *Ca-Ira,* 80 guns, and the *Censeur,* 74 guns. The ship sunk was probably the *Alcide,* which surrendered after an engagement on 13 July 1795 but caught fire, exploded and sank with the loss of half her crew.
11. Philip Syng Physic (1768–1837). An eminent American surgeon. He studied under John Hunter during Clift's first eighteen months in London, until Hunter's death.
12. *g*owling:* the verb *to gowl* is recorded in the *OED* as being of dialectal origin, chiefly Northen and Scottish. It means 'to cry bitterly' or 'to whine'. This seems to make sense in the context of Elizabeth's letter but is not recorded as being used in the South West.
13. The punctuation in the postscript appears to be Joanna's even though it is unusual for her to use punctuation of this kind.
14. Robert had been on the *St George* all the time since he left England, as the muster books show. He was never mustered on the *Windsor Castle.*
15. *Condin:* condemned.

VII. JANUARY TO DECEMBER 1796.

William wastes no time in seeing to his brother's affairs but he is hampered by lack of sufficient information. In his letter to Elizabeth in January he discloses the strange coincidence that Mrs Adams, still housekeeper in the Castle Street house, has a brother who is the First Lieutenant on board the *St George.* Unfortunately for Robert the lieutenant leaves the ship shortly after and before William has time to make Robert acquainted with the fact.

Having dealt with his brother's enquiry, William proceeds to dwell on his own difficulties. During the early part of the year he becomes exceedingly worried about his future and, after Everard Home prevents him from continuing with his drawing lessons, he writes to Mrs Gilbert for advice. This move brings about some improvement in his situation and it is arranged that he shall have twenty pounds a year in addition to his board wages and be allowed time off to attend various classes. However, the Collection, visited at this time by no less a person than the Prince of Orange, whom William has the honour of conducting round, is no nearer being disposed of, and in spite of Home's reassurances, there is no guarantee that the purchaser, whether it be the Government or a private person, will keep William Clift on to look after it. There is a suggestion, made by Everard Home, that William should learn accountancy and take up banking as a career, but here William's dislike of responsibility once more asserts itself. He does not wish to have the handling of other people's money and prefers to learn anatomy and remain with the Collection as long as he can. It was an irony, unperceived by William at the time, that having sole charge of the Hunterian Museum was to prove a far greater responsibility than any mere bank clerk would be likely to meet in the whole of a lifetime and one which, happily for the history of surgery and medicine, as well as for the nation, he was discharging with supreme excellence. Throughout his letters written to Elizabeth in the early part of 1796 we can sense the perplexity as he laboriously reasons out the various aspects of his position and seeks to protect himself against all eventualities.

In all his uncertainty about the future William never apparently considers returning to Cornwall but instead begins to make plans for Thomas and his sisters to join him in London. Thomas, after living in Bristol since before William left home, suddenly writes from Southampton to say he has left Bristol during a general strike of craftsmen and that before returning he hopes to come to London to see his young brother. This news sets William building his 'castle in the air' as he calls it and suggesting that the other members of the family (John is never mentioned in this connection) join him and settle in London. There is an immediate and enthusiastic response from Joanna, now living in Plymouth. Elizabeth does not comment. She has now left the Eyres and gone to a place at Linkinhorne, eight miles from Launceston. Thomas proceeds to Portsmouth for a short while and eventually arrives in London in July, the first of the family that William has seen for over four years. Strangely his arrival seems to arouse little excitement.

Apart from William's problems and the movements of the others, the letters continue to give the usual snatches of local news. In one we get an unexpected glimpse of Billy Hocking's father. We now learn that he is a stay-maker and has set up a shop with a 'mantua maker', although William seems uncertain if this lady is the same one who appeared earlier in the letters. The general attitude of the Bodmin people to the behaviour of Mr Hocking is seen in an incident tersely described by William. The Bodmin fraternity in London seems to be considerable but it is clear that on the whole William has little to do with them.

In September he is visited by his cousins from Fowey, James and William Puckey, now converts to evangelical religiosity and eagerly setting out as missionaries to Otaheite in the South Seas. From William's account of the meeting it seems that they are not given a very warm reception by him and Thomas. His comments on their fitness to proclaim the Christian gospel are finely contemptuous. In a letter to Joanna he clearly expects her to appreciate his witticisms at the expense of his country cousins but his remarks to

Elizabeth are so caustic that she takes them as a personal affront. Her indignation is such that she does not reply until the following June and the letters for 1796 come to an end in October.

65. *William to Elizabeth. 3 January 1796.*

Late John Hunters Esqr N° 13 Castle Street Leicester Square London

Sunday January 3rd 1796.

Dear Sister

I, as you may see, have not been long in Answering your letter as I know you will be impatient to hear from me for more reasons than one – I receivd yours yesterday, – I had a letter from Joanna last week and she told me that you had received one from poor Brother Robert and desired me to write immediately to Leghorn but as I had no particulars from her and it being wrote so long before you received it I did not know where they might be by this time and therefore thought it would be best to enquire farther about it – I told you some time ago that I knew a person onboard the St George and which I think may be very lucky for him The person who lives in the House with me and whose name is Mrs Adams is particularly acquainted with the first Lieutenant of the St George, and his Sister; and as he is the Second officer in the ship, that is, if the captain should die he will be made Captain and therefore he may perhaps do my brother any little service for he is a very good sort of a Man as I have been told and I wish we had been certain he was onboard the St George Sooner because I am very well acquainted with Mr Fortune's sister that is, the first Lieutenant's sister and she could have readily told me where to have wrote – however, as soon as I received your's I went to the Admiralty (as Mr Fortune's sister directed me) to enquire where the ship was now; as I had never been before and did not know the way to the office I enquired of a Gentleman at one of the doors who was coming out which was my way to the office for that I wanted to enquire after a certain kings ship – he asked me what ship – I told him – he asked who I wanted on board her, for says he I left the St George the other day. I told him Lieutenant Fortune, as I thought by asking for him he might more readily tell me what I wanted to know – he said he knew Lieu^t Adam Fortune very well – and by that alone I knew he must know for I did not call him by his Christened name – I then told him that what I wanted particularly to know was, that I had a brother onboard the same Ship and he asked his name I told him Clift – what says he are you a brother of Bob Clift – and therefore I was sure that he could not be making a fool of me – (as is the case with a great many wits in London) by being so familliar with their names, he told me that If I wrote to him at Leghorn he would be sure to get my letter. I should have asked him if he knew any thing of the Galleon if I had had time but it was very well that I learnt so much as I did, for the gentleman went into a coffee house and therefore I could not ask him any more for we only talked as he went along.

I went likewise to an Agency Office in Arundell Street in the Strand to be more sure and they told me that he was at Leghorn. It is a foolish thing to send to know about the Galleon without any date or its name or any thing else for unless one could tell all these things it will be no use to go to the admiralty or an Agent to enquire after any thing unless we can be very particular for they will hardly take the trouble to look over their Books when you do know, and pay them into the Bargain I have this day wrote the answer to his letter as you desired and told him that I daresay Lieutenant Fortune can tell him about it if he has a mind to ask him – I shall make all the enquiry I can against I write again to him and I have sent him all the news I could think of and every thing as you desired me – so that I hope you will think as I do, that I have not delayed any time and that I have done all that lay in my power. I have likewise sent a message from Mrs Adams to Lt Fortune which will bring them to know each other. Dear Sister, you desired to know what is the matter – for I find that Mrs Gilbert has not told you I should have wrote to you before but I wished to have something worth writing to you – I was doing some writing for Dr Baillie – he is the other Executor with Mr Home, of Mr Hunters affairs – and he asked me when I had finished my writing, how I intended to get my living when the Collection was disposed of and so on. I told him that Mr Home promised me, when Mr & Mrs Gilbert was last in town & spoke to him about me that I might depend he would do every thing in his power towards my going with it to take care of it when it was settled, and Dr Baillie who is I believe a very good kind of a Man told me that it was impossible that either him or Mr Home could have the least Idea how it would be settled or whether Mr Home would have the appointing of any body to take care of it or no, and that I ought to study something by which I might be able get my living if Mr Home's promise should fail me – He said I wrote a good hand and that I should endeavour to improve it as much as possible and practice arithmetic I told him I wished to improve my drawing as well, but that Mr Home never asked me any thing about how I went on with it and never said any thing about sending me any where – I told him that Mr St Aubin and Mr Batty had promised to give me a lesson now and then if I could get time to come to them – but I rather wished to wait till Mr Home spoke to me about sending me somewhere first or that the Collection would soon be settled one way or other and then there would be some alteration but as neither came to pass I asked Mr Home one morning when he sent for me if he would give me leave to go an hour now & then as I had been promised a lesson now & then if I could come – he said I should remember what he told me concerning my going with the collection when it was settled but that it was not his place to encourage it neither was it his interest – for I suppose he thought if he learnt me any thing by which I could get my living any other way I should be for leaving them – So I wrote Mrs G and let her know all the particulars and that my time was throwing away at present because I was learning nothing and that if I went with the Collection and staid with the Collection for a few years and then if I should disoblige any of the people who have the Superintendence of it I should then be out of Bread and too late to learn any other Business and that I could never expect but to have all the work to do and that it would be the place of the Executor to account to who ever gets it, the expences it will cost to keep it in repair as low as possible for their own sakes and therefore I should only have a bare Maintenance – I said that I only wished to have her advice and that I should always be willing to abide by her Judgement – So I got an answer to it desiring me to make myself easy about every thing and rely on them – that they thought the contents of my letter very reasonable and that they would take it into consideration and write to Dr Baillie about me So last week Mr Home said to me that Dr Baillie had got a letter from Mrs Gilbert about me and he gave me five guineas – which is I suppose for wages since Mr Hunters death and for which I gave him a receipt and which only mentioned that I received so much, not telling what for – for I desired him to give me a copy of how I was to write it – He has since told me that he thought I had better study Anatomical Drawing than Miniature Painting as he says there is not a good one in London and asked if I should like to learn anatomy I told him I should wish to learn something by which I could be sure of getting a living – he said there was no fear of that and bade me consider which I should like best – A Counting house, or anatomy. Anatomy is undoubtedly preferable to the other if one was sure of Learning it to perfection and as I have been so long accustomed to it – and as to the Counting house I do not much relish being entrusted with other peoples Money & goods for fear of any mistakes &c whereas if I studied the other there would be none of those fears Mrs G says she has Hack writing to an attorney but I am told they only give 12^d a week but however I do not fear of getting on in one way or another for my letter has done some good. Mr Home does not carry on Dissecting as he used to do but I suppose he intends to do it again or else he could not learn me – and he then could not think of giving me less than a guinea a week besides some perquisities which would fall in now & then I shall know farther about it against I write again as Mrs G promised to let me hear from her again soon and then I shall hear what they intend to do. When I received the five guineas Mr Home said that he should talk to Mrs Hunter and Dr Baillie & see if they would allow me any more because he said I served them instead of another Person – I know they do not wish to lose me as I know their ways and the way of every thing about the house and they would not get another so cheap – Dear Sister, I wish to keep my five guineas whole till I see what way matters will take – or I should have sent you a christmas Box but I want some more to it to buy me a Watch if I could – I shall see how things go & then you shall hear from me again I have not at this time enough to pay the letter but if I get any tomorrow before Post time you will see – I cannot save any thing out of my 7 Shillings a week though I frequently (as I do not work hard), go without dinner If I stay here I shall strike for more for every thing is nearly half as dear again as it was two years ago I had a letter from Brother Thomas 22 Novr he was pretty well –you told me he was coming into Cornwall – he told me to see if there was room enough to hold him in London

I remain Y^r affectionate Brother

William Clift

Brother John being always a slave to his word has not answered my letter yet. Please to remember me kindly to all who enquire for me.

66. William to Elizabeth. 21 March 1796.

Dear Sister

I daresay you think I have quite forgot you by this time but I now write to let you see I have not I have been so very busily employed of late that I have scarce had time to think of any thing but what I was about. We have at last some hopes of getting ride of our charge – the *Collection*; that is, it has been brought forward again in the Parliament House, who appointed a Committee of 30 Gentlemen of the House of Commons to examine a Committee of Medical Men on the worth, and use, of the Collection to the Nation and who have spoke much in its praise So that we shall know in the course of a few months whether they will take it or refuse it. I have been very busy in getting it in order and cleaning it ever since I wrote you last so that I have not had time to go to any school nor do I know when I shall for Mr Home and some other Gentlemen are now going to make the Catalogues complete, and some or other always falling in, that it is very inconvenient to be out of the way, – It was but last friday or Saturday that His Royal Highness the Prince of Orange,[1] who was like, or the same as, a King in Holland, called at Mr Home's House and he not being at home they sent a servant with him to me, so that it is very inconvenient to be out of the way. When the Medical Gentlemen were examined about how much they thought it would cost yearly to keep up the Collection in its present state of preservation they reckoned about £200. that was, about 100 for a Person who would devote his time to the care of it and the other hundred for Spirits and other things Mr Home asked me last week whether I thought of going with the Collection or not, (this was when I asked him about going to school for we had agreed before, that I was to go two hours a day after the Collection was cleaned) he said it would be a comfortable situation for somebody and that we should know in a few months how things were to be I told him that I had no objection to go with it but that my reason for going to learn accounts was, that I was not certain of the Situation He said nothing was certain in this world that him or me might die before tomorrow but that as there was no body who had any thing to do with the Collection, knew any thing about it, so well as him and me, he thought I had a better claim to the place than any other, and that he could not see any reason why I might not get it, and that he always was a man to his word, and as he had told me before, he said he would do every thing which lay in his power towards it, but that he thought I had better keep my mind open till we saw what change took place than draw off my attention to any thing else till then. When I wrote to Mrs Gilbert there was no appearance of any alteration which was the reason which made me do it, but now I hardly know what to say to it I went to a Schoolmaster last Saturday and he told me it was a guinea a Quarter, now I should be obliged to go thro all the different rules which I have already gone thro', and a great many more before I should be learnt Merchant accounts, and perhaps before I had been long enough to learn what would be of service to me; this may be settled, & besides I know Mr Home does not wish me to be out of the way when any Gentlemen call at this house, and should I still be desirous of going to the School he may think I do not think enough of his offer, and that I should not wish, as he might not be so ready to serve me in that or any other thing I should be very sorry to put my best friends to any more trouble than I cannot avoid and therefore I think I must trust to kind providence which hath favoured me greatly beyond what I could ever expect, and trust to chance.

I shall be able improve myself in a good many things at home and should this fail I shall not starve though every thing is very dear. I am young and the World is wide. I am to have at the rate of £20 a year while I remain in this place It begun a New Years day and I am to provide myself clothes I have began to recruit a little with the Money I received at Christmas from Mr Home and which I was much in want of.

Dear Sister I believe I told you in my last that I had wrote to Brother Robert at Leghorn &cc. but I have not received any answer as yet. Let me know how you get on, when you write and how all the people in Bodmin are, and *all* enquiring friends, and write me as soon as you can *   */ If you see Mrs Gilbert please to give my duty and return my most gratefull thanks for her kind endeavours which has been so very successfull – and I hope all the People at Priory are very well, please to remember me kindly to Betsy Nicholls when you see her and to all enquiring friends.

and remain your affectionate Brother
William Clift

Late John Hunter's Esq[re]
   13 Castle Street
      Leicester Square
         London.
March 21st 1796
Tuesday Night

Nancy Gilbert of Priory, Bodmin, benefactress of William Clift

67. *Elizabeth to William. 16 April 1796.*

Bodmin

Dear Brother this Comes with my Cind Love to you hoping it will find you in Good health as this Leves me at Preasent I bless the All Mighty for it Dear Brother I receved your welcom Letter a Goodfriday an I am happy to hear that there is some hopes of an alteration wich I hope will be for youre betterment my Dear it has Given me a Great deal of uneaseness to think that your time was Passing a way and you Learning of nothing my Dear it would be Great satisfaction to me if you was settled in some way or other so that you might Geet a Living when you are of from them but my Dear we must trust it all in the hands of the Lord who will due more and better for ous than we Can think or Even desire I saw Mrs Gilbert before I receved your Letter an she told me you was to have £20 a year an two ours of a day to Goe to Practies she told me she had receved a letter from you an she was very much Pleased with it she said she had answered it an she had wrot to one of the Gentel men in troust over Mr hunters affears an she said that they ware not willing to Part with you an she said she was not willing you should leve them a Easterday I was down to Priory an saw her a Gain she was very Glad to hear from you an she said Mr Gilbert an she should alwise be very Glad to heare from you she said she receved a letter Last wick from Mrs Hunter who said she hoped that the Collection would be soon settled I Gave your Duty to Mrs G an returnd her thanks for her Cindness she desird when I did writ to you to Let you know that she should not think it any troubel for you to writ to her she desired if any thing Ley in youre mind or you wished for any altration she hoped you would writ to her an not take any steep without her knoledg an she would all wise be a friend to you Mr and Mrs Gilbert is very well Betty Nichols an all the sirvants Give thir Love to you My Dear Brother when Mrs G told me you was to have £20 a year I had not the Preaseants of mind to ask what you was to have for youre Board for £20 a year will not Provide you meat as Every thing is so very dear wheat was £1-13s a bushal in our market Last Satuarday an Barly 15s an butter 13d a Pound an Beef an mutton 6d an veal an lamb just the same milk 2d a quart I hope you will writ to me soone an Let me know if you are to have youre Board Paid for or not an wether the £20 is to Provide you meat or Clothes or both an let me know Every Particular my Dear I should have wrot to you before now but I have not time to writ nor due any thing for my self the work is so very hard we are Eight of ous in famely an no one to due any thing but but me when she asked me to Come to Live with her she said I should not wash nor due any drugery I should only look after the Children but now I moust Look after the Children an due the work two my year was out yestarday an I due not think to stay a Gain I have three Pound a year an the Gifts I have had 15d an four yards of ribben an a yard an half of lace so I Count it a bout three Pound Eighteen shilings an six Pence the work is hard but the Living is much harder I never lived so hard in my life as I now due we Eat barly Bread that is me an the Children an I have not tasted a Beet of butter since Christmas to my knoledg of theres sister Joanna would have me Come to Leiscard to Live I will writ to you again soon an then I will writ more Particular I have not seen Brother John but once since I wrot to you Last tho he is frequently in town he was in town Last Satuarday an in town to day he was in to Mrs Mendsis a drugist that Lives in Part of our house an he never so much as Came in to see me nor I have not hard from Brother th^os since Joanna is very Cind to me she writes Every upertunity dear Brother you told me in your Last that you wrot to Brother Robert the same day you wrot to me this Eving as I was Going down prison lane John fourd Came to me and asked if I had wrot to you I told him I had a letter in writing to send to you he desired his Cind Love to you an to let you know that all thir branch ware turnd out for to rise ther wadges and that All the Masters in town have Entered in to an artical on stamp Paper not to Give any more wadges an how it will be we Canot tell there is but three Journeymen[2] at work in town four are Goon off to day to Geet work an several more are Going to morrow he desired you would writ to him and Let him know how times are in londoon not that he thinks of Coming to London till next spring nor he due not wish to Leve Bodmin till thin if his Master an he Can a Gree he told me he never would work in Bodmin on Less he hath one an six Pence a Pare fore mens shooes but he said he would not Leve the town till he heares from you Sam Pope him they ust to Ccall Cestell he workes in London he was home to see his mother a bout six wickes Past howe died two days after he Came home he made a Great showe as if he had been a Genteel man he said it was not Posabel a man Could boord him self for Less then 15s a wick he told John foard that if he was to Come to London he Could not Geet so forrid in work as he was for ten Pownd so he said he should be Glad to heare from you to know wether it is so or not he said he Could writ to Pearce or hambly or John Warem to know but they are such whose Company would not a Gree with him so he dus not wish to have any Conversation[3] with them he wishes to hear from you and to have youre advice a bout it he is a very sober Good behaved young man as any in town he is the Cindest to me of any of your acquantences he is not Proud an above speeking but he is all wise Glad to see me an to inquire for you Eesterday Miss Maria Bellringer was Maried to Mr David Lewelling Last Sunday Sally Coping was Marid to a young Gentellman that is a Prentis to Mr Liddel he is a son to the Rev^t Mr A*nna* of St Austell wm hoskin was Maried a Month Past the Master hambly is Childs Maid she Lived there be fore you went away the young thomas Roberts you knew him very well when he worked with Nichlas Sibely at the work house making Ruggs well he now Ceeps his Coach he went to Wales as one of the Round Preacheors Belonging to Mr wesleys an thire he Maried a Ladey of thirty thousand Pound forting he had one Child by her an then she died an son after the Child died an now he is a young man a Gain he now has twelve hundred a yeare he was hoome this spring he has settled thirty Pound ayear on his father an his sister Betsy is maried to the young Nicholas Sibbly he hath Given them a great deal hes sent them fifty Pound at a time he sent his sister so much Cloths that was worth Fifty Pound just be fore he was home that was his wifes an Childs he was down to St Lorance on Sunday to dine at the old Nc Sibblys an he hired Achase to Care his sister for feere she should Geet a Cald John Jefferys wife was tok the friday after the fast with the dead Palsey she did not Live but 24 ours after she was tok John foord disird you would writ as soon as Posabel if you writ to him dont say any thing to him Conserning our selves dear Brother writ me soon as you Can Dear Brother I Conclud with my Love an affection to you youre Ever loving and affectnot Sister Eliz Clift

PS   Friday Night
         Aprill 16 – 1796

*68. Thomas to William. *29* April 1796.*

Southampton April *29*th 96

Dear Brother
                        I have took the oportunity of writing you those few lines hoping it will find you in good healh as I Bless god this leaves me at presant and to let you Know that I am Now in Southampton about a month since All Crafts at Bristol struck for more wages as thare ware aplenty of room as Every thing has Been so Excessive Dear of late most part of the Crafts that were unighted for raising the wages have left the City and I am arived here and I have a very good seat of work But as I have But 75 miles to London I have a great Desire to see you before I Return to Bristol But I have one thing against me that is I have No Cloathes with me But Just my working Dress and a few tools when I left Bristol I intended to return again soon and I thought It useless to Cary a great Burthen of Cloathes as I Knew the trouble and Illconvenienances of Caring heavy Burthens Dear Brother I hope you will grant me the favour of afew lines as soon as you receive this as I Dont Know how long I may stay here as we Expect trade to be Dead this being
                              All at presant I Conclude
                              Your Affectonate Brother
                              Thos Clift

Direct At Mr Swets shoe maker Back of Gloster Square southampton Hants

69. William to Elizabeth. 3 May 1796.

London May 3d 1796

Dear Sister
                        I have taken this opportunity of writing to you, hoping this will find you in good health as this leaves me. I received a Letter from Brother Tho's:/ yesterday. He has left Bristol, he tells me that all the Craft in Bristol struck for more wages and the greatest part had left that City, and he is now at

133

Southampton, 75 Miles from London, in Hampshire; he says he has a good seat of work but that they talk of work being dead there. He says he intended to return to Bristol again soon after he left it but that being so far towards London, he should wish to see me before he returns to Bristol, but that as he did not expect to stay long before he went Back again he only took just his working Dress and his Tools, which he says is the only thing against his coming. Now I have been thinking, that he might as well get work in London as any where else, now he has left Bristol, and that he could come here and get work and then send to Bristol after his Clothes &c and he could Sleep and live with me till he could get a Situation which is more than every one can get that comes to London, and if he should come and settle here I do not think but that we may get you a place in London where you will be certain of getting more wages, living better, and not work so hard and then, Joanna can come next, and then we shall all be together – I say I do not see any thing impossible in it and I have seen far more unlikely things come to pass, but nothing that I think would give me greater happiness/ There are a great many places in London that would be certain to Suit you much better than that you are in at present I have so far built a Castle in the air, and you may pull it down again if you can. I hope I shall hear from you soon and then I shall hear what you say to it. I am afraid Our Collection will fall through, this Session of Parliament which is nearly at a Conclusion I believe, and then nothing can be done till they meet again which will not be till next Spring I suppose, for I do not hear of any thing being done about it at present, and they are wanting more money than they can get to carry on this infernal war, to let us have any, and therefore I do not think any sudden alteration will take place But I do not care so much about it now I am a little better settled, I am very much obliged to you for being so fearfull of my being Starved on £20 a year, but that is only to provide me Clothes, or else I should soon look thin indeed – for money goes but a very little way in this place – I have been laying out all my money on Clothes which I very much wanted and which makes me very poor at present but I shall get round again by next quarter day, I have got a new Suit and a half a Dozen Shirts and some other things which has ran away with nearly Ten Pounds. But one good thing is that I have credit for as much Tea & Sugar, & Bread as I can use, and which is my principal living or else I should be badly off. I shall write to Southampton to morrow if I can, and hear what he says to my castle – Dear Sister I wish you was a little nearer hand & I would sent you some butter, for we can get it as cheap here as in Bodmin I hope the bread is got lower with you as well as here, for it is got down from 15^d to 9¾ the quartern loaf within this short time, and we can get milk here for 2½^d a quart but every thing else remains very dear, I do not eat much meat & yet I can but badly live on 7 Shillings a week but as I do not work hard, and as the Family has no income at present I cannot say any thing about it, – John Ford desired me to let him know what I am very little acquainted with, for I do not keep any acquaintance and I have not seen any person I know, since I saw Wm Tabb which was before Christmas. But I do not think that there are many Journeymen Shoemakers which can afford 15 Shillings for Board However I know this, that in London you can lay out your money to greater advantage than in Bodmin, as you can buy meat ready drest in ever so small quantities and any thing else in the same way Nor do I understand what Sammy Kessel meant by his getting so far forward in work I did not know that it required any money for a man to get work in any place, especially shoemakers, – But I believe all our Town men drink what they do not eat, for I saw a whole parcel of them together a great while ago on a Sunday, who were both shabby & Dirty – they did not see me neither did I wish them. I have nothing particular to write at present but I shall write to Southampton to Brother Thomas, tomorrow. There is a person who is now in Town who used to live at our house in Leicester Square when Mr Hunter was alive, who was Housekeeper there, She lives with a Lady whose Residence is at Southampton and they go down into the Country this day week & I shall get her to call upon him. She is a very Good kind of a woman, and will be somebody for him to speak to, as she knows the place, as she was born in it, and she will likewise be able tell him about London as she lived here many Years. I have wrote to Joanna by this post. I hope you will write me an answer as soon as convenient and let me know all the newest news you can think of. Remember me kindly to all the people at priory and John Ford & his mother as to what prices they give I am utterly a stranger, for making shoes in this place, but I have a very small foot, & I give 6^s6^d a p^r/ for common shoes, – I believe Brother Thomas works upon womens shoes, and I have a Friend who I daresay could get him work * * acquaintance of theirs who carries on a great Trade and he would be able work in the room with the man who makes my shoes I Daresay, as he has not any body working with him now. I shall hear what he says to all these things by the time I write to you again and in the mean time I remain your ever

affectionate Brother
William Clift

When you write to me I will be glad if you will write your Direction as I place it underneath because you put the Cart before the Horse and makes it look foolish, and endeavour to put each line in its place.

William Clift
Late John Hunter's Esqre
N° 13 Castle Street
Leicester Square
London

You always put Castle Street N° 13 instead of 13 Castle Street – Come now dont be afronted for putting you right, but if you are I hope you will be pleased again when I see you.

I hope Willm Hoskin bought a new Wig to be married in I should like to have seen how the Old Queen Dido Cockd her China.[4]

Remember me to Kitty & Ann & Onion & her Mother.

70. *Thomas to William. 29 May 1796.*

Portsmouth May 29th 1796

Dear Brother
            Ive took this upertunity to send you those few lines hoping they will find you in good health as I Bless god this leaves me a presant I left southampton last monday week and am Now at portsea otherwise Portsmouth Common But I Do Not Intend to stay long here Before I see you If the Lord permit I hard since I have Been here that the straight Fleet is Expected home Every week and if I Did think the would arrive hear in the space of 2 or 3 weeks I would stay as I have plenty of work here then I might have the pleasure of seeing Brother Robert as the st george I hear is in that fleet that is Expected Home[5] But whether the Come or Not I hope to see London in the space of a month or thare about you mentiond that I Could sleep with you for a small time and that you Could Derect me to Place to work and that is the upertunity I shall be hapy to Except of as I shall be Hapy to be Nigh you as I shall want no other Company I have a shop mate with me which I call on at Bath and he Intends to Come with me to London but If I Can have your Company I would rather then aney other persons and I Dont Care whare I works If it be a Quiet place and the less Company the better you mentiond that you Did think womens work was the Branch I Did profess But it is a branch that I am Quite a stranger to as I have Not workd on it since I left Bodmin I have hard By them that have workd in London that this is the most Deadest time of the year for trade in london but if trade is scarce I must goe a small way in the Country Mens work is the Branch I profess at presant I Expected Mrs Martin to Call on me at Hampton But I had Not the pleasure of seeing her—

Portsmouth is a very Prosperous place and worth aney persons view—
I shall be glad to have afew lines as soon as Convenient
            this being all at presant
            I Conclude your Affectonate
            Brother Thos Clift

Derect At Mr
Hores Dean Street
N° 1 the town of
Portsea Nigh Portsmouth

136

Liskeard June 12 1796

My Dear Brother

I am happy to inform you that I rec^d your Most Agreeable Letter Likewise to
hear that you Enjoy a good state of health gives me great satisfaction indeed as
there is not a greater blessing the Allmighty god Can bestow upon us then our
health Espesialy as we are at so great a distance one from another and
Perticularly Poor sister betty as My Dear you Know what A sickly state of
health she Enjoyd for some years before you Left Bodmin and to think she has
stood in such A Place as where she Now is at Present Poor soul I often feel for
her and Could wish she^d Leave them as I have done what Lay in My Power for
her she wrote Me she was determined to Leave them when her year was out
and Indeed I so depended on what she told me that I got a Place for her directly
in Liskeard with one Mr and Mrs Chob and I am sure she Could have done
there verry well as they are only M^r and Mr^{rs} and 3 Children and they allways
Keep a Man and two Maids servants the Lady waited a fortnight for an Answer
to My Letter but to no Purpose she did not Come tho I Could wish to My
Heart she would Leave them or I am Much afraid the work she does with such
Bad Living will disenable her of doing in another Place Now If youve not Rec^d
A Letter from Sister since I wrote to you Last I shall be happy to inform you
that she has heard from brother Robert not that she has had A Letter from him
but Mathew Climo sent home a Letter to his wife and Desir^d her to Let us
Know that Robert was very well and that he was then at Fransey Bay[6] his
Letter being dated the 2nd of feburary Last My Dear I,me happy to hear that
brother Thomas is so Nigh London and I hope he does not think of going back
to Bristol untill he has seen you If he Does I shall think it verry unkind of him I
Could wish I were so nigh to London as him tis not Cloaths or any thing Else
should Ceep Me from seeing London not My dear Brother that I have the
Least Ambition or idea of seeing London if you were not there beleieve me My
Dear I would as soon be In the smalest vilage Ive Ever seen as in London for I
only wish to be with you My Dear I hope My Master will Call to see you Before
he returns again as he Promisd he would if Posible time would Permit him he is
gone so far as London with one of my young Mast^{rs} to Put him on board A
Merchantman thats bound to the East Indies Poor Lad he is but twelve years
old I supose theyre in London by this time I beleieve he will sail from
Deptford[7] But I do not Know the name of the ship My Dear I must Now Let
you Know what I think of your Castle I think the discription of it Is
remarkeably Funny but I Must needs say with you that I Can see nothing
imposible in it and since you have begun to build it in the air from this time I
am resolved to do My Best Endeavours to see it finish,d on the/ the Earth as I
Can asure you My Dear thers nothing I Can see or Desire in this world would
give me the Least resemblance of its hapiness as that of our being once More
one with another

My Dear I am happy to Inform you that I have been Inform^d since My
Master has Left Liskeard that our Family is Comming to London and that
Mast^{rs} greatest part of his buissiness is to settle affairs Concerning it now I
know he is in som *B   rth* there that brings him in between two and three
hundred a year M^{rs} told Me som time ago that when M^r was setteld they should
Leave Liskeard and if twas agreeable to me I should go with them not saying
where and if so twou^d Compleat My hapiness so you shall know More of it in
My next

this being all
at Present I remain your
Affectionate Sist^r
Joanna Clift

PS   you desired to Know what was become of betty yeo she,s still In bodmin
she has been Living with Mr tho^s Stone for som time but she Is off from them
now Sist^r told me in her Last that she said she was Coming to Liskeard but Ive
not seen her as yet

Jack williams daughter betty Came to Liskeard with Me where she work,d at
the woolen buisiness for some time till at Last she Turns out very Bad indeed
she is Just now gone home verry Large with Child. She has sworn one Mr
Andrews Father but she was Common to Evry one I suppose youve heard of
*   *irgin Mary Bests havin a Child

Adieu

72. Robert to William. 7 April 1796.

Saint Fiorenza Corsica April 7th 1796

Dear Brother

This Come with my kind Love to you hoping it will find you in good health as
it leaves me at preasent thanks be to god for it i have taken the Opportunity of
Sending this by the 3^d Lieutenant of our Ship who is going home i should have
sent to you sooner but no Opportunity has offered since as we have not been at
Leghorn i receivd your letter the 12th of Febuary dated the 3d of January and
was verry glad to hear from you You wondered the reason that you did not
receive the Letter before i sent it home in the Sincure[8] and she was taken by the
French and carried into Cadiz a Port in spain and sent from there home i have
no Opportunity of seeing Richard Levers since i Receivd your Letter please to
acquaint Walter Craps Mother that i have not seen him since i saw him at
Torpoint Mathew Climo is on Board the Bombay Castle and desires to be
Remembred to all enquiring Friends give my kind and affectionate love to my

Brothers and Sisters and let them know that i am well and in good health please
to acquaint Mrs Addams that Lieutenant Fortune left the Saint George and is
Gone on board the Britannia about a fortnight before i receivd your Letter
and have not had an Opportunity of seeing him since So no more at
Preasent

from your Loving Brother Robt Clift

73. *William to Elizabeth. 25/6 July 1796.*

Monday July 25th or 6th 1796

Dear Sister

   I suppose you have received a letter by this time which I sent by Mrs
Hunter. I received a letter from brother Robert last Saturday week dated St
Fiorenza, Corsica, April 7th 1796 and saying that he is very well, he says he
should have sent sooner but that he had not an opportunity of Sending till now
by a 3d Lieutenant who put it in the Post office at Portsmouth he got my letter
dated 3d January, on the 12th of february. He says the reason that you did not
get his last letter for so many months after it was wrote, was by the ship being
taken by the french which was to bring the letters, and the ship was taken into
a Spanish Port and the letters sent from there home He has not had an
opportunity of Seeing Richard Leavers since, nor Walter Crap since he saw him
at Torpoint. Mathew Climo is onboard the Bombay Castle & desires to be
remembered to all enquiring friends Brother Robert desires his kind love to
you all but does not say any thing about coming home, he says they have left
Leghorn but does not tell the reason, perhaps he did not know that the french
have got it,[9] because the Sailors & Soldiers are not let know of the great french
Victories unless they are at the engagements, that they may not lose heart, and
as four fifths of them are not able read, and if they could they are not allowed,
they are kept ignorant of what is going on. I have hardly had time to write to
him since I got his letter having had to go to enquire at several places for
people that have friends onboard the same ship. Besides I have had all my
leisure time taken up by going about with Brother Thomas who is arrived here
at last, he came here last Tuesday or wednesday and a Shopmate of his at Bristol
came with him so they lodge together not a great way from our house he is
very well and desires his kind love to you. He has not got any work as yet but
has been making me a pair and other odd things. Work is rather dead for a
month or so, till the gentry begin to come into Town again. I thought he used
to be so big that I should never overtake him in growing, but I suppose I am
the biggest in the family now for my Coat is full large for a great coat for him. I
have nothing more particular to write at Present but I shall write to Brother
Robert either to day or tomorrow I have not heard any thing from Brother

John since he got well as he promised you, nor for a few years before he was taken ill, but it is no matter, it saves me the Postage I wish you would write me soon and let me know how you are all going on. I saw John Warem last week, and he desired to be remembered to you he has been in work ever since he came here but I never saw him before. Harriet Jeffery or Stokes is living in Portsmouth, and Mr Jack Hocking the Staymaker is living there with his wife or washerwoman or what you please to call her, he keeps a fine shop full of stays on one side & I think his wife the other window full of Bonnets &cc she is a mantua maker[10] but whether it is that one that lived with him in this place or no I cannot tell If his wife in Bodmin does not know where to find him I can get her the directions to him but I forgot to ask Brother Thomas when I saw him last. Harriet is just such a wild devil as she used to be she went into Jack Hawkings shop one day on pretence of looking at a bonnet or something or other and asked for Jackey Hocking as she called him, so he came into the Shop for Ma'am had called him out to her so harriet says, Lord Jackey Hawking how d'ye do; when did ye hear from your wife in Bodmin He did not stay to say a word to her but Ma'am and him both were nicely put to the blush and went out of the Shop, and so did harriet because she only went on purpose for the sake of the Joke Billy Butler is living in Portsmouth I am going on here as usual and am very well Please to remember me to all enquiring friends. Let me know what is become of W Roberts & family I hear Kate Drews husband is in the cornish Milittia I was told that they were coming to London to be reviewed in Hyde Park before the king I do not know whether it is so or no. They are somewhere in this quarter of the world now about 30 miles from London. Be so good as write soon and then I'll remain

your affectionate Brother
William Clift

74. Elizabeth to William. 5 September 1796.[11]

My Dear Brother
I have once more took an oppurtunity of writing a few lines to you hoping it will find you and my Brother thos in Good health as this leves me at Preasent I Bless the Lord for it my dear Brother you moust think me very on Cind in not writing to you before as I have recived three Letters from you an I have not answeard nether one for I Could not have time to writ whilst I was in Bodmin I left Bodmin the 8 of august and I am now at Linkinghorn with the Rev^rd Mr Coffin we are 9 in famely an they Ceep But one maid an a man servant heare is five Children so I have not Changed for a Easear Place of work But much Better Living Mrs Barron Got me the Place Before I knew any thing of it she was at Lanceston some time before an she desird of Mrs tithe if she knew of a

good Place she would Geet one for me for she did not wish for me to stay wheire I was so she Goot me this and sent to Mrs Barron for me to Come as soon as Posabel I was to fix the day an they would Come to Cap^r Broads to fetch me an I knew nothing of it till the Letter Came an Mrs Barron Came up to Mrs Mendes is and sent for me an told me she had Goot a Place for me an desird I would tack my self of an Goe I did not know what it was best to due nor how to Geet off for Mrs Eyre had Goot Child But four days an she was very Bad her Breast Brook twice so I could not say any thing to her till she Goot Better then I told her the work was to hard for me an I desird she would Geet some Boddey be fore the sizes I said as I did not think to stay any Longer I did not wish to take the Preivlidg but she said she should not Geet any one till she was abel to Come down stars an Lok after the house her self and the Gifts I was welcom to for she should not trust her house with strangers so I staid seven wickes an Mrs Coffin waited all that while we Parted in very Good friends she desird when I Came a way that if I Came home while she was in the town I would Come there an sleep an tak it for my home I came to five Lanes[12] in the Coach tho I was not to Come any farther then Cap^r Broads the man was waiting thir for me but the driver would not stoop thir and drove as hard as Ever he Could so the man did not know where I was in the Coach or not so he waited ther till it was all most night an I at five Lanes freetting finly if I Could have Goot a hors I should but I Could not so I did not know what to due it was Eight miles an I did not know the way nor no Person when I Came there just as it was dark the man was Come to see if I was ther I was very Glad I ashoure you it is very wisht[13] it was on moneday night I Came thir and the thursday morning Mrs Coffin Cald me up stairs to her an she said she thought I should due very well an she hoped I would not Leve her an this one of the Girls said she hoped I should stay with them as Long as I did Live for Mother did Like me very well if I did Like them I should not Like half so well if it was not for that they are a very Good Living Peopel.[14] Mr Coffin is one of the finest Chourch men you Ever hard we have Prayers Morning an Eving in our family and wensday Evings we have a Publick Meetting in our Parlour if it was not for that I should not stay it is the wishtes Place you Ever saw the vickerig hous is all most a mile from the Church dear Brother I am very happy to hear that Brother thos is with you and Likewise to hear from our dear Brother Robert how thankfull should we be to the Lord for Preserving him in the midst of so many dangers my dear I often meditate on the Goodness of the Lord to wards ous all to think that we are speared an Preserved in health and saftey whilst thousands Cut down sister Joanna is Goon to Plymouth to Live she went thir the thursday after I Came hear so our man brought me word a satuarday he was at Leiscard market and I desird him to Call on her so if you have hard from her let me know where to writ to her as she due not know where I am nor I due not know where to writ to her I saw Brother John the wick before I Came away he was very well I was at Priory the day before I Came a way I did not see Mrs

Gilbert but they ware all very well Mrs Hunter an they ware Going to the west
the next wick Joan told me they had been to see Roachrock[15] Jack williames
had a Letter from tommy the same time you receved our dear Brothers Letter
he was then at Gibaltar he gives his Cind Love to his dear friend thomas Clift
dear Brother writ me as soon as Conveant and Lett me know if you have
seen our dear Cousens James an william Puckey I wrot a letter to them by
there dear mothers derection that they might find you

Dear Brother you moust derect for me at the Rev^d Mr Coffins Linkinhorn
to be Left at Lanceston Post office till Cald for as that is our Markit it is Eight
miles from hear Dear Brother Give my Cind love to Brother thomas an ask
him the reason he never writs to me

this being all at Preasent from your
Ever Loving and affectnot Sister
Eliz Clift

75. Joanna to William. 19 September 1796.

Plymouth Sep^{tr} ye 19th 96

My Dear Brother
this being the first opportunity of which I am happy to imbrace to inform you
of my arival at Plymouth where I never form,d the Least thot of Comming the
Last time I wrote to you as my M^r was then at London when at his return I find
Every thing did not answer his Expectations for which I was realy sorry for as I
did not wish to Leave them as I had Lived with them Just a year and half; and
five Months of that time I were the only servant but I allways thot they meant
to Keep another untill the time us parted as I told them I were more Like a
slave then a servant us were 12 in family and my M^{rs} verry Large with Child
again and My wages was only 3 guinas a year which made me verry uneasy
indeed tho at the Last they were verry unwilling to part with me or Even that I
should Leave the Town and desird I would stay with them untill I had got a
Place but as I thot to get better wages then they give in Liskard I told My M^{rs} I
meant to go to Plymouth so after a while she told me If I were determined to
go to Plym^{ot} she knew they wanted a Childs maid at her Brothers and If I had
no obgection against going there she would send Mrs Lyne a Letter of
recommendation so I returnd her thanks and Excepted the offer I Came of the
9 day of Last Month I Left them on friday the Sunday following My M^{rs} desird
me to Come in townd as she Expected a Large Company to Drink tea and
desir,d I would Lend my asistance in tending them which I readly did as she
behaved Exceeding kind to me Indeed in Every respect so she told me she had
wrote the Letter for me to take to Plym^{ot} with me but If I,de stay in Liskrd there
was not a better Place in the town then she had got for me and that I was to say
that Evening whither I would Come or not according I did say I Could not

Come for my Mind was so intent on going to Plym^{or} that I Could not think of staying is Liskard where I now am and hope I shall have a verry good Place

time will Permit mit me to say no more
at Present only that I am
your affectionate Sis^{tr}
Joanna Clift

you will Please to give my Love to Brother Thos and write to me as soon as Posible as I Long to hear from you both

Direct for me at Mr *J* Lynes In new Church Lane Plymouth

76. William to Elizabeth. 26 September 1796.

Dear Sister
        I should have wrote before but I wished as well as yourself to know first what Joanna was about I received a letter from her last Saturday and she says the reason of her leaving her place in Lisk^d/ was that for five months past they had kept no other servant but her & till Mr Hawke came back from London where things did not turn out as he expected, she always thought they meant to keep two because they were twelve in family and she had only 3 guineas a year She says they were very unwilling she should leave them but that she was so entirely a slave that she thought she could not be worse off by a change Her mistress desired her to stay with them till she got another place in Liskeard & that she would try to get one for her, but Joanna said she was resolved to go to Plymouth where she might get more wages than she could expect in Liskeard so Mrs Hawke said then if she was resolved to go to Plym^{th} she had a Brother who she said wanted a childs maid & if she liked would write to Mrs Lyons and give Joanna a letter of recommendation with her when she went, which she readily accepted She left them the 9th of last month and that they parted very good friends She says she hopes she shall have a very good place where she is which is all she says about it and says Direct for me at Mr Lyons in New Church Lane Plymouth – this is very nearly all her letter I shall write to her either to day or tomorrow & let her know where to write to you.
        I hear Mrs Hunter is returned from Cornwall but I have not seen her yet I am still here and still like to be for some time to come as we hear of no alteration and I am very well in health, as is Brother Thomas who desires his kind love to you.
        I had almost forgot our dear Cousins from Fowey as you call them they called upon me the day after they received your letter and such two pitifull

143

downlooking fantastical fanatical ragged dirty hungry religious rascals I never saw in my days;[16] they told me they were going out in the mission Ship to Otaheite to preach the gospel of their Lord & master/ Now I know you will dislike this way of reasoning but I cant help it I do assure you that I do not know any thing under heaven that would give me more real pleasure than to hear they never reached Otaheite. I know their drift too well; one can see by their looks which would be enough to hang them in any court of Justice that they had rather do any thing than work and with their pretended religion which they call "divine illumination" will introduce among the harmless people which they are going among every vice which it is possible for human nature to commit It has always been the case and it always will be. What can be expected from such stupid raw country blockheads; boys who I'd lay a 12 months wages cannot read a chapter in the Bible as it ought to be – but any thing is good enough for a Preacher or else so many who are not able read at all would not get a living by it – But it is greatly to be hoped and wished that we shall have a reform in the Church as well as in other matters in the course of a few years There is a young fellow gone out in the same ship as a Minister of Grace who has scarcely left any crime unperpetrated; but as Bags of Bristol calls it he is recalled into the fold It is by seeing Religion thus made the Tool and Cloak of Knaves & fools that most people are brought to think so slightly of that religion which is good & true. And I verily believe that the man who shows the greatest appearances of religion is the man who ought to be most narrowly watched and I had rather deal with a man who is esteemed a rogue or rascal by all the world than with a man who pretends to much religion for in dealing with a rogue a man is upon his guard when he has any thing to do with him but with the other you are taken unawares I need not tell you all this as you have seen more of it in certain families than I could be expected to see and as I suppose you are as weary of the subject as myself I drop it. But the more I think on them, the worse I think of them.

I had nothing particular to write only I thought you would expect I should write something and as I suppose this is already too long I shall (probably) not make my next epistle so long and at
present I remain your ever affectionate
Brother till death
William Clift

13 Castle Street Leicester Square
London
Sept[r] 26th 1796.

I shall expect to hear from you soon and let me know all the news you can think of that is worth sending. W.C.

I have not heard any thing of Brother Robert since I wrote last.

77. William to Joanna. 9 October 1796.

London October 9th 1796

Dear Sister

      I received yours and should have answered it long before, but I have had a good deal of writing to do for Mr Home for this week or two and Mrs Hunter is returnd from Cornwall and I have been a good deal employed by her ever since I received yours. I received a letter from Sister Betty about a fortnight before I received yours and she told me that she had left Bodmin and was now in a place at Linkinhorn; it is not a great way from Lanceston as that is the Market Town – she said their man was at Liskeard the week before she wrote to me and she desired him to call to enquire for you but they told him you was gone to Plymouth – so I waited to hear from you before I answer'd her Letter as she wished to know very much what you was doing – so perhaps you have heard from her before this, as I sent her your direction If you have not heard from her & wish to write to her, her address is Eliz[th] Clift at the Rev[d] Mr Coffins, Linkinhorn to be left at the Post office Lanceston till called for. they send once a week – that is – the market day to the Post office. She says she has not got an easier place by the change but that they live much better – Mrs Barron got her the place before she knew she was looking for one for her so they had to wait several weeks before she could leave Mrs Eyre who was laying in. She is quite in her Sphere where she is, though the Master is a Church-man, for they have prayers every night in the Family and a Meeting in OUR parlour every wednesday Evening If it was not for this I dont think I should stay long because the work is very hard. being 12 in family and only her and one manservant.

      I do not know whether I told you that Brother Thomas is in London or not – that is whether I have wrote you since or no he desires his kind Love to you.

      I saw our dearly beloved Cousins in the faith J. & W Puckey who are gone off to Otaheite near Botany Bay 12 thousand miles off as methodist preachers to convert the Blackamoors Perhaps this is news to you – if not hang the Crier.[17] Religion is come to a fine pass when such blockheaded country Boys turn ministers – But if rags & downlooking humiliation be religion – they have it. I never saw such a pair of sanctified rogues in my days. Brother Thomas told me that when he was at Portsmouth just before he came here & Harriet Jeffery told him she heard they were going some where as methodist preachers but I did not believe it 'till they told me so. There is a fine Posse of them gone off; about Seventy preachers most of them young hearty rascals who would rather do any thing than work – when they called upon me I shew'd them to Brother Tho[s]'s Room where he was at work. He asked them what they were going to do there – that is, what work they were going to do and what kind, to hear what they said – James who was spokesman very gravely said We are not going there to work but to fight the Battles of our heavenly master – So they intend the poor negros shall maintain them a whole ship Load of them too, for preaching to them & teach them to be unhappy like themselves for it is no wonder if one half of them hang themselves or drown themselves before they get there, through despair, as the smart Tom Pinch *   *

I hope you intend to send me some more Plymouth news than you did in your last, the next time you write Let me know what is become of E. Yeo if you can – I hear her old Beau[18] is going on as usual at Pencarrow – Tell me what is become of Rose Butler as I know you & her were old Cronies and all the news you can think of and I'll mend my Pen against I answer your next. but with this Ill remain

till I hear from you, your loving & affectionate
Brother
William Clift

You might have had the good
manners to write your Directions
plainer & have sent the number.

NOTES SECTION VII

1. The history of the House of Orange, the hereditary governors of the small principality of Orange, which was assigned to France after the peace of Utrecht in 1713, is long, confusing and interesting. For full details the reader should consult the usual sources. Its history impinged upon British life with the accession of William III (William III of Orange) and Mary at the 'Glorious Revolution' of 1688. By 1796 the title was nominal only and Clift overstates it importance. He is referring to William V of Orange, whose son, William VI, became William I, King of the Netherlands in 1815.
2. *Journeymen* has been superimposed on a word, now indecipherable, probably by Clift.
3. Written above, probably by Clift, is *orrespondence*.
4. *the Old Queen Dido cocked her China:* This has the ring of a proverbial-type saying but no record of it has been found. *China* is Cockney rhyming slang for 'mate' from the full form *china plate*. Is it possible that *Queen Dido* should be *Queen Dinah*? This term means 'best girl' or 'sweetheart' in London slang. *Cotch'd* or *cotcht* was a dialectal or vulgar form of the past tense of the verb *catch* and it is possible that Clift misheard this as *cocked*. One can imagine Cockney street urchins following a wedding party, chanting, 'Old Queen Dinah/ Cotcht her China' and that Clift may have heard this. It could be another instance of his possible showing off to his

provincial sister. If this is a correct guess, why he substituted *Dido* for *Dinah* is a puzzle. Perhaps he again misheard the word, or his educational aspirations led him to insert the classical name of a real Queen. According to K.C. Phillips, *West Country Words and Ways* (Newton Abbot, 1976), pp. 41–42, it has been suggested that the queen is referred to in the Cornish phrase 'kicking up a dido'. This seems unlikely but it could be where Clift got the word from. It is at least interesting to speculate that this is a hitherto unrecorded street rhyme.

5. The *St George* was in the Mediterranean Fleet. Is this another name for the Strait Fleet?

6. *Fransey Bay:* St Fiorenzo, Corsica.

7. *Deptford* has been heavily written over and one letter obliterated.

8. *Sincure:* the *Censeur*, 74 guns, which had been captured from the French off Genoa by the Mediterranean Fleet under Vice-Admiral Sir William Hotham in March 1795, but, as Robert records, was recaptured by the French on its voyage to England.

9. The Mediterranean Fleet left Leghorn after the French retook the port on 27 June 1795.

10. *mantua maker:* a maker of mantuas, long loose gowns worn by women in the 17th and 18th centuries. The word is a corruption of French *manteau* probably by association with the place name *Mantua*.

11. The date is taken from the postmark.

12. *five Lanes:* at Altarnun, Cornwall.

13. *wisht:* S.W. dialect, meaning 'dreary, dismal, melancholy, wretched', according to the *OED*.

14. The punctuation has probably been added by Clift.

15. *Roachrock:* a famous rock about 100 ft high at the village of Roche, a few miles south west of Bodmin. It has the remains of a hermit's chapel on the summit.

16. The Puckey brothers, James and William, were amongst 30 missionaries who sailed for New Zealand and the South Seas in the *Duff* on 10 August 1796. The project was sponsored by the London Missionary Society, which had recently been founded by the Independent and Anglican Churches. The eulogistic public records of the Society contrast strangely with Clift's caustic comments.

17. *hang the Crier:* the second part of the saying 'Roper's news' – 'if not hang the crier'. *Roper's news* is no news. See Section III n.6 and Section IV n.2. Presumably, if you have not already heard it, the *Crier* (Town Crier?) should be hanged for not doing his job properly.

18. Presumably John Clift.

VIII. JANUARY TO DECEMBER 1797.

By 1797 a coolness and even at times a certain feeling of uncomprehending resentment seems to have arisen between William and his sisters and brother John in Cornwall. This was perhaps inevitable. To keep up a close correspondence for over five years and at such a distance is no easy task, and William had by this time moved into a completely different world. Although he had largely educated and improved himself by his own efforts – he tells John that he had had no drawing master and certainly his formal instruction since Hunter died had been spasmodic – he had acquired the attitudes and manners of cultivated London society from such people as Home, Baillie, and the Hunter family, with whom he was still in close contact. He scarcely seems to be talking the same language as Elizabeth, especially when it comes to matters of religion, and it is not surprising that he accuses her of misunderstanding him. The dispute over the worthiness of the Puckey brothers continues altogether over the space of eighteen months, followed by a silence of over a year. Although specific in origin, the larger issues the quarrel raises are indicative of the gulf which now lay between them, both socially and culturally. Unfortunately, one of Elizabeth's letters, written in November of this year, has disappeared but one can guess its drift from others which survive. Joanna joins in the quarrel on her sister's side and in this atmosphere writing becomes strained. John, with whom William had never been on very close terms, does not take part in the dispute but he too clearly feels that relations between himself and his brother are not as cordial as he would like. Beneath the surface one senses a desire to get back on a friendly footing but unfortunately each writer is anxious to have the last word and the 'paper war', as William later describes it, continues.

Meanwhile the writers do not neglect to pass on any news which may be of interest and most important is that concerning Robert, from whom Elizabeth receives two letters in this year. The second contains the information that he is at last sailing for England and hopes to arrive shortly at Spithead. Two characters who have figured in earlier letters now turn up in the navy. Robert Haynes, previously employed by John Hunter, is a surgeon's mate on board the *Zealous* and is able to give William news of Robert when he comes home from Lisbon. William also comes across Thomas Williams, the young man involved in the brothel in Bristol. That he left Bristol after his release from prison and joined the navy is recorded in an earlier letter. Now he appears in London, having been wounded in an engagement with a French frigate and discharged from service. He has been granted a pension but is preparing to sail again as a ship's cook. By a coincidence Elizabeth mentions him in her letter of June in order to underline her grievance at her brother's neglect of her.

The Clift family themselves are more settled on the whole during this year. Joanna is still at Plymouth, although she complains that it does not suit her

148

health. John has succeeded to the position held by Mr Tabb (not the William Tabb employed by the Gilberts) and is now presumably, foreman in charge of the Pencarrow estates in Cornwall. Elizabeth is the only one who has moved and she has rather surprisingly gone to Penzance where she is working in the house of an attorney. William writes to John (only the draft survives) that he is fairly confident of going with the Collection when it is sold, although he sees little likelihood of that taking place until a peace with France is concluded. However, there are rumours of peace and a hopeful spirit in the air. Of the various members of the family, Thomas alone remains a shadowy figure in the background. No more of his letters after his arrival in London have come to light and news of his activities is henceforth confined to comments made by the other writers, who refer to his doings surprisingly little.

78. Robert to Elizabeth. 23 February 1797.[1]

St George Febr^y 23rd Lisbon 1797

Dear Sister I Know take the Oppertunity of riting these/ Few lines to you, Hoping the will find you in Good Health,/ as I am at Present thanks be to God for it, we sail^d/ From Florenzy the 2nd of Novemb^r last and/ Arrive^d at Gibraltar the first of the Ensuing month/ During our stay *At* Gibraltar we Had some Heavy/ Gales of wind in somuch that the Cougeraux[2] was/ Oblige^d to Put to sea and unfortunately was drove/ On shore on the Coast of affrica, which I am sory to/ Inform y^u that there Has Been But Very few of the/ Ships Crew saiv^d Be Plaised to acquaint Mrs livers/ That I Have made all the Enquiry that Possible/ Laid in my Power about Her son richard and Can=/=Not Get No Intelligience of Him, we left Gibraltar/ On the 18th & ariv^d att Lisbon the 22nd of Decb^r/ In Coming over the Barr of the said mentiond Port/ The Bombay Castle of 74 Guns run a shore/ and was lost But thanks Be to God the ship/ Crew was Sav^d Mathew Climo Belong^d to/ The Bombay But what ship He Belongs to Now/ I Cannot Inform you at Present The ships Company Being Distribute^d amoung the fleet We ref=/=ited oure shiping and the fleet Put to sea In order to Cruise/ off the Spanish Coast^s But In Going oute over the Barr/ we run a shore & lay 2 Days & 2 Nights and with a dale/ of trouble & the Healp of the st aulbins[3] of 64 Guns/ We Got off and Now up in the Harbour repairing oure/ Damage^s & with God^s Healp I Hope that In/ Less than two months we shall arive to England Further/ more I Have to Inform you that oure fleet under the Comman^d/ of admr[1] Jarvis Has fell In with the spanish/ Fleet & Had a Heavy Ingaugment[4] & Have Sunk taken & Burnt six Sail of the line which I Hope will Be a great means of Puting an End to the/ warr Dear Sister this is all I have at Present to/ relate to you Only Be Pleas^d to remember me/ To my Brothers & Sister and Give me Every Particu/=lar

Concerning them So Nomore att Present/ From your Ever loving Brother
Untill Death

Robert Clift

P,S, Be Pleas^d to Direct for me on Board H,M,S, the st George at lisbon
PortinGel[5] with all speed

79. Elizabeth to Robert. 8 March 1797.[6]

Penzance

the
March 8 1797

Dear Brother this Comes with my Cind Love to you and to Let you that I am
quit happy to find by your Cind and welcom Letter that the Lord hath still
Preserved and Procted you in the midst of so many dangers dear Brother I
receved a Letter from a young man[7] dated Febuary the 7 howe [who] said he
saw you the 18 of December at Gebelhalter he said you was very well an you
told him you had had a Letter From ous he said he had not much talk with you
for you was Cald away while you an he was to Geather he be Longed to the
allowence[8] his M[9] ship she is at Portsmouth she is feeting out to Goe up the
strits[10] again I was very happy then to hear from you an to hear you was still
Preserved but much more so to have a Letter from youre own hand an since
this Engagemet an to hear from you that you are Comin home to England the
Lord Grant if it be his heaveanly will you may come home at the Expected time
as I hope you will Come to Plymouth an then you will I hope have the
happyniss to see sister Joanna she is Living at Plymouth New Church Lane
with one Mr Lyne and I am very searting that thir is nothing in this Life will
Give her more real joy than to see you I had a Letter from her January the first
she was then very well she said she had thin been ther 4 mounthes but Could
not Geet any a Count whire you was an she desired if I should I would Let her
know so I have sent to her my Dear Brother I have Left Bodmin some time
when first I Left it I *went* up to Linkinhorn wich is 8 miles from Lanceston
to Live with the Reverent Mr Coffin but that Place did not a Gree with miy
health I was home but two days before I Came heare I was at Mr Barrons when
Mr Paynter wich is my Master Came ther his wife is asister to Mrs Barron they
wanted amaid so I Cam a way with him I did not know of Coming not one our
be fore I Came a way I thank God for it that have my heath much better since I
Came heair then I have fore years Past I Like Penzan very well if it was not so
fare from all my Brothers an sister it is such an out away Place an such a
distance from home that I dont think I shall Live heair 7 yeares[11] fore I Canot
Expect to see you or any of my Brothers or sister whilst I am heair my Dear
Brother I hope you will writ to me as soon as you arive in England Brother
william is in London still at the same Place at the Late John Hunters Esqu^r N^o

13 Castel Street Leicester Square an Brother Thomas is in London two he went ther in August Last he is nigh Brother william they are alwis inquiring after you they will be very happy when I writ to heare from you an more so if they Could see you Brother John is at Pencarrow still I have not seen him nor hard from him since I first Left Bodmin only by sister she informed me that Mr Tabb[12] is diad an that Brother John has Goot his Place I Could wish him to tacke Care of his Place now he is in him or Elst it would be better he had never had it Mr Pinchs famely was All very well when I was home I belive I told you that Polly was married to the young fisher he was in Prison when I was home And she hath Goot two Children an betty is Going to be maried to a friench man Cittey Climo an Thomas williamson is in the Cornish milita they are some where nigh London joseph hick is Living here an his famly to day I saw the young henery I did not know him he is very tawl he asked for you very Cindly and the young william wardling is Living in Penzance but I have not seen him since I Came heire I Cam heare the 14 of Jan^{ry} my deair brother I receved youre Letter the 6 of this Instant so I Conclud with my Prayers to God for your health and Prosperity and a safe an speedy return if it be the will of our god who hath Ceept an Preserved you this fare who I trust will never leve you nor forsack you but in his tender mercy will bring you back to your native land once more whire I trust we shall meet and see another with Joy after so many years seperations is the Constant Prayers of your Ever Loving and Affectnot sister till death

Eliz Clift

derict for me at Mr Paynters Penzance Eturney at lawe

80. *Joanna to William. 27 March 1797.*

Plymouth 27th of March 97

Dear Brother

I am happy to imbrace this opportunity of writing to you and I hope twill find you and brother Thomas in good health as I bless god this Leaves me Much better Then I have bin for some time past an I think Plym,t does not agree so well with My health as Liskard I have bin verry ill Indeed and obledgd to have the doctor twice since I have been at Plymo^t I have been so ill this time that I have been obledg to Ceep my Bed for Just a week tho I blless god I am quite recoverd to My health again My Dr Brother I am happy to inform you that I have heard from brother Robert by Thomas Teague[13] on board the alliance who Enquired him out when he was at giberalter which was no Longer since then the 18th of Last december he was then in Perfect health and said he hoped they should return to England soon he is still on board the St george My D^r

151

Brother I am grieved to think how we are seperated one from another I Could wish it were posible we Could meet once More in this world which I fear we never shall yet I hope wee shall Meet with greater Hapiness in the world to Come My dear Let me hear from you soon and Let me know if you have heard from Poor Sist^r Elizth who I were greatly surpized to hear of her being at Penzance tho I hope god allmighty orders Every thing for us according to his own will it [   ]^{14} to Let you know that Brother John Came to see me about a month since he was in verry good health and told me he should write to you soon

My Dr Brother write to me soon as I Long to hear from you and Let me know how you are situated at Present and wheither things are answerable to your former Expectations or not I mean as to your drawing and whither your M^r and M^{rs15} does for you as they usd to in bringing you on in your Buisness and Let Me know how Long you have got to serve of your time

this being all at Present
I Conclude your
Ever Affectionate Sist^r
Joanna Clift

you will Please to give My Kind Love to Brother Tho,s and Let me know how he is

you will Pleas to direct for me at Mr Lynes in New Church Lane our house is not numberd

81. Elizabeth to William. 24 June 1797.[16]

Penzance   June 24 97

                                                            this Comes from your unworthy
Dear Brother   sister Eliz Clift[17]
I have now tuck this upurtunity[18] of writing you a few lines hoping you will answer this and let me know what or whrein I have offended you I must Intreet you will deal Plainly an let me know for I did not think once to have bin slited so by you I should sooner thought all the world to have deserted me then you I have receved but one letter from you since may 96 an that I Could hardly Call one that was Septr 26th you said you had nothing Particular to writ only you thought I should Expect you to writ somthing you said you was in Good health as also was Brother Thomas who desird his love to me wich was all you wrot Except abusing them that I Esteem let them be what they will they behaved more like brothers to me and you then some I Could menchon they did not treat you nor me so when we ware at thir Fathers house[19] if you did not like thir Profshion nor thir going a broad you should have treated them as they treated you when you was at thir Fathers house and that was with the Greatest

sevility and Cindness I should have thought you would have shoon some
respect to them as being related to you by your once tender mother had they
bin in Newgate[20] I would have Goon to them and treated them as Brothers for
they was to me as such not long before I left Bodmin I was very Poorly I had a
very bad hand they sent the Poast man to see me and sent me mony by him and
desird if I wanted any thing I would let them know and I should have it that
was more then my own Brother did that was so nigh me he did not Come to see
me nor sent to ask for me and as for Brother Thomas he did not treat Thomas
williams so when he Goot him self in to troubel by Ceeping bad Company[21]
but they that seek the Lord shall be Persecuted even with them of thir own
houshold I make no doubte but I should be treated Just the same if I was to
Come to london for I think if Brother Thomas had any regard for his Brothers
or sisters he *sh   ely*[22] would have wrot to them in so many years I wrot to
him till I was tired and receved no answer an now I have bin in Penzance Ever
since the 14th of Jan^{ry} an never hard from Brother John nor nether of you wich
makes me writ this scrawl with tears to think how much I am slighted by you all
tho Undeserved I have done what Ever ley in my Power for you all since our
Father and mother died and wish it had bin in my Power to have done more for
you all I should have bin happy to have done it.[23] I littel thougth once to writ
to you an receve no answer this Brings to my mind what a Gentell man said to
me just after you went a way he said if you was to meet me in the sreet in seven
years time you would not speak to me I did not think it then to be true what he
said, I thought you was to Good natured Ever to forgeet me as you often youst
to say you never would be like Broher John you alyse wrot an behaved like a
Brother before Brother Thomas Came to london an what is the reason you due
not now I Canot think I never due any thing to him or you to hinder you from
writing to me Except it was to recomend James an william Puckey to you and I
did not think it any Crime as they had a desire to see you before they left
England as to thir dirtyness or rages[24] I know nothing of for the last time I saw
them they ware drest as well as any trades men in the town but if they are Gone
out in the feare of the Lord an alwise Ceep the End in view as I trust they ar it
maters nothing what they have on wether they are in rages or in silks if they
have Christ they have all Lazras on the dung hill was better in the sight of the
Lord then the rich man in all his Pomp and Grandyear[25] the lord of his tender
mercy Grant that you and I with all them that are near and dear to ous in the
ties of nature may be found of him in the last when he shall Come to make up
his jewels, o that we may be of that happy Number home[26] he shall say Come ye
blesed inherit the Cindom that was Prepard for you be fore the foundations[27]
then we shall not Care what men hath said of ous or what name we have Gone
by, the unsertinty of life shews ous daily that we have no Contunience hear and
that this is not our rest thire fore we ought to seek a place of reast when this
veain world shall be no more the lord Grant that tho we are seperated one fare
from another that we may meet in the realmes above whare true joyes shall

never seace and we shall meet to Part no more is the Constant Prayer of youre onworthy sister as for my Part I have greater reason then all the world be sides to be thank full to the lord for his Goodness to wards me I bless the lord I have Enjoyd my healh better since I have bin hear then I have for years Past I/ I had not a months health out of the five I was at Linkinhorn wich made me leve the Place I was home but two days be fore I Came heare wich was reason of Great thakfulness but what is more our dear Brother Robert is still Preserved in the midst of so many Dangers as he hath bin Exposed to I receved a letter from him in March he was then in Lisbon he said they hoped to be in England in less than two monthes he is still on Bord the St George he is in Admr[1] Jarvis is fleet he said they saild from Florenzy[28] the 2 of November last and arived at Gilbraltar the first Decm[br] during thir stay thir they had several very hevy Gales of wind in so much that the Courageux was forsed to Put to sea and unfortnatly was drove on shore on the Cost of affrica wich ime sorry to inform you that thir was but very few of the men saved Richard Levers belonged to her he said he had made all the inqure that Posabel ley in his Power a bout him an Can Geet no acount of him they left Gibralter the 18 and arived at Lisborn the 22nd of Decem[br] an in Coming over the bare of the said menchend Port the Bombay Castel run ashore and was lost but thankes be to God the Crew was saved Mathew Climo be longed to her but whire he is now he Canot till the ships Company being distrabeted amongist the fleet and then the fleet Put to sea in order to Cruse of the Spanish Cost but in Going out over the bare the St Georg run ashore an ley 2 days and 2 Nights but with agreat deal of troubel an fertuge an the help of the St Aulbans[29] they Got off and he said they ware then up the harbour reparing he said in Feb[ry] they fell in with the Spanish fleet an had a hevey Engagment they sunk took an burnt six sail of the line he Gave his Cind love to you and all his Brothers and sister an desird to know how you all ware they soon left Lisborn and I saw on the Paper that they ware of Cadiz blooking up the Spanish fleet an that they had taken in six months Provisions so thir is littel hopes of thir Coming home thir has a very maloncoly sean hapned here this wick at the factury ther is a mesheen wich is worked by horsies an ther was a littel boy about five years of age was Goot in thir at Play an he fell in be tween the works and his head was Crushed to Peacies that his Braines run out to his Ears I never new so many acidents to hapen in my life as I have since I have bin hear ther was a Brother son to Mr Tuck drowned at newland[30] an aman an a woman drowned in a shaft an one man Ciled an the man that did it is sent to Jail and a boy was murdred and I am shore there hath bin more then ten Cild in the tin works my master is Coreiner[31] he hath/he hath held three inquests of a wick; about a month Past we had two doges beet with a mad dog one was drowed Imedenly an this night the other is Come made she is screeching so I Can hardly bear it it is now 2 in the morning so I must Conclud with my Love to you and Brother Thos hoping you will writ to me *to* your onworthy sister this once if you never in tend to no more the last

time I hard from sister Joanna she had bin very ill
derict for me at Mr Paynters Penzance this is sufficient there is no more of the
name

82. William to Elizabeth. 1 July 1797.

London July 1 1797

Dear Sister
   And I hope as worthy to be called so as ever; I received a letter
yesterday and I should have wrote by the return of post if I had not been so
much astonished at its contents. I must say I was astonished very much and
more so the longer I look at it, and that I thought it would require some longer
time than an hour or two to take into consideration the different charges that
are there brought against me tho' I must beg leave to say as undeservedly and
more so than you who complain so much as I believe I shall make appear pretty
plainly before I have done, – And first, for I shall follow your letter – You
desire to know wherein you have offended me and did not expect at one time
to have been so slighted – I could almost send back the same words – I find you
yourself do not say you have ever wrote to me since you received my letter at
Linkinhorn for if you had wrote, & with the same direction as you used to put I
do not doubt but I should have got it, and I here declare I have never received
any letter from you since that informing me of your journey to Linkinhorn nor
did I know you had left that place till yesterday when I read your letter. I
received a letter from sister Joanna dated Plymouth 27th March 97, desiring
much to know if I had heard from you and testified a great surprize at hearing
that you was in Penzance, and that being all she said, I concluded she did not
know how to direct to you nor did I then suppose you was there, but that she
had been wrong inform'd, and in my answer to her I complained smartly of
your neglect and which she can answer for me if ever you write to her, and
when Mr & Mrs Gilbert were in town about two months ago, they could only
inform me that they had heard you was in Penzance, and when I told her I was
very uneasy at not hearing from you she said she dare say you were well and was
unwilling to put me to expence for she knew, she said, that you was very
considerate, but I beg no such consideration may be an excuse for neglect in
future My last letter was very short and had nothing particular in it; if I had
nothing particular to write I could not write it, nor do I suppose I shall have
any thing more particular for some years to come for I see no likelihood of any
alteration: You next say I did not treat the two Missionaries as they treated me
when I was in Fowey If they told or wrote you so, they lied; They had every
thing I had in my power to give except my good wishes for they had both to eat
& drink, I gave them a portfolio – drawing papers, & several Miniatures worth
as many shillings to me, but I will yet say and always say that they like a lazy
indolent life better than honestly working for their bread, and to my

Sept. 10. 1793   266

Dear Sister.

I received your kind letter dated August 8, and was very glad to hear that you enjoyed a good state of health as this leaves me at present. — I received a letter from Brother John since I received your first in which he told me proper news that you and him had had a difference about his going up to Billy Bonadys. he said he only went in to get a glass of gin just as you he was going out of town, & that he put down an old pocket handkerchief with an old pair of shoes and stockings in it, upon the bench while he went to the bar, and in the mean time, a Baggage cart with a company of soldiers stopt at the door and when he turnd round, he missed his bundle and could not find it any where, and to add to his misfortune, you came in and abused him like a pickpocket and forced him out of doors. — He says he intends coming to London when Sir Wms. Family comes to town which will be in a Month or two's time and if he cannot come then he shall try what he can do when the Furniture comes, to furnish Sir Williams new new house in Mary-bone fields. The furniture is coming by water from Towey and then he says he will come if it is only for a day or two — but he does not consider how he is to get back again I suppose, for I daresay he will not save money enough to pay his carriage back tho' he gets it up, for nothing. I wrote him an answer that I am sure he did not like, I never wrote him such a one before but as I am not much afraid of his coming up to tell me of it I do not care. — I have not seen Mr Hawkins since I received your first letter, for as I do not go to Great Marlborough Street to draw as I used to, for I have a master at our house, he is a French Gentleman who was forced to leave his own country because of the disturbances there, and therefore I do not now have time to call as I used to do for I am generally pretty busy all the morning till twelve or one o'clock and then I go to draw till dinner time at five, and then I go to write for Mr Hunter till at 8 tile 11, and on sundays I have for these several past been at earls court our country house to do any thing for Mr Hunter (as he always dines there on sundays) such as catch Insects as Bees &c and if I was to call any week day at Mr Hawkings I should be sure not to find him in, and Billy would never tell me any thing of the manner how his father lived, who and what the woman was that lived with his father nor even her name for he always said he never knew. The reason why I wrote the letter for him was because he desired me and said he did not know how to do it himself and then he would not have said half as much if I

Specimen of William Clift's handwriting

156

knowledge most of the Missionaries as they call them selves, are gone more on this consideration than any other. Religion is on its last legs indeed when such ignorant pretenders who have not even had a common education, Boys who cannot read a Chapter or a paragraph as it ought to be, or understand it when read to them, shall supercilliously arogate to themselves a knowledge of things above human capacity & in which the greatest men are lost whenever they resume the subject to trace it to its source/ Every one may see there is a divine providence attendant on all the creation, the different motions and movements of all bodies celestial and terrestial are guided and performed in a wonderfull manner but by what means we shall be for ever ignorant, at least on this side of what we call eternity, and by some invisible power – and which power we call God – thus far we may go – but when we come to argue and reason on things which cannot be demonstrated such as the shape, materiality, co-partnership and co-this and that, the residence &c of this invisible being; the state of the soul after death, its pains, punishments, and rewards, and even whether we have a soul or not – all these things are not demonstrable by us and what are called and what are called revelations &c &c &c are only the wild suppositions and enthusiastic rant of bigotted men, and designing ones – for all these things are known only by that almighty power alone who directs and governs all things, and never was intended by god to be known by us, they are above human reason & capacity – but I was told the other day by a young woman who calls herself a Dissenter and who I believe wants to convert me, that by acting according to the dictates of human reason we shall never reach heaven – or which is the same thing that we must believe every thing told us, so as it comes from the Pulpit, without reasoning upon it right or wrong. but I always thought that the end or sum of all religions, the aim of Philosophy and the essence of Libraries was to endeavour by every means in our power to make every one happy and to do to every one as we would be done by – how far this has been accomplished every one knows – ever since the creation according to all accounts, religion – that is – proffessed Religion has been made a cloak for the most unheard of cruelties and Barbarity and for every knavish action under the sun. This differs widely from true religion; God never made us to mortify ourselves and make us unhappy in this to ensure happiness in the next world, which is giving a bird in the hand for two in the bush, neither in making ourselves happy here, are we to go beyond Temperance, there is a middle path which is very smoth, the two side ones are very dangerous – some on one side hanging themselves thro' despair; and the other bringing themselves to the gallows for misdeeds.

If you were to come to London you suppose you would be treated in the manner as some others, and I would not have you think otherwise on any account for you may always rest assured (bad as you think me) of my doing every thing in my power which might contribute towards your happiness, for nothing but civility and kindness passed from me nor was it in their power to inform you to the contrary I only gave you my opinion of them. I am very much obliged to the gentleman who told you I should not know you in 7 Years hence, perhaps I may know him better between this & that – You say again that you have not heard from either of us since you have been in Penzance but I will still maintain that it is your fault in neglecting to put a proper direction upon my letters, if you sent any – neither could brother Thos write to you for you could not write to him without his direction & I am certain he did not know you was in Penz^{cc} – Mr Haynes[32] you have often seen me mention in my letters went to Lisbon last Jan^{ry} and I heard from him in March last, his letter was dated the 3d, he told me that having heard me frequently speak of Brother Robt being onb^d the St George, and he being onboard one day to dine enquired for him & saw him he was then very well; this was after they had put back after the accident of running across the sand bank, and either you or he has misstated his being in the engagement on the 14th of Feb^{ry} off Cape St Vincent with the Spanish fleet for Mr Haynes said it was in going out to join the fleet before the Engagement that the accident happened – but if he was in it and is now safe and well it will be much better for him. Mr Haynes is now a Surgeons mate onboard his Maj^{tys} ship Zealous, Capt Hood – Tom Williams[33] is now in London – he came here last week – came from Gibraltar & he says he hears the St George was coming home immediately – The spanish Prizes that were taken were put into Lisbon to be repaired and are now refitted and are expected home every day and I suppose the St George will come as part of the convoy. Tom W^{ms} went out in the Terpsichore, a frigate – they had an engagement with another Frigate and has had his right hand shot off near the elbow and two fingers off the left hand & had the left arm broke in 3 places, he has been in Gibraltar Hospital ever since and is now come home, he has got his discharge and has now since he has been here got the Pension of I believe 15 Pounds a Year and has got an appointment to go out again as Ships cook at 30 Shillings a Month. I have seen him but twice he called on me when he first came as he had my address from his father but you need not be afraid, I do not keep such company.

I am still in the same place and I do not know when there will be any alteration I saw Mrs Hunter this last monday and she told me she did not hear of any likelihood of any alteration; she said there was a talk of Peace and some Noblemen &c are set off this week for France[34] but if a peace is made immediately it is very probable nothing will be done for us for sometime – I hope you will own I have now wrote to the purpose and that I have sent you something particular besides saying

I am well, and wishing this may find you in as good health
I remain your still affectionate
Brother
William Clift

I shall expect to hear from
you soon, to know whether
you got this letter or not that
it may not be imputed to
neglect.

83. Joanna to William. 6 July 1797.[35]

Plymouth 6th July 97

My dear Brother

I am hapy to imbrace this opportunity of writing you this I Must asure you I
should have done long before now but I suppose by your Last you dont trouble
Much at the not hearing from any of your Brothers or sist[rs] at Present as I fear
by your Manner of writting that London has Engaged so much of your
attention which has Entirley banishd your Every regard from us that you once
Pretended Espesialy on perusal of your letter it realy grieves Me to the heart to
hear you speak in such slighting Manner of Poor Sister as to say what you did
yet I hope she,s not the worse for that in the sight of god or man for My own
part I Cannot forget what she has done for all of ous since it Pleasd god to take
our dear Mother from us I am shure then she ought to be Counted no Less by
us then a mother and sister too[36] as for Brothe Robert tho you thot he had not
the good Manners to write us yet he (I Bless god)[37] writes in the Most
affectionates Manner tho at such distance if you have not Rec[d] A Letter from
Sister since I received yours I will Let you know what she told me Concerning
his Letter that when she heard from him he was then at Lisbon and (I bless
god)[37] in good health and still preserved from Every danger and that he still
remains on board the St george and that they Join,d Lord Jervis before the
Engagement and that he has received no harm he said he hoped they should be
in England in 2 Months butt[38] they soon left Lisbon and saild to Cadiz he said
they saild from franzey[39] the 2nd of November – 96 and that they arived safe
at Gebralter the 1 of the Ensuing Month during their stay at Geberalter they
had Many heavy storms so that the Cognanc[40] was obledgd to Put to sea and
was unfortunatly drove on shore on the Coast of africa and that he was sorry to
say ther were but few of the Crew saved this I suppose to be the ship Poor
Richard Leaves saild in as Robert said he had Made Enquirey but Could get no
account of him the St george Left Gebralter 18th of Dec[r] and arived at Lisbon
the 22nd of the same and Comming over the bar of the said Port the bombay
Castle run ashore and was Lost but all the Crew was saved Poor Mathew Climo
did belong to her but he does not know what is become of him as they ware all
draughted about in the fleet the St george in Crossing over the bar she
ranashore where they Lay to two days and two Nights and with a great deal of

trouble and fatigue with the help of the St Albins of 64 they got off and were then up the river repairing when he wrote to Sist' he desired his Kind Love to his Brothers and sist' and to Know where we all were and hoped she would writ to him soon as Posible they talk of Lord Jervis fleet Comming in at Plym[ot] but I beleieve there is no dependance of it you desird I would send you some News but I hope you wont Expect to hear [Much at][41] Much at Present as I Can find nothing but what Is verry bad Indeed and what is worse I am obledged to sit up in My Bed to write with a Little troublesome boy by me so I hope you,l Excus what Ever may be displeasing to you however Just when I received your Letter a young Lady in the garrison Most unfortunatly shoot[42] her Maid with a Pistol thorough the breast the ball Lodging in *   *[43] so that no doctor Could get at it she L*   * days and then Expir,d in great agonys *   * dreadful accident had allmost taken *   * night was Come wherein Every one both *   * Dock and Stone house Must have Perish,d by *a* plot that 4 irish Men had Laid to set fire to the Magazine but they Led[44] a Cornish man in to their secret and he Most hapily for us discoverd it before twas two Late this being the begining of May they were Imeadeantly taken and Confind in the garrizon[45] and Last Thursday they took their trial where they receievd their Most dreadfull sentance and to day they were shot on the Howe[46] where tis supposd some thousands of spectators went to behold it.[47]

   we have had great doings with the Mutineers but they are very Peaceble at Present Let me know when you write how they have went on at London I am your affectionate Sister

Joanna Clift

I forgot to say there were but 3 of those unfortunate Men shot the 4th is[48] this day took 5 hunderd Lashes and as soon as he is able bare it he,s to have 5 hundred more and then he is to be Transported during Life he,s about 60 years of age the others I believe to be young of years I never saw them tis said they were well resignd to their unhapy fate My Kind Love to brother Thomas tell him I shoud be happy to have a few Lynes from him in [*which I hope he will Let me know when hes going to be Married as I hop to Come to wedding*][41]

{ Adieu then My D' Brother }
{ Excuse haste and Bad writing }

84. *John to William. ?27 August 1797.*[49]

Dear Brother
I have once more taken Pen in hand to Enquire after you though I find you were not so good as to ask for me when you were at Sir W[ms] House with E Nichols, the Serv' tells me you were there but you never ask'd if there was such

a one liveing – But I forgive evr'y person Even my Greatest enemy & I am happy to say that I have the best of Friends at present in this part of the world I am bound to say there is not a Gentleman & Lady in Britain can show Greater Respect to any person than they do to me, I suppose you have heard by some person or other before this time that I am Successor to Mr Tabb he Died about Christmas last – I hope your Goodness will Excuse me for my neglect in writeing but if you will be so Good to Excuse me at present I hope we shall be better friends in futur/ I were at Plymouth this spring to see Ioanna she was Quite hearty, I Intend to write to Sister E verry soon but she doth[50] not know where to direct to me I have been at Tregonna a little Country House Sir W^m hath near Padstow for two or three days past where I have been Painting but I am sorry to say that I am verry unwell at present the Greatest reason I can give for it is, (the occasion of it) I have been boiling some Vitriol by Lady Molesworth's desire for makeing an Illuminary Green[51] the Effluvia of which is of a most poisonous nature it is a Beautifull Colour but I hope I shall never have an other such a Jobb I know you will be so good to Excuse this Scroll if I tell you I have not two minutes before the post Goes of I returnd from Tregonna last night & Sir W^m hath desir'd me to go there to morrow to finish a Jobb I have in hand there I hope you will be so good to write me a Letter as Soon as possable if you can Possably read this abrupt Confused Scrol from me and am happy to say that I shall have a Chance to see you yet if ev'ry thing answers my Expectation
so I must conclude your most affectionate Brother
Jn° Clift

85. *Robert to Elizabeth. 30 September 1797.*[52]

Septm^r

Torbay st George the 30th 1797

Dear sister I Now take the oppertunity of righting These few lines to you Hoping the will find you in Good health as I Have Been but very Poorley this while past Dear Sister it Gives me a deal of Pleasure to Have the Hapness of seeing a sight of my Native Country after the absence of almost five years I rote a letter to you last Feb^{ry} But Never rec^d No answer[53] which I would Be Glad to No from you whether you rec^d it or Not we Expect to sale from Heare to spithead in a few Days and when you rite to me you must Direct There and Give my Kind love to my sister & Brother and let me No where the live I Have Not rec^d No letter From you or any of my friends since september 95 which I think it very Hard that you Could have no oppertunity of righting all that time

Dear sister as soone as we arrive to spithead I shall Have an oppertunity of Giving you Particulars of Every thing that lyes in my Power

So Nomore at Present

From your loving & Effectionate Brother till

Death Robert Clift

P.S. Be pleas^d to Direct for me on Board of H.M.S. the st George Spithead or Else where

86. *William to John.*[54]

Dear Brother I *[have]* rec^d your letter 27th August but *[which has]* and should have answered it much sooner but that I expected soon to have had something more worth writing as I heard that the St George was coming home and afterwards that she was come & I expected to have heard from Brother Robert but I have not heard any thing of him nor can I tell the reason of it. *[I sent]* Edward Wills that served his time with Mr Barron called upon me two days before I rec^d your letter and said if I wished to send to you he would willingly take a letter for me & would deliver it to you as you & him he said were well acquainted I wrote a Letter & took it to his Lodgings & left it with the young John Waram who served his time *[to]* a √ with/ the Young Neddy Hawke & he gave it him & I have *[just now]* heard a few days ago he is at Plymouth & therefore I do not know whether you have read the letter I sent by him but I should expect he put it into the Post office for you & not keep it which letter would have cleared up all our misunderstanding *[I told]* you in that letter that I called at Sir W^ms house with Betsey Nichols & what passed there. Now you say that I called there & that the Servants say I never asked for you Now there was but one or two besides the Coachman that I had ever seen before & they were too much taken up with E Nichols for me to have any talk with them but I expect you will enquire of the Coachman If he & I were not talking about you all the time I was in the house I Warrant he has not forgot it *[meeting]* & I have a better opinion of him than suspect he said I never enquired for you – I said to him that I had never rec^d a letter from you since some time before you sent me the Buckles for I had no letter with them – *[and he said that he coul]* & I did not know any reason for it & he said neither could he tell why you did not write as you was very friquently speaking of me. *[I am]* So much for that.

I have now to tell you that I am still in the same situation or nearly so – that I was when I wrote you last – There is no appearance of any alteration taking place in this Collection till a peace comes & of which there is not much appearance at present but which I do not think is far off for we must have it soon one way or another. and then it may be a good while ere they do any thing for us as they have so many ways of spending their money at present & will at any rate for some time to Come. [*   * I see many thousands] We must always hope for the Best – yet at present I [find there was] see thousands worse off than me I have had for these two years past £20 a year[55] & 7 shillings a week board wages & find myself but every thing is at such an enormous price that I make it do and that is all – but I live in expectation of seeing times alter. I Cannot possibly live on 7/0 a week & therfore I *   * on my £20 but what with that & some small trifles now & then for Drawings &c I make it do. I shall at some future period when I shall have a fit opportunity & something worth sending – send you some specimens of my handy work. I have [*it all*] never had a proper Master but I never the less have got on fairly well by dint of application and do a little now & then in Oil Water & Miniatures. I shall perhaps never make it a study for my kitchen I expect [g] share the fare & Fortune of the Collection when & wherever it goes – they might possibly have some difficulty in procuring another, as there is but one more in the world so well acquainted with it) & which I expect will be something handsome come when it will. I have a plenty of time. Besides keeping every thing in proper order & repair in the Collection and whatever may happen or the worst come to the worst I do not fear of being left destitute [besides] for as Sterne says "I [am quite a f*ellow* &] can do every thing"[56] & some I believe) as they ought to be done.

Brother Thomas is still here & is very well he desires his kind love to you and he talks of taking a turn round your part of the Country next spring but I do not know – he always speaks of a thing long before he does it [he] As an Instance – he has made my shoes since he came to London when he has made a pair I bespeak another & by the time my feet are thro the Bottom he has perhaps bought the Leather & cut them out & by the time they are made I have worn out a pair or two of shop shoes that I am obliged to buy between whiles. I shall conclude with returning back your own words "Forget all that is past & I hope we shall be better friends in future. I have not recd a Letter from Sister Betty since √last] June 30th; she was quite in a huff because I had not wrote to her for some months. She was at Linkinhorn near Launceston and the last letter I got from her was from penzance – She said she had been ther ever since the 14th of Jan – & never heard from one or any of us – I did not know she was at Penzance till she wrote me from there I desired to know in answer to it how I was to know she was in Penzance [if] without her sending me word but she has not [sent] wrote to me since. [I had a letter from Sister Joanna] I sent you her direction in the letter I told you of but if you have not rec^d it & wish to write to her Direct at Mr Paynters Penzance – that is sufficient there is no other

NOTES SECTION VIII

1. The letter was addressed to Elizabeth at Bodmin, but she was working at Penzance by the time it arrived and it was redirected. All line endings have been marked in this letter of Robert because of the frequent 'abbreviations' of words indicated by raised letters, although these do not always coincide with the end of a line.

2. The *Courageux*.

3. The *St Albans*, 64 guns, had been waiting for the Mediterranean Fleet to assemble at Lisbon since December 1796.

4. The Battle of Cape St Vincent, 14 February 1797, from which Sir John Jervis took his title of Earl St Vincent when he was elevated to the peerage in recognition of his services to the Royal Navy following this successful battle.

5. Portugal.

6. This is the only known extant letter *to* Robert from any member of the family. It seems unlikely that it was ever sent – there is no evidence of its having gone through the Post Office – and that it remained for some reason among Elizabeth's belongings.

7. The 'young man' was called Thomas Teague and he is also mentioned by Joanna in her next letter. Elizabeth had spoken of him earlier in December 1795 when she asked Clift to enquire about him. See Letter 64. At that time she believed he was on board the *Intrepid*.

8. The *Alliance*?

9. A word of 4 or 5 letters is written above the *M* in Elizabeth's hand but is illegible.

10. *strits*: the Straits of Gibraltar. Thomas talks of the 'straight Fleet' in 1796, by which he seems to mean the Mediterranean Fleet. See Letter 70.

11. *yeares* is superimposed on another word, almost certainly *Eares*. Both words seem to be in Elizabeth's hand.

12. Mr Tabb who worked at Pencarrow should not be confused with William Tabb who worked for Mr and Mrs Gilbert, although they may have been related.

13. See n.7 on Thomas Teague.

14. One or two words have been crossed out, probably by Joanna, which accounts for the lack of cohesion.

15. *M^r and M^rs*: Master and Mistress. Joanna seems to have forgotten that Clift's master, John Hunter, had died over three years earlier in October 1793.

16. This letter, the first from Elizabeth to Clift for nearly a year, shows that she had been greatly offended by his remarks about their cousins, the Puckey brothers. Clift's growing irritation on reading the letter is perhaps indicated by the increasing 'corrections' made, presumably by him. We may picture him jabbing angrily at the paper with his pen as he read the letter.

17. This addition, one feels, is at least partly sarcastic. Elizabeth repeats the phrase in the letter but her angry remarks scarcely bear out the sentiment. Her resentment at Clift's comments, which had been smouldering for over twelve months, runs throughout the letter.

18. Elizabeth appears to have written a *u*, which has been joined into an *o*.

19. At Fowey.

20. Newgate Prison, built in 1188, was at one time called the 'English Bastille'. In the 18th century it was easily the most notorious prison in England and was one of the sights of London, a fee to the gaoler giving entry to sightseers. Defoe spent six months in Newgate in 1703 and based the prison scenes in *Moll Flanders* (1722) on his experiences there. Elizabeth Fry began her work on prison reform there in 1813. It was finally demolished at the beginning of the 20th century. See Rosamund Morris, *Prisons* (London, 1976).
21. This is a reference to the episode when Thomas was living at Bristol and helped Thomas Williams when he was in prison. See the letters of early 1793, Section III.
22. The word, which is partly illegible, looks like *surely* but Clift has written *certainly* above it.
23. The full stop and the following punctuation marks have been added, almost certainly by Clift.
24. *rages*: rags.
25. A reference to the New Testament story of Dives and Lazarus: St Luke, Chapter 16, verses 19–31.
26. Above *home* [whom] Clift has written *to whom*.
27. St Matthew's Gospel, Chapter 25, verse 34.
28. St Fiorenzo, Corsica.
29. *Albans* has been written above.
30. *Newlyn* has been written above. Newlyn is near Penzance on the coast of Mount's Bay and looks on to St Michael's Mount.
31. *Coroner* has been written above this word which is not very clear in the original.
32. Robert Haynes had been Clift's superior in the Museum at the time of Hunter's death but was dismissed in October 1794 for petty theft.
33. *Tom Williams*: a reference to Elizabeth's letter of 24 June. See n.21.
34. Diplomatic negotiations were conducted with France by Pitt through William Lord Grenville in an attempt to bring about a settlement but they were unsuccessful.
35. Clift appears to have 'corrected' Joanna's letter in the same way as he did Elizabeth's. Joanna's criticisms of his behaviour towards Elizabeth probably roused his irritation once again.
36. The second *o* seems to have been added.
37. The brackets appear to have been added.
38. There seems to have been an attempt to erases the second *t*.
39. St Fiorenzo, Corsica.
40. Added above *Cognanc* in Clift's hand is *Courageux was the Ship*.
41. Crossed out, probably by Clift. Both crossings out are in the same ink.
42. Written above is *shot*, probably by Clift.
43. Here and following the ms. is torn.
44. Clift appears to have added the word *let* above the line.
45. The *z* is superimposed on an *s*, almost certainly by Joanna.
46. *Hoe* has been written above, probably by Clift.
47. The punctuation is probably added by Clift.
48. An attempt seems to have been made to obliterate the *is*.

49. John has not dated this letter. Three dates have been added in other hands: *August 27th 1797* on the outer sheet of the letter, (*26th August 1797*) and *1797* at the head of the letter. It appears to have been received by Clift on 27 August (see Letter 86) and so must have been written slightly earlier.
50. Written over *doth* is *does* but whether by John or William is not clear.
51. Vitriol, a name given to certain hydrated sulphates, is an irritant. A theory has been advanced from time to time that the green paint on the walls of Napoleon's quarters on St Helena was a cause of his death.
52. Robert again directed his letter to Elizabeth at Bodmin and it was forwarded to Penzance.
53. It seems clear from this comment and from Robert's direction that he did not receive Elizabeth's letter of 8 March 1797-
54. This is a draft letter and is clearly in answer to John's letter of August 1797. It is not signed and was probably written sometime late in 1797. As it is a draft, Clift's crossings out and additions have been incorporated to show how he composed his letters. [ ] represents a deletion and √] an insertion.
55. The Trustees of the Collection, Everard Home and Matthew Baillie, had agreed to allow Clift £20 a year in wages after he had written to Mrs Gilbert late in 1795 about his difficult financial position and the uncertainty of his future.
56. This alleged quotation from Sterne has not so far been traced.

IX. 1798 and 1799.

Only three letters survive from 1798 and the last of these is dated April. After this there seems to be a break in the correspondence until the July of 1799, apart from one letter written by William to John sometime between April and December, which is unfortunately missing. This is partly due to the ill-feeling between William and Elizabeth. His only letter to her in 1798 is in reply to another missing one which she wrote in the November of 1797. William's letter is in much the same strain as his previous one. One feels some sympathy with Elizabeth when he chastises her for her poor spelling and little surprise that she does not reply.

The two letters from John contain news of the illness and death of his master, Sir William Molesworth, following which the two households in London and at Pencarrow are greatly reduced, the heir Sir Arscott Molesworth, being a boy of only seven years. John himself is retained to see to the general upkeep of the Pencarrow house. His letters also give the first hint of any of the family marrying, but in the following year we learn that it is Thomas who has quietly got married, neither John nor Joanna.

Both John's and William's letters of 1798 report that the *St George* is at

Chatham but that nothing has so far been heard from Robert. Sometime early in 1798, or more likely at the end of the previous year, he has become caught up in some kind of trouble. Unfortunately the letter giving details of this is the missing one written by William to John later in 1798. In February 1798 Robert was transferred from the *St George* to the sloop, *Echo*, having spent a month on the depot ship, *Zealand*, a fact unrecorded in the letters. The *Echo* then cruised off the Yarmouth station, and during an expedition ashore, Robert took the opportunity to abscond. He became technically a deserter, although he returned for duty after only a fortnight's freedom. That William knew more of this than he tells early in 1798 is evident from a close examination of the sequence of events in the letters and consulting the naval records but, again, the reason for William's concealing information from the rest of the family must be purely conjectural. The family in Cornwall are shocked at the disgrace, although not unsympathetic towards their brother. They express the hope of hearing news of him but after this there are no more letters from him and only an occasional rumour of his possible whereabouts. The rumours, however, are unfounded. Unknown presumably to his family, he was drowned at sea off Cuba in 1799. (See Frances Austin, *Robert Clift of Bodmin, Able Seaman, 1780– 1799* (Dorset, 1983))

It is possibly the news of Robert that finally moves Elizabeth to write again to William in July 1799, although she allows six months to elapse after hearing the news from John before she writes. William immediately replies with a conciliatory letter and the correspondence is resumed. Elizabeth writes now from Plymouth where she has gone to join Joanna. On her way from Penzance she visited Bodmin where she stayed with the Eyre family, and it was here that she saw John and read William's letter about Robert. She writes of her initial misfortunes in finding a place in Plymouth and of an illness, both of which have proved expensive. William, who has heard from Mrs Gilbert that his sister is comfortably settled in the same house as Joanna, is full of concern and immediately sends money to help her buy shoes which she needs.

By this time William is twentyfour and feels confident of his future as keeper of the museum, negotiations for the sale of which are now nearly concluded with the Government. Fully established in a secure post in London, he no longer it seems feels the need to assert himself and his advice is friendly and assured. We catch a glimpse of him through the eyes of a native of Bodmin, William Williams, who tells John that his brother is 'Quite a Gentleman behav'd young man' with a 'solid manner'. William tries to dissuade Joanna now from coming to London where suitable places are not easy to find and he promises to make up the difference in wages for his sisters. After over three years with the Lynes family, her longest stay in one place, Joanna announces that she has moved again, still within Plymouth, but her next letter finds her back with the Lynes following the clearing up of a somewhat melodramatic misunderstanding.

There is some excitement towards the end of the year with rumours of plague in London and Joanna beseeches William for a letter to tell them that he and Thomas and his wife are all well. The rumour is not mentioned again and appears to have been a false alarm.

Late in 1799 the Collection was finally bought by the Government for the sum of £15,000. Its care and upkeep were entrusted to the Corporation of Surgeons, newly constituted as The Royal College of Surgeons of England, and in December William Clift was appointed to be its first Conservator at a salary of eighty pounds a year. It was considered that because of the diligence with which he had discharged his duties the Collection was in a better state of preservation than at Hunter's death in 1793. Thus ended six years of uncertainty for the young apprentice.

87. *John to William. 8 January 1798.*

Dear Brother,

I am certain by this time you think that I never intend to write you any more I shoud have writ long before now but I have been at St Kew for some time Painting for our Steward, & our People were not so kind to send me your kind Letter which gave me a Great deal of pleasure at my return to find a letter from you was left at Pencarrow for me, I am verry happy to hear that you enjoy your health which I cannot say I do at this time so well as I coud wish I caught a Great cold about aMonth ago in Geting wet in going to wood after Timber which I have not Quite rub'd out yet I have a smart pricking pain in one side but if it doth not leave me verry soon I intend to get some Blood taken off which us'd to relieve me, I have rec^d a Letter from Both Sisters since I rec^d yours Sisters are both in good health they both complain of your not writing to them I find Joanna intends to Get Married as soon as her Sailer (as she is pleasd to call him) returns from Sea she hath desird to know if I am Just going to be married if not till spring she says she will come home and make one of the party – but my wife is now in London if ever I marry and a worthy Girl as any in London I wish I were so near her as you are—

I am Sorry to inform you that my most worthy Friend & Master Sir William is now at the point of death if not dead in London, when that is the case I expect there will be a great alteration soon as I suppose there will not be much doing at Pencarrow untill Mr Arscott Molesworth is of age which is near 14 years to it—

Cousin peggy Bate is married to a Soldier and is sent abroad she hath had a Child and hath been home with her parents for some time but is now gone to Glynn to be nurse Mrs Glynn Died in Child Bed some time ago about 3 Months

I wish I cou'd be so happy to see you I cou'd tell you a Thousand things which must be omitted here I hear Uncle James Puckey is dead – N Pinch's Daughter Betty is with Child by a Frenchman but they are all put of from Bodmin to Mill prison[1] she says she did not think she was with Child when they went away as Monsieur told her there was no possable she could be vid Shild but shes likely to prove him a liar I should be glad to know when you next writ how Brother Tho[s] Goes on whether he is married or in what p[t] of London he resides I hope ere now you have seen Brother Rob[t] as he is at Chatham, when you write to him please to give my love to him and tell I shoud be verry happy to hear from him I have have the pleasure to tell you that I verry seldom Drink anything but Tea or clean water which I find agrees with me better than any other Liquor, I hope you will be so good to write me next post which will further oblige y[r] Most affectionate Broth[r]

J Clift

Pencarrow Jan[ry] 8th 98
please to call at Sir W[ms]

88. *William to Elizabeth. 9 January 1798.*

Dear Sister

I received yours dated Nov[r] 6th[2] and should, as you say, have known better how to have answered it before now, had you kept off the first half sheet of it, as the second contains all that I have not heard many times before and as you say what I wrote last was so very disagreeable. I should expect you would have dropped this kind of Paper war, without which it is almost impossible we should be better friends—

It has been about some Idle trifling differences in opinion in Religious matters that were the cause of the greatest mischiefs and cruelties that ever were committed – but I shall never be convinced to the contrary of what I now think, by you, unless you learn to mend your Orthography or spell better; because No person on earth I am very certain can understand the true meaning of what they read unless they read it right and unless they understand its true meaning it is impossible their Ideas of things can be rightly formed, and if not rightly formed, it is, of consequence that they cannot be sufficient judges of any thing of consequence: Now you surely do not understand the true definition and derivation of the words Lutheran, Calvinist, Methodist, &c, otherwise you could not spell them wrong – your Quotations from the Scriptures are the same; and a great many people liking to be thought of a religion that has a pretty sounding name without understanding its meaning, is just the same as people here buying old Shop worn goods because the

Shopkeepers stick them up in their Windows and call them Duncans greys;[3] Duncans, hats Caps &c &c – I also see that you quite misunderstood some parts of my letter. I think also you talk very absurdly when you say we must not act according as our reason directs us; and that our reason may lead us astray; if we are not to act according to reason, what were our reasoning faculties given us for? Reason points out to us that there must be a supreme being; Reason tells us that if we do to our fellow creatures as we would be done by were we in his place must be pleasing and agreeable to the Deity if we can for a moment suppose him to be all goodness and mercyfull, as I think we ought or if he has any superintendance over us or any thing to do with us it must be pleasing to him to see us do well. It is by acting contrary to our reason that all the mischief which happens to mankind do arise and for which we shall be deservedly punished. Again If God calls any particular men to become preachers he would most undoubtedly call those who are not entirely void of Sense and abilities, as some I know. They are preachers of their own appointment they/ they have called themselves. God would not appoint men and boys as preachers who could not read a Chapter in the Bible or a paragraph in a Newspaper as it ought, and some who are hardly able to Spell their own Name. It is very easy to pick up enough of true Methodical cant by constantly attending Meetings 5 or 6 times in a week to enable any man to be able repeat the same – A Man may have attended Medical or Surgical Lectures for many years and yet remain a Bungler in his profession all his life unless he has good sense, and takes reason to his Aid in every thing he does; and the same thing must apply to a preacher who only preaches what he has learnt by Rote and a Parrot may therefore be called an Orator or a preacher with the same propriety. I again say that God might find men of as accute judgement and sound argument among the middle Class as among the rich and great; for in general the rich and great have but very little else than their riches to recommend them – but these you say are secluded from divine knowledge – and only gave it to those who could not understand it; but if as you say, God sent poor men, as the Apostles were, yet you will see by their writings that they were men of common sense, whether the tenets they upheld were right or wrong; I hope therefore you do not intend to put the Missionaries on a footing with the Apostles. Many of them left a real comfortable home and peaceful habitation for to gain an Ideal one, and engage in a thing they did not know its end; while the Missionaries all of them left theirs for the sake of being better clothed and fed, and to lead a Lazy indolent life. We are not to employ our reason – again you say, Search the Scriptures and hold fast that which is good – now I will maintain that reason is necessary, and with it some more sense than many preachers I have heard harrangue to a gaping audience to select the right from the wrong, as you allow with every body else that some part of it is wrong, or else we might hold fast the whole – You must also have heard, or you have heard very little, that there have been men who have died in support of principles which are now exploded and thought absurd and ridiculous all over the world; and I will still suppose that there are some good – of every persuasion however they differ in opinion from you or me. Dear Sister I have stretched this letter to an abominable length and hope this will be the last of the sort we shall send one another.

I have not heard any thing of Brother Robert since I heard from you. I hear the St George has come into the River Medway which is near Chatham about 60 Miles from here I shall write to him whether he is there or no. I believe they are not yet paid off and I suppose they will not pay them off till they are turned over into other Ships for fear if they let them ashore they would not get them again – The Brittania which came home in company with the St George is at Portsmouth and is not yet paid off. I had a letter from Brother John since I wrote to you last and he was very well then but had been very poorly as usual – I have not heard from Joanna lately.

Brother Thomas is very well and desires his kind love to you as I told him I was going to write to you – I Show him those of your letters which I thought I might – If you write to him I suppose the post may find him direct to him N° 15 Moors Yard – St Martins Lane London or you send it to my care and then direct as usual to me.

I have nothing very particular to write respecting myself but that I am very well (I hope you will not be offended because I have nothing particular to write as you were at Linkinhorn) I wish I had but there is nothing doing at present concerning the Collection as the governors have too much to do with the Moneys at present to think of us.

Mrs Hʳ was down at Teignmouth in Devonshire last summer and Mr & Mrs Gilbert came up from Priory and staid with her a few weeks but went back again as Mr G. was taken very poorly; our family staid there some months, it is the lowest watering place on the Coast. I expect we shall see Mr John H⁴ home again soon as he was at Lisbon with his Regʳ but all our Troops there have been ordered home, that is, they have been ordered to leave that place, by the Queen of Portugal,⁵ of which Lisbon is the Capital, as London is of England.

I shall expect to hear from you soon and hope I shall find
    you in a good humour – Please to remember me
        kindly to every one I know & you see and I remain
           your affectionate Brother
             William Clift

London 13 Castle Street Lʳ Square.
  Janʳʸ 9th 1798.

You should always leave a space for the Seal or wafer as I have done⁶ which prevents any of the words being tore out. and fold your letter as this is Done.

171

89. *John to William. 6 April 1798.*

Dear Brother,

As I have not heard from you since your favor of the 23rd of Jan^{ry} I have again taken Pen to enquire after your health & welfare as it is the greatest Happiness I enjoy at present to hear from you so often as convenient, I cannot think the reason I have not yet heard from Brother Robt yet I expect^d to have heard from him long before now if he had been in England as I were Inform'd, may God protect him be where he will – please to let me know in your next if you have heard from him – I writ to Sister Betty at the same time I did you last but have rec^d no ans^r I suppose she is displeas'd with me as well as you but I suppose it is not Suitable to their religion to forgive small faults as perhaps she may have seen some in me which puts me in mind of Mr Rundle's words Viz

    Men have many faults, Women have but two

    That's nothing good they'l say nor nothing good they do

Mr & Mrs Gilbert I hear are gone to Bath in the road to London Wm Tabb desires me to give his kind love to you he is still Footman to Lady Dowager Molesworth[7] but his wife keeps a publick house near the house where he lives which is at the Rev^d Mr Molesworths[8] St Breock near wadebridge

I dare say before now you have heard of the death of my good and worthy Master Sir Wm Molesworth – he died the 22 of Feb^{ry} in the 40th year of his age – his death will make great alterations in the family the Steward is now in town I find Settling matters, he hath dischargd four of the Serv^{ts} I find which is Mary Edwards house maid & a Laundry maid Likewise my worthy friend the Coachman & Jas Netting the Groom & we expect to know who goes & who rem^s at Pencarrow in the course of a few days – we have Just rec^d a letter from the Coachman in which he says he left his place last Saturday but (I suppose throug haste) forgot to mention where to direct to him for which reason his wife wou'd esteem it a great favour if you woud be so good to enquire where he is and be so good to let me know as soon as possable – as he is desirous for her to come to London, but as he is out of place and it being verry uncertain how long before he may get one worth notice she says she wou'd much rather for him to come down into Cornwall please to give my love to him and let him know that we are all well & desirous to see him, his wife wou'd not wish you to say any thing to any of the Serv^{ts} only to ask where you migt see him please to say his wife hath called on Geach but I believe of no use at present if you see any of the Serv^{ts} please to give my love to them—

I have for some time past been taking up the weekly Numbers of the Encyclopaedia Londinensis or Dictionary of arts & Sciences[9] I see in the Anatomical parts there are Many of the copperplate prints representing the different parts of the Human Body Dissected by Dr Hunter which I suppose was your Master[10] and also please to Give me your advice on the Subject whether I had best continue them or not I have 27 or 26 Numbers some parts

of the work I like verry much but there is a D—d parcel of Algebra Anatomy &
a deal of useless *   * and am not so far as B–– yet – so that I *th   *
almost Endless work—
so I must conclude with my best wishes for your Health & prosperity & ever
remain your most affectionate Brother

John Clift

Pencarrow
April 6th 98

90. *Elizabeth to William. 1 July* *1799*.[11]

Plymouth July the 1 99[12]

Dear Brother
I once more take my pen to writ you a few lines wich I hop will find you in
Good health as like wis my Brother Tho[s] and to let you know that I am livin in
Plymouth I Came hear to Christmass I should have wrot to you as soon as I
Came hear if things had answard my Expectation but far from it Every thing
seemd to be a gainst me but I hop it is all for the best Joanna sent to me time
after time to Come to Plymouth to Live she sent me three letters to desir me to
Come to live at Mr Lynes with her her Master an Mistriss desir her to send for
me and they would Pay my Expence and Give me five Guines a year an they
would wait for me till such times as I Could Come and Every thing should be
made a Greabel but when I Came I found it otherwise thir maid was Maried to
Thomas williamson and they had a nother in her Place so I might due as I
would for they I Got a Place in two days after I Came hear but I had a fortnight
to wait for it an if I had known what a Place it was I would have waited till this
time be fore I would have Gone to such a Place I did not stay but a month and
that was long a nough to allmost kild me I Goot such a vilant Cold I have not
been well since I was three wickes then before I Could Geet a Place so I was
Pretty well off by this time what it Cost me in Comin hear and my lost time and
what it Cost me hear while I was out of a Place it was near fifty shilings an they
never Gave me a farthing which I think the Least they Could have dun after
takin me out of my Place was to have Payd my Expence up but I bless the Lord
for it I have a better Pace now then thirs is tho I have but four Pound a year I
have been in this Place since 27 of Feb[ry] and in this time they have Changed
their Citchin maid four times and the fifth Gave warning last Sunday an Joanna
hath warnd her self off twice she sais she will stay no longer with them she
desirs her cind love to you and to Brother Thomas she desird me to ask you if
ou thought well of her Comin to london and if you think she might due better
thir than hear and if she was to Come wich way you think would be best fore

173

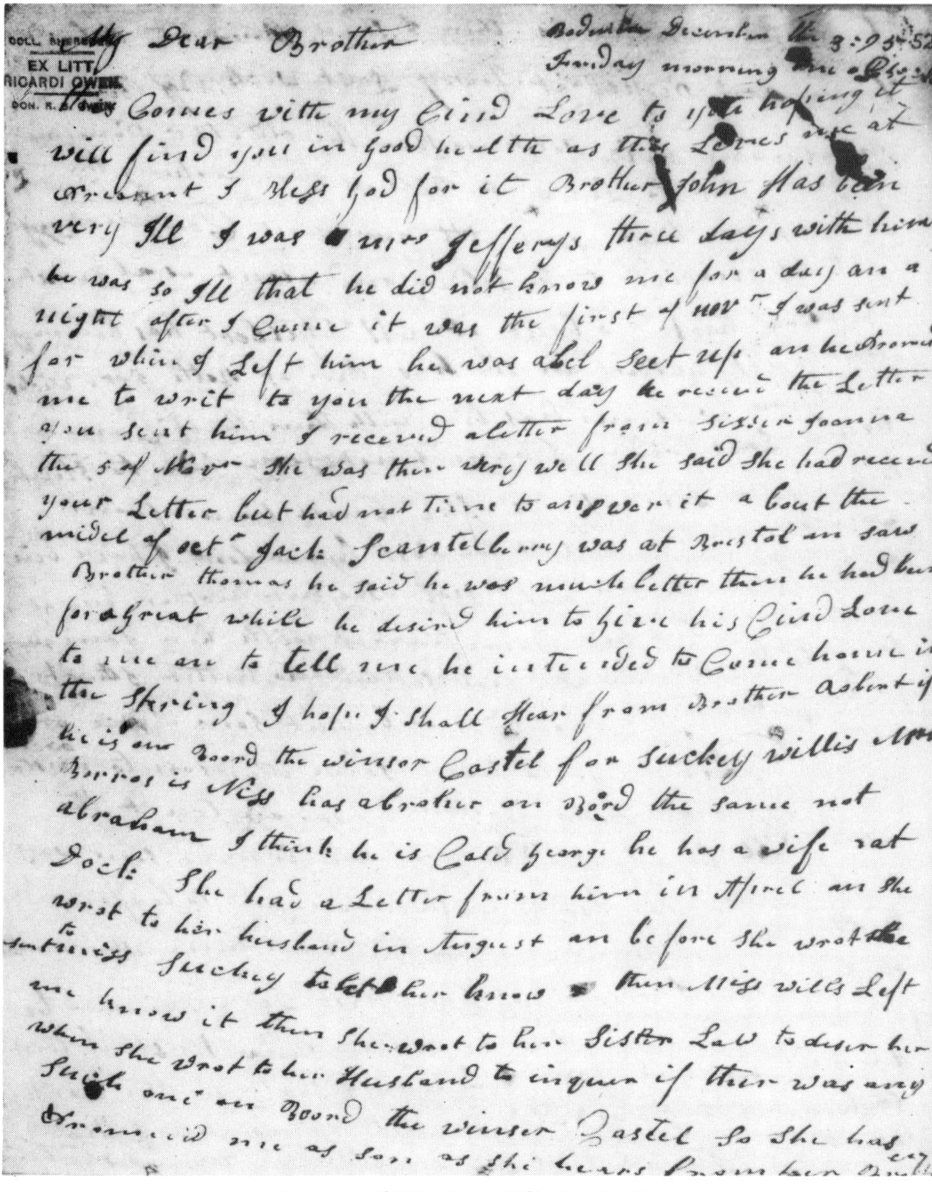

Specimen of Elizabeth Clift's handwriting

her to Come Dear Brother I should be Glad to know what is be Come of my unfortunate Brother Robert if I had seen him or had known any thing of his misfourtin I should have wrot to you I saw Brother John at Christmas showd me the Letter you sent him wich all most Brock my heart to think what my Brother had brought on him self Brother John was very well then he had Partly wrot a Letter to you wich he said he was Going to send to you in a few days I saw John foard last wick he lives a Dock he desird to be rememberd to you and to Brother Thomas an he told me that Mr Gilbert famly had been at London an ware returnd so you knew I ware at Plymouth by them Give my Cind love to Brother Thomas and tell him I should be much obliged to him if he would send me a Pear of shoes as they are very dear hear and money is very scarce with me at Preasent he knows somthing what travling is I was told a Stuarday By one of Bodmin that Thomas arther was sent to Exeter Jail the day before with several others for tring to Geet some of the frinch men out of Prison and that he was the ring leader and tis thought that nothing will save his life he was living at Dock he is but Just out of his time I hope you will be so Cind as to writ me afew lines as soon as you receve this to let me know how you are an how you Goe on now and if thir is any altration a I have not hard from you since your time was Expired Mrs Gilbert told me that you was Lerning somthing in the surgery Line wich she hoped would be better for you

if you Pleas to derict for me at Mr Hamblens upaset the Guildhall Plymouth

I still remain your Ever Loving and affectnot Sister till death E Clift

91. *William to Elizabeth. 12 July 1799.*

London July 12th 1799

Dear Sister

I received your kind letter yesterday and according to your desire I have not been long answering it. I have often been thinking of writing yet I did not know whether I had better do it or not because I could not find any satisfactory reason for your not writing to me for so long a time as I wrote to you since I had received any answer, and thought from the kind of jangling way of correspondence we had fallen into that I had better wait to see when you would write & then I should see what sort of humour you were in – as I thought of course you was too much affronted or too proud to write. I always thought all along since I saw Mrs Gilberts people that you was very comfortably settled in the same house with Joanna or else I should have sent at any rate before this time to know what you were doing & how. I cannot give

175

you any particulars concerning Brother Robert as I have not heard any thing whatever of him since I sent to John & which you say you saw. I should suppose he is onboard the Echo Sloop of War, as that was the Ship he belonged to and to which he said he was to be sent as soon as it came back from a Cruize[13] He promised very faithfully to write to me when I saw him wherever he should be but he has never done it. The Echo comes to Plymouth occasionally and if it should come there you may probably be able to enquire if he is onboard or not – I shall make all the enquiry I can against I write next. The letter you tell me John intended writing to me has not been finished yet, or at least has not come to hand. The last time I heard from him was when Sir Wm Molesworth died and he wanted me to find out the coachman as he had left his place, that his wife might know where to write to him I heard by Mrs Gilbert that he is still at Pencarrow – I should like that Joanna and you would keep near each other till you both could be provided for in any better way than you are at present – I believe good places here are not always to be met with any more than in the Country and I see that in many places they are great slaves. I do not know of any thing at present by which I could advise either you or Joanna for the better tho I am very sorry to find you so ill off – but I shall probably have it in my power shortly if you could find a Place where you could make yourself more comfortable, and I will endeavour to make up the difference of wages between what you might expect in London, from Plymouth, as I find that at last our collection is likely to be shortly settled and at present I see nothing against my being settled at the same time – Government has at last agreed to take it and most probably in the Course of Six months every thing will be settled and I shall then know whether I am settled for life or whether I am to begin the world again. However time will let us know all these things – and as long as I keep my health & hands I am not afraid of living whether or no.

I have not had an opportunity of seeing Brother Thomas since I rec^d your letter as I have not seen him for above a fortnight and he then told me that he was then looking out for a lodging as the Landlord of the house where he lodged was leaving it, and all the lodgers were obliged to move. He was to let me know where to find him but I have not seen him since, however I may expect he is very well or I should have heard. I may suppose that you have been told that he got married about 15 months ago or some such time. I think he might do much better now than when single for I always used to find her hard at work when I went to their lodgings – and I believe they live very comfortable, at least as far as I see and they seem to agree very well She was an old Bristol sweetheart I believe, and I suppose it was the principal reason of her coming to London. She was sent for by an old Mistress of hers who had come to London some time before, and when she came they did not use her so well as she expected or else she wanted to get married or something but so it was that they got married a good while before I knew any thing of the matter – She is one of Somersetshire and appears to be much about his own age. I suppose a pair of Shoes would cost as much sending as they are worth and perhaps you would want them a good while before he would find time to make them for when I used to bespeak any of him I often had to buy a pair from a Shop & wear them out before I got the others – besides I found that he got more by making shoes only – than buying the leather & cutting them out &c and would have been out of pocket by selling them at the price I could get them at at a shop so that for some time he has not made me any.

You will see I have sent you two guineas which will buy a pair of Shoes & any thing else you have most need of and if you get this without any trouble as I hope you will it will not be a great while before I shall have it in my power to send again As I must take this letter to the post office to pay the money I do not know whether they give me an order[14] to put in the letter or write upon this same paper but you will see that when you open it. I expect Joanna is not in want of any such remittance because she is too proud to write to me however I expect to hear from her soon, when I hope her & you will let me know, and I shall send her something to buy a new gown as soon as convenient after I have received an answer from you to let me know if you get this & whether you have any thing to pay at the office or not, but I hope not as I pay for sending it at this General Post office

I shall expect to hear from you soon and having nothing more particular at present to write – but remember me to all enquiring friends
I remain your affectionate Brother
William Clift

Direct as before
   Late John Hunters Esqre
     13 Castle Street Leicester Square
      London
July 12th 1799.

92. Elizabeth to William. 21 July 1799.

My Dear Brother
I receved your Cind Letter and order the 16 & the next day I went to the Post office they told me the order was for Plymouth Dock I told my Master I must Goe to Docks and he was very willing I should Goe he told Mistress that I Must Goe to Dock but said I should not Goe till such time as I had Put away the Clothes for it was our washing wick we wash once in three wicks so I finishd a thursday Eving by six oclock an then I went over to Dock Poost office I showed them the order they asked if my name was Elizth Clift I said it was they told me to sine the order so I did and they Gave me the two Guineas so I had no troubel to geet it nor any thing to Pay and I had a Pleasant walk I was back

177

to Plymouth by Eight oclock my Dear Brother I return you my sinceer thanks for this favour and I hope you have not streitned your self to send to me I hop I shall recover this a Gain if the Lord is Pleased to send me my health I have been hear all most five months and I hope I shall see this year out for I canot bear Changin Placesis if I Can help it an thir may be Greet altrations by that time for I littel thought this time twelves months to be in Plymouth at this time we are But a small famly only Master Mistress and my self I have a Great deal of Confinment I seldom Goe out side the door from one end of the wick to the other It is very seldom I see sister Joanna Except when I goe to church then I run in to see her they live Just by new chruch Mr an Mrs Lyne seem very glad to see me and all wise speek very Cind to me when I goe in she hath asked me down many times to drink tea with my sister I am sorry that Joanna is Comin Off tho they did not use me well he is a very quick temperd man and Sister is very quick to an I am afraid she will not Geet a better Place she is Coming off next wick I belive she is very well an Gives her Cind Love to you and she will writ to you as soon as she is setteld dear Brother if you should Geet any acount of Brother Robert I hope you will let me know if he should Come in hear I should supose he would let us know as he knows Joanna is living hear if I should Geet any a count of him I will let you know I hard from Brother John since I wrot to you a woman he desird to Call on us at Mr Lynes he was very thin he is to Contune at Pencarrow to look after the hous and to Ceep it in repare what he Can and the old Mr Rundel an one man more there is no fire to be lited in the Great house for one year An Brother John said at the time I was thir he thought it would be Great Part of it down it Lookt very wisht[15] then all the Plastering in the frunt was falling down then – if I was to remember Every one to you that desird to be when I was at Bodmin I might fill this Paper with that only Mr and Mrs Eyre deseird to be Rememberd to you an Frances an Joseph an John Mr and Mrs Eyre was very Cind to me whin I was at Bodmin they would scarce Let me Goe out of ther hous to Eat or drink if they Could help it – it was verry lat at Night whin I Came at Bodmin Every Person ws Gone to bead so that I scarce knew whir to Geet a bead I went up at Jacob hockens an nocked[16] an Jenny asked who was thir I spook she knew my voice an nancy run down Nacked to let me in wich was very Cind an said I should be welcome to sleep thir as long as I staid in town but in the morning when I Came down to Mrs Eyres she was very angery that I did not Come thir and Nock them up she said if it had been two oclock in the morning she would have Come down and let me in she ordred the maid to make a bead for me in one of the best rooms an saw me to bead her self an tuckt me up for fear I should tack Could an would not let me sleep any other Place whil I was in town an desird when Ever I Came home I would all wise Come ther an the Poor Children ware over joid to see me they thought I was Come ther to live a Gain I drank tea twice at Priory I supose w^{m} an betty told you that I was down to see them they told me that w^{m} was Goin/ to be maried to Jenny that lives at Mr

Flamicks Tho⁵ Arther took his trial last wick at Exeter sizes he is imprisend 6 month/ an find £20 Pound Dear Brother when you writ me a Gain I should be Glad to know if you saw Brother Robert after he was Confind if you Please to Give Joanna Cind love and mine to Brother Thomas and his wife an tell him he might have left us know he was maried wᵐ Roberts an his wife an Catty Row desird to be rememberd to you

time will not Premit me to writ any more at Preasent But I Remain your Ever Loving and affectnot Sister

Eliz Clift

At Mr Hamblens
opposit the Guild hall
           Plymouth
Sunday Eving
July 21 1799

93. John to William. 11 August 1799.

Ford Augʳ 11 99¹⁷

Dear Brother,

I suppose long before this time you must think I have entirely forgot you but believe me my love for you is just the same, though so long since you had a Specimen of my rememrance I shall not set about finding excuses but own my fault, & hope you will forgive my neglect in time past, I have defer'd writing so long I am almost asham'd to write at all but it (I hope) never shall be the case again, I did not know of Mr Gilberts going to London till Just as they return'd I hapend to be at Bodmin when William return'd at Mrs Tabbs I were Just got in to the house speaking to Mrs Tab/ when the Coach stop'd at the door, I went out to see who the Pasengers were as I thought it might be some person or persons I knew I met a young man at the Door who took me by the hand and askd me how I did (it being verry dark I did not know him at first but on entring the house he was soon Surrounded there was Mr T Pearce desirous to hear from his son Tho⁵ who I find is in London myself in great hopes of haveing a Letter from you, Mrs Tabb & Daughters to Enquere after Sally & Mrs Williams (formerly Arthur) to enquire about her husband who I find is in London with Miss Hannah Beard his Housekeeper—

I were happy to have so Satisfactory an accᵗ of you by W Williams but I thought I shoud have had a Letter by him though I had not writ you so long, I recᵈ a letter from Richᵈ Branch (Lady Molesworths Footman a few days ago who (I am happy to say) speaks highly in your favor – he says I met or saw your Brother the other day who is Quite a Gentleman behav'd young man I like his Solid manner verry much – I am really sorry for Brother Roberts misfortunes,

179

I shoud be verry happy if I could hear the same Character of him as the above – please to let me know when you write whether you know where he is my love to Brother Thos & let him know I shall Trouble him with a Letter soon, please to let me know whether he is married or not & how he goes on I am still at Pencarrow as usual but shoud be much happier if the family were here as usual, when I lost Sir W^m I lost a good Master & a True friend but its vain to repine – I hope I shall do verry well if please God to bless me with health—

Sister Betty calld on me at Christmas as she returnd from Penzance she Slept at our house at Mrs Jefferys – one night I woud have had her stay longer but she wanted to be at Plymouth as soon as posable, I went as far as Bodmin with her, I slept in Town one night & returnd the next morning I expected she woud have staid 3 or 4 days at Mr Eyres they were verry kind to her & desir'd her to stay for a week I promis'd her to come again to Bodmin before she went but before the time appointed she was gone & I have not heard from her since

There is a Camp on Bodmin Race Ground in which is the Artillery, the Stafford, Millitia the Radnor D° & Cornish Supplementary D° it is the first of the kind I ever saw I think its a verry pretty sight, Wm Tabb always enquires for you & desires to be rememberd to you, I hope shall hear from you soon so I must conclude with my best wishes for your Health & prosperity and am with great respect your Afeitionate Brother

Jn° Clift

shoud wish to know if you shoud like to venture in ye Lottery as I shoud wish to buy a Sixteenth share of a Ticket[18]

shoud you pr chance see Mr Branch or any of the family please to give my love to them

94. Mary Trebilcock to Elizabeth Clift. 15 October 1799.

Penzance October 15 1799

My Dear Betty

I sit down with Pleasur to write you a few lines as I hope you will excuse my not writing you before as I did not recieve your letter till last Saturday it lay in the post Office nearA month I am sorry to hear your sister and you do not seem a bit to Friendly as that seemed to be your only Object of going to Plymouth. Nothing greives me more than to hear you have had so much illness and difficulties since you left Penzance but however if you will come down again I do not know anything that would give me more Pleasure and as to a place I should not be much afraid of geting one for you I still live at my old place we have been but one maid this five months Joan is married this fortnight ago tho she has been married so short a time she expects to lyein in two months, we badly agreed while she was hear you know when you and I fell out no person new any thing about it but us for Joan she was a tale bearer Mr B is not married but going about it very soon you know when we was together we always agreed and do still and because of that their was many lies told upon me tho the could not make any thing of it—

I am very glad to hear your Brothers behave so kind to you I supose the think so well as my self that your Sisters marring a Foreigner cannot be a very desireabel thing I am glad to hear that your brother Robert is well—

But my dear Betty sad news I have to tell you I wish I had taken your advice in Answering the letter I recived you told me perhaps it would be the last and truly it was so for he has been dead about nine months he died sudently he was carried Ashore in the Turkish land were he was interred but my Dear Friend we must think it al for the Best tho it Shocked me when the letter came his Freinds have not Spoken to me since the melancholy news came I bless God I seem pretty well reconiled to it now my dear Freind the Lord gave and the lord hath taken blessed be his name tho I hope we shall see each other again at that awfull day when the Hearts of all men will be known and while we are about this awfull Subject I will just say that poor *Norelley* was laid amongst the Tombs a very littell while after you went away but we will drop this Subject our Edward is grown a fine young man as bubish as you please And is gone out of the house to Board at Mrs Saundres he desired me to give his kind love to you and to say that he his very much obliged to you for sending the letter to Stephen we had An answer a great while ago we are all very sorry to hear that he has hut him self I do not know whether you knew Miss Nicholas that Boarded at Mr Polgreans Mr Edmonds is married to her and great fetting out their was the was married and set out for london from the Church Stile were the spent a month the keep two maids and their house is furnished very handsome Mr and Mrs Paynter desires to be kindly remberd and are very sory to hear you have been so unwell Miss Fanny desires to be affectionately Rembered and every one of the dear Children espicaly dear little John you would be surprised to hear how Jhon is grown he is almost so big as henry Master and Mistress are talkin of puting in a coat and Breeches Poor Charles is going to sea in a twelf months time the Children all had the Scarlet Fever expect Miss Judith *   * about three months since I think the Children all got pretty well over it excepct Miss Fanny and she was so ill that Docter Penneck did not think she would get over it she has been obliged to have her head shaved the littel ones are but Just getting over the Hooping Cough I think you do not give me much encouragement to come up to Plymouth Mr Hall gives is love to you and that he is going to be married soon but that if you will come down he will wait for you Their is more talk of wars here than ever tho it is at present no Object to me Master was taken ill a very littell while after you left us and was confined upstairs near three months you will not be a littel

181

Surprised when I tell you that we had a Gentelman and his lady in the house boarding for two Months the were the most amiabel Peopel I ever met with the hapend to be hear Just has the melancholy news came of poor Jimmys death I belive I should not ben abel to have past it over so well the Gentelman has been in a decline for three years and was just come from Lisbon were he had been for his health after the left us the went near Bodmin as it was nesesesary for him to have change of Air or else I belive the would never have left us for my Part I did not care if the had said with us till now you must Judge that I had a great deal of work as we never hired without it was to wash and Iron and to milk it is imposibel for you to judge the feelings of the house went the account of his death came tho he was an entire Stranger

My dear Betty I wish you would write me often as I should never begrudge the Postage of letter and not neglect sending me when ever you do hear from your Brother Robert as I shall always be glad to know how he is I asked Edward to enquire at the Post office and I supose I should not have had it now if I had not went myself Uncle William and Mary Nicholas desired in love to you together with all the neigbours round about Mrs Hick is much Better than when you left Penzance She desires her kind love together with all her Family I have not seen any of Daniel Drew Family as yet But when I do I will rember what you said DB do write as soon as Possibel For nothing will give us more Pleasure than to hear from you Jenny and betsy desired their kind love to you Mathias is Just saild for Plymouth I desired him to call at Mr Lynes to enquier for you and to say that we thought you was very ungratefull I should be glad to know if you have heard any thing of Billy Yalls and his Wife My Dear Bety I must conclude your sincere

             Freind and well wisher
             Untill Death
                   Mary Trebilcock

My Dear Bety I will let
you know all the par
ticulars of James Ricks Death next letter
So soon as you will write me

95. Joanna to William. 10 November 1799.

                             Plymouth Nove[r] the 10

My dear Brother
I have once more took the Liberty of writing to you which I hope will find you in good health as thank god this Leaves Sister and my self at present I should have wrote you Long before now but I have for some months past been rather

unsettled in service not that I have been out of a place at the same time I thot of Leaving my Last place for 2 months before I did and now I have been where I now am for Just those 3 months and I dont Like it very well but shall If posible make it doe for the winter It/ tis so verry disagreeable in Living as a single ser^nt/ which I have under took for with an Adm^l and his family and I have scarce time allowd to Eat drink or sleep therefore I humbly hope you,'l Excuse this my very bad writing and as for poor Sisters place if posible ten times worse then mines for which I am realy sorry for

My dear billy I hope to hear from you as soon as posible and hope never to be so Long without hearing from you again as I have since I receieved your Last and I should be hapy to hear peticularly how you,re going on and in what manner as I have not had a Letter for so Long a time you will please to give my Kind Love to Brother Thos Likewise to my new Sist^r tho unknown
time will permit me to say no more at
present I Conclude your Ever
Affectionate
Sist^r
Joanna Clift

you,l direct for me at
  Adm,l valiants
    georges Street
     Plymouth

96. Joanna to William. *December* 1799.[19]

Plymouth the   1799

My dear Brother
I Can nolonger with patience wait the return of an answer to the Letter I sent you 3 weeks since and this morning my M^rs told me the dreadful news of the plague being in London[20] and if so My dear brother I shall be miserable to think of my shamefull neglect in not writing to you since I received your Last Letter I must therefore desire you my dear billy to answer this by return of the post and Let me know Every thing peticular you Can as I shall be verry unhappy till I hear from you, and poor Brother Thos and his wife and desire him to write me as I should be happy to hear from him I hope you,l Excuse this sad scrole of writing as my heart is ready break while I write to you fearing this may be the Last I may be permited to send you as I am sure all Letters will be stop,d imeadently if this dreadfull news is true tho I hope and trust in god tis not so poor sister is Just distracted Likewise about your wellfare she desires her Love to you and Brother most Affectionately My dear i desired you in my Last to direct for me at Adm^l valiants where i have been only 3 months and this

week I think to Leave them again to return to my Last place at Mr Lynes as they geatly desire me to Come back again nor should I have Left them at first had I Left my M^{rs} know the real Cause of my Leaving her which was no,other then thatt of my Fellow servant^s daily threatning to poison me on account of a young man^s paying more atenshion to me then she Cou^d wish so I undertook as a single servant with an adm^l and his family where I thot have Continu^d but to obledge Mr and Mrs Lyne I must disobledge them where I am at present
time will permit me to
say no more at present
I Conclude your
Affectionate
Sister
Joanna Clift

My dear write as
soon as posible and
direct as usal at
Mr Lynes
new Church Lane

NOTES SECTION IX

1. *Mill prison*: it was decided in 1776 to build a new gaol at Bodmin at Berrycombe or Burcom, near the mill where John had grown up. In 1778 the land was acquired and the prison was officially opened in 1780. This must be the one to which John is referring. He would be likely to call it *Mill Prison* in view of the family connections with the area and this would identify it to William. However, Bodmin was a Depot for French officers who were Prisoners of War, about 400 being in the town, and they were normally on *parole*. They were only committed to the gaol if they showed signs of riotous behaviour. Their servants were probably treated as ordinary prisoners and John may be writing about these.
2. The letter of Elizabeth dated 6 November 1797 is no longer extant.
3. *Duncans greys*: no reference to these outside this letter has so far been located and the usage remains obscure. Possibly it has something to do with Admiral Duncan and seamen's clothing.
4. John Banks Hunter (1772–1838), John Hunter's only son, who was in the army.
5. The Queen of Portugal at this time was Maria I, who suffered from fits and bouts of melancholia. Her son, later John VI, became Prince Regent in 1792, when his mother's mental illness worsened.
6. Clift has drawn a dotted line round the space where the seal goes and left it blank.

7. This William Tabb is probably a different one from the William Tabb who was footman to Mrs Gilbert and he may be mentioned in a later letter from Elizabeth of 21 July 1799. See Letter 92. However, the William to whom Elizabeth refers could be William Williams, mentioned on 11 August 1799. See Letter 93.

8. The Rev[d] Mr Molesworth could be a brother of Sir William, who is referred to again on 30 November 1806. See Letter 104.

9. *Encyclopaedia Londinensis*: this is the *Encyclopaedia Londinensis: or Universal Dictionary of Arts, Sciences, and literature*, compiled by John Wilkes, 1810–1829 in 24 vols. Vol 1. (1810) contains a very lengthy section on anatomy. John's letter is dated 1798 and obviously the weekly numbers of the Encyclopaedia came out some years before it was published in volume form.

10. *Dr Hunter*: probably William Hunter, the elder brother of John Hunter, who taught his younger brother when he first came to London. William was a well-known anatomist but also a celebrated gynaecologist and accoucheur to Queen Charlotte, wife of George III. Four of the plates in the anatomical section are described as being 'Dissected by Dr Hunter'. As these plates show the female pelvis and various stages of pregnancy, it seems more likely that it was William's work than John's. In addition, William was known as Dr Hunter whereas his brother was generally referred to as Mr Hunter.

11. The year 1799 is confirmed from internal evidence, relating to the incident when Robert deserted from the *Echo* in May 1798.

12. *99*: this may have been added by another hand.

13. *a Cruize*: after Robert had deserted from the *Echo* it sailed for Cuxhaven and returned on 25 July 1799. The whole episode is fraught with complications and Clift's letter here is evasive. The letter to John which Elizabeth read at Christmas 1798 may hold the key to many of the questions which arise but it does not, unfortunately, survive. See Frances Austin, *Robert Clift of Bodmin*, pp.31–36.

14. Money Orders were first issued by the Post Office in 1792 but the service was not fully established until 1838, when it was taken over by the Government.

15. *wisht*: South West dialect. The meaning here would seem to be 'dismal, wretched'.

16. The final *d* seems to be written over a *t*, probably by Elizabeth.

17. *Ford*: almost certainly Croan Ford, about half a mile north east of Pencarrow. John may have been working there.

18. This may refer to a National Lottery. Lotteries were started in England as early as 1569 and discontinued by the Lottery Act of 1823.

19. The letter is undated but is clearly written soon after the previous letter of 10 November. The postmark is 5 December.

20. The Plague retreated from England in approximately 1720 but there were repeated scares about its reappearance.

X. 1800–1802.

The letters for the three years following William's official appointment as Conservator of the Hunterian Museum are mostly concerned with plans for Joanna and Elizabeth to come to London. Joanna is the first to remind her brother of his 'castle in the air' in May 1800 and, after many vague hints over the years about coming, she now completes her arrangements with surprising rapidity and arrives in London towards the end of July. Her letter to Elizabeth recording the details of her journey and first impressions of the city recalls the early letters of William. She sends news of her two brothers, Thomas and his wife now having a little boy, and speaks warmly of the welcome they have given her. William is apparently courting a young lady called Caroline Pope and, although not mentioned in the letters here, he marries in the January of the following year. That Elizabeth must have been informed of his marriage is clear from a letter written in the September in which he tells her of the birth of his daughter, another Caroline.

This letter, in answer to one of hers which is missing, also contains news of the Puckey brothers. James is still living abroad, near Botany Bay, and has turned to the building trade, but his brother William, whom William Clift meets in London, has returned to England and is working on board a coastal vessel plying between Falmouth and London.

William makes no mention in this letter of any possibility of Elizabeth's coming to London but Joanna has clearly been expecting her and is disappointed at her failure to arrive. She begs her sister to leave her place in Plymouth and assures her of a welcome from Thomas and his wife, with whom she can stay. Of William's ability to provide a similar welcome she seems doubtful and she does not altogether approve of the ways of Mrs Clift – evidence, perhaps, of suspicion of a sister-in-law from a different social background. This letter, written on October the 12th 1801, describes the celebrations at the news of imminent peace, although the Treaty of Amiens was not signed until March 1802. Another interesting paragraph contains a brief description of the Hunterian Museum, the fortunes of which have for so long dominated the correspondence. We realise for the first time that the family in Bodmin must have heard of the Collection and accepted its importance in the life of their young brother without ever forming any clear idea of what it consisted. Obviously Joanna was surprised when she first saw it.

As late as 1802 Elizabeth is still in Plymouth and William writes to ask her to come and keep house for him, a proposal which she agrees to accept. At this point the letters between Elizabeth and William, which have for so long formed the backbone of the correspondence, cease. By the end of 1802, with the exception of John, who was still employed at Pencarrow, and Robert, the family was united again.

Dear Brother,

I have once more taken my Pen to Solicit the favor of an other Letter from you, though I must confess myself unworthy of it from your hands, as I'm sure you must think long before now that I have quite forgot you, as not to have answerd yours before now but I hope never to be so negligent in future, as I have now the pleasure to inform you that I am verry happily Situated – the Coachman is living with a Mr Carpenter in Tavistock in Devon he puts off his family at Michaelmas, I was verry to sorry to p^t with them but it's all for the best, I am now liveing in the Garden with Mr Bevan the Gardner where I am treated with the Greatest respect, I have washing, lodging, making/mending, milk for Breakfast ev'ry day if I chuse & all kinds of Garden stuff of the best for 1s/6d pr week which you will say is beyond what any person cou'd expect & I thank God am well respected by our Stewards, I have a long troublesome Job in the painting line to do this Summer which I do not much like as it doth not agree well with my Constitution it was Sir W^{ms} pleasure to put me with Several Painters to improve in that buisness & to oblige him I work'd mostly in that way for two or three years past, about two years ago I had a Severe fit of the Gout but I thank God have been quite hearty ever since till now I have a great deal of pain in one foot but I hope it will pass off again as I am much better to day than I were yesterday, I verry seldom drink any sort of Liquor, especially spirit, though I have heard its nothing but drinking to Excess that brings the Gout but this I can prove to be entirely false for I know many people that have had the Gout to a verry great degree that Scarce ever drank any kind of Liq^r in their lives, but at the same time I know it's not Hereditary but I have great Reason to believe it is mostly owing to the bad effects of the Paint Joind to inactivity in working it as I find a vast difference in my Constitution when at work in our own line

I suppose by this time Mr & Mrs Gilbert is in London I saw Willm Williams Just before they went off & propos'd to see him again before they left Bodmin but was oblig'd to go to St Kew to our Stewards as I frequently do about some Jobb or other I am verry much in his favour & I hope I shall always Cont/tinue so he says he will ever be a friend to me as to the news in Bodmin Serjeant Arthur died a few days ago likewise Mr G Ley Hatmaker Mr Slogget & his wife & I must not forget to say something of Minorca alias Hoskin who was married some time ago to an old maid that liv'd some time with Dr Hambly but not being Satisfied with her he got about a mare that belong'd to the Surry light Dragoons, was caught in the act & they being determin'd to make him a publick Example Drag'd him through the Streets like a dead dog through ev'ry Dirty place they cou'd find till they cou'd scarce perceive any life in him, when some person interfer'd & got him out of their hands I find this is not the first time by many that he hath been Guilty of the like crime—

I find Sister Joanna is Return'd to Mr Lynes again I had a Letter from Betty not long since they were both verry well but had no Inteligence from Robert at that Time I hope Brother Thomas, his wife & Child are well Please to Give my love to him & tell him I shall Expect a Letter from him Soon – Ev'ry kind of food is at a shamefull rate at present here wheat at £2:2s p^r Bush^l Barly £1:4s – Meat 7½ & 8d p^r lb Butter 1s – 13 & 14d p^r lb be so good to let me know when you write how things of that description are in London, though I suppose as to Corn you know nothing about – as I have heard Jeffery say you Londoners Scarce know what your Bread is made of

I have a favor to ask which I shoud Esteem a great one if you can possably Grant me my Request it will be ever indelibly fixd on my memory as I shall see that when I cannot see you but will be ever dear to me which is your likeness – which I long to see for believe me my Dear Brother though I have so much neglected in writeing you my love is still the same, & must for ever last whilst I have a being – all our old serv^ts have left Lady M Except one that is my worthy friend Mrs Mary Clements I shoud be quite happy if you coud make it convenient to call on her before Mrs Gilbert returns from London, I love her as a Mother – perhaps you may have seen her she is a verry fat stout woman she is Ladys maid & I believe housek^r/ at present – I likewise must desire you woud be so good to send me a few good Crayons, a Map of London & an Inch & Quarter Centre Bit – I desir'd Jeffery to Get me a good Stock & Bits which he did at one Shepleys I believe its near portman sq^r he is Supposd to be the best Tool maker in London & I have great reason to think so for I Suppose you never saw any thing better set out of hand, & if he hath any Good Scribeing Gouges in Sets (I mean numberd from 1 to 8 – shoud wish to have a Set of them & please to send me the Bill, as I Expect a young man from Wadebridge will be in Town soon an Intimate acquaintance of mine he is a Clock maker by Trade his name is Cholwell Billing a Farmers Son & I will send you something adequate to it

my Candle is Just burnt down so I must conclude with my best wishes for your wellfare and ever remain your most affectionate Brother
Jn° Clift

Pencarrow April 27th 1800

if you think a H172[1] or any thing of that sort woud be wor*t*h sending I will send it with the Greatest pleasure be so good to send me all the news you can
NB: Quite Hearty this morning 28th

98. Joanna to William. 27 May 1800.[2]

Plymouth May the 27th 1800

Dear Brother

I must Confess our Correspondence has bin very unregular and very unkind for some time past yet I hope twill not allways be the Cause as I,ve now to remind you of that building you so Long ago spoke of I mean the Castle in the air as twoul,d be my greatest hapiness to see it Compleatly finishd as at present I dont form an Imposibility of its not being brought forward I asure you my dear brother I have thot of it I may say a thousand times over but could never think it Conveient as now I thank providence I have good Cloaths and I hope money suficent to pay for a pasage up by water and to defray my Expenseses untill I get a place which I should hope I might go to Brothers as he is maried there – to stay for the Course of a week or so not that I would wish to rely on them for any thing but I would pay them for it If you see Brother you,l please to give my kind Love to him and his wife and tell them my Intentions of Coming to London I shall therfore wait the return of your answer and aprobation to my Coming as I shall Leave my place about the End of this month or begining of June against which time I will get Every thing ready as far as my abiliteys will permit me if you will Consent to my Coming as I should wish and humbly hope you,l have no objections to my proposals you will therefore answer this as soons Possible at the same time I must not forget poor sist[r]/ betty who desires her Kind Love to you and also to Brother Tho[s] and his wife she allso desires to know if tis settld Concerning the Collection she is very agreeable for me to go to London and if I was there I think twould be no hard matter to get her Thire Likewise

in Expectation of an answer to this
I Conclude being your Ever
Affectionate Sist[r]
Joanna Clift

Ps
if you,l please to Excuse this sad scrole of writing I,le be much obledg,d to you

Adieu

99. Joanna to William. 19 June 1800.

Dear Brother

to Let you know I receieved your Welcome Letter the 2nd of June dated the 29th of May in which I am realy hapy to find that my Letter met with your aprobation and am greatly obledg,d for your kind Invitation and proposals toward,s my Much wishd for intended Journey and at this time I hope the time is not far distant that will permit me to return you thanks personly as I with

great hapiness Look forward to that hapy time when I shall once more have the
pleasure of seeing you after so many a Long and *teideaus* year as I,ve not seen
you to Let you Know I dont Look on this time to be the Latter End of May or
the Begining of June yet I hope before the Latter End of this Ins,t^{nt} to be with
you as there,s a servt Coming in my stead on Monday next at which time I shall
have to agree with a master of a vesell which as yet I,ve not done as I promis,d
not to Leave Mrs Lyne till she was suited with a servant as I have liv,d in the
family Just those six years and I have Every reason to hope that we shall part
with that same degree of friendship as we first met as that will ad greatly to my
satisfaction respecting my Cariter My acquaintance here in plymouth advise
me to go to portsmouth by water and from there Come in the Coach to
London but as I first propos,d Coming by water – that I shall trust too and I
shall if it please god Leave plymouth the Later end of next week and I hope we
shall have a good pasage up and then I dont mind it but they rather disharten
me by saying we are Liable to be a month or 6 weeks on the pasage yet I trust
that will not be the Case with us as I shall Expect to be sik Best part of the way
as I,ve never bin much on the water since I,ve bin in plymouth I have only to ad
my sister is realy agreeable to my Coming to London she,s in good health and
spirits as I,ve Ever Known her to be for these years she gives her Kind Love to
you mary Hender allso and george desire their Kind Love to you they have
Lived in plymouth only since Last March Mary Keeps a Large Milliners
shop
      time will permit me to say no more
                  but Conclude with My prayers to god
                  for your health and welfare and
                  our hapy meeting and beleive me
                  to be your afectionate Sist^{r}
                  Joanna Clift

my Kind Love to Brother Thos
June the 19th 1800

100. William to Elizabeth. 25 July 1800.

                13 Castle Street Leicester Square July 25 1800

Dear Sister
            I have now the happiness to inform you of Sister Joanna's safe
arrival, after a passage of 9 days of very fine weather; having only been sick for
the first few days is now in perfect good health as we are all at present I have
only a few minutes to spare before the post goes – Joanna will write you all the
particulars in a day or two only we wished to make you easy with respect to her
safety

                            190

Brother Thomas & family are all very well & desire their kind love to you
You may expect to hear from us again very soon and in the mean time
remain your affectionate Brother
Willm Clift
Friday Evening.

101. *Joanna to Elizabeth. 30 July 1800.*

London July 30th 1800

dear betty
this I hope will find you and poor Boice well as this Leaves me and Both
Brothers at present I thank allmighty god for it I now mean to send you Every
thing that has hapend since I saw you Last and hope you will do the same as I
Long to know Every thing that Concerns me from plymo^t and tell Mr B I have
Expected a Letter from him some days past and if he,s not wrote that I Expect
he writes as soon,s posible as a Letter from him now will be much more
Exceptable then wen I were in plymo,t tho I want for no hapiness nor pleasure
that Life or London Can produce and wish from my soul that you and poor
Boice were here to share the Compleat hapiness and pleasure that I now Enjoy
with my Both Ever dear and more thend afectionate Brothers had any one in
plym° told me twere posible for them to receieve me with or in the maner they
did I shou,d have thare thot twere Imposible and I trust god before many
months is Expired you shall be with us and Experience the same hapiness as I
now do for tis unexpressable I therefore begin from the time I firs Left you
and find by Experience that a bad beginning makes a good End so bid you
adieu from the Howe I have now to begin I,de not bin onboard Pasing an
howr till I was as sick as sickness Could make me but I think twas partly by
reason of my being hurried away so sudenly so I wer soon glad to go to bed
where I Lay untill friday afternoon when we Came in sight of the Islle of white
of which I took a view of with the spyglass I then as twas a most delightfull
Evening wallk,t the deck till 10 oclock and then went to bed again where I Lay
till the wendsday following sick Enoug as you will Imagine we were by that
time got in the Thames when I began to get much beter and by the time we
Came to London bridge I bless god I were quite recoverd but I still think if the
Capt,n and pasengrs had not behaved as they did to me that I never shoud have
reach,d London but I realy am at a Lost for words to tell ther goodness to me
the Capⁿ if he,d bin my father a thousand times over he Could not have done
more for me then what he did in Every respect and I hope when you Come you
wont think of Coming with any other Captⁿ but him as for Mrs Brown and
Little mary they were sick on times but twas only when we were tosd pretty
much and hapy for me that they were not sick as she Behaved with the greatest
and most kind bhavour to me all the way on our pasage I wanted for no kind

asistance from her or the Little girl and all the rest behaved with the greatest sivility as people posible Could so when we Came at the warf twas about 1 oclock I dind with the Captn and mate the rest were all gone on shore so the Capt,n sent for a Coach the hansomest I Ever rode in which tookt me and my Box and all my things for 3 and 6d to Sq^r Hunters in Castle Street when the Coach stopt at the door the Housekeeper a most kind and Motherlike woman ran and opend the door and my Brother Came imeadently and spoke to and bid me welcome to London and went to take my Box I said Sir I am much obledgd to you the Coachman will take it so he staid to setle with the Coachman this while I Enquird for my Brother as I Could not think that gentleman at the door to be him but the housekeeper told me ther was no other william Clift but him however I believe youd not Know him more then I did he,s Just so tall as Boice and much stouter however I was soon reconcild that he was my Ever dear Brother in about an hour after we went to se Brother Thos and his wife and they have the pretiest Little boy I,ve seen for some time he,s a Little spritley Creature you Ever saw so we drank Tea at Thos,es house then we walk,d to St James park which is well worth seeing Next Evening we went to Sadlers wells and Last Night we went to Ashleys riding Scool[3] which was well worth seeing and on Last Sunday Brother Thos and his wife and Child and me went in to the City to see Mrs Godfrey she desird her Cind Love to you hopeing you would soon be there and to day we have been to St Jamses with some Thousands more to see the King where we acompanied him to the parliment house which was a verry good sight I am Just now going again to Thos,es to drink Tea tis not many streets from Castle Street so now I Can go Just when I please as I know the way he Lives in Chandos Street at the Ship Inn I Like his wife much shes a desent Endeavouring Carefull woman she behaves Exceeding kind to william and me both and treats us with the greatest Civility Thos and william Live verry hapy and agreeable with Each other william is remarcably kind to them the dear Little angel knows him and Cries after him william is not Maried as yet but he keeps Company with a verry smart young Lady she is Cald Caroline pope[4] and what is better then all this I was informd of a plase the day after I Came and Last Saterday I went and was Excepted of where I shall go Next munday its with a french family only 3 doors from Mr Hunters in the Square at 12 guineas per year they keep about a dosen servants I might go if I would to day but I have not seen anough of London yet nor will my Brothers agree to it youl please to Look out for Captn Heale in the Course of a fortnight or so as we shall bring something to him for you as he promisd to take any thing for me to plymouth I shall allso send some Little toys to My dear Little Jeny and Richard Lyne of which youl be so good to give it them with my kind Love to Mr Boice Likewise My duty to Father and Mother to Jenny at mrs Sanders Church Lane and all others and poor Carckling so I must conclude your affectionate Sister

Joanna Clift

102. E. Yoe to Elizabeth Clift. 8 February 1801.

Lostwithiel Feb^ry 8th 1801.

My dear Betty,

I received your kind Letter and was happy to hear you were well I was very much supprised to hear that your Sister was gone to London therefore I should be glad to know whether she is married or gone to service I was very sorry to hear she was so unwell as she is so far from home Beleive me my dear Betty I should have written to you before but as I have written to Joannah and have never received any answer I thought she would not trouble herself about writing to me If I had known were to direct to you I should have writen to you many times before this I should be glad to know when you write again whether you intend staying at Plymouth or returning home If you please when you write to your Brother and your Sister to give my Love to them and tell them that when ever it is convenent for them to write I shall be happy to hear from them as I shall be always very glad to hear from any one of the Family as any People I know I should be very glad if it was please God that we could one day all meet together it would be great pleasure to me as we have had so many before at Bodmin if not the Lords will be done but I did not think we should all be seperated from each other so far I should be glad to know how you have got your health now My dear Betty I am sorry to say your Brother is very idle still I have enquired and by what I can find is the same for my part I have not seen him to speak to him this three years now I never wish to see him again I was told he was obliged to leave his Watch at a Public-house at Bodmin for 16s but he has redeemed it again for this two Months My dear Betty when you write do not let him know that I told you any thing about it as I do not wish that he should know that I enquire any thing about him believe me it was only for your sake as you wish to know but I hope you will not trouble yourself as I think it is not worth a while about him I sent him word that I thought he was very ungrateful in not writing to you as yous are all alone and has been so good a Sister to him W: Wearam is going in the Dock-Yard that used to live at Mrs Baron's and I desired him to call to see you M: Rob/berts was here last week she desired her Love to you the family is just as the were I must now conclude your ever Sincere Friend and well Wisher

E. Yoe

103. William to Elizabeth. ? September 1801.[5]

London. Saturday Septr 1801.

Dear Sister

I received your kind & affectionate letter yesterday, and have taken the earliest opportunity of answering it especially as you seem so anxious about Joanna who is still where she was – Mrs Brown's, N° 1 Baches Row Hoxton,[6]

London. I saw her last wednesday, when she was perfectly well and came to this end of the town to see us, and Brother Tho⁵ & family; but as it is such a great distance from this, that we do not see each other so often as we otherwise should. I most undoubtedly ought to be ashamed of having neglected writing for so long a time, but you must know by yourself that the longer you put it off the longer you may; besides if you knew but half of what I have continually upon my mind, and hands, you would very readily find an excuse for me.

Let me hear from you very soon, and write more to the purpose, and let me know what you intend, or wish to do; and whatever it is, if I can be of any assistance you very well know it will not be wanting. I suppose you will hear from Joanna about two days after you get this, as I have wrote to her since I received yours.

I three weeks ago received an addition to my family of a little girl, who with her mother desire to be kindly remembered to you. Brother Tho⁵ and his family are well. I have neither heard from Brother Robᵗ or John since I heard from you. About 10 weeks ago Wᵐ Puckey was in Town for several weeks; he came up as Mate to a Vessel from Falmouth he was very well, and came several times to see us. He told me that a few months before he had been in Plym° for some time and went before your Door almost every day but did not know you was in Plym°. His Brother, James, is still at Port Jackson in Botany Bay and has turned builder of Ships and Houses, which they found to be the most profitable;⁷ for Religion is not so good a Trade there as it is in England – Aunt Betty, and Polly Stevens, are still living in the same house in Fowey that they used to do and were very well when he heard from them. Peggy Bate's husband the soldier is dead and she is married again to some one in Bodmin as much against the old peoples will as at first. However, of all these things you probably know better than I.

Let me hear from you soon, and
'till then I remain your affectionate Brother
Willᵐ Clift

PS

Every time I write to you I have to remind you of my direction. Write it in this manner.

> W. Clift
> late John Hunter's Esqʳᶜ
> Castle Street
> Leicester Square
> London

Plymouth 27th of March

97
75

Dear Brother

I am happy to imbrace this opportunity of writing to you and I hope twill find you and brother Thomas in good health as I bless god this leaves me much better then I have bin for some time past as I think Plymouth does not agree so well with my health as Sicard I have bin very ill indeed and obledged to have the doctor twice since I have been at Plymo I have been so ill this time that I have bien obliged to Cepe my Bed for just a week tho I blifs god I am quite recovered to my health again

My Dr Brother I am happy to inform you that I have heard from brother Robert by Thomas Langin... onboard the alliance who Enquired him out when he was at gibralter which was no longer since then the 18th of last december he was there in perfect health and said he hoped they should return to England soon he is still onboard the St george My Dr Brother I am grieved to think how we are separated one from another I could wish it word posible we could meet once more in this word which I fear we never sha yet I hope we shall meet with greatter happynefs in the world to come My dear let me hear from

Specimen of Joanna Clift's handwriting

195

Batches row Hoxton October 12th 1801

My dear Betty

to Let you know I recd yours but to my more then great disapointment as I realy did Expect to find its Contents so verry diferent I so depended on being inform,d by it that you were on your pasage and with unexpressable pleasure I Enjoy,d my thots to think I should so soon have the pleasure of Conversing with you personaly and shuch were my real Expectations that I had fully determin,d not to get a days Liberty untill your arival and form,d in my mind where I would take you as I have allready Learnt Every Capital place and pleasant walks and and am so well accustom,d to the ways of London that I Can with pleasure pass without the Least interuption Either night or day I had therefore the greatest hapiness to think of your Coming however I find my self much disapointed indeed but shall not reflect on that allwise providence and whose Heavenly Care and protection is allwise for the Best I shall therefore hope this to be the Case at present but I sincerly Beg and desire you do not put up with shuch unnatural and unbecoming insults as I fear you have of Late as there,s the same way for your Coming as well as mine and in me you shall Ever find a sister and a sinceere friend if you thin proper to remain where you are a small time Longer if not only Let me know and I will do what Ever is in my power for you if you should want money to free you Either by Land or water Let me know and to the Last farthing I am posest of is yours to Comand was it a Thousand times more then I have you desir'd to know what Willm said in answer to my Letter I asure you he was verry angry at my proposals of your going at Brother Tho^ses he said you should never be at a Lost for a bed or yet a dinner while he had it for himself and was sorry to say he was then short of mony and it was not in his power at present but hoped he should soon have some to send you but poor fellow he is maried now and Cannot do as he Likes in allmost any respect but as she Likes he shou,d Tis therefore in Vain to reflect on Time past as that is not to be recald Brother Thos and Mary were quite pleasd at your being with them and Both promis to make Every thing so agreeable as Their Little room would admit of this I proposd as I wishd you to Come to Town and I am well asured you would find your self much hapier with Thos and his wife then at Will^ms she is so much the fine Lady and if he got a Thousand pounds a year she would make way with it tho I dont wish to interupt them I go at Tho^ses 3 times where I go there once tho you may form diferent ideas of things as you Can,t form it as I do as to the house Brother Willm Lives in tis as Large as Tho^ses is small but they have scarce room to sleep its so occkeypied with Surgeanry Combustables I never as yet told you what the Colection is perhaps you think of it Just as I did once but were much deceieved There,s Thousands of Large Bottles with both Fleash fish and fowls perservd in spirits its sertonly verry Courious with a quantity of

Scelletons great and small) Mrs adams still Lives with them I mean she is still in the house with my Brother) Wi^llms Child is the Least Child I think I Ever saw but tis a sweet Little girl I were at Their house this day fortnight they were then all verry well I shall Conclude this and think of something better I have to Congratulate you on this Happy news of peace which has bin so Long Expected and Come at Last[8] tis not as yet proclaimd but we had here on Satuarday night a most Lovely illuminaton with the most Elegant Transparencys Lik that of italia*n Shades*/ representing peace and plenty with Thousands of varigated Lamps fix,d in the most magnificent *   *[9] the Bells ringing in Every part of the Town with the Tower guns and Every other gun with Blunder Busses and grand Fire works and what was more wonderfull the Heavens seem,d to Join this unspeakable hapiness with Thunders and Lightning. Lightnings of the strangest Coollour Ever seen and Come on Early in the Evening and Continued all night

time will permit me no Longer at present
but hopes to hear from you
soon I am your afectionate
Sister Joanna Clift

my kind Love to Boice when you see him

to Let you know I this instant rec^d a Letter from poor Boice who I am hapy to find is safe arrived in the Sound But am supriz^d to think he says noth^r word Concerning Peace. He says he shall take the Liberty to Call on you should you see him tell him I shall write him in a day or two but at present we are in shuch a bustle about this illumination as twill to night be worth notice

adieu

Monday october the 12th

NOTES SECTION X

1. This word is written in the code that Clift used to transcribe the early letters from Bodmin and shows that John also knew it and treated it as a family code. The word is *Hare*, 1 being *a*; 7, *r* and 2, *e*.
2. There are several slight alterations in this letter, probably made by Clift, but as they are mostly erasures of letters it is impossible to be certain. As they seem of little consequence, they have been silently incorporated to make a readable text.
3. *Ashley's riding School:* Joanna has written *Ashley* but almost certainly intends *Astley*. Astley's Theatre was opened in 1770 and was known by various names until it was closed and demolished as unsafe in 1893. It was never officially called Astley's

Riding School but the entertainment featured equestrian events. The name derives from Philip Astley, who constructed the second building, which was opened in 1784. This was destroyed by fire in 1794 and Joanna is referring to the third building, which was opened in 1795. This, in turn, was burned down in 1803. There is a description of a visit to Astley's by Dickens in *Sketches by Boz* (1835).

4. This is the first mention of Clift's future wife, Caroline Harriet Pope. They were married at St Clement Dane's on 21 January 1801.

5. The letter has no day in September assigned to it but it must have been fairly late in the month. Clift was married in January and his first child, Caroline Amelia, was born early in September.

6. Hoxton is an area in the north east of London, just north of Shoreditch. One wonders if the Mrs Brown mentioned is the Mrs Brown whom Joanna met on the boat from Plymouth to London.

7. William Puckey had gone out as a missionary to the South Seas in 1796 but returned to England in 1797.

8. This was probably in anticipation of the Treaty of Amiens of 1802, which resulted in a short period of peace between France and England until 1803.

9. The letter is damaged at the edge of the sheet.

XI. 1805–1817.

Between the years 1805 and 1817 there are only six extant letters, five from John to William and one draft from William to John. Apart from Robert, all the brothers and sisters were in London and William and his eldest brother had never been regular correspondents. That other letters were exchanged between various members of the family and John in Cornwall is evident but it is from John that we now learn news of the family in London. A son of Thomas's dies about 1812 and by then Joanna is apparently married, but whether to Thomas Honey with whom she eventually lived at Gerrans in Cornwall is not clear. This information comes incidentally with no details and, almost as casually, John tells his brother in the first letter of 1805, that he too is married. News of Robert's possible whereabouts, an indication that the family did not know of his death, is conveyed with more elaboration and this is the last mention of Robert in the letters. Other family news, exasperatingly slight, is passed on. John has been in touch with the Bates family, more cousins, and the Puckeys at Fowey – Cousin Thomas has apparently died. John has also seen an Uncle Phillips and his wife, presumably relations of their mother, still living at Cardinham.

John is able to give little news of Bodmin since his visits there are few, but he tells of the large number of houses being built and of a rumour that the Church and tower are about to be taken down and rebuilt, an event that took place between 1814 and 1819. Some familiar names reappear. Mr Salter, William's schoolmaster and Parish Clerk, has died and been succeeded in the latter office by his son. Mrs Gilbert is still carrying on her good works among the poor in Bodmin as late as 1814 (she died in 1818). Sir Arscott Molesworth, last heard of as a boy of seven, is now married and his family seat at Pencarrow is refurbished prior to his taking up residence there.

A recurrent theme in the letters is that of John's illnesses, mostly gout, and this greatly incapacitates him as time goes on. There is a reference to treatment by electrification, which was then very much in fashion, and John seems to derive great benefit for a time from this new cure.

His letter of 1817 is the last, as far as we know, that he wrote to William and two years later he died, the only one of the family never having left the neighbourhood of Bodmin in which he was born.

105. John to William. 31 March 1805.

Egloshayle March 31st 1805

Dear Brother,

I suppose by this time you must think that I have Entirely forgot you but I hope you will be so good to excuse me for all past faults & I hope in future never more to be so negligent I rec^d a letter from Sister Betty in the beginning of Jan^{ry} last (which I am sorry to say I have not answerd yet) in which she gave me the melancholy acc^t of Brother Thomas's misfortune but I thank God for his great Providence in preserving their lives – I hope their loss was not great Sister informs me that Joanna lives at Cornhill & hath a verry good place which I am verry happy to hear – as to Bodmin I can give you but verry little acc^t of as it is scarce once a year that I go there you wou'd be surpriz'd to see what vast number of houses there have been built in the course of a few years, poor old Mr Salter is dead and his Son James is his Successor as Clerk I find Sally Tabb is married to Wm Berry a mason and I had almost forgot to tell you that I have took a wife my self, & am happy to say so good a one I believe as any man can have, I thank god we live verry happy we keep a Cow & a Pig the latter of which I have the different p^{ts} of a verry fine one Just over my head which I wish you may have one Equal to it – we have no dairy at pres^t/ but I was in great hopes of Seeing a Calf by the Cows Side this morning—

I Saw mathew Climo a Small time since he askd me when I heard from Brother Robt I told him what I knew respecting him he said the last time he saw him was in the mediteranean but that was a great while before you saw him there was another Sailor with Climo when I saw him on hearing me mention the Echo he said what the Echo Brig I said yes so he told me that she was in the west Indies about 6 months before that time when himself was there – so this being the case Brother may be still on board her,[1] I recollect you menton'd Clouted Cream in your last Letter which I suppose is a Scarce Article in London, if there was any possability of sending you some I shoud be verry happy to send you some, but it woud give me far more pleasure to see you here, I Saw Mrs Gilbert at Dr Hamley/ some time ago she ask'd whether I had heard from you lately or not, and likewise if I knew whether you had another Child I told her I understood you had one she said yes she knew you had one but she hop'd you had not another[2] I suppose you know before now that Mr Wm Tabb is living in London with some Lady

I am happy to inform you that I have not had a fit of the Gout this twelve month past which is more than I could say for Seven year before I shoud suppose by this time you could give me some directions respecting that dreadfull Complaint – I have got in to the way of prepairing some most Excelent pills of Dr Reeds prescription it is Composd of four ingredients Viz Assafatida/ Aloes, Rhubarb & Castile Soap[3] – I hope you will never be troubled with the Gout but I shoud suppose you can have but verry little Exercise, I shoud be much oblig'd to you if you will be so good to Let me know when you write, the nature & dose of Rochelle Salts[4] as I have a nice lot of it which I dare say is verry valuable I believe Sir W^m used to take it as Physic – Please to write me as soon as Possible Please to give my love to your wife, Thomas & his wife, Elizabeth & Joanna & I remain with due respect your Affectionate Brother

Jn° Clift

P:S I shou'd be glad to receive a letter from Brother Thos I shall write to Betty soon nancy desires to be rememberd to you all

106. *John to William. 30 November 1806.*

Dear Brother,

        I am happy to say I have Just rec^d your verry acceptable letter safe with poor Sisters kind favour inclos'd which will ever be Indelibly fixd on my memory as long as I live, I wish it were possable for me to see you all again though most likely I never shall, in this vain & Transitory life, but hope we shall all meet in that which is to come which is far better I am really sorry to hear that Mrs Clift and my dear little niece is so much indispos'd as well as yourself, but yours I find is verry different from theirs, and hope you do not want for the best of advice, I suppose you never tried the effect of Electricity[5] as for my part it hath perform'd what I may Justly call a miracle on me after Physicians & Doctors had tried ev'ry thing else in vain, but it is much that no

200

one of the faculty shou'd never have propos'd it in so long a time However after I had spent 6 or 7 months in that helpless state providence brought Mr Molesworth (Sir W^{ms} Brother[6] to Pencarrow he ask'd me how I did he said he wou'd advise me to Be Electrified So then I was determin'd to try it & Set off to wadebridge at Dr Clements – & on the first trial I soon found a most wonderfull Change, for my poor hands that were entirely useless and Cold as a dead mans in all respects, soon began to show some life and the blood which seem'd to be Congeald began to circulate apace, it gave me great Consolation when I were able to put on and take off my Cloaths without help for it seem'd a long & miserable time to me, my God Grant that wee never may meet with such an affliction √Excuse blunders] I have a friend Just calld to see me, so must keep on when I begin as you plainly see, you say that Joanna is living at a Mr Hadleys in long acre but please to let me know in your next whether that is Sufficient for a direction, to her please to give our kind love & Sincere thanks to Sisters both, and love to brother Thomas & his wife & little boy as to news I Cannot Say that I know of any worth Sending at present as to Bodmin I know verry little about for I hardly go there twice a year unless on any verry particular acct/ But you wou'd be Surpriz'd to see what Building there hath been in that Town since you Left it – we were at Cardinham last whitsuntide at uncle Phillips he is pretty lusty still And aunt Considering their age—

Cousins Thomas & Humphry are verry fine young men They both work with uncle still, Henry Jane & martha live at the the Rev^d Mr Stephens's at the vicariage house – Cousin Peggy is Married to Robert Hoar Commonly calld Noble – which almost broke Aunt & uncle's heart, but have pretty well past it off again – I heard from Fowey not long ago by Cousin T Bate Cousin M Pukey is left a widow & lives home with her mother and that the above Mr Stephens's mother (an old Lady that lives at Fowey) is verry good to her & the Child on uncles acc^t Cousin William lives at Penryn he is Captn of a Trader there Cousin Thos I hear is dead, so I must Conclude

> your most afectionate
> Brother J Clift

Pencarrow Nov 30th 1806

The old proverb is – 'tis good to mend and here you will see mending Enough God knows

Please to give our love to Mrs Clift and accept the same to your self

107. John to William. 1 July 1812.

Dear Brother,

I am verry sorry it hath not been in my power to send you a letter long before this time, which I Certainly shou'd if please God I had the use of my hands or cou'd prevail on my wife to write but she always makes this Excuse that she cannot spell well enough to write to you, which I know you wou'd Readily Excuse if I cou'd Get her to write, as for myself I can but Just put on my Cloaths with out assistance, at this time though thank God am much better than I have been for nine months past, in Septr last I had a Rheumatic fever so bad that the Doctor had verry little hopes of my Recovery it deprived me of the use of my hands so much that I cou'd not even feed my self no more than an infant and as I were Geting a little better I were seized with the Gout, when I made trial of the Gout medicine which you were so Good to send me by Poor Wm Menhinnick who is no more, he died of what they call the Brain fever – sincerely lamented by Rich and Poor who had the Pleasure of his acquaintance, as to the Gout medicine it gave me instant relief as it did when I made a Trial of it before but then I were never well after untill I had the Gout severely & left it take its Course – I have been in Expectation of seeing you down for some time past[7] I Sincerely hope you will have an opportunity of coming Down soon as I long to see you, I have a Great deal of news to tell you if I could use my pen but my right hand is still so num'd that I cannot keep my own accounts – only with the pencil, I am verry sorry to hear of Brother Thomas losing his Son as A Miss Henwood Caled on me during my Illness she told me of it and said he was a verry fine Lad she told me her father & Brother Thos^s were Good acquaintance before they went to London I know her Grandfather verry well he lives not far from us, I promisd to send Brother a Letter by her but before she went of I was verry ill indeed, we expect Sir Arscott & family here verry soon but dont expect they will stay long in Cornwall for the house is not furnishd yet at Pencarrow, I suppose their stay will be at at Costislost, a small distance from here, the place Mr Gilbert had of Sir W^m, before Mr Pennington[8] died but that is too small for such family they are now at Tetcott[9] in Devon I think that is so large a house as Pencarrow – but not half so pleasant a Residence, My Dear Brother I hope you will endeavour to come down if possable, I think we shall find many things in Cornwall worth notice of what you mean to take off you will find great alteration in & about Bodmin, please to give my love to Brother & his wife, I shoud be glad to have the street & N^o where he lives & shall write to him I find by Sister Betty he hath had some fits but I hope it is not the opopletic kind I desird to know in my last but had no ans^r to it please to let me know in your next, I am verry sorry to find you have been confind by Sickness but I trust in god by this time your health will be restord as I think health greatest Blessing on Earth, of which I have had a small share for some years past I heard from Fowey this week by Geo^e Hockins Daughter she saw Aunt Pukey she was verry well & promised to send me a letter by her but she had not writ it when she came away, I rec^d a Letter from Sister Betty the same time I did yours which I hope to Answer in a few days when you will have some news from Cardinham, please to give my love to Sister Joanna & her husband – my wife Joins me in Dutifull Respects to

Pencarrow, the country seat of the Molesworth family for whom John Clift worked

Mrs Clift & Children & I remain Dear Brother yours most affectionatly
Jn° Clift

Pencarrow
July 1st 1812

108. William to John.   *1814.*[10]

Dear Brother,
          You have no doubt expected to hear from me long before this
and I have at last sent you the box which I promised to send two months ago
and I have been prevented from sending it sooner by a thousand
circumstances, having been so busy √exceedingly busy] I have not had leisure
to get together the few little things you will find in it till now. One principal
thing which prevented me writing to you was that I wished to ask Sir Everard
Home who has been in the Country about your cough and Gout – and he has
been so good as to give me a memorandum for your/your guidance as to your
mode of living which I hope will you will find of material service
     I have sent you some warm stockings and gloves for the winter and I hope
you will find benefit from them –, and if your shoes admit of it you should
wear socks made of old hat or something similar

You will also find some materials for drawing and writing, and I hope you will have regained the use of your hands to use them by the time you receive this letter.[x]

I have sent you a print of Mr Hunter, and one of Sir Everard Home which I know you will set a value on for my sake & take care of them as they are both very fine prints being engraved by Mr Sharp[11] who is one of the best Engravers England ever produced; and these are esteemed of his best performances.

I have sent you a print of my own engraving – of the Shark which was caught at Brighton the dissecting of which was one cause of my illness. I engraved this soon after my recovery. It will give you some Idea of its immense size by comparing it with the man in front of the print I have sent you two or three little pamphlets which will explain themselves – and a very interesting little History of the County of Cornwall which I have read myself with great pleasure.

As I know you are fond of Curious experiments I have sent you a receipt for making instantaneous light which is very much in use in London though the manner of doing it is known to very few; and I have sent you some matches ready made and a little of the liquid in which you dip them to make them light but which you must keep close corked, and do not let it get upoon your hands or your clothes as it will burn them, being very strong vitriolic acid.

Caroline & William have sent you some little drawings [and things]

[x]I have sent you some Writing paper folded properly that you may see how they are done; the thick edge being always to be put under the thin edge where you seal it

109. John to William. 9 December 1814.

Pencarrow Dec[r] 9th 1814

Dear Brother

I have now the Pleasure to Say that I have rec[d] your verry acceptable presents all Quite safe for which we Return you Our Sincerest thanks, but not untill last wednesday Evening, I was verry much afraid that the Box had been lost in Carriage as I sent to Bodmin so long that I had almost given it up for lost, I sent my wife to Bodmin with Mrs Gilberts Parcel last Saturday, she says when she came to priory Mrs Gilbert was home but she did not see her, she was with the Children which she pays Schooling for – Examining their work, E Nichols gave her the parcel and told her it was from you but she said she Suppos'd it was from Mrs or Miss Hunter—

Nancy desir'd E Nichols to give my Duty to Mrs G & let her know that I should write to you immediately & if she did wish me to say any thing to you I shoud be happy to do it, but she said she shou'd write Soon

My dear Brother I hope you will be so good to excuse my many faults & imperfections which you will find in this Scrole, as Assure you I'm verry unwell at this time, about the 8th of last month by 4 oClock in the Morning I awoke by a violent pain in my head so bad that I could not Suffer to speak or be spoken to, & in a short time became Quite insensible to every thing, however Nancy as I commonly call her (My wife) got up and applied a Blister to my forehead which had a verry good Effect I soon became Sensible & found it to be the Gout, which was remov'd to my feet, which soon left me & I have been Tolerable well Since, untill last monday morning when It returnd to my head but not So accute as at first – when I got another Blister to my Back which bro[r] the Gout to my feet again where it Still remains, I am not in much pain in my feet though I can hardly cross the room, I have been takeing the magnesia[12] for some nights past, for which I give you my most Sincerest thanks – for procuring it, likewise the Chamomile flowers[13] as I never saw any so fine at this time of the year I hope it will have a good Effect, as my Cough is not so severe I cannot sufficiently Express my feelings for your goodness to me, the Stockings & cap are most Excelent – as well as the Gloves, verry few in this Country Ever saw any thing Equal to, it's admir'd by Ev'ry person that hath seen it, I am delighted to see your dear Childrens Drawings which I think verry few can Equal at their age, you will soon see I am verry badly able to write as I have only a Thumb & fore finger to use – I know of no news from Bodmin at present only the Church & Tower is to be Taken down this next spring & rebuilt,[14] the Great Hall[15] hath been us'd as the Church I find for some time past – Mr Gilberts family were all well when Nancy Deliverd the Parcel my wife desires me to give her love & thanks to Mrs Clift, to you & the dear Children for the many favors you have Confer'd on us, I hope I shall have an opportunity soon to send something as an acknowledgment I hope you will be so good to Excuse many Blundes as I see I have made, Please to give my best respects to Mrs Clift and Children & accept the same to yourself and I remain Dear Brother yours Affectionaly

Jn° Clift

please to give my love to Brother – & Sisters & let them know I shall write to them Soon

I want to write a great deal more if I were able

110. John to William. 7 March 1817.

Pencarrow March 7th
1817

Dear Brother,

      I am sure you must think that I am verry ungratefull in not answering your verry Satisfactory Letter of the 12 of Dec[r] as I found what

Sister told me was a mistake for I was verry much hurt when I understood that you had not rec[d] my letter, I shou'd have wrote you long before now if had not been prevented by Sickness, Just as I rec[d] your last, I was Siez'd with the Gout which I had verry Severely in every part Except my left hand, but I soon got so well as to be able get out again, which was a Great Consolation to me as I have so much Busines to mind now Since the family hath been down – as I Superintend all the work & keep the acct[s] of Every thing Bro[t] in & Carryd out of the place, & to what use apply'd, Soon after the family came down Lady M—h Calld me in and told me she Entertain'd a verry high Oppinion of me from the Character she had of me from some friend She told me they did not wish for me to work any more, as she said all they desir'd me to do was to take Orders from them to give to the Tradesmen, as she thought I should find plenty to do without working, I got out too soon after my illness which was likely to have Cost me my life, for my disorder returnd & Seizd me in my Stomach But by the care & attendance of Dr Kingdon (who is our family Doctor I thank God I am able to walk agan though verry Badly, Sir Arscot & Lady M have been Constant visitors to me during my illness, Dr Kingdon seems to know you well & allways asks me when I See him when I heard from you & how you are, I think he is a verry nice young man, he is much respected by the family Sir Arscot being now going to town rather unexpectedly, I have taken this opportunity of writing, to let you know things are but I long to See you then I should tell you a Great deal more than I can possably do at present, Mr Brooks the Bearer of this is Sir Arscots Butler he is a worthy man as I Ever had any acquaintance with he says he will gladly do me any favor that lies in his power for me, as I askd him whether he Could make it Convenient to Call on you, it was late at night before I knew whether they intended to go or not so you will be so good to Excuse Blunders as it is near one Oclock in the morning when you write me please to let me know how your Cough is, mine is Bad still the Magnesia I took according to your direction, but soon after I took it I was taken Ill of the gout – then I left off taking it & after the Gout left me I took it again & then I found it only Bro[t] the Gout to me instead of relieving my Cough, as to the night Cap and Stockings you was so good to send me I Set a great Value on, But am Sorry to Say I was oblig'd to have one p[r] Cut off my legs they Swelld to that Degree – Please to give my most Dutifull respects to Mrs Clift & love to the Children

And I rem[n] Dear Brother yours Sincerely

Jn[o] Clift

please to give my love to Brother & Sister

NOTES SECTION XI

1. In fact Robert had been drowned from the *Echo* N.E. of Cuba, between Saddle Hill and the Isle of Pines on 4 July 1799. See Frances Austin, *Robert Clift of Bodmin,* p.38.
2. Clift's second child, a son, William Home Clift, had been born on 20 May 1803, but John appears not to have known this. More surprisingly, perhaps, Mrs Gilbert was also unaware of it.
3. This concoction is still occasionally dispensed today as a purgative, although myrrh is substituted for asafetida, both being oleo-gum-resins. Castile soap is named after the province in Spain where it was originally made. It is a hard soap made from olive-oil and soda.
4. *Rochelle Salts:* named after the port in western France and similar to Epsom Salts and Seidlitz powder. Rochelle Salts were popular from the mid 18th century and are still used today as a saline purgative.
5. The use of electrical treatment in medicine, especially for rheumatic conditions, dates from as early as 1766, when it was described with illustrations in J.G. Schaffer, *Electrical Medicine.*
6. This could be the Rev[d] Mr Molesworth referred to in a letter from John of 6 April 1798. See Letter 89.
7. Clift did in fact visit Bodmin and his brother in February 1813. See Frances Austin, ed. *The Letters of William Home Clift 1803–1832* (Dorset, 1983), pp.11–12.
8. *Mr Pennington:* this may be Mrs Gilbert's uncle, William Pennington of Priory, Bodmin, who left his niece the house in his Will.
9. Tetcott was one of the Molesworths' family homes. The parson-poet, R.S. Hawker of Morwenstowe (1803-75), wrote a poem entitled 'Arscott of Tetcott'.
10. This is part of an undated draft letter. It must have been written before John's acknowledgement of the parcel on 9 December 1814. The whole has been crossed through but most internal crossings out have been omitted.
11. William Sharp (1749–1824), the well–known engraver.
12. *magnesia:* various forms of magnesium are used medicinally, mainly as a mild laxative and antacid.
13. *Chamomile flowers:* these have various uses in medicine, particularly as a remedy for indigestion. Applied externally, as a poultice, they can relieve inflammation. However, John seems to be taking them for a cough.
14. *Bodmin Church and Tower:* the Church of St Petroc at Bodmin was restored in the early 19th century, between the years 1814 and 1819.
15. *the Great Hall:* this probably refers to the old Assize Hall, which was part of the Old Friary Church and was in Mount Folly Square at the east end of Fore street. A new hall for the Assizes, Shire Hall, was built on the site in 1836.

XII. 1818–1836.

The next batch of letters, spreading over nearly twenty years, can best be characterized by Joanna's phrase which occurs in the last of them: 'the death of so many Dear relations as you mention', and there are, besides, some whose deaths are not mentioned but which we know took place during this period.

By 1818 Joanna was back in Cornwall, living on the coast at Portscatho near Gerrans and married to Thomas Honey, who was part owner of a seaning vessel. It is possible that he was the Thomas Teague, mentioned by both sisters in earlier letters of 1797 when reporting news of Robert. Their brief prosperity and subsequent time of hardship as the pilchard fishing failed occupy much of the correspondence. Elizabeth, who was by then far from well, joined her sister and brother-in-law in Gerrans in 1818 and news of her safe arrival is swiftly followed by an account of her last illness and death. It comes as something of a shock to find that the stern and religiously minded Elizabeth indulged in smoking a pipe. Just a year later, her death was followed by that of her brother John and there is a single letter from William to his widow, Nancy, offering his condolences.

Just before his brother's death in 1819, William made his first visit to the continent to Paris, and this he obviously felt as a landmark in his career, making his Will before he set out. Twenty years later he mentions the anniversary of his crossing the Channel, which by a strange coincidence falls on the day that his wife makes her first crossing. By the time he arrived back in England John had died and any account of the visit which might have appeared in the letters – indeed, he says he had started writing one to John before he learned the sad news – is naturally superseded, although letters relating the events of the journey to his wife and son are in existence. His daughter, then aged eighteen accompanied him.

From 1822, when there is a mention of the unfortunate Bodmin boy, Billy Hocking, until 1827 there is a gap in the extant correspondence and Joanna's next letter is written from Truro. No reason emerges as to why she and her husband have moved from Gerrans. The strain of melancholy which marks all this section of the correspondence is again in evidence. Joanna seems to have lost the flamboyance of her younger days and becomes in old age an echo of her religiously minded elder sister, sprinkling her letters with quotations from the Bible and devotional exhortations. In 1827 she, herself, is far from well and her husband, Thomas Honey, is failing. One brighter prospect is the proposed visit of William Home Clift (then a young man of twenty-four) to Cornwall in the coming summer and Joanna expresses the hope that she will see her nephew. There is no evidence from the letters that the visit ever took place.

After two letters in 1827 there is again a long gap until 1836, although whether the correspondence lapsed or the letters written have not survived is impossible to tell. The latter is the more likely since William seems to have sent money regularly to his sister in the later years of her life. In addition the death of William Home Clift, William's only son, in 1832 would surely have been the occasion of an exchange of letters.

The letter of 1836 again contains news of deaths. Mr Gilbert of Priory has been dead since 1827, his wife having predeceased him in 1818, nearly twenty years earlier. Some of Caroline Clift's relations, including her parents, are also among the number of those recently dead, and a young nephew of hers, Richard Pope, who lived with the Clifts, had died much earlier in 1829. The last misfortune is not mentioned in these letters. The most significant death referred to in the letter of 1836 is that of Thomas, tidings of which have been sent to Joanna and William. With the passing of Thomas the accounts of the deaths in this Cornish family, closely bound in affection for over fifty years, in spite of the immense distances which often separated them, come to an end. From now on the remaining letters between William and Joanna, the only two of the family remaining, enter a new phase.

111. Joanna to William. 29 July 1818.

Gerrons July 29th 1818[1]

My Dear Brother and Sister—

I once more imbrace the opportunity of writing and we Sincerly hope this will find all the family in Perfect health as I thankfully acknoledge this Leaves us at present I hope to hear that Master and Miss Clift got safely through the Measels without any other afliction) ariseing from it we shall be glad to hear that Master William Enjoys much better health then he formerly Did – The last time I wrote to you I had Every hope of seeing you all) this Summer But Now I greatly fear that we never shall have the Hapiness of Ever seeing you any more and therefore since it is the will of –God – we are Content – He has Bin our greatest friend since we came Here—

I told you my Dear friends what success we meet with Last year which Enabl,d my Husband to Become one of the owners of a New Float mackrel Sean – which has Bin very fortunate indeed for us they have Caught above Thirty Ninc Thousand mackerel this season and they sold well and Last monday they begun the Pilchard seaning which makes this place very Chearful here is 2 fine french Brigs now at the Beach with salt there is several New fish Cellars Built since Last year this Place is said to have one of the finest Bays for fish that is in Cornwall – and there is a point of Land that runs out from the which you will have the full Command of the Bay – on which Hill I have intended for a Long time Past to have a Beautiful Country seat or Summer

House rather for your Family Built on that Lovely point it is all throw the summer Coverd with Trefoile Flowers and sea Dayses and then we shall be sure to have your Company with us Every summer I hope) and now I may say from the most sincere wishes of my Hart O that this was an House and not a Castle But my Dear friends many – many times have I thot how very much you would Like to walk on our Lovely Beach of a sumer Evening it is at Least a quarter of a mile in Length Coverd with shells

My Dear friends Let us hear from you at all times when Conveinent we should be very thankful for a Paper once on a time if you please as I am at all times hapy to hear any news from London and I find my Brother Thomas is maried of which I am realy glad to hear[2] my Love to them if you please at present I Conclude with

Being your Ever afectionate Brother
and Sister) Thos and Joanna
Honey

PS—

I am sincerly sorry to hear that my sister Elizth is and has bin for this great while past Dreadfully afflicted and therefore as it is our Lot to remain Here we are willing to have her here with us if she is not to ill to undertake the pasage perhaps it might Be a means of restoreing her health and if so I should be glad for her to Come away imeadently for what Can she Do poor Dear Creature to be afflicted and out of place the Little that she had Carefully reserved must be nigh spent then what Can she Do this I will Promise she shall not want for any thing that Can be Done for her sick or well and we Beg it as a favour that you will Let us know what to Expect as soon as Posible – at the same time I will write to her imeadentl*y   * I Dont rightly know Her address

we keep a plenty of Ducks and fowls Both french and English – and a Beautiful – Portagees Dog—J

Please to tell Mrs Clift I have Just Bot a new Bonet from London – Cost me near £2 pounds I have sent a small Bit of the ribbon for Her to see Inclosd

112. Joanna to William. 24 August 1818.

Gerrons August 24th 1818

My Dear Brother and Sister

This will Inform you that we rec^d yours on Satuarday the 21st whire my sister and we were *   * at dinner which Proved to us a Better Desert then all the fruit that Could be Laid on the table) we so Enjoy^d it with the sight of our Dear sister who arived at Falmouth on wednesday 19th and there she was

210

most kindly rec^d by our most worthy friend Mr John Turner a Custome Hous Officer and he with His Eldest daughter accompaniyd Her to his House where she was Excepted as a Sister and not as a Stranger) a 2nd daughter of his then at our house on a visit a most beautiful young girl about 15tn years of age they are I beleieve as sightly a family as – is in Falm^th My Husband has known him for 30ty years at Least³ Should you have occasion to send any thing that may remain of my sisters Direct it to His Care if you please as this place is 12 or 14 miles from Falmouth) she remaind at Their House untill the next day when she was most Carefully – with Every thing safe and well sent up to us by the Market Boat She was as may be suposd after a six days Passage very fateteagued But the next day she was much Better then might Be Expected Poor Dear Little Woman our sittuation I hope will be much in her favour tis a healhy place indeed and she seems) to Like it very well,) we shall get her about I hope) that she may Enjoy her time for many years to Come) she had a most Beautiful passage Down as Could possibly Be which was very much in her favour she intends to write to you as soon as she is got better in which she will give you Every peticular Concerning her little Voyage our Friend Turners Eldest son is/ is a Planter in – Jamaecka – I am sorry to say that the Pilchards are rather Backward in making their appearance we have not as yet Caught any But the weather is still in their favour we Live in hope that they will begin to Come with the spring tide – which will be next week
my Dear Brother

Please to give our very kind and Best respects to Mrs Clift and our Love to Master william and Miss Clift tell them if you please that I should Have thot very highly of a Drawing or 2 from them as the only one I have is a Cat – that Master Clift gave me some years ago – and She takes Her seat in the most Conspickous place in the Palour which is – opisite the Door and indeed She is greatly admired as all other things are that Came from London—

This Being all at present
we Conclude with our Love
to all and remain your
Ever affectionate Brother
and Sisters
E Clift and Thos and J Honey

Please to direct thus
  Mr Honey Gerrons
    nigh Tregony
      Cornwall

Please to give all our kind Loves to Brother Thos and his wife and Dear Little anna⁴ tell her after a Little while I hope to send for – Her—

Fowey Sep^t the 10 1818

dear sir

I hope you Will pardon my Long silence though it is not Neglect for I have becom so unwell that I have not been Abell to Writ and it is with Much pain I do this Now dear Cosen I More *pictlour* Wish^t to answer your Last sooner and to send it by Capt bone but Could not but i desired E *gillists* sister to give my Love and tell the Cause which I hope she did – for to Neglect you would be in gratitude indeed for your great kindness to us and in time of Need when Most wanted god will bless you without doubt in your Casket and your store is my prayers for my benefactor and friend my dear Cosoon you have taken great troubell about John Nickells but I fear it will be of No use I recaved a Letter Last Week from them and my daughter is brought to bed with a boy she had a good time and I thank god very well in her present state the Menchen that the had given up all hopes of Coming back as the doctor would not give a Certificate for any illness but he Could have don it for the Child have been ill with a fever since the have been there and the have writen me several times that the have been unwell, perhaps have not told the doctor of it I know my daughter has got a Complint on her breath and I thought the *Coulm* which the b*   *n did not agree and I know one family have been sent back on that account but dear sir it Cannot he helpt if we Never see Each outher again in this Wourld I will resing Every thing to kind provdence that have hetherto don all things Well – but John and my daughter is greatly Obliged to you all the same for the think you would have been happy to have succeeded for my own part I do not have any doctor to atend me since about 3 years ago for all Im greatly afflicted for in my Complint it would be of No use dear Cosen E gillists sister told me that you had recave^d a Nother Letter from my brouther since you Wrot me telling how his Littell stock is increaceing it gives me pleasure to here the Gaine a View of doing well Im thankfull to you in sending me a Copy of his Letter but my brother talks rather Light aboute a thousand pounds to be Left him poor soul he has No reason to Expect souch a thing but it was Just I sopose Wile he was in good spirits for he sais he is sometimes very sorrowfull – it is No Wonder indeed when he Looks back with sorrow how i^t have been in times past but I hope god will bless them and grant the May do better but Now the are gon for Ever I Never Expect to see one of them again I wish he may Content himself to stay where he is it is a blessing the injoy good health and I hope he will not Neglect to do Every thing he Can that you have desired of him if it *   * don for it would grive me if I knew he had Neglected any thing I told you that I had a Letter from him I recived it on the first of March and it was 12 Months coming but I hope he have receive some from som of us by this time I have had 2 from him I hope I shall be abell to send one to you and one to my Brother when Capt Bone goes Next my

daughter joins in Love to you and your famly and dear Cosen I desire kind remembrances to your dear famly and to my Cosons and
Wee Conclude your Loving Cosens
Mary & Betsy Stephens

114. *William to Joanna. 26 October 1818.*[5]

Dear Sister

        I received your Letter informing of Sister Bettys safe arrival which I was very glad to hear and hope before this that she has recovered from the fatigue. *[of her journey.]* Having had a weeks holiday immediately after she left London I have been obliged to work night & day ever since to fetch it up and I have never had a moments leisure to sit down to write till now I hope however that this will find you all in good health and that the Herring season is likely to turn out profitable, I supposed that you were all very busy as I have not rec[d] any letter from Betty since you wrote and therefore suppose she has not written.

    I have just seen Brother Thomas who with all his family are well. He says Anny is always inquiring if there is any news from you. I have sent you a this days newspaper we have very little news stirring except that all the Troops are leaving France.[6] The Queen still continues very ill as you will perceive by the Paper.[7] We have all of us very bad Colds; and as I am afraid of having a Cough for the Winter if I get a Cold at this part of the Year; I am therefore doing all in my power to avoid it. I have not heard from Brother John since I heard from you I have intended to Write to Sir Arscott Molesworth to know if he is living if I knew whether he was at Pencarrow or not as I have written to John two or three times without receiving any answer. Mr Gilbert was in London about a month or 6 weeks ago in his way to the Continent where he will remain for some time on account of his health.[8] He is exceedingly low spirited & melancholy still. Tell Betty that we forgot to send her great arm Chair after all and that I wish she had it to sit & smoke in, of an evening but do not know how to send it. Remember me kindly to Thomas & Sister Betty and I remain Dear Sister
yours very sincerely
W.C.

Oct 26 1818

115. Joanna to William. 13 January 1819.

Gerrons Jany 13th 1819

My Ever Dear Brother
      I wrote you a Letter Dated Decr 15 to inform you of My Dear sisters heavy affliction and I have waited for an answer – until now I were in hope that I should have heard from you Much sooner that she might have heard Likewis–But Now — she is nomore forever in/ in this life – an inflamation in the Bowels and then a mortification took place Decr 28th and she Lived only 2 Days after the inflamation took place while that Continued she sufferd most – Dreadfully yet I Bless the Lord she was Entirely – resigned to his will and she was sensible Even to the Last Dear tender Creature for me to describe her sufferings is not in my power she was allways a great sufferer after she Came Down at first But the Last 2 days was worse then all) the mortyfication only took place a few minutes Before her death or she would have had Ease sooner she Died without a sigh or a groan holding my hand in hers as Composd as if she was only Falling into a sweet sleep and the night my Dear sister Died I heard the Lovelyest museick that Ever any mortal heard it appeard to me Entirely over our House as the voyces of a Thousand Little Children all Joind in one – Hovering kind of – sound my Dear dear Brother this with Every other Tryal was allmost two much for me alltogether one of the heavyiest Tryals I Ever meet with in all my Life she Desired some time Before her Death that when she was nomore that I would write to you to Let you know of her Death and give her very kind Love to you and allso to her poor Brother Thos as she should never more write or speak to you again in this Life – Every one that Came to see her said she was more patient then any one they Ever saw all the Neibours were Extremly kind and attentive in Calling to see her) Dear Creature) and a Mr Dugless a Calviness minester after first being introduced to my Sisters acquaintance he thot so highly of my Sisters religion – that He allways Came to see Her when Ever he Came to this place – and went to prayer with her as Did allso a Mr Jennings and a Mr Billing some of the most respectable people of this place their Families Likewise were very attentive) my Dear Brother I Did mention the Chair – & – But now Let all that remain if you please untill a more Convenient opportunity only Let us hear from you as soon as Posible you Can make it Convenient please to give our very kind Love to Mrs Clift and Master and Miss Clift
      and Except the same to your
self and we remain your
Ever affectionate
Brother and Sister
Thos^s and J nna
Honey

He [Mr Dugless] has since preach^d her funeral sermon his text was taken from the 23 psalm – 4 verse[9] from words that my Dear Sister said to him when he had Been to prayer with Her and all Her sayings he thot much of seeing her great Hope on the Lord – through all her Tryals and sufferings[10]

116. Joanna to William. 10 February 1819.

Gerrons Feb^{ry} 10th 1819

Mr Dear Brother

This will inform you that I rec^d yours of the 4th on Satuarday the 6th and the inclosed allso – which for that and the – 1 – I Could wish it was in the power of My hart to return you thanks for But Indeed tis not) If I had ask,d the trifeling favour of you on my own account I should not have so severly felt the Dissapointment as I well know I never had it in my power to merit your kind attention as you well know my sister Did and its Equally Known to me that she has bin a friend to the friendless and as a Tender mother to the Motherless Child and this – and this only is the return for all her kind attention that unless she had Earnt it of her hard Labour she is not thot worthy to be Laid in the grave after all she has Done and sufferd But Blessed be the Name of the Lord In Him she hath found a friend that sticketh Closer then a Brother and Better is a friend that is near then a Brother afar off and tho you May immagine that I have Done this To Exact money from you as being the only sister you have) But no it was my Dear sister that Desired me to Do it and that a 2nd time after she Came to us she said when I am no more write to my Brother and he will send you Money to bury me – and I said Do you think he will – she answer^d I know He will For where should my Brother think that I should have it) as Ime sure no one Ever gave me £5 pounds at once in all my Life and he knows my wadges has been very Little—

This as near as I Can possibley) recollect was the request of my Dear Dying sister and that is thot to great – well be it so I know I have Done my Duty as a sister in Life and Death Neither have I Done it for sake of gain But – Rather when I sent for My Dear afflicted sister the Lord – that knows my hart He knows it was to keep her from the workhouse to where she must very soon have went if she had not Come to us) or Did she Ever say to me that she was sory she Left London no Dear tender Creature she knew that it was wisely orderd for her good she well knew that the Littl she had reserved was wasting fast and being at Lodgins and – afflicted – and after she Came to us I sincerly accknoledge she was at a great Expence as she Could not mak use of such things as was in our power to provide – tho had she recoverd or Lived for years she should never have wante^d for any thing that we Could have Done for her Dear Creature as I think its our Duty to Do for one another Espesialy where the Lord – has given us a talent–and tho it was his will to withold the Blessing from us Last season) we have Every hope of a Blessing at his hands – This – If we are spared – If not – His will be Done—

I therefore Conclude
your affectionate
Sister
J Honey

PS
my husband gives His very kind respects to you

PS you Desired to know Concerning the postage of the Letters the first – one shilling and the 2nd *   * shilling[11]

my kind Love to Brother Thomas and his wife to whom I will write very soon But not untill I return from pencarrow to where I intend to go very soon perhaps Next week

117. *Mary Stephens to William Clift. 10 May 1819.*

Fowey May the 10 1819

Dear Cousin
I once more take this opportunity to send you as Capt Bone intends to sail to Morrow I should have sent by him Last time but I was afraid you would think me troublesome but Now dear sir I hope to be Enabled to writ you though but badly while Im so un Well my infirmitys raign so hard upon me and Im very weak my daughter is very un Well indeed also May god be our helper I hope all your dear family are Well dear sir Im sorry you should have had so Much troubell about John Nickells and all to No purpose but your goodness is the same and I have not the Least doubt but you Would have felt happy if it Could have been done and the are all the same thankfull to you I had a letter from them a Week since their youngest Child is very ill but the are Well I thank god for so great a blessing dear sir your Last Letter informd me that you received a Letter from my unfortunate brother home [whom] I find still Continues with his Wife in their old Course I was in hopes that the dear Childs death would have been a Call of reformation to them but the Lord have still Left them but I trust by this time there is some alteration with them how sorry Im that the did

not do better in that Country and Endeavoured to have *desced* themselves but Now the Cannot Expect any favour from you nor the gentellman you recommended him to What I have heard have grived me very Much oh What pride have done the Lord have sufferd this to pull down her pride which was the Cause if my dear Cosen you was at Penryn you would be able to Judge how these things are he tells you that the dear boy is on trial at sidney I hope he will have a better Example than he have had years past what must them dear Children have felt to see their Parent in the state the Lately have seen them dear sir these things are a secret to all but ourselves he did ought to have been doubly atentive but Im sorry it should be so and May god turn them from their Evil Ways with a true repentance I sopose the have heard by this time of my dear Mothers death our kind Love to all your dear famly and our friends and betsys duty to you and I desire to remain dear Cosen your

 Humble servant

Mary Stephens

Sir I shall here from you again I hope

118. *Ann Clift to William Clift. 13 December 1819.*

  Pencarrow Dec^{br} 13 1819

Dr Brother & Sister

   I have the Malcony News to acquaint you of the Death of my Poor Husband he was taken ill with the Gout about two Wheeks before he Departed but ware a Great deal better and we thought the worst was over but he fall back again and the Surgeon supposed the Gout was in his head and he lay for two Days & two Nights without any Sign of Motion or speech and Departed the first Day of this Mounth – so Dr Brother I am left in avery Malancony State of Life—

my Poor Husband wrote to Sister Johana this Summer but Rec^d no Answer so I do not know where she is

So I hope Dr Brother and Sister this will finde you in Good health and all the Family as for my Self I am very poorly at present – I should be very glad to have a few lines from you in way of Answer as soon as convenient

So I have no more at Present to Say but Remain your

 Loving Sister till Death

Ann Clift

Direct of me at
Pencarrow

The front of the new premises for the Royal College of Surgeons, Lincoln's Inn Fields, designed by George Dance

119. William to Nancy Clift.[12] *20 December 1819.*

My dear Sister

        I received your very kind though unwelcome letter on Thursday last which brought me the tidings of my poor brother's death √I regret exceedingly that I did not write to him two months ago, before I set out for France on business but having put off writing for so long a time in consequence of not hearing from him, as I wrote two letters to him since I received any from him; one of which was to inform him that I had had the pleasure of seeing Sir Arscott Molesworth in London, and which I hope he received I intended to wait till my return and had actually begun an account of my travels to Paris and back again which I hoped would have amused him poor soul,*]*[13] I was happy to understand from your letter that he did not appear to suffer much towards the last; as he had been a great sufferer for many years. I received a letter from my sister Joanna a considerable time since and my brother Thomas received one about the beginning of October in which she informed us of her having been for a week or two with you at Pencarrow and of your both having been ill but that you were recovering. My brother Thomas

218

wrote to Joanna the day after I left London, in consequence of a Letter, which she wrote to him in June last, never having arrived and he has not heard from her in return so that a fatality seems to have attended all our letters, as you say that she did not answer one which you wrote to her last summer and which probably never reached her. I believe she is still living at the same place Her direction is – Mr Thomas Honey Gerrons nigh Tregony/ Cornwall.

I shall write to her this day to acquaint her of the Melancholy news which you have communicated in your letter and you will probably soon hear from her. I hope you will write to me again soon and let me know more particulars respecting my poor brothers illness & how & where he is buried; and what was done for him by Sir Arscott, who promised me when I saw him that he should never want anything in his power. I am afraid that Sir Arscott was not at Pencarrow at the time of my Brothers last illness, as I was told a week ago that he was now or lately at Edinburgh in Scotland. I returned to England on the very day that my poor brother died and had very near been washed away in the Packet which brought us across the Channel. My dear Sister I hope you will write to me very soon and acquaint me if you have any wish respecting my Brothers memory, or if he had any himself which I can in any way satisfy, and it will be a great satisfaction to me to do whatever lies in my power; and if ever I have sufficient spare time to come into Cornwall nothing should prevent my coming to see you; as I am sure that nothing was left undone that lay in your power to do, with regard to my poor brother during his long illness.

My Brother Thomas, Mrs Clift and my Children sincerely condole with you on account of your trouble and we hope that your health will shortly be reestablished. I have inclosed a £1 note to buy any little trifle that you stand in need of for the present and If you will let me know if you receive it safe; I will write to you again shortly. I hope you will bear up the best you can under the affliction which it has pleased god to afflict you with, and to which we must all submit sooner or later. I hope the people at Pencarrow have been kind to you. Pray let me know all particulars when you write, and I remain my dear Sister

yours very affectionately
Wm Clift

Royal College of Surgeons
  L I F.
    London.

Decr 20 1819.

Sent a £1 note. No not taken. Changed £30 note at young Shu*rr*'s

D° to Joanna same date.

120. Joanna to William. 9 December 1819.[14]

My Dear Brother

This will inform you that yours of the 20th Came safe to hand and I am – greatly oblidg[d] to you for – the same I accnoledge I were in Expectation of hearing from you at your return from Paris as Brother Tho[s] informd me of your Being gone there I were sorry you Did not go in the sumer instead of the autumn But I must know that was not your fault and tho you Did not say much Concerning your passage From France I know it was a great Mercy that you Ever Reach,d London in safety – for we Experin[d] that Dreadfull storm as our Little village of Portscatha Lieth Entirely Exposd to the North East wind But – am sincerly glad to hear that you are returnd – and now my Dear Brother Begins my – heartfelt Trouble – to write of the Death of my Dear afflicted Brother John tho I have bin writing on not knowing how to Begin to speak of him Dear tender afflicted Creature – o that I had known of his being so ill or of his Death that I might have seen him once more Little Did I think when we Last parted that it was for Ever in this Life tho he was heavily afflicted Dear Fellow when Ever I heard him Coming up the stairs I ran to assist him and he us,d to say in the most affectionate manner) O My – Dear Jo – I Can get up Tollerably well Consideringly and so glad whilst I staid with them and unfortunate it was for me that I went so Early in the year But as it was Expected the mackre season would begin the Latter End of March and then the pilchard season But as the Lord would have it He has witheld the Blessing from this place for these two years past therefore I may Justly say one Trouble or Tryal Comes not allone to me But in yearly succession Last Dec[r] my Dear, dear sister was taken from me and now my Dear Brother who weept Bitterly when I told him of her Death and now to speak of my other afflications which I Count the Least of all – for 3 weeks I have been very ill – indeed and now whilst I write this I am not able to sit up But yet I hope I am somethg/Better But There is no Doctor within 3 or 4 miles of this place Therefor the inhabitants must suffer – Hopeing to hear from/ I Conclude with   to you and all the Family I am sory to hear of Mrs Clifts affliction) and Love to Brother Thos and Family I will write to him as soon as I am able from your affectonate Brother

    and Sister J and T

    Honey

121. Joanna to William. 22 February 1820.

Gerrons Feb^{ry} 22nd 1820

My Dear Brother – and Sister

I have taken the Liberty of writing once more to Inform you that as we were going in to Church on Sunday Last we meet with a Captⁿ May of this village who very kindly told us if we had any Commands to London he thot to sail – Next Day I therefore gladly imbras^d the opportunity of sending a few things to my poor Dear Brother Thomass Children I would have sent many more things to them But I had not time or a Convenient package Box I therefore filld the one I had and the Capⁿ Desired to have a Letter to put in the office when he Comes to the warf and that will be at one of the Fruit warfs they are Laden with fruit from the Indies its Name is the Dove Scooner tis his own vessel) and he has a Large But a most agreeable family they Live in great stile – Not withstanding they have Ever treated us with the greatest respect since we have bin here) and should it please god to send a good mackrel season we shall get forward again I hope But those Blessings being withheld for 2 years past – our poor Little village Looks quite Disstrest had it not bin for our trifling Income we shou^d be worse off then they as we Dont belong here and therefore He Could not have any work was it Ever so trying for the men of this plase must not Look for work But where they are sent by the vesstry – and they get only – 5 – and some 6 shillings p^r week My poor Dear Creature has had But one weeks work Ever since the Last seaning time for which he recd 7 shillings and tho we have £18 pounds p^r year we pay 4 for rent and allmost Every quarter we have £1–0 to pay for rope and twine for the Craft so my Dear friends I asure you our situation is at present very trying But we Live in hope that one month more will give us great incouragment I hope sometime in march to go to Bodmin – tho most Likely twill be the Last time forever and am sure twill be a great tryal to my mind as my Dear Brother was become as Natural to me as tho we had never been separated – But now we are seperated forever in this Life and am sure twill appear to me when I go as tho I were going to his funeral Dear afflicted Creature His poor aged widow sent me a most affectionate Letter Desiring me to Come as Early in the spring as possible as the family were in Scotland therefore poor Creature I hope she will allways Continue there as Long as shes able to stand it I asure you she is a Compleat slave when the family is there tho they all like her very much she is allways Dairy maid still But she has a great deal of other work to do – Lady Molesworth and me had a great deal of talk Last time I were there) Had I Bin at Liberty I might have had a situation at once and now my Dear Brother I hope you will if possible see Brother Thos as soon as you receieve this as he must go as soon as possible when he receieves my Letter that the Capⁿ will put in the office for he will return again imeadently after unlading his Cargo and Let Brother be sure to Cary the Letter to the warf to show that he is the person as I have Directed the Box the same as

221

the Letter My Dear Brother I have sent you a present and that as a keep sake Both for me and my Dear Brother John as he gave it me when I were there to keep for his sake it is a Beautiful tothpick Like anharp and a Queen Elizabeths Coin – Little thinking it was the Last time forever in this world that I should see him tender man soon after I rec^d his Last Letter I allso recd a Letter from Brother Thos saying you were gone to paris and at your return you would Be able to give me all the peticulars Concerning your Travels this I thot would be a very agreeable account to write to my Dear Brother therefore unfortunately I never wrote to him any more this my Dear Brother shows us the unsertanty of Every thing in this life

This being all at present I Conclude
your Ever affectionate Brother
and Sister T and J Honey

Tho here we are Calld Mr and Mrs Teague more then By our own Name on account of My Husbands relations of that Name[16]

our kind respects to Master and Miss Clift please to tell Brother Thomas that I am sory I Did not send him any thing or did I in my haste think of it But I hope I shall be able to send him something shortly please to tell the I forgot to say anything about the stockings – gloves or Ribon that allso is for anna and the Flanel peticoat is for my Brothers wife If she will please to Except it—

122. *William to Joanna. 10 November 1822.*

Written Sunday 10. 1822

Sent Wednesday Nov: 13 1822

My dear Sister

        I received your letter of October 17 and would have answered it sooner if I could have found a minute's leisure to do so but every day brings me three days work, and I am almost driven out of my senses by its continual increase. I have really no time to write to any body and hardly any for eating or sleeping; having for a long time past seldom more than four or five hours for sleep. I am sure I have the best possible reason to wish that the labour and the good things of this World were more equally divided, as I know I have more than my share of the first, and not so much as I ought of the last, or I should have more power to assist those who are not able to help themselves. However I ought not to complain, for if I have no opportunity of getting money, having but barely sufficient to carry me on – yet I have that which pleases me better as far as concerns myself – peoples good opinion in regard to my profession[17] – and now the Museum is becoming so well known all over the world I have so many people continually sent to me by those who have been here before that it leaves me hardly a minutes leisure through the day and obliges me to work most of the night to do that which would be otherwise done in the day. and this being of a nature in which no body can assist me I am obliged to do it myself or it must remain undone. But though this increase of business, brings no increase of income but only credit for being better acquainted with various subjects connected with my employment than other people; it gives me the opportunity of associating with and being looked up to those who are infinitely my superiors in every thing else and has been the means of my being admitted a member of several societies into which many who have large fortunes cannot get admittance and makes my situation desirable on that account only, which would otherwise be too much for any one to encounter. But as it was by being more industrious than other people that Mr Hunter acquired his reputation though not riches I cannot do better than follow his example when I find that I must get that or nothing. and think myself very well off too This however necessarily increases my expences and prevents me from saving money and sometimes from having enough for present use but being so situated I cannot go back, but must go on, and trust to providence for the rest.

I am sorry to hear that things go on so badly in the Country, and wish it was in my power to mend them: but I believe there is very little difference in that respect either in Town or country. Brother Thomas has left the House in which he lived which may be one reason why he has not received the letter which you say you sent him in June last, but he still lives in the same Street N° 10 Haughton Street Clare Market and if the letter had come to London & not found him there it would have returned to you at Truro unless you paid the postage, if so it would go to the dead letter office and afterwards be destroyed. therefore the best way is never to pay a letter unless you are sure of the address, as the Postman will take no pains to find the person if it requires any trouble.

His wife's eldest Boy has been seriously ill and was for a good while not expected to live, but has now recoverd All the rest of his family are very well, and he himself looks better than I have seen him for a great while past. But he complains sadly of having very little to do and has been in very indifferent circumstances which has made it necessary for me to assist him toward the rent, &c. His eyes begin to fail him and he cannot see so well as could be wished, or his business requires. My own family have all had bad colds – and Caroline is just recovering from the hooping Cough which has left her in a very delicate state of health I have been several times inclined to be ill but have really had no time to think seriously about it and so have got well again. I have lately had 2 or 3 letters from Mr Gilbert of Priory whose health is far from good and he unfortunately does not now grow younger.[18] He wrote to me to purchase some things for him to be taken to him by a Lieutenant King who is a relation of old Mrs Stone's and is now settled in Bodmin you will perhaps recollect him though I did not. He says it is about 30 years ago since he left the Town. He was lodging at Mr Sam Stones in St Georges Fields who I believe carries on the Watchmaking Business. He is grown so old and lusty, and dresses so unlike what he did when I before knew him that I should not have had the slightest recollection of him. I called there to see Mr King, and talked over some of his old rigs[19] with poor old Jonathan Ham & Walter Crap, and some other of the Bodmin worthies in his younger days I have not seen him before for near 30 years, at the time that he brought up the son of Hawkins the Staymaker to London who brought letters for me from home.[20] I have not seen any one from Cornwall for a great length of time. If Mr Jo. Eyre still lives in Truro I beg you to remember me kindly to him when you see him. I sent you a Newspaper giving a long account of the Death of Lord Castlereagh about 10th of August[21] and directed it to your former address Lemon Row but do not know if you received it. I have never set eyes upon that Vagabond Mackenzie and perhaps it would have been to purpose if I had. I have sent a £1 note which has been in Cornwall before – which I rec^d from Mr King for things bought for Mr Gilbert

123. *Joanna to William. 6 February 1827.*

Truro
Fairmantle Street
Feb^{ry} the 6th
1827

My Dear Brother[22]
this will I hope once more find you and your family in good health and asure you I Could have wish^d Long since to know) as I realy Long to hear from you But my dear Brother this I am sure that on account of your situation and family you have but Little time to write or think – of me I thot my self alltogather forgotten untill I rec^d a paper of the Death of HRHighness the Duke of York[23] – or Did I think that I should bin Liveing to have wrote to you Concerning it untill now and yet I – did hope that I should have recd – His Funeral prossesion for the which I so *   * Enquir^d after and if its not to Late now I should be glad to receieve it – as I asure my Dear Brother I never hear of anything worth – hearing in this Place or Do I Ever see a Newspaper But when I receieve it from you I think I did not miss any thing in the Last paper for it was all news to me and – Nothing Can please me so well as news from London—

I am thankful – that I am a Little better in health then I were when I receiev^d the paper as I have bin very much afflicted for a Long time – with a severe – weakness at the pit of my stomack it takes me at first with – something similar to the hooping Cough and what is strange it seiezes a me in the night when sleeping – and seldom at any other time and when it takes me I think I never shall Draw my breath any more in this world – people here Call it the riseing of the Lights[24] be what it may it makes me so weak and Low spirite[d] for a great while after that I dread it more then I Do the thots of – Death as I Can Justly say – that the Lord has in great mercy Deliverd me from the fear of Death For Death is nomore the king of Dread since our Emmanuel rose He – took the tyrants siting away and spoild His H[st] – Foes[25] so that when Ever the Lord thinks fit to Call me I am fully resignd to his will – and I sincerly hope that all – them that I hold Dear to me in this Life Can or will be inable,d shortly to say the same Every one for themselves as the Lord has Latley shown us that He is no respector of persons no for Kings an Prince *ses* all must Die and that is to show us what sin has Done – to know that we must Die as well as they is not the worst – thing to know no my Dear Brother But to know that we shall not Die Eternaly is Better or more then the gift of Ten thousand Earthly worlds and my Dear dear Brother and friends Let me Beg of you – as it may be the Last time I may Ever write to you in this world of unsertanteys that you will read the Epistle of St paul – to the Colossians and may that grace and peace from god our Heavenly Father rest on you and your Dear family – forever in this world and that which is to Come – I hope my Dear Brother will not think that I have bin Led away by a people Cal[d] the methodist no my Dear Brother I never go to hear their pernicious Docterine But the precious Bible I find – being instructed of the Lord shows us the only true way of salvation and that allone Through a precious Redeemer – my Dear Brother its now a fortnight since I begun to write to you and since that I have bin very ill indeed or you wou[d] have heard from me before now – and I hope I shall hear from you as soon as it may be Conveineint and please to Let me know how you all are and how my poor Dear Brother Tho[s] and his family whome I thot to have wrote to Long before now but I were sure that if it was not in my power to pay the postage of my Letters to him it was not posible for him to receieve them as I allways have Endeavourd up to this time) as allso my Dear sisters and Brother Johns I have allso since my sisters Death Paid for the Keeping up of her grave at gerrons the reason is my poor dear partner has bin failing for this Twelve months past and when he is not able work it is hard times with us as we have only seven shillings p[r] week to Live on and Every thing is – in this plase very Dear 6 – a gallon for potatoes Even now and not Long since they were 10d/4 and Every thing in propotion

   my Dear Brothers—
      We remain your most affectionate
         Sister and Brother
            J and Tho[s] Honey

I hope to write to my Dear Brother Thos very soon—

Fairmantle Street
truro
april 6th 1827

my Dear Brother
This will inform you that I rec^d your kind Letter with what was inclos^d therein
as allso the News paper with it and to be suficintly thankful for tis not in my
power but I sincerly hope that the Lord will in great mercy reward you for all
the favours that you have Done for me and should I never hear from my dear
brother any more in this Life – your Last Letter fully perswades me to believe
that your brotherly – friendship is not in the Least alterd tho since I wrote my
Last Letter its not in my power to tell you how my mind has troubl^d me to
think in what an uncouth manner I wrote in some respects tho far from my
hart to offend Either my Dear Brother or his – Dear family if they did know
what I wrote I mean with respect to my speaking of them in rather – Distant
manner but my Dear Brother I realy think my self unworthy to speak of them
as I Could wish only this I am sertain that if I Could But see Mrs Clift once
more I am fully perswaded in my mind that she would forgive me and I hope
she will if I never see her any more in this Life – as I fear I never shall if Mrs and
Miss Clift will please to Except my sincere respects I shall be glad I am realy
hapy to hear that Master Clift thinks of Coming to Cornwall this summer I
hope he will and if he Does not intend Coming Down so far as Truro I would
go to Bodmin to se him There) I supose my Dear Brother knows that the
young parson Gilbert and his family Lives at Priory with Mr Gilbert[26] I seldom
hear from Bodmin now as Mrs Billing has Left it for some time past she Lives
at Lostwithel with her son he is a surgeon – she has very often wrote to me and
was allso very kind to me when I were in Bodmin) however I wish you and
Master Clift Could Come to Cornwall togather if it were posible But I fear
that Cannot be I supose Master Clift is so alterd that I should not know Him
any more than I knew my Dear Brother when I first Came to London I am
supris,d when I Consider where he has bin Traveling allready for one so young
as he is tho I Dare say he Likes it much and I hope the Change of Air will be a
means of preserving his Health I hope my Dear Brother should I be spared to
see the hapy period of your Comming to Cornwall that Mrs or Miss Clift will –
Come with you I only wish it Could be this summer as I may say whilst there is
Life there is hope – and now my Dear Brother I hope that you will never any
more get in to a throng no not for the first grand sight that England Could
boast of – I read the rest of your Letter with great pleasure but when I saw
what Danger you were Expos<d> to my Dear dear Brother that Cut me to the
hart so that I forgot my affliction and Every thing Else I thot had my poor
Dear Brother Thomas wrote and told me that you had lost your Life in that
Dreadful manner I am sure it would have bin my Death allso I dread to think

226

of it now But as King David said my dear Brother will I hope from his hart say
the same He took me out of an Horable pit and did set my feet upon a Rock He
put a new song in my mouth Even a song of praise and thanksgiving[27] and
when Ever I think of it in future I hope I shall Ever give praise to The Lord for
your safty and may the Lord Ever preserve you and your family

is the sincere Desire of your
Ever affectionat Sister
Joanna Honey

PS
my Husband desires to Join me in Love and kind respects to you and all the
family as allso to my Brother Tho[s] and his family—
I am hapy to say we are Both Better then we have Bin through the winter He is
able to go to work again

I will write to Bro[th]
Thomas next week

125. Joanna to William. 28 January 1836.

1836
Portscatha Gerrons January 28

My Ever dear Brother
this will inform you that with thankfullness I recciv,d your Letter with the
inclos[d] But the Contents of it has Brot me so dreadfully nervous that I Can
scarsely write or atend to any thing that I have to do and being so Entirely by
my self night and day having none but strangers around me[28] that I Can
scarsely bearup under it having no one to Comfort me in this time of Distress
no none but the Lord – therefore I will look onto the Lord I will patiently wait
for the god of my salvation the Lord will hear me – as the prophet micah says
Chap[tr] 7 verse – While I Consider how all my dear family is taken from me
one/ one after another that somany as we once were and now only 2 Left one
Dear brother instead of 4 while I am Left Like a poor Pellican in the
willderness[29] of this world for only a short time I sincerly hope as there is no
Lasting hapiness for any one this side the grave its only one trouble on another
and I believe its only to make us all to Look more at the Eternal world where
true hapiness is only to be found, and in all the tryals in Life that my Dear
Brother Thomas must have sufferd that he did not forget what I once heard
him say to me and my Dear Husband as we were walking Down parliament
Street and we were talking of religious subjects But this is all I Can recollect
He said I know in whome I have believed and am perswaded he is able to keep
that which I have Comited unto Him against that Day – which is sertanly

meant the Day of Judgment) and now the Distress of those he has Left behind greatly ads to my distress knowing its not in my power to do any thing for the poor dear dear Creatures The Lord Has said in his Blessed word that He will be a father to the fatherless and a Husband to the widow If they Call on him in faith and attend to His ordnances in the House of prayer – I allmost fancied my self with them yesterday the whole day and as wretched as they Could posibly be, and I only wish it had bin True, Tender dear Creatures, and when you see any of them that is poor anna or mary please to Desire Either of them to write to me) my Dear Brother I feel for you with the most sincere affection for the Bitter Tryals you have had as well as the great Expence you must have atended to at the death of so many Dear relatives as you mention and tho Mrs Clifts Parent must have bin very aged it must have bin a great tryal to part with a Dear parent and sister yet she has a Dear friend to soothe Her distress besides Her dear Daughter and Husband[30] I hope they are well and will remain so for your sake as well as their own – I find Mr Gilbert of pryory has bin Dead a great while[31] and one of his Brothers sons has full posesion of pryory and Live in the greatest stile imaginable, they keep their Coach and Pegy Bates Eldest son is Coachman there he is Call^d Nicholas Hoar he Left them once and Came to this Parish as Coachman with a Squire Johns hes a well behavd young man he Lived here 2 years and then went to Live at Mr Gilberts again I have now to go two miles or more with this letter Therefore – my Dear dear Brother I Conclude with my kind Love and affection to you and your Dear family and remain your affectionate Sister

Joanna Honey

NOTES SECTION XII

1. The date of Joanna's return to Cornwall is not known but it may have been about 1817.
2. It seems that Thomas's first wife has died and that he has married again. As there is reference later to his wife's children, it seems that she too must have married before.
3. Joanna had been married in London and it is not clear if this is the same husband or if she, too, had married a second time.
4. Anna is referred to fairly frequently until her death in 1837. Probably she was the child of Thomas and his first wife or just possibly of his second wife.
5. All Clift's letters from this time are drafts. Deletions have generally been ignored and insertions silently incorporated to make for ease of reading, unless they seem of particular interest.
6. Peace was established in 1815 with the Settlement of Vienna but English troops remained in France, initially under the command of Wellington, for a further five years.

7. The Queen was Charlotte, wife of George III. She died on 17 November 1818.
8. Mrs Gilbert had died on 8 April 1818, aged 73.
9. Psalm 23 verse 4 is, 'Yea, though I walk through the valley of the shadow of death, I will fear no evil; for thou art with me; thy rod and thy staff they comfort me'.
10. From *when Ever he came* to *Tryals and sufferings* appears to have been added as an afterthought. It is written opposite on the facing page but as placed it carries straight on. This accounts for the disjointed reading at the end of the insertion.
11. The ms. has been damaged here.
12. Nancy Clift was John Clift's wife. She signs herself *Ann* in the preceding letter.
13. These lines seem intended as an insertion where Clift has marked the draft with an **a**.
14. Written on the outer sheet, probably by Clift, is *Rec^d Jan. 1. 1820.*
15. *1819* has been written under the year, probably by Clift.
16. This remark leads one to surmise that Joanna's husband may have been the Thomas Teague mentioned in 1797 by Elizabeth and Joanna. See Letters 79 and 80.
17. Clift was elected an F.R.S. on 6 May 1823.
18. Mr Gilbert lived until 1827, when he was succeeded at Priory by his nephew, the Revd John Pomeroy Gilbert.
19. *rigs:* this word has many meanings, the most obvious, perhaps, being 'prank' or 'frolic', a dialectal usage. In this sense it is first recorded in the *OED* in 1811 but is, presumably, much older. In dialect it can also mean a wanton girl or woman and the *OED* records its use in this sense from Elworthy's *Somerset Word-book* (1886).
20. See Section III, the letters for the first half of 1793.
21. Castlereagh died on 12 August 1822.
22. Written above the greeting is *Answered April 2. 1827.* and *money letter office £1.0.0.*
23. Frederick Augustus, Duke of York, was the second son of George III. He was born in 1763 and died on 5 January 1827.
24. *the riseing of the Lights:* the name given to a complaint suffered by women, which consisted of choking in the throat and inability to draw breath. The *OED* also terms it 'hysteria'.
25. *Dr Wats* is written below in the margin. The verse is taken from Isaac Watt's *Hymn and Spiritual Songs* Book II and is the second verse of No. LXXVI. 'The Resurrection and Ascension of Christ':

> Death is no more the King of dread,
> Since our *Emmanuel* rose,
> He took the Tyrant's Sting away,
> And spoil'd our hellish Foes. (5th ed., London, 1716)

26. *young parson Gilbert:* John Pomeroy Gilbert, a son of Mr Gilbert's brother, the Reverend Edmund Gilbert.
27. Psalm 40 verses 2–3. This could be taken from the Bible or the Book of Common

Prayer, the wording not matching either exactly.

28. Joanna's husband, Thomas Honey, must have died sometime between 1827 and 1836. Joanna seems to have returned to Gerrans to live.
29. *a poor Pellican in the willderness:* Psalm 102, verse 6. This is Coverdale's version from the Book of Common Prayer. The Authorized Version has '*of* the wilderness'.
30. Clift's son, William Home Clift, had died after a coaching accident on 17 September 1832, hence he is not mentioned here.
31. Mr Gilbert died on 2 February 1827.
32. Added, almost certainly by Clift.

XIII. 1837–1846.

The letters of the last ten years of the correspondence, between William and his last surviving sister, are spasmodic and, unfortunately, many letters referred to are missing. The ones that survive, tell of present matters both personal and public, as well as giving glimpses of the days of their childhood in Bodmin. William, in particular, shows a tendency to recount memories of his childhood escapades when he writes of Bodmin.

The impact of the public world is, as always, a source of comment. The increasing speed of steam trains is a matter of interest to William, at the end of whose garden in Regent's Park ran the main line from London to Birmingham. Neither he nor his sister shows a great enthusiasm for travelling by train and when William and his wife take a week's touring holiday in 1839 they stick to the conventional coaches as well as taking a steam packet on a crossing to Calais. In the same year William speaks warmly of the Penny Post which was scheduled to be introduced in 1840.

Of the family's personal fortunes more has to be deduced than is actually stated. By 1837, from Joanna's references to Mrs Owen, it is clear that William's daughter Caroline has married Richard Owen, who had succeeded to the position of William's son in the Museum in 1832 and by 1834 was elected a Fellow of the Royal Society and appointed to the Chair of Comparative Anatomy at St. Bartholomew's Hospital. The marriage took place in 1835. By 1837 Caroline has a young son, another William, who was to be the only child of the marriage. In 1842 Owen succeeded Clift as the Conservator of the Museum and William went into semi-retirement. As the Owens then took over the Clifts' apartments at the College, William and his wife moved to a cottage in Regent's Park and relinquished their quarters in the College.

In 1837 Joanna was living once more in Gerrans but returned to Truro by 1840. Part of the Eyre family of Bodmin had settled there and in 1840 William received a letter from Thomas Eyre (presumably a son of Joseph Eyre) informing him that his sister was ill. By 1845 she had returned to her native town of Bodmin and married one of the notorious Soady family. The marriage was not a success and in her final letter in 1846 it is clear that she and her husband are living apart. William expresses no surprise at the outcome of this late marriage and expatiates at length upon the infamous doings of the Soadys, who have hitherto received no mention in the letters. Even at this late stage he reminds his sister of her own hot temper, which no doubt did not improve the situation, but he still sends her money from London and is anxious that it should reach her safely.

Most of William's letters surviving from this time are drafts and one, which appears in two separate drafts, is of particular interest for showing how he elaborated on a topic in successive reworkings. The letters are filled with complaints about the ever increasing work at the College, his own consequent lack of time, and the innumerable calls on his pocket in the way of taxes and bills. Some of the letters contain pages of the names of people he remembers from Bodmin before he left in 1792 and one includes an extensive inventory of road names as he endeavours to place Turf Street where Joanna is living.

Over the years both city and country have seen many changes. London has grown to twice its size since 1817 and the new houses have water on the first floor, or even, in some cases, on the second and third. In Bodmin there have also been changes, and there are new faces among the inhabitants. Another Sir William has succeeded Sir Arscott Molesworth at Pencarrow and Mr Salter's voice is heard no more intoning the responses in Bodmin Church. The old names are recalled before they are finally laid to rest. Even Catty Pinch, the Prentice girl who lived with old Mr and Mrs Eyre, is not forgotten as Joanna remembers the 'many happy Days that are gone and past'. Joanna died in 1846, a few months after the last surviving letter, but her brother lived on for another three years when, in 1849, both he and his wife died within a few weeks of each other.

126. Joanna to William. 22 May 1837.

Portscatha Gerrons
May 22 1837

     My dear dear Brother
This will inform you that I rec^d your most kind and welcome Letter dated the 12 and for the Letter as well as the inclos,d I am most sincerely thankfull as Every time I Look it over it Cheers my poor heart Except that of Mrs Clift and Mrs Owen[1] being so very unwell for which I am sincerely sorry But when the weather allters I hope they will get much very much better and that soon as I

am sure that you and Mr Owen are not Comfortable while they are so unwell and when I Consider the Confusd state of Every thing around you at present and the very Little time that you have to spare and the trying Difficulty at the postoffice the time being so Limited that I realy wonder that you my dear Brother should be able make your mind up to write atall tho for some time I might not have known the Cause and tho its not in my power nor Ever will be to show suficently the gratitude thats Due to my Ever dear Brother for what you have Ever done for me yet I am fully asured that – the Lord will do more for you then I Can ask or think for the great kindness to many poor widdows that you have done at all times) for The Lord hath said) that if its only a Cup of Cold water in His name that the giver thereof – shall not Loose His reward for as much as ye did it to one of these ye did it unto me[2] and as the Lord hath prosperd you and your dear family I sincerly hope He Ever will) when I read that delightful account of the unspeakable satisfaction you do and will injoy in future with respect to that dear young – gentlemans proceedings allready it does my poor heart good)[3] my dear Brother I think if you had made Choice for your self and family you never Could have made a more suitable request and still as there is another blessing promisd after a few months more that will Compleat your familys Hapines[4] – and I sincerly trust in the Lord that you will spend many very many Happy hapy years togather—

I am glad to hear that poor Mary is Likely to do well[5] I wish twas no worse with Her sister anna poor dear and sory I am to hear so Bad an account of my Dear Brothers widdow and her daughter poor girl I have not seen Ether of mr Eyres family since I were at Truro Last which was twelve months Last Sep[r] but they write to me still and Ever have treated me as one of their own family Dear people—

I think if – Lady Ker acted as a Lady ought to do she migh have wrote to have Let you know what her unkle thot of your Letter for she knew that you had bin very familar with Him I supose Miss Eyre inform,d you that Her unkle andrew Lives at St alena and is a great man Ther he Caries on a great Brewery

> at present I Conclude with my
> most affectionate Love and kind
> respects to you and all the Dear family
> J Honey

my Dear Brother I hope you will please to forgive my Bad writing as I Can scarsly Hold my pen haveing almost Lost the use of my right hand by the reumatic and my sight is Just as Bad But rather then suffer another to write for me I have bin several days writing this miserable scrole

127. Sarah Clift to William Clift. 26 June 1837.

7 Cross Court
Vinegar Yd.
Drury Lane

Sir/
These few lines will acquaint you my poor dear Girl is no more; she died this morning at ½ past 12 oClock; she had had long and deep suffering and for the last seven weeks has kept her bed.

In addressing you now Sir, I do it with the greatest humility, intreating your aid in the *hour of Death*; which I am assured from the kindnesses I have received from you, will not be witheld in the hour of a widowed Mother's trials; in consequence of her extreme illness I have necessarily been confined to my home, that my own industry & exertions have been straitened – I have no means of placing her under ground – I hope you will be a frind; the friend of your poor Brothers Widow; I am desired by the persons who reside in the same house with me to say how much they feel my situation they all have witnessed my sorrows, and been eye witnesses to my beloved childs sufferings and release.

Thus Sir trusting to your human and Christian feelings, and *hoping you will come and see me.*

I remain Sir
Yours respectfully
Sarah Clift

"Aged 23."[32]
next October.

26th June
1837

128. William to Joanna. ?26 1839.[6]

My dear Sister
I received your Letter of July 18 and take the earliest opportunity and first minutes leisure to quiet your fears about our health which is as good as can be wished or expected notwithstanding the rough weather which has done as we hear so much mischief in various parts of the Country, though I have seen little of it and heard almost less, as I have very seldom time to read a Newspaper. Mrs Clift and myself had been up to the Regent's Park on the Sunday afternoon which you mention to see Caroline and drink Tea with her in her new Cottage, for they have got a very pretty one on the edge of the Regent's Park with a rail road at the back of them and the

233

Regents Canal on the front; at least within a stones throw of each. We escaped the rain thunder & lightning by getting a Coach about half a minute before it begun & got home quite safe & I afterwards saw no more of it. They removed away from the College at Midsummer, and have what I wish I had, the advantage of fresh air, as well as day-light, which they were very deficient of in Lincoln's Inn Fields, where they had hardly the one or the other – The little Girl which we expected about this time has not made her appearance yet though we are weekly & daily expecting her. [7] Both Caroline and Mr Owen are very well, and little Willy is growing away, and just beginning to run about nicely: and has a mouthful of teeth and half a dozen words. It must be quite nonsense and fancy to talk as you do about growing old and infirm when you cannot be more than four years older than me at the most,[8] and I was 64 on the 14th of February 1839 and must not talk of growing old and useless until I give over eating and hard work:– for without the one I have no chance of doing the other, as far as I yet see: and every year adds considerably to the labour and anxiety of all that went before. Every week now brings as much work, and requires as much attention as a month did when I first began, but as it is *still only the Museum*, no alteration as far as regards myself has ever been mentioned, and as I am always alive and in my place, and have no time to think whether I am ill or not, and still less to take Physic, and few people have taken less or needed less than I have: as exercise, though almost intirely within doors, has been fortunately Physic enough for me. I almost envy you your journey from Truro to St Austle and Bodmin, though I should have perhaps regretted it afterwards, as you did, to find so many old friends and acquaintances in half a century dead and gone: and I suppose I should scarcely find one that I know, or one that would know me, now Poor old Mr Gilbert is gone:– as I know none of that Family, and from what I hear I scarcely need regret it.

Several of the Old friends you mention I cannot well recollect. I do not know what Mr Billing it can be with 12 Children:– Not old Mr Billing the Watchmaker who lived opposite to Mrs King! I knew him & recollect him very well, and some of his funny Stories about London which he told me when I was coming away. Poor Polly Godfrey & Honour Williamson I should have been glad to have heard they were living. Jenny Leavers, and Poor Betty Williamson I think I recollect hearing of their death many years ago. I recollect the name of Miss Mitre though I do not recollect who she was or where she lived, though I recollect Hannah Popham, and Mr Gurney the glover next door who made me a shilling pair of gloves worked with sky-blue silk on the backs to come to London in, in 1792. I was much pleased to hear that you found Betty Hoskin alias Oliver alive. I suppose that Harry is dead, as you did not mention him. It was poor Harry that I was riding behind, when Mr Mudge's horse ran away with us, and we fell off in Back lane where I received such a blow on the temple as I shall never forget for I have the mark there still, and I was obliged to walk as gravely as an old man for a year or two afterwards. Poor old Jack Pearn that kept so many Cats in St Nicholas Street tried to stop us, but the Horse ran straight between his two pitchers of Water & did not break either of them in coming down St Nicholas Street. When we got to Mr Moore's at the corner of Back Lane & Mount Folly the horse turned suddenly down Back-lane instead of going down Prison Lane & threw me off my balance & my short legs could not regain their position – Poor Harry leant off the other side until my head hit against the Moor Stone Pillars near the lower end of the lane, and when I came down, he went over on the other side, and the horse ran home to the Stable in Great Bury Lane with the Halter between his legs. Poor brother Thomas seeing the Horse run by at Church Stile with the halter trailing, ran to see what had happened and found me at Mrs Blakes in Back lane apparently dead. I was taken to Mr Mudge's where I kept my bed for I do not know how many days vomiting bile, and I have no doubt with my skull fractured, but luckily there was no surgeon to trepan me,[9] & Mr or Dr Colville or Colwell opposite Mr Mudge allowed me to take my chance, and so here I am still.

Mr Barron had no business to die he was not many years older than me. I bought a book of him at an Auction in the Town hall all about London & Greenwich, long before I had an Idea of seeing either. I ran after him in the Street soon after I came to London stumping along with a Great stick

129. *William to Joanna. 25 October 1839.*

£1: 19: 11.

My dear Sister

No doubt you expected the present letter a week or two before this time, but I was prevented from writing sooner on account of being far removed from the Post Office and could not obtain this Order until to day, and the reason was this:–

I was glad to avail myself of the first Opportunity of enjoying my holiday after the affairs of the Quarterly Boards and Meetings were all over, and the weather promised to be fine; and I most fortunately did so; for the eight days we were on our travels were among the most beautiful that this dull summer has produced, and we luckily returned to London on the very last day that was fit for travelling, and it has continued raining most dismally ever since and is continuing to do so while I am writing or rather scrawling this, on this most abominable Post Office Paper, which however answers the purpose of saving Double Postage,[10] and therefore we must not grumble more than necessary, particularly as they give us the paper, and have reduced the amount of Insurance for the *above sum*[11] to Sixpence when formerly I used to pay for two pounds, *Insurance two Shillings* and postage of the double letter *two shillings* more. But in this present way it is now reduced to one shilling and sixpence:

and in a short time it appears that the Postage af all letters to every part of England is to be reduced to one Penny,[12] as most of them will be carried a great part of their journey by rail road conveyance on which I have no compassion, as the weight of the additional letters that will then be sent, will not break the backs of the poor *Post-Horses* much more than at present; and this will be a great blessing to many a poor family who will be then enabled to correspond with their distant friends who could very ill afford to pay a day, or two day's wages for the Postage of a Letter, however anxious they might be to write or to receive a letter from their friends or Children, who too often made this an excuse for not writing at all, and thereby, in time, neglect and forget each other. But to return to the fine weather of last week;– it enabled Mrs Clift and myself to enjoy ourselves completely like Children let out of School:– after having been shut up in London during the whole Year with hardly one day's sight of the Country, or a green field except that of Lincoln's Inn Fields:– and *bating the fatigue* of packing and unpacking, night and morning, and clambering to the tops of Stage Coaches and down the Ladders of Steam Vessels and up the ladders of Piers of Harbours which necessarily accompanied our pleasure, as during our intire journey we never stayed longer than one intire day in one town, in order to see as much as possible in the shortest time, which would have been delightful and not so fatiguing, thirty or forty years ago:– but nevertheless we had the pleasure of seeing some very pretty *places* and things that were not in existence at that time. Although we were absent from home only eight days we accomplished about three hundred miles, by water and by land; and once we had to get up at five in the morning to be in time for starting at Six:– which was any thing rather than a Joke as Mrs C was very unwell at that time, and in *a Foreign Land*! for we were then in the French King's Dominions:– vizt From London we set off by a noble Steamer for Herne Bay near the mouth of the Thames, and from thence across the Country to Canterbury which is one of the Oldest Cities in England, and which neither of us had seen before:– saw the fine old Cathedral in which Thomas a Becket was murdered at the foot of the Altar, and touched the spot where he fell, and from whence his Title to Martyrdom or Saintship took its Origin;– and this spot became so sanctified that such Myriads of Pilgrims and Devotees resorted to this place from all parts of the World, that the steps leading to his Shrine are nearly worn out by their crawling on their knees; and which is quite evident at the present time. The Cathedral is still very beautiful, and *was* immensely rich 'till Harry the 8th plundered it. The City is prettily situated, but small compared with London and many others. From thence we went on to Dover and the weather being very beautiful though rather *blowy*, we set off at a Short notice by a French Steam packet for Calais, as Mrs C had never been in France and we crossed the Channel which is here two or three and twenty miles wide in about three hours, on, I believe the *very day* of the same month that I crossed it on my way to Paris just Twenty years before, vizt 1819. I believe each of us could sail to America without being *Sea-sick* which rendered the Voyage to us delightful, though the Mops and basons were travelling every minute for our less fortunate Fellow-Passengers all the way there; and the same on our return. They were chiefly in the Cabins below, or cooped up in their Carriages on Deck, but as the weather was chiefly beautiful we of course kept on Deck always. We remained one day in Calais and saw their fine old Cathedral and all else that was worth, and a great deal that was not worth seeing; as it is a very old and much neglected Sea Port though a great Thoroughfare from England to Paris and all parts of the Continent on account of the narrowness of the Channel at this part. We returned to Dover – saw Shakespeare's Cliff – went up a tunnel of Steps half as high as St Paul's, to the Barracks, from whence is a delightful prospect. From Dover we returned by Deal, Sandwich, Ramsgate, (with its beautiful Stone Pier, the two parts of which are nearly a mile long, and is esteemed the finest in England, and has cost little less than a Million sterling) From thence we came across six miles of East Kent to Margate and from thence to London by the Royal George Steamer nearly 80 miles in little more than 7 hours, with the wind right a-head, to London Bridge,– and were glad to find ourselves at home again safe and well, and to find all those we left behind in as good health as ourselves. My little Grandson Willy runs about and begins to say a hundred things and understands twice as many:– and we are all *quite well*.

This is all the news I have, worth sending. I hope I shall have as satisfactory a letter from you as soon as you receive this. I remain my Dear Sister

Yours ever truly
Wm Clift

Lincoln's Inn Fields
  October 25. 1839.

Joanna Honey
N° 1 St Mary's Street
  near the Latin School
    Truro, Cornwall.

130. William to Joanna. 5 February 1840.

My dear Sister, I receivd a letter from Mr Thomas Eyre & I wrote an answer to him yesterday, and answered the same day, and requested him to acquaint you that I had written to him, and that I would if possible also write to you by the same post, but which I afterwards found to be impossible to be written in time for the Post and I had still less time to get as far as the Post office, and I thought it would be useless to write to you unless I could Do that first. I am exceedingly sorry to hear that your Cough has continued so very distressing, and I had been hoping from day to day that you would have been so much better as to have been able to write to me a few lines only, to say you were better as in the letter which I received from *Mrs* Pascoe on the 23d of January at your request in which she acquainted me that you had received my Letter, which I had sent about a week before. If I had been certain that it was a Lady that had written the Letter I should have endeavoured to *have* answered it if I could have found a minutes leisure, but except from the delicate hand writing I could not tell, as it had only the Initial letters S.D. Pascoe, and I put off writing from day to day till I received Mr Eyre's Letter yesterday, which I answered immediately: but I naturally deferred writing as long as I could, on account of having so much writing to do for the museum lately which keeps me employed as usual a great part of the night, and I have now many letters lying by me which ought to have been answered from a week or two or three weeks ago: and which if I had help I could not avail myself of, to assist me in answering:– I have had a young man for a month past to help me in copying some writing for the museum, and he has done it so very badly that I have been obliged to rewrite and correct it so much before it could be put into the Printer's hands, that I might have done it all myself in nearly the same time; which has kept me in continual plague till three or four o'Clock every morning lately. So that I have had very few minutes to attend to my own affairs for several weeks past. I hope that Mr Eyre's medical/–man Mr Spry's prescriptions will have done you service and relieved your very troublesome Cough. I mentioned in my Letter to Mr Eyre what I thought might be of most service in order to procure you some sleep at nights and relief from pain and the Cough,– I am exceedingly obliged to Mrs or Miss Pascoe for her Kindness in Writing for you and also to Mr Eyre and his family for their goodness and attention to you, and trust they will meet their reward for it hereafter. We are all as well as can be, considering the strange and unseasonable weather and except slight colds and rheumatism we are all in perfect health and my dear little grand/ son in particular. I shall hope for a few lines from your or some of your kind friends to tell me you are better and I remain my dear Sister yours very faithfully Wm Clift

5 Feb^y
1840

131. Joanna to William. 25 October 1841.

Saint mary^s Street Truro
Monday morning oct^r 25 1841.

My Ever dear Brother
   with my most sincere thanks and gateful acknolegement of the receipt of your most kind and welcome Letter this morning and as it is the only hapiness I

Can posibly desire whilst hear on Earth to hear that amidst Every tryal and difficulty in this world of – Tryals and difficulties – that you and your Ever dear family are still preservd in Life and health and tho trying as your situation is and has Bin for so many years I sincerly hope that the time is not far distant when you might Expect a superanuation after so many years of slavish servitude and to me its realy strange that such a Body of Gentlemen should not have Considerd you as a Brother not in word only but in deed and in truth and it realy grieves me to hear that they are still adding instead of Diminishing – the work may the Lord give you patience to Bare it a Little Longer it Can not be forever I am allso realy sory to hear of Dear Mr and Mrs Owen haveing had such an unpleasant Excursion[13] the dear Creatures they will not I hope Ever undertake such another it was a saying in former times – Haste makes waste[14] – I hope it may be a means of preventing you and Mrs Clift from Ever going anymore by steam by sea or Land if opportunity should permit I would much rather Travel a Little way in safety then go a great way in danger on Tuesday the 21st of Septr I left Truro for Gerrons and returnd on Tuesday the 19th which was one month I had not bin there for 2 years Therefore I were the greater stranger among them and were most kindly receiev,d by all the people from the Esquire and all his family to the meanest in the village I know and am sure that Lady Hartley has never bin so kindly receiv,d as my self amongst all the people tho she is Extremly rich and keeps her Coach the name of her Country seat in Gerrons is Called Roseteage and antient built house about half a mile from the Church Town she has one son and brot him up Like herself to do no good for King or Country My poor Rich Sisterinlaw is Dead some time since and one of her Daughters keeps the Publick House in the Churchtown Her Husband is a Carpenter a well looking young man as any in the parish both steady and sober they have 2 dear Little Children Boy and girl the younger is maried to one of Devonshire a farmer said to be of a Thousand pounds fortune my poor sisterinlaw was remarkeably kind to me 2 years since when I were There she was afflicted Last winter when I were so that we Could visit one another and tho in her Life time she was one of the strongest women In Gerrons and yet Cut down before me she Left all she had To her to Daughters and they sent me 2 shillings to buy morning I Did not send it Back no – I took it from whence it Came—

My Dear dear Brother
Please to give my most sincere Love
   to all your dear family and when you write
   me pleas to Let me know how that dear dear
   Child is and if he is able read yet
     I am your sincere and most affectionate
               Sister Joanna Honey

January 10. 1845.
Stanhope Cottage
Mornington Road
Regent's Park[16]

My dear Sister

I had intended to have written to you at Christmas, or the New Year at farthest, but I have been prevented for several reasons, and among the rest, my being hindred from getting so far as the Post Office to procure the inclosed Order, on account of my being so very lame and unwell from Rheumatic Gout in my joints, and pain in my teeth, and face, which has prevented me from doing, or attending to almost any thing. Illness here has been so very universal that hardly any one that I know, has escaped altogether. Almost every body has been suffering of Rheumatism on account of the dampness of the Season, instead of the good old-fashioned dry Frost and Snow.

We are now all of us getting better. I hope you have escaped better than we have, as you are so many hundreds of miles nearer the Sun, though we keep ourselves as warm as fire and flannels will allow. I have no news worth telling you though, I fancied I had before I began to write. I was much pleased to learn that Poor old Bodmin has been so much improved in its Streets and Buildings – though I suppose they have not yet advanced so far as to have any *foot pavements* on the sides of the Streets, which I recollect used to annoy the London people so much, when they came down to attend the Assizes or the Races. They used to complain sadly of the Streets being paved with flints, with the sharp points upwards. No doubt they felt it thro' their thin London Shoes and Boots, and no wonder as I can now perfectly understand what they meant.

I have lately been reading a Book which I wish you had. It gives a good account of London as it was in 1817 describing all the old and new Buildings and Improvements *to that time* and *you* have not seen it since: though it *now* has so increased, as to cover nearly twice the extent of ground, that it did then: there having been several hundred miles of Streets built, of a very superior kind to those you can recollect. I was almost in the Fields when I came to this House two years & a half ago, and am already shut in by new Streets in almost every direction: containing perhaps five hundred new houses within musquet shot, all excellently wide, well paved at the sides for foot passengers and macadamized[17] in the centre,– well lighted by Gas, & watched by the Police – and supplied with water as high as to the first floor in most of the best houses: *and* to the third and fourth story in many that lie towards Lincoln's Inn Fields and the Strand. Many miles of streets have been paved with wooden pavement[18] which prevents the noise and dust which used to stun and annoy us when paved with stone in former times, and vast numbers of others are made like the best turnpike-roads to prevent the noise and jolting which formerly almost jolted us out of our Skins. When you knew London there was *just One thousand* Hackney coaches and no more with 2 Horses. Then was added five hundred Chariots & two horses – Afterwards were added about an equal number of Cabriolets with one horse – Then followed some thousands of Omnibuses with 2 horses each which are licensed to carry fifteen, besides the Coachman and   .[19] The Hackney coaches are allowed *one shilling* a mile with no more than four passengers – The Cabriolets & chariots carry 2 (or sometimes 3) for 8 pence per mile. The Omnibuses run right through/

Rent – Taxes – Rates – Mr Guillemard – Mr Webster) and/ Hills. &c. &c. &c.

133. William to Joanna. 10 January 1845.

Stanhope Cottage, Mornington Road,
Regent's Park, London.
January 10 1845.

My dear Sister

I had intended to have written to you at Christmas, or at the New Year at farthest, but I have been prevented by *several* good and substantial reasons; and one or two among the rest shall serve. My being prevented from getting so far as the Post-Office to procure the inclosed Order, on account of my being so very lame and unwell from Rheumatic Gout in my joints, and severe pain in my face and the three or four Teeth who are grateful enough to remain in my Service: all the rest have quitted me as *civilly* as it was possible;– only two or three required to be taken into Custody, and *put in Irons* by the Dentist, much against my wish, as they had for many long years been my faithful assistants; and never rebelled before: but like a falling house, or a sinking Ship, (when the Rats are said to *take to their heels*) – my Teeth chose to give me warning all at once: supposing, *I suppose*, that Victuals was becoming scarce, because I only troubled them much less than I formerly did. However, I am well quit of them—

Illness here, of one kind or another, has been so universal that hardly a single person that I know has escaped altogether. Almost every body has been *suffering*, from Rheumatism; which they, and myself attribute to the *damp* coldness of the Season:– How *unlike* the Good Old-Fashioned Frost and Snow of my *young* days, when I did not *much* mind breaking though the Ice of the Pond at the Top of Saint Nicholas Street; and after having my Jacket, my Shirt, and unmentionables wrung out by my good-natured schoolfellows, retiring to my good old friend *Grace Ham's* Oven-door for an hour to render me presentable at home!!!

If *Young* Jonathan Ham brings you *this*, I request you will give him a Shilling to drink my health. He may, and has, no doubt forgotten a little fellow like me so much *his Junior*, for I am *only* Seventy in three weeks hence; but I recollect him, well enough, when dancing a *hornpipe* in Old Otho Popham's parlour – the 15 Balls (Cornish Arms *One and All*[20] in Prison Lane opposite my *good* Mr Salter's School.) in *Dancing Pumps* of *his own* making, with *buckles* that *scraped the ground* at the Corners, (nearly as big as ones hand.) You will not have forgotten the fashion of that day.

Being in Prison Lane – what has become of Mr Flamank, Old Roger Dawe,– Mr Salter's Family. Mrs Northey,– Mrs Jack Hocken, the Staymaker:—and Josey Leavers, who sold milk at the Prison-Lane-Bridge? What has been done with the Prison,– and the *Stinking* prison-pools, where they used to *preserve* Carrion for the Gentlemen's hounds? (They would be prosecuted here now for such *Savoury* doings as were *then* tolerated.)

Betsy Blight I think you told me was *dead*;– Blue Peter Rescorla, not yet gathered to his Fathers. Jack the Giant and his Wife Nanny, and Family are they *all gone*?

Down Back Street – the Staymaker from Mount Charles Turnpike,– Nell Philp the Slater, and Betty Cook the Mutton-Pie-and-Cow-Heel-Maker,– Nanny Cook's mother next the *"Old Meeting"* – The *Trescotts*;– Old Jonathan Fry, next door to Mr Barron's Meeting house,– *Mr Jack Starr* Butcher, next door. *Willy Sweet, the Clerk* and Patten & heel-maker; Mrs Northey, and all *the Pearses'*, Malsters:– and the Wheel-wright opposite:– And *Deborah Ford*, and John, her Son – and poor *Deborah Lord* and her Sister Molly (Something) *Gadd?* who lived at *Lanivet* or *near it*. Have they *all gone* and *escaped your remembrance* or *have they not?*– Jack Clemo or *Climas* of *Bury-Lane* – his Son *Dick* and Daughters *Katy* & Sally:—&c. Jack Williams – and his Daughter Mary who married Richard . . . . at Luxillian: and *Sally and Lovey*, and his graceless Son *Tom* – who lost an Arm at Sea. And John Coppin the Grocer, and his *daughter* who *married* Robin Granville:– and Tammy *Bonney* who *married Mr Williams*, Mr *King's* foreman, who became Gingerbread-maker *for love of her.* and Billy *Bonney* and his strapping Wife, who used to throw the Sledge hammer *to him* (not at him). And *Drum-Major* Wills at the *Butter-Market*, and his Sons *George*, and *Jack*, and *Richard* – with large foreheads when they were young;—and Mr *Tabb* at the *Queen's head* – And *Willy Saunders* at the *George and Dragon*, Mount-folly;– and *Coade* the Smith, and *Jonathan Elicott* and *all the Elicotts* of Penbiggle (or Penbugle) where we used to knock about the *Red Streaks*; and feed the *Shot* in the *Well.* Have they forgot to put *rush crosses* in the *Holy well* in a field near poor old *Bury tower* on Good Friday?? to learn *who* was to live *till* that day *next year?*[21] I know we we used *to do it in fear and trembling*, because if any of us had fallen in we should have been *too stupid* or too *frightened* to help one another out. Does poor old Bury Tower *stand* with one two – or three pinnacles standing?[22] I hope the Town will *still* increase on the *Sunny side*. When I once begin to think or write on my favourite Subject *Poor old Bodmin*, I do not know how or where to stop. I am glad to hear that they have originated a *Society* whose meetings are to be held in the Old Workhouse in St Nicholas Street; and I wish I may be able to contribute something in furtherance of their Views; but I have all my life had *too many Calls* upon me to do *much when competing* with People who have Thousands to my Pounds. My good will and good wishes are with them *nevertheless*. I had *intended*, because I fancied I had nothing to say, to have *said* something about the Improvements which, I hear, has taken place in Bodmin. I am afraid they have not yet so far advanced as to have any *flagged* foot pavements on the sides of the Streets, which I recollect in my young days used to annoy the London Visitors so much, when they condescended to come so *far down* to attend the *Assizes*, or the *Races*. They used (and not without reason) to complain, sadly, of the *Streets* being paved with *flints* with the *Sharp* edges upwards! No doubt they *felt* it through their *thin London Shoes and Boots*. (*Stream-workers* in Boots with *Soles* of *three inches thick* could only *laugh* at this *sensibility*, who *could* have *none* of their own.)[23] We can *all, now-a-days* perfectly comprehend *this*.

I have been, lately, *reading a Book* which I wish you had to read, though I do not know how *to send it* to you without more trouble and expense than the thing is worth, unless it were for the benefit of your *good neighbours* who would take proper care of it for you. It gives an excellent *account* of London *as it was* in the Year *1817.* describing all the old and new Buildings and Improvements to that time. And as you have not seen it *since* it would amuse you, to get any young friend to read it to you. (There are many engravings to shew the New Buildings which you have not seen.) *London* has since that time so amazingly increased, as to cover nearly twice the extent of ground that it did in 1817. there having been *several hundred* or *miles* of Streets built, of a very *superior kind* to those you can recollect. I was almost in the *fields* which I first came to this *House* (for I must, or ought not, to call it a *Cottage* at Sixty Guineas a year.) Besides Taxes of all kinds (But in two years and a half I am *already* shut in by

134. *William to Joanna. 11 April 1845.*

Stanhope Cottage, &c April 11. 1845.

My dear Sister

I received your letter of March 25 and was glad to find that you were so much better than I could have expected. This has been in London a very long and *trying* Winter. Every body that I am acquainted with has been ill more or less from Coughs, Colds, Rheumatism and other accompaniments of five or six little winters in Succession, which has made many more people ill, and carried a greater number to their long home than I almost ever recollect. A shopkeeper in the Hampstead Road opposite St James's Burying Ground with whom I occasionally deal for Pocket handkerchiefs, &c – being himself unwell & unable to go from home told me that he had seen I think eleven funerals one Sunday, and eight on the next; but that of course is not usual – and many are brought from considerable distances to these comparatively Cheap Burying grounds. This was, however, a month or six weeks ago.[24] I am very much obliged to you for your very satisfactory account of the alterations and improvements in Dear Old Bodmin – and I sincerely hope that I shall yet see it once more if not oftener, though there are very few now remaining that I should recollect, or they recollect me – and that would be rather dreary work now when travelling is tiresome and *expensive* into the bargain; and the very little money I have to spare is better laid out in sending to you than coming to you. I have, however, lately learned that by a *fast train* on the Great Western rail-way, I could get to *Exeter* in about Five *[or Six]* hours √193 & ¼ miles*]* by the way of Bath and Bristol; and from *Exeter* to Bodmin by Coach is about 60 Miles – but I am horrified at such *fly-away doings* – it almost takes away one's breath even to think of it by *Coach* nearly 3 times as fast as a Racehorse The Birmingham Rail-way at the foot of my little garden is just going to put on a *fast-train* which is to do a hundred and odd miles in *three hours* stoppages included. There have been too many things to think of and attend to at the College to have time to think of *holidays, travelling,* or *pleasure* – Food, Rent, Bills, Tythes, & Taxes of all sorts and kinds put all other things out of ones *thoughts*, and *out of one's power* – when we get past 70. Three score and ten is the age of Man, and when we get past that we are all old women together: and I have no desire to be jolted, blown up, boiled or broiled to death, by any *rail road engine* or engineer whatever. You have given me an excellent account of the Alterations, and certainly Improvements in Bodmin though *sorry* to hear of the Destruction of the *Butter-Market*.[25] Where are the Boys on a winter-evening to find the Stocks, round which we used to play *Old-Fox*?? Tom Low, a Plymouth-Boy brought home by Purser Slogget, used to put pebbles in the fingers of *his Gloves*, of which his *Fox* was made, and *pretending* he had been flogged by the Purser we all *spared* his *Cowardly* shoulders: while *we simpletons* allowed, or rather did not *allow* or *like* him to lay in into ours; but so he did: a Cowardly Scoundrel. Many a half penny and farthing did we subscribe for Candles bought at Mr Bligh's, and many a bit stolen from a poor old souls Lanthorn, when pretending to borrow a light & then stuck up in a Clay Candlestick in the Poor old *Buttermarket*. I am glad that Mr Collins of *Truedale* has subscribed to the Clock. I think I recollect his Mother, a pale pretty woman. Old Mr Brown the Lawyer, just above the *White Hart I think* in Fore Street, made out my Indentures of Apprenticeship to Mr Hunter, and *James Webb* was his Clerk. Poor old George Brown said to me "You are going to London;– when you come back hereafter in your own Carriage/ "you will

244

hardly know us, but don't forget your old Friends" Dear Mrs Gilbert said to him "For god's sake Mr Brown don't put *such Nonsense* in the poor boy's head." Mr Gilbert signed his name to Witness my Indenture as did poor Sister Betty. Mr Brown, who of course *in those days* wore a Wig, had instead, a magnificent Crimson Velvet Cap, on – I recollect him perfectly – *a magnificent old Man* in his Cap and Scarlet Morning Gown. I made a drawing in my early days of *"A Perspective View of Truedale the Seat of George Brown Esqr."* What became of it I do not know. I little thought then that he was afterwards to bind me a "London Prentice" or of pulling a Lions Tongue and Heart out like the *Original* London Prentice, but which I have since done many Times (after the Lion was dead, however.)[26] I am answering your Letter as it follows: We have had a plenty of very bad cases here and near London at the *Assizes*. I will send you a Newspaper on Sunday – I am sorry for the Death of poor Mr Grills – he was a very intelligent man too good to be buried alive at Cardinham – What has become of all the Bates's. Thomas, Phillip, and Phillipa, (Philly and Fillipey as they called her) and Humphrey, and some others if I recollect. and the Puckeys of Fowey. If any are surviving. Poor Mr Salter and his good gentle wife,– and Betsey, and James and My favourite Molly,– and Richard, and Mr Jack, and the youngest, Sally. I delight to think of them and my young Days notwithstanding my failing in *Boxing the Compass* of the Multiplication Table *backwards,*[27], and *Zigzag* after I had it *so perfect* straight forwards. Mr Salter I believe was almost as sorry as I was myself. I had never *then* felt any grief *equal to that* of being *sent back* but I soon conquered it, and he was *doubly kind* to me afterwards for what he had made me suffer:– and many a thump I got from some of my bigger school fellows because I was permitted to accompany him many times to Dunmeer after school hours, and carry his beautiful Fishing-rod, ornamented with ferules of Silk of all the Colours of the Rainbow – and artificial flies made of Cock's neck hackle and Peacock-feathers. How happy was I then!! and to have the loan of his next

135. *William to Joanna. 13 March 1836.*[28]

March 13th 1836

(*Tom Mitchell* a Scotchman
an adventurer into Cornwall
as a gardener or Nursery
– man. Fanny – Betty
with red Carrotty hair
Deborah Lord.[29]

My dear and only Sister

I received your Letter this morning I am only distressed, but not *disappointed* at your unfortunate connection with the Soady family.[30] I *foresaw* what was likely to happen: but who ever *interfered* in *family quarrels* that did not get the worst of the Battle. I saw poor *red haired* Betty Soady get her head and neck knocked between the rails of somebody's garden gate between old Betty Soady and old Mrs Blake's in Castle Street by interfering between *Kitty Climmas* and his strapping *Ann Pollard* his wife.

Every body believed the Soadys to be a *bad set* when I left home and how you *conceived* them to be *otherwise* I cannot *now conceive*: except that it might be the *means of restoring you to dear old Bodmin*, where our father and mother were buried. You could *never* have *forgotten* the saucy Red Haired Betty Soady coming and insisting on examining Poor Deborah Lord's Box for a Flannel Petticoat without any *Warrant*. (*they* were too ignorant to think such a thing necessary) *but so it was*.) You might have been present for aught I know but I recollect seeing Betty Soady turn over a pair of Tin *Shoe-Buckles* in Poor Deborah's box to *be sure* that her *lost*, or *not lost*, flannel petticoat was not hidden beneath them. I was a *comparative* child then, but my blood boiled when I saw poor Deborah Lord *suspected* of such a dishonest action by such *a sett* as the *Soady's*, for I am sure that every body in Bodmin had heard of the honest proceedings of the elder Brother *Edmund* in his *Bum-boat proceedings* at Plymouth.[31] You *knew* these things, and ought to recollect them better than I do: but people are not Wise at all times and *forget* things and themselves. Your man was *too wise* for you, because *he had probably learned* that you had a small allowance from London; or depend upon it *he would not* have gone to the *expence* of a Journey to Truro in search of an *Old* Sweetheart. Depend upon it I shall never answer any Letter from him in search of *Money*: I would see the whole of them in Purgatory first. Only let me know who I may write to, or depend upon when you send to me next time in case of your being *unable to write* yourself. I am glad to know that you have one or two good natured Souls that still stand your friends, in spite of old age, and *ill temper,* because you know, and I know, that there was always a little *too* much *Capsicum*[32] or *Cayenne Pepper* in your *Temper*, to jog on quietly; I have found good temper best, in *all my quiet Long Life.*

I never lost a friend that I ever gained: and I have gained many: If I wanted their assistance I think I should have it still but I always did, and hope I ever shall trust to myself. I have helped many, but never *required* the assistance of any,– or never applied for it. I hope I am now so near my Grave that I shall have no reason to alter my Opinion of the world which I have enjoyed. There are a *great* many *Selfish* and *Bad*, and a Good many *good* and kind-hearted. I hope the latter are the most numerous after all!!

I am, &c

I have bought two *Books* which I intended to send for your *amusement*. One, a history of Cornwall, many parts of which you know better than I do. The other is a History of London, which I ought to know best, but do not *half* know, though I have lived here *so long*. I hardly know how to send them *at present*

Carriage Paid, but must inquire. They will amuse you, and any young person you may get to *read them to you*. Or you can lend them to any of your friends who will have the good Sense to read them *with clean hands*; for they are *too good* to be treated as a Newspaper usually is.

W.C.

136. *William to Joanna. 6/7 April 1846.*

Stanhope Cottage, Mornington Road
Regent's Park, London –
April 6th 1846
& 7th

My dear Sister

I would have written on Saturday last, had there been time, after the Bills were paid, as I know that every day after Quarter-day appears to count *two*. But as this is now, *and always has been* the Case, on account of allowing the quarter-day to pass, before the Bills can be collected and examined by the Board and then re-examined by the Auditors before being paid,– always drives off *a week or ten days before they are finally* settled. We must however think ourselves favourites of Fate and fortune, to get our bread so regular and constant in *our old age*: and thank God and pray that it may be so *regularly* supplied as it has hitherto been:– but on which we *must not reckon too surely*: for all the medical world has been, and are in a disagreeable ferment, at present, and have been for some time past:– and if the College funds fall, *mine* will of course fall with it:– but we will hope better things. Do not show this to any body, as there are *so many busy bodies* in the World who love to make *mischief* though it does *themselves no good.*

Our Lectures are now proceeding, which occupies every hour and half hour until past the middle of May so that I have no time to write more at present. I had *intended* to request *Mr Pearse* at the Post Office to deliver you the Money I send, but you think it *safe enough* in this way. If it ever fails in reaching you, recollect it will be your *own fault*, and I shall send *no more* until I can be quite sure of its reaching *your own hands*: as I have no money to *throw away* on any body, not even myself: for I have Rent, Poor's Rates, Paving and Lighting, Coals/ Candles, Water, Window-Tax, Income Tax, and *twenty other* beautiful things to pay, that *formerly* I had nothing to do with, or care for; I have not time to write any more at present; only *let me know* either by *your own hand*, or by *some* friend that you can trust, that you have received *this* safely: *as soon as you can.* We are all pretty well at present.

I remain my dear Sister
Yours very sincerely
Wm Clift.

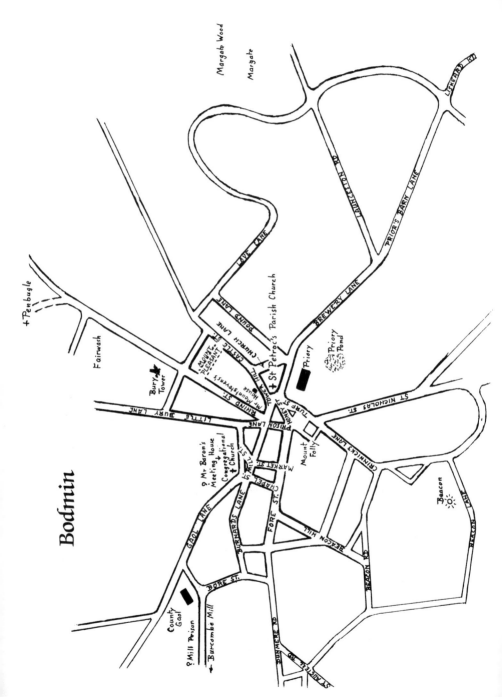

Street map of Bodmin, showing the streets named in the letters

Mrs Joanna Soady,
  Turf Street
Bodmin,
  Cornwall.

P.S.

After so much has been said about *Turf*-Street, I should *like to know* where it
is *situated*. It is *not* I dare say, upon the *Race-Ground*!!! I have asked two or three
times, but I cannot *make it out* from *your description*: Is it the *Back-Lane* leading
from St Nicholas Street and Mount Folly, by Mr George Moore's and Mr
George King's Nursery Gate, down by Mary Rescorla's, Hatter Ley's, Mr Tabb's,
Mrs Blake's, Jack Parnell's, and Betty Wennan's (or Wendon's) round a corner
into Honey Street?? If there had been any *Turf* there, about the year 1786, when
Mr Mudge's Saddle horse ran away with poor *Harry Oliver* and *me* from
Careland, and broke my *head* against the Moor-stone posts at the foot of some
Steps *opposite* to Mrs Blake's, and next door to *Jack Parnell's*, I should have
probably fallen *softer*, and avoided two or three years severe *head aches*; after
galloping between poor Old *Jack Pearn's* two pitchers of Water without
breaking them or knocking him over, though he poor soul, tried to stop us:–
neither could *his Cats*.

There was also *Back-Street* leading from the foot of Great Bury-Lane
westward, past Nanny Giants (and Jackey) and Staymaker *Rowe's* at the foot of
Little Bury-Lane, and Cornelius *Philps* and *Aunt Betty Cook's*, and Nanny *Vice's*:–
and the Old *Meeting House* – and the Scantleburys, and the Phillips's, and the
Garvours, and the *Blue Bells*; and the *Jack Starr's* (*Brother Sixfoot*); and Mr
Baron's Meeting-house, and Mild *Willy Sweet* (the Patten, Clog, and *Women's
Wooden-heel*-Maker) and George and *Mary Hender*: and *Jonathan* Fry, and his
Daughter, and *Grand*-Children, *Jonathan* & *Betsy* – and *Deborah Ford* and *John*;–
and *Deborah Lord*; and Mrs Bet Northey – and the Wheelwright *on the right*, and
Malster Pearse's on *the left*. With *John* or *Thomas*, George, and poor *Peter*, whose
funeral *I attended*.[33] And *Lewis* Roscorla the Roper, and *Roper's thread* maker,
and his *afterwards pretty* Wife *Betsy Bligh*, the Exciseman Shallcross's *Daughter-
in-Law*, at the foot of Prison-lane-Bridge. After *all these recollections, where is
Turf Street*? It *is n't Carter's Lane*, nor *Prison-Lane* nor *Meeting-house Lane*; Nor
Mary Carpenter's Lane; nor *Beacon Lane*; nor *St Nicholas Lane*; nor *Priors-Barn
Lane*; nor *Love-Lane*; nor *Dark Lane*; nor *Honey-Lane*; nor *Starmar's Lane*.
Where can *this confounded* Lane called *Turf Street* be? I think it must have been
some *Irish Street* that has slipt across Saint George's Channel *since I left home*. We
had no such saying as *"Bother and Turf"*,[34] when *I left home*!!!– though I have
heard it *sworn* since.

NB. *Write to me* soon, and let me know how my Letters may *reach* you *safely*,
or I shall *not write again* in a *hurry*, as I have *bother* enough *here*, without any from
the *West of England*.

I am my dear Sister
Yours very affectionately
Wm Clift.

Mrs Joanna Soady
Bodmin Cornwall.

137. Joanna to William. 4 June 1846.

Bodmin June 4 1846

My Ever Dear dear Brother
This will I sincerly hope find you and your Ever Dear family in perfect health
that you may all be able Enjoy this more than delightful weather I offten think
of your Lovely garden and wish were it posible that I Could Look at it there are
some pretty Little gardens in this street with pallasades in front of the Houses
poor Miss Sally hambleys is the first which stands Just where Mr Kings
Nursery gate once stood I said poor Miss S hambley they have Just Buryd
*   * one of the 4 sisters of a Decline she has bin ill a great while and they
all have bin Extremly kind to her she was the yougest of them and yet now not
very young about a fortnight since poor Katey Clima Died she had bin maried
but the husband had bin Dead som years since) his name was Cottell she was
seventy 7 years of age she had no Child But she has Left 2 sisters Betty and
fancy and a son to Dick Clima Lives Down in the Back Street with his family
next door to where Mallster pearce once Liv,d poor old Jellin Climas and I
have bin talking of Dear old Mr and Mrs Eyre and Katey pinch the prentice
girl – at present if a family wants a girl they may go to the union and take one
for meat and Cloaths no wages Expected my Ever dear Brother I have Just Bin
Looking at your Letters as I have now no Controwler as in times past[35] and it
put me in mind of many hapy Days that are gone and past and as I now go to
the Dear old Church once more instead of the Chaple and there I Do – realy
miss Dear old Mr Salter and think he has not Left his Equal for a pleasing voice
and good Delivery one popham I think his father was a glaizer there were 2
Brothers Jack and Tom this is a son to Tom he is positevily Like one Crying as
he reads with the minister Mr John wallis is the vicar But he never preaches
hear one Mr Taylor from up the Country is the Curate a man very much Likd
He has many times invited me before I Came into this street we have had
Churching tho not with a sermon Every Day no – since Last Satuarday Sunday
monday Tuesday and wensday Tis a most Beautiful Church and Churchyard
for the 2 Trees at the stile – are at this time a most Loveley shade But one thing
is shamefully neglected that is that they are filling up that small Churchyard
and not to get a proper Burying place for so many strangers theirs the Asylum
the union and the Jail untill there is scarcly room for the Towns people they

250

Dont Let fellow Creatures more then one year untill they are Dug up again I am hapy to say that I paid 20 years for my Dear sisters grave neither do I think they will tuch her grave no I know they will not Because theres plenty Room There – Then I am Led Back to that Lovely day that you and I went to Slades Bridge not wade Bridge[36] and next Day you Drew Dear old Mr Iris' Little Cottage house and it was so good a Liknes that I knew it the instant I saw it – since Sir william Molesworth[37] got maried Pencarrow is not Like the place it us,d to be no he takes such Delight in it from the Beautiful account I hear that it Exceeds Every Jentlmans seat in the County who his wife is I know not she was a young widdow very Rich and realy good to the poor as yet they have no Child I allways Enquire when I have opportunity at the priory a Brother to that Mr Grills who once Livd at Cardinham he is the Minester at N Lanhidrock or lenitherick[38] he Does not Enjoy good health But hes a good Man

I am thankfully glad that the Lectures are are all Ended before now that you and your Dear family may Enjoy this Delightful season my Sincere Love to all and not forgetting the Dear youth he must be Dear to you all I know he is as tho I were with you

I remain your Ever Affectionate

Sister Joanna S

my Ever Dear Brother will please to Excuse me for writing in this manner which I Did not intend to do I am glad to inform you that old *   * Never Came nigh my new Dwelling But has Done all he Could to tempt me Back he *   * saying he was shure I Could not Live on what my Brother sent me if that would not do if I would Come Back * with him* again He would mentain Me if you Never wrote to me again at the same time He has had *to get in from *   * for those 2 years at Least he Enjous good health But he has bin a grat sufferer But my Dear Brother I firmly abide By your good advice in not saying any thing to him nor go where he is tis as much as I Can do at present to do the Little I have to Do for I am so weak I Can scarcly walk the Room without my stick my poor feet and ankles are so very weak *but   *[39] throw mercy I have no *wound*[40]

138. Marey White to William. 27 September 1847.

Sep 27th 1847

Dear Uncle

I hope you will Excuse the liberty i have taken in writing these few lines to you hoping this will find you in good health as it leaves my family at present Except my self for i am still Suffering with my heavy affliction and I am Afraid I shall never have the use of them any more in this world wich is a Great loss to me

and my family as i can do Scarsely any thing for them and my Husband haveing
so little work to do makes me very unhappy for his trade is so bad that he as
Scarsly any think to do if this should meet your kindness to call on me I should
be Very thankfull

I Remain Yours
Marey White[41]

NOTES SECTION XIII

1. Caroline Amelia Clift had married Richard Owen on 20 July 1835. Richard Owen
    was at the time Assistant Conservator of the Museum. For further details of his
    life see Brief Biographies.
2. This seems to be a conflation of two biblical quotations from St Matthew, the
    first part being Chapter 10 verse 42 and the second Chapter 25 verse 46.
3. Clift's grandson, William Owen, was born in 1837. This appears to refer to an
    earlier child born to Caroline and Richard Owen, but no record of any seems to
    exist.
4. This refers to the birth in October of William Owen.
5. Mary, who has been mentioned previously was presumably Anna's sister and
    probably Thomas's daughter by his first wife. See Letter 119.
6. The letter must have been written between July and October 1839.
7. This probably refers to a maid, expected perhaps from the country.
8. In fact, Joanna, born in 1765, was 10 years older than Clift.
9. Trepanning was an operation performed with a trepan, a surgical saw, usually on
    the skull, and was resorted to for removing pieces of bone.
10. Enclosures were charged double postage at this time and the Money Order that
    Clift is sending seems to have space for a letter to be written on it.
11. The sum refers to £1.19.11 written at the head of the letter. In old money this was
    just one penny short of two pounds.
12. Following the Postage Act of August 1839, a national pre-paid postage system
    came into being for the first time and the much cheaper 'penny post' introduced
    by Rowland Hill. At first postage stamps were unavailable and letters were
    marked 'Postage Paid' but the famous Penny Black stamp finally appeared on 6
    May 1840.
13. In August 1841 Richard and Caroline Owen toured the West Country, staying
    with the Quaker Fox family at Falmouth and taking in Bodmin. Nothing
    particularly untoward seems to have occurred during the visit but they evidently
    did not have an entirely comfortable journey from London to Plymouth on a
    steamship, with a cabin possibly too near the boiler.
14. *Haste makes Waste:* this seems to be a variation on the proverb 'More haste, less
    speed'.
15. By this time Joanna had married again. On 20 September 1842 she married

Thomas Soady or Sawdy, a shoemaker of Bodmin, at St Mary's Church, Truro.

16. Clift moved from Lincoln's Inn Fields to this address in July 1842, when he went into semi-retirement and Owen was appointed Conservator of the Museum. Caroline Owen and her husband moved into her parents' apartments in Lincoln's Inn Fields.

17. *macadamized:* the method of making roads named after its inventor John Macadam. It was first introduced about 1820.

18. *wooden pavement:* this may refer to the road rather than the pavement as we understand it. Clift usually makes clear when he is referring to pavements for pedestrians. A citation in the *OED* for 1841 says 'The wooden pavement, properly so called, seems to have been first used in Russia'. *Penny Cyclopaedia* (1833–43). This reference from a contemporary encyclopaedia seems to indicate that wooden pavements had only recently been introduced into England. Clift's remarks in this letter on methods of making London streets are of particular interest for the history of urban development.

19. *Omnibuses:* horse-drawn omnibuses were first used in London on 4 July 1829, when one ran from Paddington to the Bank.

20. The Cornish Arms still stands in Bodmin and is still known also by its alternative name, The Fifteen Balls, which is the device on the Coat of Arms of Cornwall. 'One and all' is the Cornish motto, and it is inscribed on the Coat of Arms.

21. *the Holy well:* Holy Rood Well near Bury Tower at a place known as Fairwash.

22. *Bury tower:* built between 1501 and 1514, is all that remains of the old chantry church of the Holy Rood or Cross. It stands in the old town cemetery. See Pat Munn, *Introducing Bodmin the Cornish Capital* (Bodmin, 1973), p.5.

23. *Stream workers:* probably another name for *streamers*, i.e. men who worked in the mining industry. They flushed deposits of earth off the ore with jets of water to expose it. Tin mining and tin streaming was carried on all round Bodmin.

24. From *A shopkeeper in the Hampstead Road* to here has been crossed through.

25. Bodmin Butter Market was built in 1679 but was superseded when Market House was built in 1839. The site where it stood is now marked by the Turret Clock erected in 1844/5 and the remains were re-erected in Crinnicks Lane. They were still in existence c.1930.

26. Clift evidently knew of a traditional tale concerning a London apprentice who pulled out the tongue and heart from a lion, apparently when it was alive. No record of this story has come to light. Clift links the story to his own dissections on dead animals, which were a constant part of his work.

27. *Boxing the compass* refers to naming the points of the mariner's compass. The 32 points are not only named in order but also backwards and in any relation to each other.

28. Clearly the date, at least the year, of this letter is wrong. Joanna was still living in Gerrans in 1836.

29. These seem to be notes of what to put in the letter.

30. This is a reference to Joanna's marriage to Thomas Soady.

31. *Bum-boat proceedings:* a *bum-boat* was the term given to a boat employed to carry provisions, especially vegetables, for sale to ships offshore. Originally it was one that scavenged filth deposited from ships in the Thames.

32. *Capsicum:* a tropical plant, known for the pungent flavour of its seeds and used as a condiment.
33. Written in the margin is 'or Peter/ *Blue Peter*'. Blue Peter Rescorla is mentioned by Clift on 10 January 1845. See Letter 126. It seems unlikely that he had attended his funeral between then and April 1846. Perhaps Clift is referring to another member of the same family who died before he left Bodmin in 1792.
34. *"Bother and Turf":* no record of this phrase has so far been found. The etymology of the verb *bother* is unknown. According to the *OED* the earliest instances occur in the writings of Irishmen: T. Sheridan, Swift and Sterne, the earliest citation being from Sheridan in 1718. 'The word has long formed part of the comic Irishman of fiction and the stage. This suggests Anglo-Irish origin; but no etymon has been found in Irish'. The earliest usage recorded of the word used as an imprecation is in 1850 from Mrs Harriet Beecher Stowe, *Uncle Tom's Cabin*. *Turf* also seems to have possible Irish connotations from racing contexts. Turf Street, which is the centre of the town, may be located on the map of Bodmin, p.248.
35. Joanna appears from this letter to have left her husband, Thomas Soady.
36. *Slades Bridge:* this bridge over the River Camel is about 5 miles from Bodmin and two or three from Wadebridge.
37. The Sir William Molesworth referred to here is the son of Sir Arscott Molesworth, who died on 30 December 1823, when his son was thirteen. This Sir William became a notable radical politician and edited the most recent standard edition of the works of Thomas Hobbes. He died without an heir.
38. Lanhydrock is about 2 miles south of Bodmin on the Lostwithiel road.
39. The ms. is damaged at this point.
40. Joanna died in Bodmin on 18 December 1846, aged 80 years, and was buried there two days later.
41. Mary White is probably a daughter of Thomas.

BRIEF BIOGRAPHIES

The following public figures, who do not belong to the Clift family, are often referred to in the correspondence:

BAILLIE, Matthew (1761–1823)
s. of Dorothea Hunter, sister of John and William Hunter and only one of the family to leave issue. She went to London in 1752 after *d.* of their Mother. *m.* James Baillie who became Professor of Divinity in Glasgow. Matthew became a junior colleague at St George's Hospital (1787) and, jointly with Everard Home, was co-executor of Hunter's Will. Wrote first English text book on pathology. *br.* of Joanna Baillie (1762–1851), whose plays Scott admired. Trustee of Hunterian Museum after it was handed over to the Royal College of Surgeons of London, 1800. Uncertainties about Hunter's Will led to uneasy relationship with Home.

The EYRES of Bodmin, Cornwall.
John Eyre (*d.* 1793) was in general business in the town. Among his sons were John (1754–1803), Joseph and Thomas. The first attended the Grammar School under Rev. John Fisher and was apprenticed to a clothier in Tavistock (1769). Returned to father's business, but preached such a radical sermon in Bodmin that he was turned out of home penniless. Received theological training through Lady Huntingdon's Connection (Trevecca, S. Wales). Ordained by Bishop Lowth. Ministered at Tregony (Cornwall), Lincoln, Homerton and London, where he had a home at Hackney. *m.* 1785. Founder member of London Missionary Soc. (1794–5) and Hackney Theological College (1803). The correspondence refers to the Hackney house. It would seem that Joseph took over the family business concerns (bark stripping, wool, farming and a retail shop are mentioned) and William Clift said that Joseph employed nearly every one in Bodmin. Mrs Clift and her *drs.* Elizabeth and Joanna were all at one time employed by Mr Eyre in his cottage wool industry. Joanna and Elizabeth in turn were employed in his household. Elizabeth, indeed, was treated as one of the family. It is almost certain that William Clift worked for Mr Eyre in Bodmin, *i.e.,* before he left for London. The Eyres, squeezed, it may be, by the onset of the industrial revolution and war time inflation, could be quarrelsome. Joseph and Thomas sued each other for debt, an episode that affected Elizabeth, who conveyed the gossip about it in her letters.

GILBERT (*b.* HOSKEN), Mrs Nancy (1745–1818)
Benefactress of William Clift. *dr.* of Rev. Anthony Hosken, Vicar of Bodmin. At school with Anne Home (later Hunter). *m.* 1st Rev. John Vivien of the Manor House, Glynn, where Robert Clift senior, William's father, worked a mill up to 1783. *m.* 2nd Colonel Walter Raleigh Gilbert (1752–1827). A child *b.* 1786 lived 25 days. Inherited from her uncle Walter Pennington the Priory house on the site of the old Priory of St Petroc, Bodmin. Through the Priory grounds runs the stream that drove Burcombe Mill, birthplace of William Clift. Walter Raleigh Gilbert was a descendant of the old Cornish Elizabethan seafaring families that produced Sir Walter Raleigh and Sir Humphrey Gilbert. He was a Gentleman of the Bedchamber to George III and often at court.

HOME, Everard (1756–1832)
s. of Robert Boyne Home and *br.* of Anne, who *m.* John Hunter. Became house pupil to Hunter 1773. Eventually, jointly with Matthew Baillie, co-executor of Hunter's Will. Undertook delivery of Hunter's lectures 1792. Like Baillie a trustee of Hunter's collection on *d.* of Hunter. Surgeon to St George's Hospital 1793. See Jessie Dobson: *William Clift* (1954) for account of Home's treatment of Hunter's papers.

HUNTER (*b.* HOME), Mrs Anne (1742–1821)
dr. of Robert Boyne Home (related to Earls of Home) of Greenlaw Castle, Berwickshire. Hunter visited the numerous and cultivated Home family at their house in Suffolk St., Pall Mall. *m.* John Hunter 1771. Held *salon* in Leicester Square, where visitors and neighbours included Mrs Thrale, Elizabeth Montagu, Fanny Burney and Sir Joshua Reynolds. Several of her lyrics were set to music by Haydn, the best known of these being 'My mother bids me bind my hair'. Her *libretto* for Haydn's *The Creation* has been praised but was not used by the composer. Her poems were pub. separately (1802; 2nd ed. 1803). Of 4 children, 2 *d.* in infancy. The eldest, John Banks Hunter, became Major in the 103rd Regiment, and the youngest, Agnes Margaretta Hunter, *m.* 1st Capt. (later Sir) James Campbell; 2nd Lt Col Charlewood. Both *d. s.p.*

HUNTER, John (1728–1793)
b. Long Calderwood in parish of East Kilbride, Lanarkshire, 14 Feb. 1728. 10th and youngest child of John and Agnes Hunter. Father *d.* 1741. Aimless in childhood and youth. Began study of anatomy (1748) in London under *br.* William Hunter (1718–1783). At St George's Hospital 1754. Short stay in Oxford 1755–6. Army surgeon 1760. Served abroad. Returned to London 1763. Mem. of Corp. of Surgeons and F.R.S. 1767. Surgeon to St George's Hospital 1768. Collection of biological specimens acc. to scientific plan dates from this time. Collection augmented with live animals – *e.g.,* leopards, buffalo, ostrich, bees – at cottage built at Earls Court. Sought to cultivate

pearls in a pond. *m.* Anne Home (14 yrs his junior) 1771. Surgeon Extraordinary to George III 1776. Vertigo (strokes) began 1777. Cures at Bath. Elected R. Academy of Surgery of Paris 1783. Moved to Leicester Sq. and Castle St. 1784. Museum housed in the intervening space 1785. Consolidated reputation in philosophical surgery which he estab. on scientific footing. Edward Jenner (1749–1823) a pupil and friend. Home undertook delivery of Hunter's lectures 1792.

The MOLESWORTHS of Pencarrow, Bodmin, Cornwall.
William Clift's *br.* John became estate manager to this old Cornish family. The 1st Sir William in the correspondence (1740?–1798 – but see John Clift's letter 6 Apr. 1798) served on the bench. A *br.,* a Rev. Mr Molesworth, lived at St Breock nr Wadebridge, Cornwall, and he or anr *br.* also advised John Clift to try treatment by 'electrification' for his gout in 1806. The family was connected with the Arscotts of Tetcott, and this Sir William was succeeded by his son, then a minor, Sir Arscott-Ourry Molesworth (1791–1823). The Pencarrow estate seems to have been looked after by John Clift. Sir Arscott prepared to take up residence 1812. Whilst Pencarrow was refurbished he and his *w.* stayed at a house nearby where the Gilberts had lived before Walter Pennington bequeathed the Priory, Bodmin, to his niece Nancy Gilbert. Lady Molesworth gave John Clift a pension 1817. She and Sir Arscott helped his wife Nancy nurse him through his last illness. William Clift saw Sir Arscott in London. Latter probably in Edinburgh when John Clift *d.* at Pencarrow 1819. Sir Arscott Molesworth so detested his *s.,* the 2nd Sir William (1810–1855), that he packed him off abroad. This Sir William became an infidel and radical (also the last editor of Hobbe's works, 16 vols, 1839–45). Hawker of Morwenstow wrote a poem entitled 'Tetcott, 1831; in which Year Sir William Molesworth Caused the Old House to be Taken Down, and a New One Built.' Radical inside and outside parliament, Sir William was accused of apostasy by Cobden for serving in government, and was a friend of the elder Mill and Grote. 'He preferred to be disliked.' (*DNB*). *m.* 1844 and made his home at Pencarrow. *s.p.* Bequeathed house to his widow (*d.* 1888) for life. Pencarrow remained in the family and is now open to the public.

SELECT BIBLIOGRAPHY

John Hunter
  Jessie Dobson, *John Hunter* (London, 1969).
  S. Roodhouse Gloyne, *John Hunter* (Edinburgh, 1956).
  George Qvist, *John Hunter 1728–1793* (London, 1981).

William Clift and the Clift Family
  Frances Austin, *The Letters of William Home Clift 1803–1832* (Dorset, 1983).
  Frances Austin, *Robert Clift of Bodmin Able Seaman 1792–1799* (Dorset, 1983).
  Frances Austin, 'Epistolary Conventions of the Clift Family Correspondence', *English Studies* (Amsterdam, 1973), Vol.54, pp.9–22; 129–140.
  Frances Austin, 'London Life in the 1790s', *History Today* (1978), pp.738–745.
  Frances Austin and Bernard Jones, 'William Clift: The Surgeon's Apprentice', *Annals of the Royal College of Surgeons of England* (1978), Vol.60, pp.261–265.
  Jessie Dobson, *William Clift* (London, 1954).
  Sir Arthur Keith, 'Life and Times of William Clift', *The British Medical Journal* (1923), pp.1127–1132.
  Royal Cornwall Polytechnic Society, 'The Ninety-second Annual Report of the Royal Cornwall Polytechnic Society' (1925) V, Part III.

General Background
  Charles Hadfield, *The Canals of South West England* (London, 1967).
  L.E. Long, *An Old Cornish Town* (Bodmin, 1975).
  John MacLean, *Parochial and Family History of Cornwall* (London, 1870).
  Pat Munn, *Bodmin Riding* (Bodmin, 1975).
  Pat Munn, *Introducing Bodmin the Cornish Capital* (Bodmin, 1973).
  K.C. Phillips, *West Country Words and Ways* (Newton Abbot, 1976).
  Howard Robinson, *The British Post Office* (London, 1948).
  Derek Robson, *Some Aspects of Education in Cheshire in the Eighteenth Century* (Manchester, 1966).
  Norman Rogers, *Wessex Dialect* (Bradford-on-Avon, 1979).
  Martin F. Wakelin, *Language and History in Cornwall* (London, 1975).

Joseph Wright, *The English Dialect Dictionary* (Oxford, 1923). 1st pub. 1898.

Joseph Wright, *The English Dialect Grammar* (Oxford, 1968). 1st pub. 1905.

INDEX

Abernethy, Ann, wife of John; 13.

Abernethy, John, surgeon; 13.

Adams, Mrs, housekeeper to John Hunter; 24, 37, 63, 85, 89, 96, 101, 115, 123, 125, 126, 192, 197.

Alcide, The; 123.

Alliance, The;150, 151, 164.

Alternun; 4, 19, 147.

Annual Register, The; 1.

Baillie, Matthew, surgeon; 7, 79, 85, 93, 102, 103, 114, 126, 127, 148, 166

Banks, Joseph; 1.

Bath; 44, 117, 136, 172, 244.

Becket, Thomas à; 236.

Birmingham-London Railway; 244.

Blissland; 65, 72, 111, 121.

Boconnoc; 44.

Bombay Castle, The; 138, 139, 149, 154, 159.

Bodmin
    Assizes; 33, 40, 43, 56, 70, 72, 73, 82, 240, 243.
    Bridewell; 49, 59.
    Burcombe; 4.
        Mill; 2, 3, 19, 20.
    Bury Tower; 242, 253.
    Butter Market; 61, 98, 242, 244, 253.
    Canal project *see* Canals.
    Chantry of St Thomas; 10.
    Church of St Petroc; 49, 75, 199, 205, 207, 250.
    Church Stile; 61, 95, 235, 242, 250.
    Fifteen Balls or Cornish Arms, public house; 11, 242, 253.
    George and Dragon; 69, 73.
    Great Hall; 59, 205, 207.
    Holy Well; 242, 253.
    Jeffery's mill pool; 44, 81.
    Margate; 70, 83, 95.
    Mill Prison; 169, 184, 250.
    Old Workhouse; 243.
    Penbugle; 50, 51, 242.
    Prison; 242.
    Race Ground; 180.
    Races; 240, 243.
    Riding; 72, 84.
    Whitehorse Inn; 86, 99.
Bodmin Streets
    Back Street; 85, 103, 106, 234, 242, 249, 250.
    Beacon Lane; 249.
    Bury Lane; 53, 235(Gt), 242, 249(Gt).
    Carter's Lane; 259.
    Castle Street; 6, 85, 106, 246.
    Crinnicks Lane; 253.
    Dark Lane; 249.
    Fore Street; 44, 207, 244.
    Honey Street; 249.
    Little Bury Lane; 249.
    Love Lane; 249.
    Meeting House Lane; 249.
    Mount Folly; 207, 235, 242, 249.
    Priors Barn Lane; 249.
    Prison Lane; 11, 38, 41, 71, 132, 235, 242, 249.
    St Nicholas Street; 50, 235, 240, 242, 243.
    Starmars Lane; 249.
    Tower Hill; 43, 50, 54, 59.
    Turf Street; 231.
Bodmin and Local People
    Baron, Mr, preacher and cabinet maker; 49, 65, 66, 67, 150, 162, 235, 242, 249.
    Baron, Mrs; 140, 141, 145, 150, 193.
    Bate, Cousin Peggy; 111, 116, 118, 168, 194, 201, 228.
    Bonady, Billy, publican; 69, 70, 76.
    Bonady, Tammy; 29, 32, 62, 106, 242.
    Brown, George, lawyer; 100, 111, 244, 245.
    Clemo, Kitty; 26, 31, ?55, 49, 82, 83, 115.
    Clemo, Matthew; 137, 139, 149, 154, 159, 199, 200.
    Eyre, John senior; 68, 70, 71.
    Eyre, John, s. of John; 5, 65, 68, 70, 71.
    Eyre, Joseph, s. of John sr.;5, 6, 23, 36, 41, 44, 65, 68, 70 and *passim*.
    Eyre, Mrs, wife of Joseph; 6, 24, 40, 65, 66, 71, 92, 95 and *passim*.
    Eyre, Thomas, s. of John sr.; 103, 117.
    Eyre, Thomas, ?son of Joseph; 230, 231, 237, 238.
    Hambly/Hamly, Dr; 95, 187, 200.
    Hawking, John, staymaker; 52, 60, 67, 71, 72, 74, 76, 77, 82, 83, 109, 124, 140, 224, 242.
    Hawking, Nancy, wife of John; 59, 66, 67, 71, 72, 74, 76, 77, 82, 83, 108, 109.

Hawking, William, s. of John; 41, 44, 49, 50, 52, 54, 57, 59, 60-4, 66, 71, 208, 224.
Hocking *see* Hawking.
Honey, Thomas, *see also* Teague, Thomas; 6, 198, 208, 209, 211, 216, 219, 221, 225, 227, 229, 230.
Jeffries, John; 19-20(mill), 59.
King, George, nurseryman; 20, 22, 242.
Levears, Richard; 59, 121, 139, 149, 154, 159.
Musgrove, Billy ?Rodney; 32, 58.
Nichols, Elizabeth, servant of the Gilberts; 108, 109, 110, 111, 117, 129, 131, 160, 162.
Ough, Billy; 43, 44, 46, 47, 54, 83.
Pinch, Catty; 24, 32, 40, 44, 103, 110, 117, 118, 231, 250.
Roberts, William, servant of the Eyres; 32, 44, 62, 70, 74, 77, 92, 179.
Rowe, Catharine, servant of the Eyres; 32, 34, 72, 74, 95, 179.
Salter, John, Parish Clerk and school-master; 10, 11, 15, 23, 32, 60, 68, 199, 231, 242, 245, 250.
Scantlebury, Bill; 43, 44, 54.
Soady family; 231, 245, 246.
Soady, Thomas; 6, 246, 250, 253, 254.
Tabb, Mr, of Pencarrow; 43, 46, 51, 70, 72, 83, 86, 89, 90, 149, 151, 161, 164, ?242, 249.
Tabb, William, servant of the Gilberts; 28-31, 33-5, 38, 46, 54, 57, 59, 65, 73, 80-2, 91,117, 135, 164, 172, 180, 185, ?200.
Teague, Thomas; 122, 150, 151, 164, ?198, ?202, 208, 209, 222, 229.
Williams, Mr, nurseryman; 20, 22, 41, 106, 109, 122, 242.
Williams, Thomas; 37, 52, 53, 56, 57, 61, 63, 65, 115, 153, 158, 165.
Yeo, Elizabeth; 29, 50, 62, 138, 146, 193.

Botany Bay; 145, 186, 194.
Brighton; 79, 81, 84, 204.
Bristol; 6, 24, 29, 33, 34, 37, 40 and *passim* to 176, 244.
  Assizes; 53.
  Newgate; 56.
Brittania, The; 171.
Broadstairs; 27.
Byard, Sir Thomas, Captain of *The St. George*; 51.

Cadiz; 138, 154, 159.
Ça-Ira, The; 123.
Calais; 230, 236, 237.
Cambridge, The; 47, 98.
Cambridge, University; 32.
Camel, River; 254.
Camelford; 59.
Campbell, Capt., later Sir James, husband of Agnes Hunter; 90, 109.
Canals
  Padstow-Lostwithiel Scheme;
  Polbrook Canal Scheme; 86, 98, 101, 102, 107.
Canterbury; 236.
  Cathedral; 236.
Cape St Vincent; 158.
  Battle of; 164.
Cardinham; 3, 4, 19, 198, 201, 202, 245, 251.
Censeur, The; 123, 147.
Castlereagh, Lord; 224, 229.
Charlotte, Queen, wife of George III; 31, 185, 213, 229.
Chatham; 167, 169, 171.
Cheshire; 109.
Clift, Caroline Amelia, WC's daughter; 1, 2, 7, 23, 186, 197, 198 and *passim*.
Clift, Caroline Harriet, WC's wife; 7, 186, 192, 196, 198 and *passim*.
Clift, Joanna, née Courts, WC's mother; 2, 4, 8, 19, 20.
Clift, Robert senior, WC's father; 2, 4, 8, 19, 20.
Clift, William Home, WC's son; 1, 7, 16, 203, 204 and *passim*.
Cornish Militia; 46, 48, 65, 140, 151, 180.
Corsica; 109, 123, 138, 139, 147, 165.
Courageux, The; 123, 149, 154, 159, 164, 165.
Costislost, nr Pencarrow; 202.
Croanford, nr Pencarrow; 179, 185.
Cuxhaven; 11, 185.

Dance, George; 7.
Davy, Humphry; 1, 7.
Deal; 27, 28, 79, 237.
Deptford; 137, 147.
Dover; 27, 39, 236, 237.
Duloe; 98, 102.
Dungeness; 27.
Dunmere; 245.

East India Company; 86, 101.
Echo, sloop; 11, 167, 176, 185, 200, 207.

Eddystone lighthouse; 27.
Edgeman, Mr, chaplain of *Intrepid*; 74, 122.
Edinburgh; 219.
Egloshayle; 199.
Electrification (medical); 199, 200, 201, 207.
Encyclopaedia Londinensis; 172, 185.
Exeter; 57, 60, 65, 92, 244.
  Assizes; 179.
  Jail; 72, 175.
Eyre, John, dissenting minister and co-founder of London Missionary society; *see* under Bodmin.

Falmouth; 186, 194, 210, 211, 252.
Fisher, George; 14, 18, 24.
Five Lanes; 141, 147.
Ford; *see* Croanford.
Fowey; 5, 22–4, 26, 27 and *passim*.
  Fowey Fair; 29, 39.
Fox, Caroline and family; 8, 18, 252.
Frederick, Augustus, Duke of York; *see* York.

Genoa; 123, 147.
Gentleman's Magazine, The;1, 18.
George III; 5, 22, 31, 32, 90, 140, 185, 249.
Gerrans; 198, 208, 209, 210, 215, 219, 225, 230, 239, 253.
Gibraltar; 105, 142, 149, 150, 151, 154, 158, 159.
  Straits of; 164.
Gilbert, Nancy; 5, 6, 7, 12, 13, 15, 23, 26, 28 and *passim*.
Gilbert, Walter Raleigh; 5, 12, 23, 26, 29–31 and *passim*.
Gilbert, Revd Edmund, br. of Walter Gilbert; 54, 229.
Gilbert, John Pomeroy, s. of Revd Edmund; 226, 228.
Glorious First of June; 96, 102.
Glynn; 3, 4, 5, 19.
Gravesend; 28.
Greenwich Fair; *see* London.
Grenville, William Lord; 61.

Hammoaze; *see* Plymouth.
Haydn; 5.
Haynes, Robert; 6, 24, 28, 30, 31, 37, 40, 47, 85 and *passim* to 165.
Herne Bay; 236.
Home, Everard; 7, 49, 79, 81, 85, 93, 96 and *passim*.

Hood, Vice-Admiral Lord; 96.
Hosken, Revd Anthony, father of Nancy Gilbert; 12.
Hotham, Vice-Admiral, Sir William; 147.
Howe, Admiral Lord; 96, 102.
Hunter, Agnes, dr. of John Hunter; 79, 81, 90, 109.
Hunter, Ann; 5–7, 23, 28, 31, 32, 38, 41 and *passim*.
Hunter, John; 1, 2, 5–7, 13, 15, 17, 23 and *passim*.
  Collection; 1, 2, 6, 7, 15, 37, 85, 90, 92–6 and *passim*.
  house at Earls Court; 47, 51, 61, 66, 76, 81.
  death of; 69, 79, 80, 81, 84, 85.
Hunter, John Banks, son of John Hunter; 32, 66, 67, 70, 79, 90, 105, 171.
Hunter, William, br. of John Hunter; 172, 185.

Illustrated London News, The; 1.
Intrepid, The; 74, 122, 164, 184.
Imperieux, The; 123.
Isle of Wight; 43, 191.

Jervis, Admiral Sir John; 149, 154, 159, 160, 164.
Joseph Andrews; 13, 77.

Lancet, The; 1.
Lanhydrock; 252, 254.
Lanivet; 242.
Launceston; 22, 56, 124, 140, 145, 150, 151, 163.
Leghorn; 118, 121, 122, 129, 138, 139, 147.
Lerryn; 69, 70, 74, 106.
Linkinhorne; 124, 140, 142, 145, 150, 154, 155, 164, 171.
Lisbon; 118, 148–50, 154, 158, 159, 164, 171.
Liskeard; 22, 103, 106, 110, 111, 118, 121, 131, 137, 138, 141–43, 145.

London
  Astley's Riding School; 192, 197.
  Blackheath; 6, 85, 89, 90, 100, 108, 109, 115.
  Bridge; 191.
  Charing Cross; 86, 101.
  Cornhill; 199.
  Covent Garden; 38, 66.
  Earl's Court; *see* Hunter, John, house at.

Greenwich; 28, 63, 235.
Greenwich Park; 28, 63, 64.
Greenwich Fair; 63, 64, 66.
Hackney; 5, 66, 68, 71.
Highgate; 97.
Houses of Parliament; 32, ?90, ?128.
Hoxton; 193, 198.
Hyde Park; 31, 109, 140.
Kensington Gardens; 109.
Knightsbridge; 61, 62.
Long Acre; 201.
Regent's Canal; 230, 234
Regent's Park; 233, 253.
River Thames; see Thames
Sadlers Wells; 47.
St Bartholomew's Hospital; 230.
St Clement Dane's Church; 198.
St George's Church; 67.
St George's Fields; 224.
St George's Hospital; 79.
St James's Burying Ground; 244.
St James's Park; 31, 32, 109, 192.
St Martin's Church; 81.
St Marylebone Fields; 69.
St Paul's Cathedral; 30.
Seven Dials; 60.
Tower of London; 38, 197.
Westminster; 33, 72.
Westminster Abbey; 31.
Westminster Bridge; 42.
Woolwich; 28.
    Arsenal; 39.
London streets
    Angel Court; 101.
    Arundel Street; 126.
    Baches Row; 193.
    Castle Street; 6, 24, 37, 38, 47, 66, 97, 100,
        108, 123, 135, 151, 192.
    Chandos Street; 192.
    Charing Cross Road; 24.
    Charles Street; 63, 79.
    Clare Market; 223.
    Cranbourn Alley; 57.
    Cranbourn Passage; 38.
    Drury Lane; 109, 233.
    Gloucester Square; 88.
    Great Marlborough Street; 49, 76.
    Great St Andrew's Street; 60.
    Grosvenor Square; 63.
    Hampstead Road; 244, 253.
    Hanover Square; 67.
    Haughton Street; 223.
    Leicester Square; 6, 24, 33, 37, 39, 47, 71,
        85, 89, 97, 101, 108, 135, 151, 192.
    Lincoln's Inn Fields; 1, 7, 234, 236, 240,
        253.
    Little Drury Lane; 38.
    Little Exeter Street; 62.
    Moors Yard; 171.
    Mornington Road; 7.
    Portman Square; 88, 188.
    St James's Square; 79.
    St Martin's Lane; 60, 171.
    Sloane Street; 62.
    Soho Square; 83.
    Strand, The; 126, 240.
    Tavistock Street; 38.
    Vinegar Yard; 233.

London Missionary Society; 5, 68, 147.
Lostwithiel; 19, 22, 56, 59, 60, 86, 107, 226,
    254.
Luxulian; 22, 242.

Margate, Bodmin; 44, 51, 70, 95.
Margate, Kent; 27, 28, 39, 237.
?Martin, David, painter; 49, 51.
Matrion; 74, 83.
Mediterranean Fleet;?136, 147, 164.
Medway, River; 171.
Mells; 7.
Melpomene, The, frigate; 115.
Molesworth, Lady, wife of Sir William; 161,
    172, 179, 188.
Molesworth, Lady, wife of Sir Arscott; 206,
    221.
Molesworth, Mr Justice; 110.
Molesworth, Revd Mr, br. of Sir William;
    ?59, 172, 185, ?201, 207.
Molesworth, Sir Arscott, s. of Sir William;
    166, 168, 199, 202, 206, 213, 218, 219,
    231, 254.
Molesworth, Sir William; 6, 24, 40, 44, 46,
    56, 69, 72 and *passim.*
Molesworth, Sir William II, s. or Sir
    Arscott; 231, 251, 254.

Newlyn; 154, 165.
North Foreland; 27, 39.

Orange, William V, Prince of; 123, 128,
    146.
Otaheite; 124, 144, 145.
Owen, Caroline; see Clift, Caroline Amelia.
Owen, Richard; 1, 2, 7, 8, 18, 230, 232, 234,
    239, 252, 253.
Owen, Willy; 15, 230, 232, 234, 237, 238,
    252.

Padstow; 36, 37, 52, 54, 55, 58.
  riots; 85, 88.
Paris; 208, 218, 220, 236, 237.
Pencarrow; 6, 7, 24, 26, 34, 39, 40, 43, 51, 53
  and *passim*.
Pennington, William, uncle of Nancy
  Gilbert; 5, 202, 207.
Penny Post; 230, 252.
Penryn; 201, 217.
Penzance; 150–5, 158, 163, 164, 167, 180, 182.
Philip Quarll; 19.
Physic, Sir Philip Syng; 114, 123.
Plymouth; 8, 27, 124, 141–3, 145, 146, 148,
  150 and *passim*.
  Plymouth Dock; 48, 51, 55, 98, 113, 116,
    119, 160, 175, 177.
  Plymouth Hoe; 160.
  Hammoaze; 54, 55.
Polkerries; 30, 44.
Pope, Caroline; *see* Clift, Caroline Harriet.
Portland; 27.
Portscatho; *see also* Gerrans; 220, 221.
Portsea; 136.
Portsmouth; 6, 124, 136, 139, 140, 145, 150,
  171, 190.
Prince George, The; 48.
Priory; 5, 6, 12, 23, 26, 44, 51, 54 and
  passim.
  maids/servants; 5, 23, 28, 31, 33, 34,
    41–4, 50, 59, 65, 72, 82, 129.
Priory Pool; 101, 107, 245.
Proceedings of the Geological Society; 1.
Proceedings of the Royal Society; 18.
Puckeys of Fowey; 5, 36, 44, 68, 198.
  Aunt; 26, 32, 111, 142, 202.
  Cousin James; 25, 26, 39, 70, 103, 111,
    122, 124, 142 and *passim*.
  Cousin William; 26, 29, 111, 124, 142 and
    passim.
  Uncle James; 24, 26, 70, 111, 169.
  Cousin Thomas; 103, 105, 107, 122, 198,
    201.

Radnor Militia; 180.
Ramsgate; 27, 39, 237.
Reculver; *see* Two Sisters.
Reynolds, Sir Joshua; 24, 30, 39.
Robinson Crusoe; 13, 19, 77.
Roderic Random; 13, 77.
Roach Rock; 142, 147.
Rowing-match on Thames; 42, 51.
Royal College of Surgeons; 1, 13, 15, 230,
  231, 234, 247.

Royal Society, The; 7, 230.

St Albans, The; 149, 154, 160, 164, 165.
St Austell; 22, 132, 234.
St Bartholomew Fair; 47, 51.
St Blazey; 22.
St Breock; 172.
St Fiorenzo; 118, 119, 121, 123, 137–9, 147,
  149, 159, 165.
St George, The; 51, 52, 55, 58, 88, 96, 98,
  102–4 and *passim*.
St Issey; 36, 37.
St Kew; 168, 186.
St Lawrance; 132.
St Mabyn; 44.
St Minver; 22.
St Veep; 73.
Saltash; 118.
Sandwich; 237.
Sharp, William, engraver; 204.
Slade's Bridge, nr. Wadebridge; 251, 254.
Somerset Militia; 70.
Southampton; 6, 104, 124, 133–6.
South Foreland; 27, 39.
Spithead; 148, 161, 162.
Stafford Militia; 180.
Start Point; 27, 39.
Sterne, Laurence; 163, 167.
Strait Fleet; *see* Mediterranean Fleet.
Swansea; 43.
Syren, The; 46, 51.

Tahiti; *see* Otaheite.
Tavistock; 186.
Terpsichore, The; 158.
Teignmouth; 171.
Tetcott, house belonging to Molesworth
  family; 202, 207.
Thames, River; 28, 42, 64, 66, 101, 191, 236,
  253.
  Rowing match on; 42, 51.
Tom Jones; 13, 77.
Torbay; 161.
Torpoint; 58, 138, 139.
Tristram Shandy; 13, 77.
Treaty of Amiens (1802); 186, 197, 198.
Tregonna; 161.
Tregony; 211, 215, 219.
Truro; 59, 91, 208, 223, 224, 226, 230, 232,
  234, 239, 246, 253.
Two Sisters, Kent; 27, 39.

Vicar of Wakefield; 13, 77.

264

Wadebridge; 22, 86, 101, 107, 172, 188, 201, 251, 254.
Washaway; 110.
Watts, Isaac; 225, 229.
Welsh Militia; 88.
Wesley, John; 132.
Whittington, Dick; 97.
William V, Prince of Orange; *see* Orange, William of.
Windsor Castle, The; 85, 98, 103, 116, 119, 123.

Wollaston, William, natural scientist; 1.
Woolwich; 28.
    Arsenal; 39.
Yarmouth; 11.
York, Augustus Frederick, Duke of York; 224, 229.
Young Man's Best Companion, The; 14, 15, 18, 24, 35, 40.
Zealand, The; 167.
Zealous, The; 148, 158.